BEYOND THE
DEVIL'S ROAD

BEFORE GOLD
California under Spain and Mexico
VOLUME 8

ROSE MARIE BEEBE & ROBERT M. SENKEWICZ
Series Editors

BEYOND THE DEVIL'S ROAD

Francisco Garcés

and the Spanish Encounter with the American Southwest

JEREMY BEER

UNIVERSITY OF OKLAHOMA PRESS ✳ NORMAN

Published in cooperation with
THE ACADEMY OF AMERICAN FRANCISCAN HISTORY
Mission San Luis Rey, Oceanside, California

LIBRARY OF CONGRESS CATALOGING-IN-PUBLICATION DATA

Names: Beer, Jeremy, author.
Title: Beyond the devil's road : Francisco Garcés and the Spanish encounter with
the American Southwest / Jeremy Beer.
Description: Norman : University of Oklahoma Press, [2024] | Series: Before
gold: California under Spain and Mexico ; volume 8 | Includes bibliographical
references and index. | Summary: "The first full-length biography of Francisco
Garcés, an important Spanish missionary and early ethnographer"—Provided
by publisher.
Identifiers: LCCN 2024007656 | ISBN 978-0-8061-9457-8 (hardcover)
Subjects: LCSH: Garcés, Francisco Tomás Hermenegildo, 1738–1781. | Southwest,
New—History—To 1848. | Southwest, New—Discovery and exploration,
Spanish. | Missionaries—Southwest, New—Biography. | Missions, Spanish—
Southwest, New—History. | BISAC: HISTORY / United States / General |
HISTORY / Military / General
Classification: LCC F799 .B48 2024 | DDC 979/.01—dc23/eng/20240520
LC record available at https://lccn.loc.gov/2024007656

Beyond the Devil's Road: Francisco Garcés and the Spanish Encounter with the American Southwest is Volume 8 in the series Before Gold: California under Spain and Mexico.

The paper in this book meets the guidelines for permanence and durability of the Committee on Production Guidelines for Book Longevity of the Council on Library Resources, Inc. ∞

For
FRED AND PEGGY CLARK

If then there be a preacher and dispenser of recovery, sent from God, that messenger must speak, not to one, but to all; he must be suited to all, he must have a mission to the whole race of Adam, and be cognizable by every individual of it.

John Henry Newman

Contents

Illustrations

Maps

Acknowledgments

This book is both an outsider's labor of love and a biographer's work of synthesis. My academic field was psychology, not history, let alone Spanish borderlands history, and despite four years of Spanish in high school and college my ability to read it is embarrassingly limited. Whatever value this volume has is thanks to the scholarly work and assistance, not always knowingly provided, of genuine experts, both living and dead.

Among the former are the wonderful Rose Marie Beebe and Robert Senkewicz, whose fine biography of Junípero Serra served me as a model. I have been continually encouraged by their interest, saved from many wrong turns by their editorial guidance, assisted by their selfless efforts, and honored by the opportunity to publish this book under the aegis of their Before Gold series at the University of Oklahoma Press. I am also thankful to Joe Schiller at the press for his interest in, and shepherding of, this project, and to John Thomas for his expert copyediting.

Rose Marie contributed substantially to this book by translating many documents. I was also helped immeasurably by translations provided by Constanza López Lamerain. She and her husband, David Rex Galindo, were extraordinarily generous with their time, documents, and advice. The orientation to the relevant literature and archives provided by David was especially valuable, even if the perspective I adopted differs in important respects from his and that of some of the field's leading academics.

I was fortunate to engage with many other scholars who graciously took time to speak with me or provide me with various kinds of help, including John Kessell, Peter Whiteley, Damian Bacich, Skyler Reidy, Carrie Gibson, Andrés Reséndez, Jay Harrison, Bob Kittle, Jeffrey Burns, Darryl Hart, Richard Gamble, Fernando Cervantes, and Darío Fernández-Morera. Many friends—some of them brilliant scholars in their own right—did the same, including Robert Dean Lurie, Will Luzader, Tim Hoiland, Helen Andrews, Josh Hochschild, Mark Henrie, John J. Miller, Steve Wrinn, Mike Phelan, Bill Kauffman, and Anthony Maza. I owe a special debt to my partners at AmPhil—Doug Schneider, Liz Palla, Justin Streiff, Matt Gerken, Chris Kuetemeyer, Josh Owens, and Kyle Vander Meulen—for allowing me to ditch work for weeks at a time in order to biographize Fray Garcés.

Many priests provided me with insights and good conversation. The list includes Fr. Bill Minkel, Fr. Michael Weldon, Fr. John Nahrgang, Fr. Antony Tinker, Fr. George Decasa, Fr. Ron Zanoni, and Fr. Charlie Urnick. I hope they think the resulting product was worth it, especially Fr. Urnick, who has made the retrieval of Garcés's legacy a significant part of his pastoral vocation.

We aren't done. Erika Castaño at the University of Arizona's Special Collections Library was incredibly helpful. I thank her and the rest of the staff there, as well as those at the Huntington Library, Bancroft Library at the University of California–Berkeley, Newberry Library, Latin American Library at Tulane University, Arizona Historical Society, and Colorado River Historical Society. Sam Stein assisted ably with research at the Bancroft, and my friend and colleague Stephanie D'Anselmi did the same at the Antonianum in Rome. I am grateful to them both, as I am to Stan Krok for his photos of the Garcés petroglyphs and to Bertram Tsavadawa for guiding me through Old Oraibi and the Hopi reservation.

I owe an even larger debt to the good people at the Southwest Mission Research Center. Fr. Greg Adolf, Michael Brescia, and David Carter did more than cheer me on; the SMRC also provided a generous research grant. For some years I have appreciated the SMRC's work, and I am delighted to have partnered with the Center to make this book a reality.

Finally, I heartily thank Tom Jonas not only for the beautiful maps he made for this volume, but for his assistance in helping me figure out Garcés's likely pathways, many of which had never been determined. Tom has added significantly to our knowledge of just where Garcés traveled.

This book is dedicated to my good friends Fred and Peggy Clark as a small token of my appreciation for the inspiriting conversation—usually about books—and unwavering support they have offered over the years.

Kara, my wife, puts up with so much. I *think* she knows how profoundly thankful I am for her editorial suggestions, indexing prowess, spiritual support, and genuine patience. But if I don't say that here, she might get the wrong idea. So: thanks, Kara.

Prologue

Más Allá

The Devil's Road is still there. It's still dry. And it's still dangerous.

It starts at Boundary Camp on the western border of Organ Pipe Cactus National Monument in southern Arizona. Swinging westward through Cholla Pass and O'Neill Pass, El Camino del Diablo—its official American name is still given in Spanish—works its way toward a parallel path with the international border, to which it finally comes within shouting distance. Passing the oasis of Tule Well, the road then heads straight as an arrow into the Barry M. Goldwater Air Force Range until it reaches the Tinajas Altas Mountains. At this remote sierra's base, El Camino del Diablo abruptly turns north-northwest for thirty miles, emerging into modern civilization at the banks of the Gila River near the small town of Wellton. In total, the road covers about 110 desert miles.

Such a matter-of-fact description makes El Camino del Diablo seem tame. It is not. Authorities warn drivers away from using

1

it. Permission must be obtained to travel through the American military's territory, where live ordnance might be encountered. Except in the winter, El Camino del Diablo is exceedingly hot. There are no settlements along the way, no services, and no easily accessible water. Smugglers—of goods, of drugs, of people—cross the road's path on a daily basis. Rock piles mark the gravesites of those travelers who met their ends here. The landscape—widely spaced desert shrubs, ancient lava flows, dry arroyos, cloud-less skies, sandy plains, seemingly lifeless mountains—is either starkly beautiful or dreadfully ugly, depending on one's tastes.

In the latter half of the 1700s, El Camino del Diablo did not yet have its name. But it was there, at the edge of New Spain's north-western frontier, like a bent spear pointing north into the great unknown. The region's inhabitants had used the trail for centu-ries, probably millennia. Only a few Spanish priests and soldiers had ever traveled it. None had gone much beyond the Gila River to the interior of modern Arizona. None had gone much beyond the Colorado River to the interior of modern California or Nevada, let alone whatever lay beyond. For the Spanish, the terminus of El Camino del Diablo marked the end of the known world.[1]

There might, they thought, be a great west-flowing river up there. There might be another great civilization like those found centuries earlier in Mexico and Peru. There might be a usable route to the South Sea—our Pacific Ocean. There might be green, lush lands worthy of Spanish settlement.

Beyond this terrible desert there were likely Russians and Brit-ish who threatened Spain's hold on whatever *was* there. And there were certainly untold thousands of natives whose souls it was the responsibility of Spain to save. For those reasons if for no other, someday, somehow, someone with opportunity and cour-age would need to go farther—*más allá*—and explore the world beyond the Devil's Road.

When a Franciscan friar named Francisco Garcés arrived in the region in 1768, that day had come.

Introduction
The Prince of Lonely Wanderers

On July 4, 1776, as several dozen sweating American colonists sat in the stuffy Pennsylvania state house wondering what would befall them for having dared to rebel against their king, a lone, hungry Spanish priest lay in the windswept stone plaza of a Hopi village wondering what would befall him for having dared to serve his own.

The cleric's position was by far the more precarious. The colonists might indeed be hanged, as one of their number famously warned, but at least that misfortune, should it come about, lay in the indeterminate future. The bearded, black-haired, black-eyed priest was surrounded by dozens of agitated warriors. He might not survive the hour.[1]

Father Francisco Garcés's Mohave Indian friends had begged him not to go to Oraibi.[2] The Hopis would kill him, they said. But Garcés had been undaunted. The prospect of death was hardly new. For months he had been traveling through the wilderness. Unarmed and hundreds of miles from the nearest Spanish soldier, it was obvious that he might be murdered at any moment. Still, he knew that by going to the principal Hopi village he was courting even more danger than usual. Garcés was a Franciscan friar, and the history of his order's interactions with the Hopi tribe was not a happy one.

The Franciscans had established missions atop the Hopis' Black Mesa homeland as early as 1629. For twenty-four years things went relatively well, with the friars apparently winning the affection of a good portion of the profoundly traditionalist Hopis. That changed with the arrival of Father Alonso de Posada in 1653. Posada took a converted Hopi as his mistress, possibly against her will. When a Hopi man began to rally the community against this transgression, Posada had him killed by two native officials. Fearing they would reveal his crimes, Posada then had *those* officials hanged.

Father José de Espeleta succeeded Posada in 1661 and repaired much of the relational damage wrought by his predecessor. But his efforts were hampered by the savagery of his colleague Fray Salvador de Guerra, who was cut from the same cloth as Posada. On one occasion Guerra drenched several Hopi men with turpentine, then set them on fire. As one of his victims ran for a spring to douse the flames burning his flesh, Guerra rode him down and killed him. In light of such crimes, it is not surprising that during the region-wide Pueblo Revolt of August 1680 the churches built by the Franciscans on the Hopi mesas were destroyed, and the four friars who served them slain.[3]

Twenty years later, the Franciscans returned to the Hopi village of Awat'ovi. Dozens of its residents accepted baptism and began incorporating Christian devotions into their sacred practices. This was not a development welcomed by many of their Hopi kin. Warriors from neighboring villages slaughtered the Christianizing pueblo's residents and laid waste their town. Since that tragedy, at least nine Franciscan priests had visited the Hopi homeland. None had experienced success in gaining a foothold for the church.[4]

In broad outline, if not in gory detail, Francisco Garcés knew this history. But neither the prospect of failure nor physical danger tended to deter him from action. During the previous eight years he had wandered on muleback and foot, often alone, two or three thousand miles through the deserts, highlands, meadows, and mountains of New Spain's far-northern, unmapped frontier—today's states of Sonora, Arizona, Nevada, and California. He had been the first European to enter what became Nevada; the first to descend to the village of Supai in the Grand Canyon; the first to cross the treacherous Colorado desert west of Yuma, Arizona; the first to describe the San Joaquín Valley and its inhabitants; the first to make contact with several Native American peoples; and now the first to enter Hopi territory from the west. In his travels he had unceasingly preached the Christian gospel of peace and salvation. He had just as unceasingly sought to serve the interests of his Spanish sovereign. To him, as to every Spaniard he knew, crown and cross were but two sides of the same coin.[5]

✳ ✳ ✳

It was as a man in the service of both his earthly and his eternal king that Father Garcés thought his going to Moqui—as the Spanish called the region where the Hopis lived—vitally important. It lay along the route from Santa Fe, the long-established Spanish capital of the province of New Mexico, to Monterey, soon to become the capital of the Californias, from which settlement, by July 1776, new Franciscan missions dangled southward like a string of delicate rosary beads.

Actually, a route from Santa Fe to Monterey did not yet exist; Garcés was in the midst of an arduous attempt to find one. He knew that to establish a road from Alta (as opposed to Baja) California to New Mexico would be to expand upon the major strategic victory he had recently helped win for Spain's King Charles III. Over the previous eighteen months, Garcés had provided crucial assistance in locating an overland trail across the uncharted, all

1782 map of the Viceroyalty of New Spain. *Map by John Bew. Image courtesy of Arizona Historical Society.*

but waterless desert from Sonora to California. He had then helped lead the first expedition of Spanish settlers across the same path. Those families were now beginning to settle a place the Spanish called San Francisco. There, it was hoped, they would check the advance of Russia down the coast and discourage England's menacing maritime forays. Drawing a more direct line between that and other new settlements in Alta California and the old ones in northern New Mexico would serve to expand New Spain's northwestern frontier and solidify Mexico City's always tenuous hold on this far-flung area.[6]

To make the Spaniards' use of this new road feasible, Garcés believed, he first needed to win the powerful Hopis' friendship, as he had seemingly done thus far with every people with whom he had come into contact, not infrequently as the first European they had ever seen. From there he could proceed to winning for

Heaven Hopi souls and the souls of the men, women, and children constituting the many peoples around them. A new series of missions might be built to minister to and protect these Indians, and the introduction of Spanish agricultural methods and technological know-how would improve their earthly lives immensely. However the modern reader might assess them, such were Fray Garcés's thoughts and motivations.

The Hopis had other ideas. It was a bad omen when, on June 28, a Hopi man he encountered on the trail refused not only to kiss Garcés's crucifix—a rare refusal, in the priest's experience—but even to come near him. On July 2, as Garcés neared Oraibi, he met with more rejection when a young Hopi refused tobacco and two others declined to shake hands. Worse, they motioned for Garcés to turn back. Six of the eight Indian guides who had accompanied Garcés thus far became frightened and hung far to his rear. Only an old man and a young boy had the courage to walk with the padre as he rode the final section of trail up Black Mesa to Oraibi. Narrow, steep, and rocky, its very nature seemed to prophesy the difficulties that lay ahead.

Curious women and children watched from rooftops as Garcés rode into the center of the village, but no one greeted him. That was highly unusual. The priest found an out-of-the-way place near the street, dismounted, and sat. Two days passed, and no Hopi offered shelter, food, or conversation. That was even more unusual, for Garcés had been met warmly nearly everywhere he went. With little to do but be patient, he passed the time reflecting on the situation. Deeply impressed by the Hopis' high degree of agricultural and technological development, he could not shake the conviction that they were fundamentally good. Only their chiefs' prejudices and interest in preserving their own power, thought Garcés, as well as the friar's association with peoples they considered their enemies, kept the Hopi people from showing the kind of curious hospitality he had received elsewhere.

Two nights passed. Then, as the sun began to rise on the morning of July 4, flutes began to whistle, drums began to beat, warriors began to dance. Garcés became uneasy. Summoning his resolve, he remained where he was and waited. Finally, seeing that he was indisposed to leave, four warriors approached him. "Why have you come here?" they asked. "Don't stay. Go back to your own land."[7]

Not a very promising opening, but an opening nonetheless. Through signs, Spanish, and scraps of local languages, Garcés communicated as best he could where he had come from, all the peoples he had seen, and how welcoming and open all had been. He told his audience, now growing large, that he cherished the Hopi people and for that reason had come to tell them about God and his crucifixion in the form of his son, the God-Man Jesus Christ.

Finally, an old man scowled. "No, no," he thundered to Garcés, his face displaying contempt for all the priest had said.[8] It was the first time the friar's narrative had ever been so decisively and disdainfully rejected. Maybe he had been wrong about the Hopis, thought Garcés. Perhaps they had not understood him. Or perhaps success would require a more holy messenger. In any case, it was obvious that if he valued his life it was time to go.

Garcés asked for his mule. He mounted, smiled, and began to leave, praising the village and the residents' manner of dress as he slowly rode away. He would do nothing to make things harder for whomever the next missionary might be to visit Moqui. As his mule picked its way down the mesa, the reflective Garcés must have mused on how profoundly his Spanish predecessors had wounded and alienated the Hopis. Perhaps he thought too about how deeply attached a people could be to its own ways, its own rituals, and its own understandings of creation, the divine, and the human journey. Regardless, here in Moqui it was clear that evangelization would have to wait for another day. So too would his martyrdom.

* * *

Thomas Jefferson, Benjamin Franklin, John Adams, and their fellow conspirators on the continent's east coast had never heard of Francisco Garcés. They knew little, if anything, about the missions he and his coreligionists were planting in the continent's western reaches, and even less about the hot, dry, brown country in which Garcés was wandering, somewhere far, far beyond the green Allegheny Mountains that marked their own aborning nation's western frontier. Yet, within a century, the region Garcés was helping to map and prepare for European habitation would be part of the colonists' new nation.

For their labors, Jefferson, Franklin, and Adams have received the pious reverence—or at least the respectful attention—of succeeding generations. The primary monument to Francisco Garcés consists of a statue in a Bakersfield traffic circle.[9] Few people outside the specialized field of borderlands studies have heard of him. Yet, as generally unacknowledged as he may be, Garcés's multiple months-long treks into what was, for Spaniards, the unknown and unfathomably dangerous wilderness make him one of the greatest pathfinders in North American history.[10] Scholars continue to unpack the precious anthropological and ethnological data gathered by Garcés on his travels.[11] And Garcés's explorations made an undeniable geopolitical impact in leading to the settlement of California. Were it not for the friar's exploits, San Francisco and Los Angeles might have been established many years later than they actually were (1776 and 1781, respectively), and a Spanish society might have failed to take root before the onslaught of the American gold rush, depriving California of a significant component of its cultural heritage.

Whether this legacy is judged good or bad, Garcés certainly matters, which is why Herbert Bolton (1870–1953), the pioneering historian of Spanish American history, longed to undertake but was never able to make time for a biography of Francisco Garcés.[12] To Bolton, as to nearly everyone else who has made Garcés's acquaintance, the Franciscan priest was a strangely compelling figure. Bolton's favorite adjective for Garcés, whom he called "the prince of lonely wanderers," was "intrepid."[13] The Spanish military men, explorers, and missionaries who were Garcés's contemporaries were hardly blushing violets, and even among them the priest stands out for his fearlessness. "No one could surpass him in courage," wrote Bolton.[14] The friar was unbelievably energetic, tireless, and "a man of common sense."[15] Others, following in Bolton's wake, have described Garcés as "hardy," "warmhearted," "down-to-earth," "peerless," and filled with "abundant energy and ambition."[16] These traits, along with his natural likeability, helped Garcés build rapport with the Southwest's native inhabitants more quickly than any of his peers. He intuited how important it was to eat what they ate, sit how they sat, converse in the way they wished to converse. As a result, he came to exceed his Spanish compatriots in his sympathetic tolerance, even affection, for the peoples he encountered. The Hopis notwithstanding, the available sources indicate that his bravery, openness, and peaceable nature typically won him natives' affection and respect.

No wonder, then, that ever since Bolton failed to complete one the lack of a Garcés biography has been lamented.[17] One gets glimpses of Garcés in mainstream treatments of the history of the Southwest, but the only published post-Bolton volume that provides an extended account of his life and legacy is a fine study of several Franciscan missionaries published by Robert Kittle in 2017.[18] Sometimes Garcés goes completely unnoticed.[19] Usually he emerges from the contemporary literature as, at best, a tantalizingly fascinating supporting actor. That, until now, no full biography has appeared indicates the low esteem colonial-era missionaries and the enterprise they represented generally command in scholarly circles. More broadly, it suggests how easy it is for certain unassuming figures to slide through the cracks of history.

✶ ✶ ✶

Francis of Assisi founded his brotherhood of mendicant friars in 1209. By the 1300s, Franciscans had arrived in eastern Europe and central Asia. A century later they were in Africa. Next came the

Americas. A Franciscan, Bernardo Buil, became the first priest to sail for the New World, in September 1493. A Franciscan friar by the name of Juan Pérez probably said the first Mass in the New World on the island of Hispaniola on December 8, 1493. On the same island, another Franciscan, Francisco García de Padilla, was consecrated as the New World's first bishop on November 15, 1504. Finally, in 1523 the Franciscans became the first religious order to establish itself formally in New Spain. There, in Mexico City, the first friars—the so-called Twelve—founded the kingdom's first schools, hospitals, orphanages, printing presses, and libraries, besides engaging in religious instruction.[20] "In the history of what has come to be known as the 'Spiritual Conquest' of Mexico," writes Fernando Cervantes, "the Franciscan order was the first and always the most conspicuous protagonist."[21]

Not coincidentally, by the early 1500s the Franciscans were firmly established as the Spanish crown's favorite religious order. Centuries earlier, Ferdinand III (or Saint Ferdinand of Castile, ca. 1200–1252) had invited the Franciscans to southern Spain and, as a third-order Franciscan himself, was buried in the order's garb. King Ferdinand II (1452–1516) of Aragón and Queen Isabella of Castile (1451–1504) continued the tradition. Ferdinand would often retreat to the Franciscans' El Abrojo, near Valladolid, for spiritual refreshment, and Queen Isabella was, like Saint Ferdinand, so devoted to the order that she asked to be buried in a Franciscan habit.[22]

Operating so close to the seat of royal power was not always advantageous to the development of Franciscan virtue. But having a front-row view of, and plenty of direct involvement in, unedifying political machinations did not prevent the order from nurturing within its bosom a startling optimism concerning the inhabitants of the New World—so long as they could be protected from the sinners who had stained the Old. And so to the Americas the Franciscans flocked—five thousand of them by the end of the 1600s.[23] The papacy had given the Spanish crown the exclusive right to colonize the Indies in exchange for shouldering the burden of the church's apostolic mission there. The friars saw themselves as indispensable in ensuring that this mission was not sacrificed to lower, mundane ends, such as the exploitation of native labor. Here was a chance to build rigorous Christian communities untouched by the Old World's rivalries, tensions, sins, and unnecessarily low view of humanity. That goal could be achieved only via the segregation of Indians from settlers. The friars therefore usually resisted the integration of native populations into broader Spanish society, even as they claimed to be preparing them for such a role.[24]

In the colonial context, the Franciscans' idealistic worldview shaped a recurring dynamic in which missionaries often portrayed themselves—indeed genuinely thought of themselves—as taking the side of the Indians in building a new Christian order rooted in justice and love, as against the self-interested views of settlers, soldiers, and royal officials. From the latter groups' point of view, the missions infantilized the natives and enriched ecclesiastical coffers at the expense of everyone but the missionaries. Spanish settlers and officials also saw only too clearly how the missionaries themselves regularly failed to live up to their high Christian ideals, whether by demanding too much native labor, inflicting cruel punishments, or engaging in distasteful power politics, all of which we encounter in the pages that follow.[25] It was a resolution-defying pattern of conflict that formed quickly and persisted across time and place. Garcés, among many others, inherited it some 250 years later. He is best understood not as a "maverick," as some writers have maintained, but as a priest trying his best to deal with this complicated legacy on the ground in a creative and faithful way.[26] In this sense, he stands not only for other clerics who found themselves in a similar situation but for all those men and women of history who in good faith have, however imperfectly, sought the good of the Other across the chasm of cultural difference.

※ ※ ※

Juan Bautista de Anza, Junípero Serra, and Eusebio Kino have been the main Spanish characters in the story of the United States' southwestern borderlands, however that story is constructed.[27] Francisco Garcés, who explored more of the Southwest and had greater contact with more of the peoples of the region than any of these better-known figures, deserves to join their ranks. Although his life and diaries have been studied in the context of specific episodes in which he participated, such as the Anza expeditions and his explorations of California's Central Valley, up to now Garcés's many journeys and his unique interactions with Spanish and Indian leaders and communities have not been brought together into one unified account.

This volume is an attempt to fill that gap. In this biography I rely on the work of scholars who have published translations of some of Garcés's writings, as well as unpublished translations from various archival sources. These documents reveal how his missionary activities and goals both reflected and diverged from the standard missionary methods of the late eighteenth century. They reveal much, when approached critically, about how the region's inhabitants lived and thought. And they allow us to peek into the minds of the Spanish Christians who brought European culture and practices to the Southwest. In short, both as a man of his times and as a man who transcended his times, Garcés's life offers us a unique view on the origins and development of the American West.

Francisco Garcés was a faithful son of Saint Francis inclined to wander and explore in order to reach those who lived in ignorance of what he solemnly and passionately believed to be Good News. No man of his age was better suited to introduce the Christian faith to the longtime residents of New Spain's northern frontier. That frontier was no place for a person of delicate sensibilities, snobbishness, doubt, anxiety, or worldly ambition—especially not that part of the frontier explored by Garcés, for he could hardly have traveled through less climatically hospitable territory had he tried. The Colorado River valley, the Sonoran and Mojave deserts, the Central Valley of California, the places that are now Yuma, Lake Havasu City, Laughlin, Tacna, Gila Bend, Phoenix, Parker, Bakersfield, Coolidge, Brawley—these are the names that show up in lists of the hottest, driest, sunniest places in America. Garcés walked or rode through all of them. Often in high summer. While wearing a wool habit. With little or no water or food. With no map. With no knowledge of what lay ahead, or how he would be treated by the people he might encounter.

Toughness, courage, simplicity, and a generous spirit were what made for success in the parched, sun-baked deserts of Sonora and Arizona. Garcés embodied those virtues better than any other European in this time and place. Even after taking into account both his personal flaws and the tragic outcomes and violence associated with Spanish colonialism, for those virtues Garcés can be admired by all. In the end, they are why he deserves our attention.

✳ ✳ ✳

It seems appropriate, at this early juncture, to say a word about perspectives and sources. Francisco Garcés and the Spaniards among whom he moved encountered and wrote about dozens of different native peoples. Needless to say, we have no contemporaneous written testimony from these peoples on what that encounter was like from their perspective. That's a problem. The best we can do is to re-create those perspectives from a critical reading of the Spanish sources themselves, from the material record, from what we know about the relevant Native American cultures, and from later native accounts. Unfortunately, in telling the story of Garcés's life and journeys the extent to which I am able to bring native perspectives to bear is somewhat limited by space, and even more limited by my own lack of expertise.

Generally, therefore, I would urge the reader to keep in mind that the story I tell is a partial and inevitably biased one. It is important to ask—even when I do not prompt the reader to do so—what motives, intentions, understandings, and strategies this or that Indian group may have brought to this or that situation. And it is important to ask the same about the Spanish actors whose documents often constitute our only (written) historical sources. Although I think the principal actors in this story—very much including Garcés himself—are usually reliable witnesses, they were certainly human, meaning that they not only saw things from particular vantage points but also communicated what they saw in ways meant to advance their own particular agendas.

Having said all that, it is also true that a pervasive hermeneutic of suspicion greets Spanish missionaries in today's literature.[28] Indeed, that they were, as a group, guilty of genocide is now a rather commonly heard claim.[29] Sober historians tend to reject this extreme charge.[30] Yet even in some of its milder forms, to the extent that it distorts our vision the dominant, moralistic hermeneutic is lamentable.[31] In any case, I agree with Fernando Cervantes that "the role of the historian is to attempt to understand the past, as far as it is possible, on its own terms. . . . It would be a very impoverished present that did not show sympathy and understanding for belief and convictions that now seem discredited to us."[32]

This understanding of the historian's role accounts for the "sympathy and understanding," otherwise in rather short supply, that I extend to Spaniards in this biography, which is to some extent unavoidably centered in their worldview. I hope it will not be read as a failure to appreciate the harm and violence the colonial enterprise undoubtedly visited on Native Americans, about which we read much—if not as much as genuine justice would dictate—in the pages that follow.

CHAPTER I

Epiphany

1738–1763

or most Spaniards, daily life in the first few decades of the eighteenth century centered around religion, the extended family, and the land, much as it had for centuries. That was certainly the case in the tiny village of Morata del Conde. Known today as Morata de Jalón, the town was (and is) located in the province of Aragón, forty miles southwest of the provincial capital of Zaragoza along the road that then as now carried travelers heading west to the national capital of Madrid. At 1,400 feet above sea level, the town—surrounded by a fourteenth-century ashlar wall, complete with battlements— experienced mild winters followed by wet springs, warm summers, and crisp autumns.

Most of Morata's families had lived there for generations as farmers and artisans. Along the Río Jalón, in stone or adobe two-story homes capped by red-tile roofs, the village's human residents lived on the top floors, its animal residents below. The people of Morata kept body and soul together by cultivating

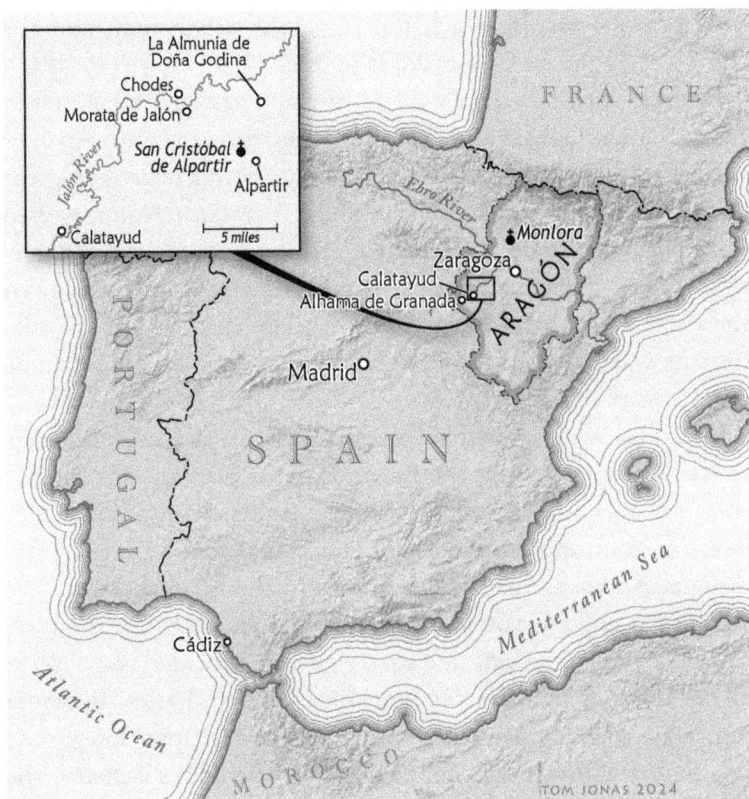

Garcés's Spain. Garcés spent his youth and young manhood along
the Jalón River in the province of Aragón. *Map by Tom Jonas.*

hemp and flax, harvesting olives and grapes, and raising sheep
in the surrounding brown, grassy, nearly treeless hills. In the eve-
nings they promenaded through the new, impressive plaza surrounded by the palace of the Count of Morata, the town hall,
and the Church of Santa Ana, the latter two buildings sending
slender, square-faced towers soaring into the sky.[1] To the count,
on whose estate their houses and farms were located, villagers
gave a portion of their harvests.[2] To the parish they gave a portion of their incomes. Existence had a simple, integrated, highly

parochial pattern in which the state, the aristocracy, and the church each had its God-ordained place.

In 1728, with the dispensation of their pastor, two Moratan cousins, Juan Garcés and Antonia Maestro, were wed. An heir arrived when Juan Francisco Dionisio was born a little over a year later. Juan and Antonia's second child, Francisca Antonia, died in infancy. Their third, Josepha Casimira, was more fortunate, as was their fourth, a boy born on April 12, 1738.[3] He was given the name Francisco Tomás Hermenegildo when, as was the custom, he was baptized the next day in blue-domed Santa Ana by a Franciscan priest.[4]

If the Garcés and Maestro clans shared in the stereotypical traits of the Aragonese—and the future exploits of Francisco suggest they probably did—they had a marked tendency toward independence of mind and doggedness of will, traits embodied in the traditional Aragonese oath of allegiance to the Spanish king: "We who are as good as you swear to you who are no better than we, to accept you as our king and sovereign lord, provided you observe all our liberties and laws; but if not, not."[5] King Charles III, whose policies would later play a determinative role in shaping Francisco's missionary career, once complained that one of his advisors, the Conde de Aranda, was "more obstinate than an Aragonese mule."[6]

That was probably not an atypical complaint of government officials about proverbially sturdy Aragonese peasants like Juan Garcés. Juan was a farmer, but a fair number of his relations, including at least two of his brothers, were priests. Domingo was the vicar in the little town of Chodes, less than a mile away. The second clergyman brother, Francisco, had the honor of serving as personal chaplain to the Count and Countess of Morata. It was this Father Francisco, along with another uncle named Tomás, for whom little Francisco was named. The child's third namesake, Hermenegildo, was a sixth-century martyr whose feast was celebrated on April 13. *Nomen est omen*, indeed, for little Francisco Garcés.

From all appearances Juan and Antonia were devoted Catholics. They brought their toddler Francisco to be confirmed by the bishop of Tarazona when he paid the hamlet a visit in September 1739, and before Antonia's child-bearing days ended she had given birth to four more children, two of whom died, like Francisca Antonia, in infancy. Because he was their second-born son, it made sense to designate Francisco for religious life; fortunately, from an early age he showed himself "inclined toward sacred things."[7] Uncle Domingo took Francisco under his wing, raising him in the rectory at Chodes. The boy assisted with parish tasks as best he could, but otherwise we know very little about his youth. One historian speculates that Francisco occasionally took "time out to join the other boys in fishing . . . beneath the ancient one-span stone bridge or assaulting the castle ruin high on a rocky summit behind the village."[8] Perhaps. Undoubtedly he joined in the village's August festival honoring both the Virgin Mary and San Roque, the second of whom had lived in France during the fourteenth century, devoted his life to ministering to the sick, and had since gained a reputation as a powerful protector against the plague.

As a boy, Francisco also would have been aware of the fame and popularity of those missionary preachers who roamed throughout Spain, exhorting their many listeners to hold fast to traditional Christian values and social arrangements amid the changes being wrought by Enlightenment thought and commercial practices. Perhaps he heard the Jesuit Pedro de Calatayud promote devotion to the Sacred Heart of Jesus. Surely he crossed paths with his fellow Aragonese and namesake Antonio Garcés, a fervent devotee of the rosary who served as one of King Ferdinand VI's court preachers. (Antonio may even have been one of Francisco's cousins.) Antonio Garcés was so popular that his clothes were ripped off his body by relic hunters after he died. It is entirely plausible that a young Francisco took note of how Antonio "shared the plain life of the poor," and how during his sermons the friar would display an image of Mary surrounded by roses and holding the Christ child.[9]

Whether because he was inspired by such domestic missionaries, because he enjoyed his uncle's ecclesiastical tutelage, or for

some other reason, Francisco decided at age fifteen to enter the
Order of Friars Minor. In his application he provided documentation of his baptism and confirmation, testimonials to his good
character, and, crucially, proof of his "untainted Christian lin-
eage."[10] He was accepted and at the age of sixteen was sent to the
convent of San Cristóbal de Alpartir.[11]

※ ※ ※

Just what attracted Francisco to a religious order rather than the
diocesan priesthood, and particularly to the Franciscans, can only
be surmised. The order had long been the most popular in Spain,
so he would have surely known some friars. Perhaps Garcés had
acquired a devotion to Saint Francis. Perhaps he was attracted
to the Franciscan course of studies: Francisco was never thought
by his peers to be an intellectual, and though the Franciscan curriculum was certainly not easy it was less academically rigorous
and less oriented toward a life of scholarly study and debate than
were those offered by the Dominicans and Jesuits. Or perhaps
Francisco was enthralled even at this early age by the exciting
possibility of preaching the gospel in faraway lands.

If that was the case, the miraculous experiences of a Franciscan
nun named María from nearby Ágreda may have had something
to do with Francisco's choice. María had become well known
throughout Spain—indeed, throughout the Catholic world—
a century earlier, and her story illustrates well the intellectual
atmosphere that pervaded that world.[12]

As a young child, María displayed extraordinary spiritual
precocity, reaching the age of reason by four years and suffering her own Saint John-of-the-Cross-style dark night of the soul
by the age of ten. Entering a new Franciscan convent founded
by her mother—in their own retrofitted home—at the age of
sixteen, the pretty, engaging María was drawn deeply into the
spiritual life. That life became so intense, interiorly, that after
taking communion she would enter into what appeared to be

trances. During these states, as the nosy nuns who took the lib-
erty of peering into her cell were shocked to witness, she actually levitated—on multiple occasions. Priests were summoned.
They saw it too. (Levitation was in the air; just a few years later
a Franciscan priest named Saint Joseph of Cupertino would
attract the attention of the Inquisition for having similar flights
of ecstasy.)

María was abashed and angry at having been spied on by her
religious sisters. A cloistered woman deserved more privacy. Still,
when pressed by higher authorities, she dutifully reported what
had happened to her during these periods of heightened experience. It seemed to her, she said, that she had traveled—not just
spiritually but physically—to the New World, a place she had
long ardently wished to visit. There, in a dry land a thousand or
so miles north of Mexico City, she had preached the gospel to
various native peoples. She had journeyed there many times—
hundreds, perhaps—between 1620 and 1623, although of course
during that period she also never left the convent in Ágreda.
These weren't dreams, she insisted. She had *been* there, feeling
the wind in her hair, smelling the flora, seeing and conversing
with the amazed Indians who gathered to hear her. To her message they had been highly receptive. She had urged them to seek
out missionaries and ask for baptism.[13]

María's miraculous experiences were well known in early
eighteenth-century Morata to peasants and clerics alike. The fact
that she had lived nearby invested María's story with additional
interest. By the time Francisco Garcés embarked on his own religious path, Franciscans far and wide had been deeply affected by
María's writings. They were stirred not just by her stories of the
New World but by her report that Saint Francis himself had told
her the Indians of the New World would be converted by merely
seeing a friar.[14] María's *Mystical City of God* was the only book,
other than the Bible, taken to New Spain by Junípero Serra, a
man who would one day be Garcés's acquaintance and peer.[15] But
she was just one of many men and women who may have inspired

young Francisco to join Saint Francis's order and eventually conceive a desire to enter the mission field.

Álvar Núñez Cabeza de Vaca was not a religious. But, to the extent Francisco thought about the souls in North America awaiting harvest, Cabeza de Vaca's story must have also offered encouragement. Having just barely survived Indian attacks and near-starvation as part of a Spanish expedition to Florida, Cabeza de Vaca and some eighty companions found themselves shipwrecked off Galveston Island in 1528. Disease, hunger, and enslavement soon whittled the number of survivors down to four. In 1534, Cabeza de Vaca and the three other surviving Spaniards managed to escape their masters. Having very little idea where they were, they made their way in a westerly direction across a vast, utterly unknown landscape before finally reencountering European civilization in the form of a party of Spanish slavers near today's Culiacán, Mexico. During their incredible journey, Cabeza de Vaca was compelled to pray over many sick and dying natives. To his own amazement no less than everyone else's, these prayers for healing had frequently seemed to work—well enough, indeed, that by the time they encountered the Spanish slavers the Cabeza de Vaca party had acquired a widespread reputation for an ability to perform medical miracles by the power of the Christian god. To the Spanish mind, the miracles worked through Cabeza de Vaca were clearly part of Divine Providence's plan to win Native Americans for Christ and His Church.[16]

Many more Spaniards and Franciscans who had won glory in the mission fields were known to Francisco and his contemporaries. The twenty-six martyrs of Japan—four of them Spaniards, all but three of them Franciscans—who were crucified in Nagasaki in 1597 had been beatified in 1627 by Pope Urban VIII and were much celebrated in the Spain of Francisco's youth.[17] Blessed Raymond Llull, a Mallorcan, made it his life's mission to preach Christ to the Muslims of North Africa; according to tradition, he was stoned by an ungrateful audience in Tunis in 1314 and died the next year. And then there were Garcés's

namesakes: the Jesuit Saint Francis Xavier, famously brave missionary to the Far East, and the Andalusian Franciscan named
Francisco Solano y Jiménez (Saint Francis Solanus), who evan-
gelized throughout South America, courageously defended the
rights of the continent's native peoples, and was canonized a
decade before Garcés's birth.

Finally, there was the scripture and liturgy of the church. Everyone knew that Christ had commissioned his followers to "make
disciples of all nations, baptizing them in the name of the Father
and of the Son and of the Holy Spirit."[18] And everyone knew that
the readings on the most important feast of the year, Epiphany,
promised that such activity would not be in vain—that, whereas
prior to Christ's advent "darkness" covered the earth, the people
of all nations were destined to worship the triune God.[19] For a
young man drawn to piety and imbued with a Spaniard's yearn-
ing for an honorable death, even martyrdom, there was no shortage of compelling stories or attractive models.

✶ ✶ ✶

Of all the many important journeys Francisco would take, the
journey from Morata to San Cristóbal—all of ten miles—was the
shortest. It surely seemed farther than that to the teenage Francisco, partly because of the very local life he had led, and partly
because of San Cristóbal's peaceful, self-contained location halfway up a mountain. The Franciscans who lived in San Cristóbal
were Recollects, a reform-minded branch of the order that had
sprung up in France during the late 1500s. The Recollects were
devoted to prayer, penance, and solitary spiritual reflection, but
not to the exclusion of missionary work.[20] By the time Francisco
was invested with their gray habit at San Cristóbal—binding
himself forever, as the vows put it, to "living in obedience, without property, and in chastity"—the Recollects had been active in
New France (today's Canada) for more than a century.[21] There
were also Recollects evangelizing in New Spain, the Philippines,

and elsewhere. Francisco heard their stories while he struggled through his studies in the classics and philosophy.[22]

"Struggled" seems like the right verb for, although Francisco seems to have taken well to the Franciscan routine of prayer, meditation, discipline, and physical mortification, he was not exactly the second coming of Saint Bonaventure, his order's most famous intellectual. Later, his simplicity would often be remarked upon, and his circuitous writing style would be considered infelicitous by those New World authorities who tried to make out the meaning of his letters from the field (one scholar has retroactively diagnosed Garcés as dyslexic).[23] Even so, Francisco did well enough to take the next step toward the priesthood. He was sent to the Franciscan convent in Calatayud—another twenty miles or so, as the crow flies, toward Madrid—to study theology, and he later merited the appellation "theologian."[24]

Simplicity has its advantages. One story has come down to us about Francisco's time at Calatayud, and like most stories about Garcés it was told to underscore how successfully he connected with the socially humble. It was Francisco's practice, we are told, to take solitary walks in the Calatayud countryside, during which he would seek out peasants—people like his own family, perhaps—to whom to preach. On one of these walks he befriended a potter, who took such a liking to the young man that when he suddenly found himself upon his deathbed he sent for "Father Garcés" to come quickly and hear his confession. It took a while for the convent's superior to realize that the priest named Garcés who was so urgently requested was in fact Brother Francisco. The potter, upon being informed that "Father" Garcés was no father at all, insisted that he would nevertheless make his final confession to no one else. Finally, promising not to leave his side, Francisco was able to persuade the potter to confess to an ordained priest, after which the forgiven man died in Garcés's arms, having instructed in his will that all his goods be left to the Franciscans—and that a painting of the Immaculate Conception be placed in the convent in honor of his young friend in the gray habit.[25]

His six years of study in philosophy and theology completed, Francisco entered the Franciscan house located in the lively town of La Almunia de Doña Godina, a few miles east of his hometown of Morata on the road to Zaragoza.[26] We have no first- or even secondhand record of Garcés's thoughts at this time. Perhaps he expected to stay in this Franciscan institution forever, praying, preaching, hearing confessions, and ministering to the sick in the region of his birth. If so, a change of heart came quickly. Francisco had been at La Almunia for only a year or two when two recruiters from the Colegio de Santa Cruz de Querétaro showed up and changed his life's path.

The *colegio* at Querétaro, a city located about 125 miles north of Mexico City in New Spain, was in 1763 one of twenty-one such Franciscan institutions in the New World. The purpose of these colegios was to form well-educated, highly disciplined, courageous missionaries for work in the field, especially on those frontiers where Indian "nations" (to employ the term most in use at the time) remained unreached, or at least unbaptized. It was a difficult life, and the recruiters were therefore looking for a certain type. They preferred men who had already been ordained as priests; who were healthy and neither smoked nor drank to excess; who had experience preaching and confessing; who had reasonably obedient natures; and who had voiced a desire to go to the Americas prior to the recruiters' arrival, thereby demonstrating that they might truly have a calling.[27]

Imagine, for a moment, the emotional appeal such an opportunity exerted on a young, zealous cleric (for at around this time, at the age of twenty-five, Francisco had been ordained to the priesthood), and how he would have approached it intellectually. Thousands of miles away there lived people who, through no fault of their own, had never heard the gospel, never been baptized. Were they to die in such a state, the church taught, they could not be admitted into Heaven. (Whether the unbaptized who died under such circumstances necessarily went to Hell was a somewhat different question. Many theologians thought they did; others thought a middle state they referred to as "Limbo" was a possibility, at least for infants; and others adhered to the doctrine of "baptism of desire," more fully developed later, which held that upright, unbaptized persons could enter the presence of the Beatific Vision.) These pagan nations lived in a state of spiritual ignorance, went the thinking, as was attested by the many stories of their depraved ways, and as could be known by simply attending to the language of the liturgy, Christian hymnody, and the Bible itself. Each of those sources of wisdom attested to the notion that a world that did not know the light of Christ, the source of light itself, was inevitably a frightful one. As the experiences of María de Ágreda (who was highly venerated in the colegios of New Spain), Cabeza de Vaca, Saint Francisco Solanus, and countless other missionaries demonstrated, pagan peoples would ultimately be immensely grateful for having been brought into the Christian fold, however much they might resist the church's teachings at first, thanks to the devil's malign influence.[28] And not just would their souls be saved. Their material circumstances would improve as well, for it was obvious to Europeans that their own civilization was more advanced in every conceivable way. What compassionate person wouldn't want to be part of such an enterprise—if he, or she, had but the courage to sign up for it?

In any case, Francisco—even though he was comparatively young and must have had little experience preaching and confessing—was offered a place at the colegio in Querétaro by Father Joseph Antonio Bernad, leader of its recruitment efforts.[29] A great adventure beckoned, but at the same time Francisco was directed by Father Bernad to meditate on his decision for four or five days, speaking only to his confessor during that time.[30] Due warning was given: life from now on would be more strict, less comfortable, more self-sacrificial. Francisco needed to consider honestly the depth of commitment being requested. Such cautions would have come as no surprise to Garcés. Everyone knew that the colegios followed a rigorous observance of the Franciscan rule and that the friars within their walls lived lives of profound self-abnegation.[31]

Garcés did not waver. On December 15, 1762, he received his patent, or license, to enter the colegio from Father Bernad. The Advent and Christmas seasons that followed must have been bittersweet, as Francisco said good-bye to his family and friends in nearby Morata. It was possible he would one day return, but not for at least ten years, the commitment that missionaries made in exchange for a modicum of financial support from the Spanish crown for their outfitting, travel, and living expenses. More probably, both Francisco and his loved ones knew, they would never see each other again. Not on this side of the veil.

On January 25, 1763, Francisco Garcés began his long walk from home. It would not be far from the truth to say he never stopped walking.

❊ ❊ ❊

Francisco had a traveling companion to Madrid, a tall, lanky, black-and-curly-haired friar named Juan Crisóstomo Gil de Bernabe who had been recruited by Bernad from another mountaintop Recollect monastery, this one on Monlora.[32] For the next decade, the fates of these two Aragonese would be inextricably linked.

It was not difficult for Fray Gil to win Francisco's affection. The former was in his mid-thirties and was both more worldly and more spiritually advanced than the young, enthusiastic priest who walked by his side. Juan was handsome, a wonderful singer, and an emotionally powerful preacher. He was also witty and pleasingly smooth in his dealings with others—a star priest, in other words, who had made quite a career sacrifice in order to discipline his soul on Monlora and was now making an even greater one in volunteering for the West Indies mission field. He was a man his home province must have been sorry to lose, and someone from whom Francisco could learn a great deal.[33]

Walking about eight leagues—or a little over twenty miles—
per day, the friars soon passed through Father Gil's hometown of
Alhama, an ancient spa town located, like Morata, on the banks
of the Río Jalón. A week later they arrived in Madrid, where they
were greeted again by Father Bernad. Juan purportedly forswore
exploration of the great city's sights, opting instead to spend
his time ramping up his spiritual exercises. Francisco probably
joined him. Soon they were on their way to the bustling port city
of Cádiz, for centuries Spain's principal port of embarkation for
the New World. Here twenty-four other priests and brothers
also bound for Querétaro joined them, including a stocky, moon-
faced, prickly fellow from Catalonia named Pedro Font, with
whom Garcés's life would become as entangled as it would with
Father Gil's.[34] Father Bernad set to checking all the necessary
bureaucratic boxes; in Spain and its overseas dominions there
was *always* an abundance of boxes to be checked. The Inquisition
must sign off on the books in the recruits' possession. Insurance
must be purchased to cover the goods being taken on the journey.
The distances the friars had traveled to Cádiz must be officially
logged. Supplies had to be gathered.

It all took time. Francisco and the others had ample opportunity to examine the colorful city life that now swirled around
them—a life that could hardly have been more different than
everything Francisco had ever known. Cosmopolitan Cádiz, in
the words of the College of Santa Cruz's chronicler, was "the
emporium of nations and the charm and attraction of taste."
A priest who had sailed from Cádiz to the New World fourteen years earlier, reminiscing about the welter of languages and
commercial chaos encountered on the city's streets, wrote that it
was in Cádiz that he "began to understand what is meant by the
confusion of the world."[35] Hundreds of ships, perhaps as many
as one thousand, flying the flags of numerous nations, sat at
anchor in the walled city's port. The narrow and noisy streets
teemed with priests, sailors, merchants, and those catering to

their needs and desires. In the months that a religious waiting to sail to the New World usually bided his time in this whirling city, it was easy to become distracted. Once again, however, we are told that Juan and Francisco sequestered themselves, using their time in Cádiz to pray and practice self-mortification and perhaps read up on missionary life in the Americas.[36] If it was not fear of the sea, perhaps it was this strict regimen that led to four of Father Bernad's recruits ultimately failing to make the voyage.[37]

Not until late July were the two frigates that would sail the Querétaro party the five thousand miles to Veracruz ready to be loaded with the two dozen or so containers of the personal effects, tools of the priestly trade, paper, chocolate, and liquor that constituted the friars' gear. Compared to the other ships riding at anchor, the *Júpiter* and *Mercurio* had to have looked "discouragingly small," in the words of historian John Kessell. "From stem to stern they measured no more than one hundred and ten feet, about the length of two Greyhound buses parked bumper to bumper. In rank cabins below decks, where upper and lower wooden planks served as berths, there was not room to stand up."[38] Besides people, each ship would transport at least four hundred live chickens. If all went according to plan, the missionaries would be stuck on board these fragrant vessels for at least six weeks. Rarely did all go to according to plan.

On August 1, 1763, the *Júpiter* and *Mercurio* drew anchor. Besides the general discomfort of their surroundings, their occupants immediately faced two concerns: seasickness and pirates. To defend against the latter, the *Guerrero*, a man-of-war with seventy-four mounted guns, escorted them for a week until they reached the Canary Islands. There was no defense against seasickness. As the small ships rode the massive swells of the open ocean, most of the landlubber recruits fell victim to vomiting, cramps, and dizziness. Filthy water sloshed continually over the floors of their berths. The accompanying stench was almost impossible to bear. The two meals provided each day, served cold out of a fear that the ship's ovens might spark a fire, did little to stimulate the appetite. Even the most pious of the friars, as he labored to recite his daily Mass and Divine Office, must have been hard pressed not to wonder why God had led him into such a hell.

Storms made it all worse. During one especially frightening mid-Atlantic tempest the *Júpiter*, on which Garcés, Font, and eleven other friars were passengers, fared so badly that its Basque captain ordered eight cannons jettisoned to prevent her from sinking. The gambit worked (although the captain would later be taken to task by royal authorities none too happy about the loss of the king's artillery). One and a half months after leaving Cádiz, the *Júpiter* limped into harbor in Puerto Rico. There, among the tropical papaya and banana trees, Garcés and the others waited out the equinox, that ancient sailor's nemesis, until continuing to Veracruz, where they arrived on November 8. The voyage had taken one hundred days.

The *Mercurio* was not so fortunate. Separated from the *Júpiter* en route to the Indies and missing for weeks after the *Júpiter* arrived in Veracruz, her whereabouts were discovered only when a messenger sent by her captain arrived at the New Spain port town of Campeche. The storm that had rocked the *Júpiter* had also damaged the *Mercurio*. The ship's captain had sailed to Havana for repairs, but unlike the wise skipper of the *Júpiter* he would hear nothing of waiting until after the equinox to sail for Veracruz. It was a decision for which those on board paid a heavy price. Blown off course by gale-force winds, then becalmed for days somewhere in the Caribbean, the *Mercurio* finally ran aground on a submerged reef near the Yucatán and capsized. Fortunately, all aboard made it to shore. Unfortunately, they soon discovered how unhealthful the New World could be. It was terribly hot, they were terribly hungry, and they were terribly lost. In a short time many of the company were struck by a severe fever—probably malaria. Each of the traveling friars somehow survived, but before help arrived death took a number of their shipmates, including the *Mercurio's* impatient captain.

Later, Father Gil would be singled out for acting with particular heroism in ministering to the sick and dying.[39] As far as Francisco Garcés was concerned, it was not the last time that Father Juan would earn such distinction.

CHAPTER 2

The Children's Padre

1763–1767

I
n more than one respect Veracruz and the lands that lay
between that disease-ridden city on the Gulf of Mexico
and the friars' destination of Querétaro formed a new
world for Garcés and his companions. Much of what they saw
along the *camino real* on which they now traveled, most likely on
horseback, in the late autumn of 1763 dramatized the differences
between New and Old Spain. Veracruz itself was more lush and
tropical than anything the men had yet encountered, save perhaps San Juan, Puerto Rico, where they stayed briefly. Then, as
they ascended the eastern slope of the Sierra Madre Oriental,
they rose to unaccustomed heights—eight thousand feet at the
pass at Perote. If and when the weather was clear, the Spanish
Franciscans gazed on mountains of unbelievable magnitude,
the most imposing being Mount Orizaba, which rises to more
than eighteen thousand feet. Finally, after two weeks of hard
travel, they arrived at beautiful, wealthy Mexico City. Here the
group likely rested at the Franciscan College of San Fernando;

this may have been where Garcés met, for the first time, the man who would become that college's most famous son, a Mallorcan named Junípero Serra.[1]

From Mexico City it was still another 125 miles or so to the College of Santa Cruz in Querétaro. When Garcés finally entered the colegio gates in late 1763, the impressively large structure stood, as it stands today, on a hill overlooking the pretty colonial city. Querétaro was a leafy and prosperous town of about 14,000 people. Sprinkled among their adobe houses were more than a dozen convents and tall churches, some of which were already approaching a century or two in age.[2] The city boasted a strikingly long and beautiful aqueduct that rose seventy-five feet above the ground and was supported by seventy-four Romanesque arches. A few years earlier, a local grandee had even had running water installed in his palace. Water, wealth, European culture and technology: life in Querétaro could hardly have contrasted more starkly with the rough and arid frontier to which Garcés would soon be sent.

The gray-stoned complex that was the College of Santa Cruz sat in the heart of the city. Founded in 1683, the colegio was the brainchild of Father Antonio Llinás, a Franciscan whose experience in New Spain had made him realize the need for a new kind of religious institution.[3] Santa Cruz's mission, according to the colegio's constitution, was "to preach the Holy Gospel to all creatures, that is: to the faithful by reforming their customs; and to the unfaithful by giving them notice and light of the faith, by baptizing them, and by adding them to the flock of the Roman Holy Church, and enlisting them to its obedience, without which none are saved."[4] As this statement of purpose indicates, the colegio was self-consciously an institution of the Catholic Counter-Reformation. Its primary goal was not to form contemplatives, to serve the poor, or to succor the sick but to evangelize—that is, to convert the hearts of Catholics and non-Catholics alike, turning them toward God and away from error. The colegio's business was to save souls and form Christians. To accomplish that end it would send missionaries wherever it could.

The College of Santa Cruz was such an inspiring success that soon after it was established the need for similar institutions throughout the Spanish realm became apparent. Twenty-eight additional Franciscan *colegios apostólicos de propaganda fide* were founded in both the New World and Spain by 1812.[5] These apostolic colleges became the principle and most prestigious training centers for Franciscan missionaries in the Americas. Recruiters had little trouble finding volunteers. At Querétaro alone, a total of 800 friars were resident between 1683 and 1829; 350 of these were, like Francisco Garcés, natives of Spain—or *peninsulares*. The 1760s were a particularly fruitful period for recruitment, with more than 150 Spanish friars arriving at Santa Cruz during that decade alone.[6]

When Garcés arrived in the autumn of 1763, he may not have been warmly welcomed. Resident friars were frequently skeptical and fearful of new arrivals, who threatened to upset existing power balances. At the time Francisco entered the colegio, debates were under way between older and younger friars over the extent to which native ways of life ought to be accommodated in the missions.[7] Francisco, fortunately, had a disarming personality. "Simple and artless" as he was, in the appraisal of one of his brother priests, he had little aptitude or appetite for institutional politics.[8] There is little reason to believe he was ever a controversial, or even an influential, figure at the colegio.

That doesn't mean he was unnoticed. Francisco's relative youth prevented him from acting as a confessor to women. He was expected instead to confess teens and preteens, so he sought out the town's boys, and he soon acquired a reputation as their special favorite.[9] It helped that he was kind to them—kindness not always being a feature of the eighteenth-century confessional, or of the eighteenth-century household, for that matter—and that he was not above winning their friendship by providing sweet treats. Before long he was being called "the children's padre," or, more literally, "the father of the boys." There could have been an element of mockery in this sobriquet, the intended implication being

that ministering to the town's youths was about all the unsophis-
ticated Francisco would ever be fit to do. But there was something
of St. John Vianney, even Father Flanagan, in Garcés's makeup.
While other friars shrank from dealing with Querétaro's urchins,
with their dirty bodies, dissipated families, profane speech, and
bad habits, Francisco apparently relished their company.[10] No one
seems to have noticed how this capacity for understanding and
tolerance fitted him perfectly for mission work.

He was certainly not noticed for his scholarship. As at Calatayud, Francisco managed to escape his academic work at the colegio without a reputation for brilliance, doubtless in part because
his dyslexia made both reading and writing rather difficult. (Garcés's later letters are noteworthy both for their creative spelling
and for their neologisms, often consisting of three or four separate words smashed into one.)[11] In addition to advanced study in
philosophy and theology, the curriculum to which Garcés applied
himself as best he could included practical courses in apologetics,
rhetoric, and pedagogy.[12] These courses were supplemented by
conferencias, seminars in which the friars discussed the practical
application of otherwise abstract moral theology in daily life.[13]
All this academic work was situated within a highly structured
daily routine that allowed for little if any idleness, a vice the friars
believed to be as evil as did the Puritans. The first wakening took
place at midnight. A period of group prayer—matins—began at
12:15, the day's first indication that life in the colegio was more
rigorous even than in other convents, where matins was not typically observed.[14]

Day after day, Francisco entered into and was gradually formed
by the monastic schedule. After matins was concluded at 1:15,
there was a half hour of silent prayer. Veteran friars were awakened again at 3:45 to celebrate Mass at four o'clock; the rest of the
community was awakened at 4:15. Choir and silent prayer took
place at five, followed by the singing of prime in choir at 5:30.
Mass for the whole convent was said at eight o'clock. Conferencia
was held at eleven, followed by lunch at noon. From one to two

o'clock, there was rest for whoever wanted it; others prayed or
conducted their spiritual exercises. Vespers was prayed at two,
followed by another conferencia. Compline was sung at five. Evening prayer was said at six. Dinner was served at 7:15, followed by
self-discipline. Finally, silence was required as of eight that evening. If a friar went to bed right away, he could get four hours
of sleep prior to the beginning of the next day.[15] We must keep
this schedule in mind later, when we try to understand why friars
complained so much about the lack of discipline displayed by soldiers, settlers, and Indians outside the colegio walls. The fathers
did not always account for how greatly their unique formation set
them apart.

Even the mealtimes at the College of Santa Cruz offered little
relaxation of the mind. As they dined, friars would have read to
them some edifying words—perhaps the Franciscan rule (the
regulations guiding Franciscan life) or passages from the Bible.[16]
Fortunately, the soup, meat, eggs, vegetables, fruit, and beans
were usually good and relatively plentiful. Tobacco could be
smoked (usually in pipes), a glass of wine might be offered, and
hot chocolate, the favorite drink of the New World's Spaniards,
was usually available.[17] This relatively generous feeding of the
stomach might have been the only way in which the colegio did
not prepare its friars well for life on the mission frontier.

One could hardly fail to emerge from this sort of spiritual
training without getting used to communing with oneself and
one's God, without acquiring the habit of partaking in long, long
periods of prayer, and without knowing how to argue for the
"holy mysteries of our faith," as a Queretaran friar would have
put it. Here is where the conferencias came in. Mandated by the
Council of Trent as a necessary part of a priest's education, these
working seminars were where questions relevant to missionary
practice were hashed out. At a conferencia, a veteran friar would
present a thesis in defense of some position. Sexual ethics, money
lending, the rights of labor—such topics and others were grist
for the mill. Students then attempted to refute the presenting

friar as best they could. The point was to make every member of the colegio a strong apologist for Catholic Christianity, ready to respond persuasively to any objection and to answer knowledgably any question, a goal further aided by the colegio's well-stocked library.[18] No latter-day Luther or New Spain Voltaire would be able to befuddle an official representative of the church if the College of Santa Cruz could help it.

It is sometimes maintained that the Franciscans, unlike the Jesuits and Dominicans, cared little about learning native languages.[19] This is not true. It is especially false with respect to the Franciscan colegios. It was plainly impossible to teach all the Indian languages a missionary might encounter on the frontier— there were, for example, at least fourteen separate languages spoken in the region of modern New Mexico and Arizona alone, many of them mutually unintelligible, and many with mutually unintelligible subdialects, and *one hundred* distinct languages were spoken in modern California—but instruction in Otomí, Nahuatl, and other native tongues was offered.[20] An even bigger problem was that many Indian languages lacked a vocabulary for abstract concepts like those at the heart of Christian doctrine, such as the Trinity or transubstantiation—at least as far as the missionaries could tell.[21] The friars were therefore directed to try their hardest to learn the languages of the peoples to whom they were assigned and do the best they could in those languages until the Indians could be taught Castilian Spanish, as official policy directed.[22] Garcés would have entered Querétaro knowing at least two languages (Castilian and Latin) and possibly a third (Aragonese, still spoken in rural areas of the province while Francisco was a youth). Later he would learn the Piman language and, somewhat surprisingly, gain a reputation as being one of the northern frontier's best linguists.[23]

Finally, to achieve a life of holiness meant adopting holy habits. One of the great obstacles to creating such habits was the desiring, demanding body—Saint Francis's "Brother Ass." Well-instructed Catholics did not think the body was bad, a misinterpretation one continues to hear today.[24] Quite the contrary. The human body, as part of creation, was good, and it had been given special status when God took on bodily form in the person of Jesus. But like all orthodox Catholics, Franciscans did think the body needed to be disciplined, since like the rest of creation it had been corrupted by the Fall and could therefore lead a person to sin. Very few eighteenth-century men and women regarded the liberation of fleshly desire as something to be wished. Furthermore, voluntarily to experience bodily discomfort was both to imitate Christ and to do penance for sin—one's own as well as the sins of others.

Even if we put such theological considerations aside, the disciplining of the body and the concomitant habits of self-abnegation encouraged by the colegios made as much sense for missionaries in training as they do for modern Marines. Conditions in the mission field were incredibly rugged. Extreme discomfort and privation were constant companions. To persevere, one needed to develop a strong mind and an iron will all but impervious to physical pain. Hence the self-mortification practiced by the Franciscans: the hair shirts, the plank beds, the scourging of backs. Such practices may seem like cruel and pointless self-abuse, but they were not so different in intent from the grueling exercise and dietary regimes zealously undertaken by today's athletes, not to mention large segments of the West's educated classes.

The saints understood. Along with Saint Francis of Assisi himself, one of the preeminent models placed in front of Garcés and the Queretaran friars for their edification was the Venerable Fray Antonio Margil de Jesús, one of the colegio's first students and its most illustrious alumnus. Antonio was purported to have taken self-mortification to extremes. On one occasion, he refused to swat mosquitoes that attacked him while praying and emerged from the garden with a red, monstrously swollen face. He once lifted the stone lid of a sepulcher in order to breathe its awful stench. When his mother insisted on paying him a visit, he dutifully walked out to see her but refused to look her in the face, saying only, "You have seen me, Madam," before disappearing within the college walls.[25]

Following their great predecessor's example, some friars would practice self-mortification by tying nooses around themselves and asking their brothers to jerk them. Others might walk around the refectory during meals carrying heavy crosses.[26] Garcés's contemporary, Junípero Serra—who had been trained at the College of San Fernando in Mexico City, daughter institution of the colegio at Querétaro—often beat his chest with a rock during his preaching. Sometimes he placed his bare chest in the flames of candles. Once, trying to inspire a congregation to greater spiritual zeal, Serra began to scourge himself during his homily. As the story has it, one of his congregants was so moved that he rushed to the front of the church, took the whip from Serra's hands, and began to whip himself so badly that he keeled over dead. Before the man expired he was given the last rites, so this was regarded as an edifying spectacle.[27]

Clearly, self-denial was absolutely necessary for a Franciscan missionary of the College of Santa Cruz to become a worthy inheritor of its tradition. Whether self-denial came naturally to Garcés or was instilled in him by his Franciscan training, it was something at which he became extraordinarily adept. It would serve him as well as an explorer as it did as a missionary.

❊ ❊ ❊

The colegios were important not only to the spiritual mission of the church but also to the political mission of the Spanish crown. King Charles II and the Council of the Indies (the supreme legislative and administrative institution with respect to the Spanish Americas) had assented to the initial plan presented by Father Llinás because the disastrous (from the Spanish perspective) Pueblo Revolt of 1680 had revealed just how insufficient and ineffective the Franciscan missionary effort in New Mexico had been. Clearly a different approach was necessary. And from the

perspective of the regime, it was obviously a good idea for some
of Spain's thousands of Franciscan friars to be pursuing not quiet
lives of prayer but the active, productive lives of missionaries who
served the government's interests by Christianizing natives and
taming its wilder subjects.[28]

When Francisco arrived in 1763, Querétaro's missionaries were
working in the Coahuila and Texas mission fields. The provinces
to the west of these—Sonora, Sinaloa, and Nayarit—belonged to
the Jesuits, who had been working in that region since 1591 and
had expanded their reach as far north as the Gila River in modern
Arizona. It was an area in which the Black Robes had achieved
great success, especially in the earliest decades of their work. It
was also an area in which there had been great disasters. Lately
the disasters had been outpacing the successes.

It wasn't that the natives naturally despised or had no interest in
Christianity. Quite a few of those in northern Mexico—especially
those who were comparatively settled, as opposed to nomadic—
had, upon their first encounters with Jesuit missionaries, manifested a surprisingly receptive attitude toward Christianity. First
reactions to contact by a missionary were often curious, positive,
even welcoming.[29] After all, Christian doctrine, per se, rarely presented a direct threat to the natives' way of life. It operated on a
different plane—a strangely abstract theological and metaphysical level that seemed scarcely to exist in many native cultures. The
implications of Christian concepts, insofar as they could be understood, must have been vague at best. But often what the Indians
heard—or thought they heard, or what the *priests* thought the
Indians heard—was appealing.[30]

Many non-Christian peoples, including those living north of
Mexico City, readily made room for more divinities in their pan-
theons, and it was obvious that the Spaniards "must have very
powerful gods who had given them many wonderful things," as
Elizabeth John puts it, including new technologies and military
prowess.[31] The Christian God represented the "manifestation of
a new power" that it would be foolish not to recognize.[32] "From

the beginning," explains Fernando Cervantes, "Christian 'magic' was believed by the Indians to be efficient, and its association with the dominant sectors of society gave it a charisma that native magic, for all its local efficacy, lacked."[33] The spiritual power of Christianity was made visually present in a particularly salient way in the buildings it set aside as sacred. The dim candlelight, rich ardornments, strangely beautiful music, solemn rituals, and emotional sermons found therein all attested "a power that merited close inquiry."[34]

Natives' attitudes toward the Spaniards' religion frequently remained positive until one of six all but inevitable things happened: their lands were intruded upon by Spanish settlers; they were impressed into labor in the mines or on ranches, or even outright enslaved; they were made to feel their military subjugation too strongly; the missionaries themselves overworked them, abused them, or restricted their movements or activities too closely; an epidemic (smallpox, perhaps, or measles, usually unwittingly introduced by the Spanish) hit the community; or their medicine men—*hechiceros*—persuaded them to return to their ancient beliefs and rituals.[35] When one or more of these factors was present, attitudes toward Christianity often became violently negative.[36] But the faith itself, when presented gently and winsomely, seems not to have been unattractive to many of the peoples living in what is now Sinaloa, Sonora, and the southwestern United States, especially if those peoples thought it could be received (contrary to the missionaries' intentions) in a nonexclusive manner.[37]

Many Indian cultures had a conception of divinity that was the same as that found almost everywhere but in the Abrahamic monotheistic faiths. In Judaism, Christianity, and Islam, good and evil cannot coexist, for evil has no real being. It is but the privation of good, and God is all-good. In other religious systems, as in Hinduism, good and evil, the divine and the demonic, are and must be intertwined. Cosmic order requires the maintenance of a healthy balance between life and death, creation and destruction, good and evil. For most native peoples of northern New Spain, the Christian god was quite acceptable insofar as he could be incorporated into this essentially non-Christian viewpoint. That is therefore how he tended to be viewed, at first—and for as long as the missionaries, or the Indians' own cognitive dissonance, would allow.[38]

Theological cross-conceptions aside, a missionary's success was made more likely if he had the courage to enter a new territory without a military escort. The few who had such courage—Garcés one of them—often yielded the best results. In the seventeenth century, for instance, Jesuit Fathers José Tardá and Tomás de Guadalajara traveled in Tarahumara lands without soldiers at their sides and gained acceptance. The pattern repeated itself when the Jesuits reprised their missionary efforts after a major Tarahumara revolt.[39] The most successful missionaries were also patient. They required their neophytes—new converts—to abandon only those ceremonies and practices very clearly at odds with Christian teaching. Effective missionaries learned the language, no easy task in communities without writing and in a region where dozens of different languages and dialects were spoken. Finally, the most successful missionaries worked hand in hand with native leaders, who were given official civil and ecclesiastical posts.[40] Among many groups the Indians of the New World were not slow to accept priests who showed them affection and respect.

Just as Christianity was made unattractive when it came packaged with slavers, soldiers, unscrupulous settlers, and abusive and heavy-handed missionaries, its appeal was enhanced by its association with new crops and animals, more secure access to food, more effficient agricultural technologies, knives and cloth and ribbons and other useful and colorful items, and the ability of its representatives to provide protection against enemies.[41] These ancillary benefits were the main reason most native groups invited and accepted missionaries into their midst, and the missionaries fully realized—and accepted—this fact. Following the examples of Saint Francis Xavier, Matteo Ricci, and Saint Paul himself, the fathers were realists to the core. That the Indians might primarily value them because they brought gifts, alleviated hunger, and offered other nonspiritual goods and services bothered them not at all.[42] What they wanted was time: time to baptize, time to preach, and time to teach. Whatever bought them that time was, they believed, fair game—including, after baptism, coercion, as we see throughout this narrative.

Even when mission life, or Christianity itself, was not viewed as offering much in the way of inherent advantages, it might still regarded by native peoples as the best choice among bad options. For if the missionaries were sometimes too strict, at least they usually took the Indians' side against soldiers and settlers, and at times the padres offered real protection against "forced labor, kidnapping, and mistreatment at the hands of Spaniards."[43] Slavery or its equivalents was rampant along New Spain's frontier, where the crown's official and oft-repeated prohibitions against its practice could frequently be safely disregarded, well into (and past) the time of Garcés's presence there. Were it not for the resistance to and exposure of slave-taking offered by (some) Catholic priests, the story arguably would have been even uglier.[44]

Sometimes because of the violent practices of the padres, and sometimes because of the abuse and oppression heaped upon them by nonclerical Spaniards, prior to Garcés's arrival in the New World the colonization of northern New Spain had sparked numerous revolts. The Tarahumaras, the Yaquis, the Mayos, the Seris, the Pimas, and others all attempted to throw off the Spanish yoke at one time or another. On one hand, whether because of fear of reprisals or because of a genuine loyalty to their missionaries or their Christian faith, many natives refused to join uprisings, and many a rebellion failed as a consequence.[45] On the other hand, when violence broke out, missionaries were often the first to be targeted. The new ways, the new spiritual practices, the new god they had introduced had upset the old order and made things worse—such went the thinking. The new religion and its representatives had therefore to be wiped out. Usually a mere slaying would not do the trick. Often, a priest's body would be mutilated. Sometimes a priest was crucified.[46] And sometimes, as at Awat'ovi, the Indians who converted to the new faith, even though they be kin, had to be killed as well.

Indian anger at persecution often, perhaps usually, resulted in generalized anger at Spaniards—cleric, settler, soldier, and public official alike. During the Yaqui and Mayo rebellion of 1740, a mob yelled at one priest, "There is no God; there is no king; there are no priests; death to the priest!"[47] But it was not unheard of for natives to maintain a distinction between secular Spaniards and the church's representatives. During the same revolt, one battle cry went "Long live the King, Long live the Blessed Mary, Down with bad government!"[48] Some Indians, it seems, were better able conceptually to separate church from state than were the Spanish themselves.[49]

✳ ✳ ✳

Because it would later be the region in which Garcés and his Franciscan allies labored, it is important to linger for a bit on New Spain's northwestern frontier and the work undertaken by the Jesuits there. The greatest Jesuit missionary to labor in this area was a captivating, attractive, erudite, thoroughly irrepressible, wavy-haired Tyrolean named Eusebio Kino. No priest would be more committed to restless exploration, be more consumed by visions of expanding New Spain's northern frontier, or have better relations with the region's natives until Francisco Garcés came along three-quarters of a century later.

Thanks to the combined efforts of Kino's Black Robe predecessors and Spanish arms, not to mention slavers and disease, by the end of the seventeenth century the northern frontier of New Spain had advanced to the southern boundary of what was called Pimería Alta—the northern part of the region inhabited by Indians known to the Spanish as Pimas (and the northern part of the province of Sonora). The Pimas all spoke a dialect of the same Uto-Aztecan language. Two or three dozen closely

Scale in Miles
0   50   100

RIO SANTA CRUZ

RIO SAN PEDRO

Santa Catarina

San Cosme • • San Agustín del Tucson
SAN XAVIER DEL BAC •

SONOITA •
Arizona
Sonora   Tumacacori •   • Sonoita
GUEVAVI

Pusanic •   Bacoancos
SARIC •   Aquimuri • San Lázaro
Cocóspera   Tibideguachi •
Adid   TUBUTAMA   CUQUIARACHI •
CABORCA •   Oquitoa   Imuris   • Cuchuta
San Valentín   SAN IGNACIO •   • Remedios   • Touricachi
Pitiquito   Magdalena   LA PURISIMA   • Bacoachi
DOLORES •   • CHINAPA   • Bavispe
CUCURPE •   ARISPE •   • BACERAC
Senoquipe   • Guachinera
• Tuape   Oputu •
Banamichi •   • Cumpas
Opodepe •   • HUEPAC OPOSURA   (Techicadeguachi) •
ACONCHI •   GUASAVAS
Naconeri •   • Baviacora   • Bacadeguachi
Populo de los Seris   • NACORI

SONORA

GOLFO DE CALIFORNIA

• URES   • Tepachi
• Sereva
Alamos •   BATUCO • Mattura
Nácori •   • Teopari
MATAPE • SAHUARIPA
Bacanora
Relbeico •   • ARIBECHI
• Onapa

RIO SONORA

TECORIPA •   • Tónichi
Suaqui •   • ONAVAS
YECORA   • Maycoba
Cumuripa •   • MOVAS
• Nuri

N
S

SEMUTAYEPO
RAHUM •   Tepahui •
TORIX •   Tecaprichi •   • Cutego
Potam •   • Cocorit   Tarachi •   • Vallumbroso
Vicam • BACUM   SANTA INES •
Conicari •   CEROCAHUI
GUAZAPARES
TESIA •   Macoyahui •   • Temoris
NAVOJOA   Caimos
• Corimpo   Huites •
JESUIT MISSIONS   SANTA CRUZ DE MAYO • • Echojoa   • VACA
Yauer   • TORO
• Choix
in   • Baimoa
Northwestern New Spain   • TEMUECO   Chicuros
1767   Sirixijoa •   CHICORATO •
MOCHICAHUI •   Oquera •
LEGEND   • Charay   Bacoburito •
Ahome   OCORONI   RAMOA
• CABECERA   GUASAVE • • Nio
• Visita   Tamazula •   MOCORITO
•Exact location not known
drawn by Don Bufkin

Jesuit missions in the Pimería Alta, so-named by the Spaniards because
it was the northern part of the region inhabited by the Pima Indians, ca.
1767. This map shows the missions—many of them established by Father
Kino—that existed there in 1767, the year the Jesuits were expelled from
Spain's dominions. *Map by Don Bufkin. From Polzer,* Rules and Precepts
of the Jesuit Missions of Northwestern New Spain. *© 1976 The Arizona
Board of Regents. Reprinted by permission of the University of Arizona Press.*

related but distinct, politically independent groups of Pimas
lived in the Pimería Alta. Four of these groups tended to be distinguished by the Spanish: the Papagos, or Tohono O'odham
(Desert People), who made their homes in the desert to the west
of the Río Santa Cruz and south of the Río Gila (the so-called
Papaguería); the Gileño Pimas, or Akimel O'odham (River
People), who lived on the Gila; the Sobaípuris, whom the Spanish found living specifically on the San Pedro River in today's
southern Arizona; and, as a general catch-all term for Pimas
who did not fit one of the above categories, the Pimas Altos (or
Piatos).[50] It was Father Kino's destiny to introduce Christianity
and European culture to this inhospitable but sublimely beautiful land of little rain.[51]

The Pimería Alta, 50,000 square miles populated by an estimated twenty to thirty thousand natives at the time a forty-two-
year-old Kino arrived in 1686, was bounded on the south by the
Río Yaqui, on the west by the Gulf of California, on the northwest and north by the hazily understood Colorado and Gila
Rivers, and to the east by the Santa Cruz or San Pedro Rivers.[52]
During the quarter-century of his enterprise in the region, Kino
founded twenty-four missions. With the founding of Tumacácori and Guevavi (1691) and San Xavier del Bac (1692), he also
expanded the Spanish frontier northward into today's Arizona.

Kino made at least fifteen expeditions into Arizona, entering
the territory on three occasions by way of the deadly Camino del
Diablo.[53] Via these colonizing expeditions into unknown territory, journeys the Spanish called *entradas*, he blazed new trails
(new only to Europeans, of course) to the Gila and Colorado Rivers; made contact at the junction of those strategically important streams with the people today known as Quechans, called
Yumas by the Spanish; and proved that Baja California was not
an island but a peninsula. He also demonstrated, by his persis-
tent inquiries into how they had obtained beautiful blue abalone
shells, that the residents of Sonora maintained active trade relations with other groups on the Pacific coast—an important fact

in that it showed that an overland route to the Pacific was eminently feasible. Finally, the winsome Kino proved that, contrary to the claims of the settlers, the natives of the Pimería Alta were disposed to be friendly. In the early years of his travels, especially, their standard greeting for Kino and his traveling party consisted of lining the road with crosses and arches, and they seem overwhelmingly to have welcomed the establishment of missions, no doubt largely because of the animals, foodstuffs, and protection that came, or were supposed to come, with them.

After Kino's death in 1711, he was not immediately replaced.[54] For a generation decay set in. Then, from 1732 to 1750, new crops of Jesuit missionaries, many of them recruited from the German-speaking lands of central and northern Europe, began to arrive.[55] Fathers Joseph Och, Ignacio Keller, Ignaz Pfefferkorn, Philipp Segesser, Jacobo Sedelmayr, Gaspar Stiger, and Juan Nentvig, among others, effectively rebuilt the missions founded by Kino. These men were not blind to the sins of Europeans. All would have agreed with Father Och that the "first conquerors of America were much less rational than the most ignorant Indians," that the *conquistadores* were "depraved" in murdering and enslaving the Indians and in regarding them as subhuman, and that "through their cruelty . . . many thousands, yes, even millions of souls were inhumanly offered up to their avarice."[56] Even so, at their best these German Jesuits lacked Kino's warm affection and tolerance for the natives of Sonora.[57] At their worst, they were nasty, abusive, and violent.

A few quotations from these Jesuits' writings suffice to illustrate their general attitude. To Father Juan Antonio Balthasar the Papagos were "servile, timid, and cowardly."[58] To Father Segesser the Pimas were "very stupid" and (if it were not un-Christian to say so) more like "unreasoning cattle" than men.[59] Father Och also thought them "stupid," and all Indians generally to be aloof, fainthearted, and distrustful.[60] "Imagine a man whose every quality of character makes him mean and despicable," wrote Father Pfefferkorn, a man who in all his human relations acts blindly, without consideration or reflection—a man whom no kindly act moves, who feels no compassion, whom no disgrace shames—a man who loves neither truth nor loyalty and who faces no undertaking with a steadfast will—a man unmoved by desire of glory, passive in good as well as an ill fortune—finally, a man whose only thought is of the present and what touches the senses, whose motives are those of the animal, who lives in indifference and dies the same way. Such a man is the true type of an Indian of Sonora.[61]

Father Nentvig, who served as visitor-rector of the Jesuit missions in northern Sonora, was even more splenetic. The Ópata and Pima Indians, he wrote, were stupid, stubborn, and cruel. He claimed that the Indians of Sonora had a nature "based upon four traits, each more despicable than the one that follows: ignorance, ingratitude, inconstancy, and laziness." He endorsed the view that, "generally speaking, the Indian is definitely a man so uncivilized that I dare say he is a never-seen monster with a wild brain, an ungrateful heart, an inconstant soul, a lazy backbone, leaden feet, and a thirsty belly. And he is inclined to imbibe until drunk. All these things transform him, in a moral sense, into an irrational being."[62]

In light of such views, and in light of credible accusations that some of these Jesuits abused their charges, it is no wonder that Oacpicagigua (Spanish name, Luis) of Sáric, the pueblo where Father Nentvig had been posted, was in 1751 able to attract others to his plan for a general rebellion.[63] Whether Luis was justly resentful of the mistreatment he and his people had received at the hands of the missionaries and settlers, as is likely, or whether he was an ambitious demagogue eager to seize power for himself, as the Jesuits retorted, the shrewd and courageous Luis decided in late November of that year that his moment had come. Having been promised allegiance by hundreds of western Pimas, he launched his uprising by inviting to his home in Sáric eighteen men, women, and children known to be loyal to the Spanish, then set fire to the house and commanded his armed guards to kill any who tried to leave.

Doubtless to Luis's disappointment, Father Nentvig was not among them. Having been tipped off at the last moment, Nentvig saddled his horse and fled to Tubutama. He did not take time to warn others in the small village, including his servants, the foreman, and the wife and children of the mission's native *mayordomo*, of the impending danger; twenty-five residents of Sáric were consequently killed. Luis then moved south to Tubutama, where Fathers Nentvig and Sedelmayr were holed up with a dozen or so settlers. After an intense battle lasting the better part of two days, the two priests were eventually able to escape under the cover of nightfall, leaving behind two wounded Spaniards.[64] There is no vocation in which heroism is not in short supply.

For ten months Luis's men terrorized the Spanish countryside, killing two Jesuits and more than one hundred Spaniards before Luis finally sued for peace. In the post-Luis years the Jesuits and other Spaniards living in the Pimería Alta routinely spoke of the province as ruined. Father Nentvig, writing in the early 1760s, claimed that in Sonora during the previous seven years more than four thousand mules and horses had been lost and three hundred or so ranches abandoned.[65] Throughout the region towns had been vacated, ranches deserted, and mines left unworked. Nentvig calculated that at the time he wrote Sonora contained 174 depopulated estates, ranches, mining sites, and other Spanish settlements—and only twenty-four that remained inhabited.[66]

The Spanish authorities clearly had a serious problem on their hands. But the Jesuits were not to be part of the solution.

※ ※ ※

On June 25, 1767, at four o'clock in the morning, doorbells rang at the five Jesuit houses of Mexico City. Moments later, the king's men rushed in. Groggy priests stepped out of their cells to find soldiers with bayonets roaming the corridors. The buildings were ransacked for much-rumored hidden treasures, officials even digging up clerical graves (and finding depressingly little except bones). Items like the fathers' rich gold ciboria, used at Mass, were confiscated. In one house, the consecrated sacramental wafers therein had to be consumed by the priests on the spot. The expulsion of the Jesuits from New Spain had begun.[67]

King Charles III, by all accounts a pious Catholic, never condescended to explain his reasons for forcibly removing the Jesuits from Spain and all its territories—or for stealing the order's property. In his decree, read for the first time by New Spain's viceroy, the Marqués de Croix, to high officials at the royal palace on the evening of June 24, the king said only that he did so for considerations he kept secret in his royal bosom. His instructions were nevertheless quite clear. In the letter Croix opened on the night of the 24th the king had written,

> I invest you with my whole authority and royal power that you shall forthwith repair with an armed force to the house of the Jesuits. You will seize the persons of all of them, and dispatch them within twenty-four hours as prisoners to the port of Vera Cruz, where they will be embarked on vessels provided for that purpose. At the very moment of each arrest you will cause to be sealed the records of said houses, and the papers of said persons, without allowing them to remove anything from their prayerbooks, and such garments as are absolutely needed for the journey. If after the embarkation there should be found in that district a single Jesuit, even if ill or dying, you shall suffer the penalty of death. *Yo el Rey.*[68]

Charles's command may have come as a surprise, but his expulsion of the Society of Jesus has never been regarded as indecipherably mysterious. At one time it would have been unthinkable for a Christian ruler to expel from his or her dominions the only religious order that reported directly to the pope. But by the middle of the eighteenth century European states had become more centralized, wealthy, and powerful. That growth, combined with Enlightenment skepticism, had weakened the power of the papacy. What reason was there for a modern, ambitious ruler—even a good Catholic like Charles—not to rid himself of a group that held so much valuable land, that educated the children of the elite, that extended its reach to the four corners of the earth, and that was intellectually highly influential but opposed to contemporary currents of thought? Especially when that group could be counted on not to resist? The Society of Jesus had, after all, been successfully expelled from Portugal in 1759, thanks to the influence of the cunning Marquis de Pombal, and from France in 1762. In following suit Charles was keeping up with the royal Joneses. Plus, he, or at least his advisors, blamed the Jesuits for instigating alarming riots in March 1766 that had caused the king to flee Madrid.[69]

Expelling the Jesuits, it was thought, would have the additional benefit of making it easier for Charles and his ministers to implement sweeping changes throughout the Americas. The crown's goal was to decrease the power of the Catholic Church's corporate bodies by reducing the role of missionaries in the colonial enterprise, for missionaries had the vexing qualities of being neither "enlightened" nor secular. The ultimate hope was to replace organized bands of religious with priests who volunteered to administer missions as individuals, or at least to graduate missions into tithe-paying parishes. These changes would break the hold of the religious colleges and provinces over the missions and their Indians, ultimately leading to higher revenues, lower costs, and increased royal power. Such was the thinking of not only Charles but his highest-ranking representative in New Spain, the man in charge not only of expelling the Jesuits but of the implementation of a wide range of reforms: Visitor-General José de Gálvez.[70]

What Francisco Garcés and his brother friars at Querétaro thought of their king's decision we can only guess.[71] (There was a Jesuit community in Querétaro, so the Franciscans at the College of Santa Cruz would have learned about the expulsion immediately; indeed, they may have witnessed the king's men in action.) Regardless, directly after initiating the expulsion in Mexico

José de Gálvez, the
visitador-general,
was brilliant and
energetic. He also
likely suffered from
a mental illness
that would today be
diagnosed as bipolar
disorder. *From
Wikimedia Commons.*

City, Gálvez began to hold secret meetings with Fray Manuel de
Nájera, who as commissary-general of the Franciscans in New
Spain was the highest-ranking member of his order in the kingdom.[72] It was not yet possible to administer the frontier's missions without recourse to the religious orders, so Gálvez worked
out with Nájera a plan for deploying priests from the various
Franciscan colleges and provinces to the soon-to-be-vacant Jesuit
mission fields in Sonora and California (which, at the time,
meant only Baja, or Lower, California). Some of these priests
would be drawn from the Franciscans' Jalisco province. But Viceroy Croix and Gálvez both agreed that most should come from
the colegios, whose friars constituted a sort of elite task force

trained for precisely this sort of moment.[73] Fourteen missionaries, it was hoped, would come from the College of Santa Cruz at Querétaro.[74]

The viceroy asked the colegio to man the missions of upper Sonora. In short order Father Guardian Sebastián Flores had the fourteen volunteers he needed for that distant mission district, plus one more: Fray Mariano Antonio de Buena y Alcalde, a tough veteran of the Texas mission field who would serve as the missionaries' president. Buena also bore the title of *prefecto apostólico* for all the colegios in the New World. That meant he was the representative of the *colegios apostólicos de propaganda fide* in the Americas, a position that conferred on him ecclesiastical powers akin to those of a bishop. At the moment of crisis, Querétaro would not stint in serving its king.

Among the friars selected for service in Sonora were old friends Fathers Juan Crisóstomo Gil and Francisco Garcés. This is why they had left Aragón. They would not miss their chance.

Over the next several weeks, preparations were made for the missionaries' departure. They must have thought they were moving with all deliberate speed, but their brothers at the College of San Fernando, spurred by their impatient mission president Junípero Serra, moved even faster. Father Serra and eight of his companions, en route to the friars' designated gathering spot at Tepic on the Gulf of California, arrived at Querétaro in mid to late July. If they did not meet in 1763, when Garcés was en route to Querétaro from Veracruz, this may have been the first meeting between Garcés and Serra, perhaps the two most consequential friars in the Spanish colonization of the American Southwest.

A great adventure was under way, and the friars were made all the more anxious when they learned it would not be business as usual once they arrived at their missions. For, to restrict the influence of the missionaries, make Indian labor more readily available to its settlers and officials on the frontier, and ultimately enrich the royal treasury, the crown had made sweeping changes. Instead of being placed in charge of both spiritual and temporal matters at their missions—that is, instead of serving as the authoritative representative of both church and state among the Indians whom they were supposed to Christianize and Europeanize—the Franciscans would be in charge of spiritual matters only. What this change in policy meant, concretely, was laid out in the instructions formally signed by Flores on August 4. No longer were mission Indians to be isolated from contact with Spaniards in the area. Instead they were to be allowed to trade with, labor for, and move among the Spanish settlers with no restrictions at all. They were to be taught Castilian, and schools were to be established that would be led by non-Indian teachers. Immediate acculturation was now the goal. The friars looked on these instructions with a mixture of confusion and horror. How could they convert the Indians, or protect them from exploitation, under such conditions? Experience had shown it was impossible. But for the moment, at least, the priests went along with the program.

There was one more thing: the instructions specifically ordered the missionaries to do what they could to learn about, first, the geography, plants, and animals of the regions to which they were assigned, and second, the lands that lay beyond the frontier. Friar Garcés would take the latter request especially to heart.

CHAPTER 3

Ende der Christenheit

1767–1768

On August 5, 1767, only a little more than a month after King Charles's expulsion of the Jesuits from Spain and its dominions, fifteen Queretarans were ready to step into the breach.[1] The entire Santa Cruz community gathered in the colegio church at 5:30 in the morning for the solemn chanting of prime. Then the departing friars prostrated themselves before the altar of Mary as the rest of the community sang the ancient Marian hymn Tota Pulchra, pleading in song with the Virgin to pray for their brothers as they left for their dangerous assignment. There were embraces and open weeping; everyone knew that this parting might be, from a terrestrial perspective, final. Sebastián Flores, the Father Guardian, gave the fifteen missionaries a special blessing—the blessing of Saint Francis—before they said their private Masses anxiously at the church's side altars. At last the friars gathered to eat breakfast in the refectory, where they were read Viceroy Croix's letter of July 8, in which he requested the colegio's help, and the official instructions signed on August 4. The fifteen then took their leave.

The well-traveled but not necessarily well-maintained camino real to the Quereterans' destination of Tepic, 350 miles away, went through Guadalajara, where the friars rested for a short while.[2] They arrived at Tepic on August 26. Perhaps the scene they encountered there reminded Gil and Garcés of the day, some four years earlier, when they had arrived at chaotic Cádiz. Tepic was not just bustling, it was bursting at the seams. The town, situated on a cedar-forested plateau some twenty miles from the gulf at a pleasant three thousand feet above sea level, had long served as a convenient jumping-off point for travelers headed north to the *tierra caliente*. José de Gálvez had selected it as the gathering place and supply post not only for the Franciscans who were to replace the Jesuits in Baja California and Sonora but also for troops he was sending north to put down, once and for all, the seemingly interminable uprising of Pimas and Seris that had been dragging on since Luis of Sáric's 1751 revolt.

That conflict was now centered in the mountains that stretched from Guaymas to Pitic (today's Hermosillo) on New Spain's northwestern coast. Twelve hundred Spanish soldiers were therefore present at Tepic when the Queretarans arrived. So were dozens of Franciscan friars. By mid-September, forty-seven of the latter were encamped on the grounds of a Franciscan institution known as the Hospice of Santa Cruz de Zacate, property of the blue-robed friars of Jalisco province. Its residents greeted the Queretarans hospitably, but they had no room to board the visitors within their walls. One-third of the priests making shift at the *hospicio* were from other houses in Jalisco; these were to serve in southern Sonora. Another third hailed from the College of San Fernando in Mexico City; these were ticketed for Baja California. The Fernandinos included Junípero Serra as well as others who were to make lasting names for themselves in the California mission field, including Serra's fellow Mallorcan and former pupil, Francisco Palóu, and his future successor as president of the Californian missions, Fermín Lasuén.

Garcés had ample time to get to know them all, for things now moved with the irritating slowness that always bedeviled Spanish activity on the northern frontier. Gálvez was obsessed with sending everyone—troops and friars alike—to Sonora by sea rather than land.[3] But neither the Spanish navy nor the Gulf of California were cooperating with his plans. When the padres arrived at Tepic, the ships that were to transport them to their missions either were not yet built or were stuck in port on the other side of the gulf. For weeks, then months, they waited.[4] Finally, around Christmas 1767, the four ships being built on the nearby Río Santiago were ready to sail from the new, stale-aired, mosquito-ridden, shallow port of San Blas. Colonel Domingo Elizondo, leader of the military expedition headed north, was the first to leave, embarking with his dragoons on the 193-ton packet boat *San Carlos* for the port of Guaymas in Sonora, some six hundred miles to the north. He was soon pushed back to San Blas after high seas broke the vessel's mainmast.

One attempt at sailing to Sonora was enough for Elizondo, who was by now thoroughly disgusted with the incompetence of the Spanish navy—and newly respectful of the treacherous gulf. The unpredictability of its winds and waters was legendary. One never knew, on board a ship in the Gulf of California, how long it would take to get anywhere. Only April, May, and June offered anything like reliable sailing conditions. Plying northward from September through March was extremely difficult because of the prevailing northwest winds, and terrible monsoon storms arose in July and August. It took eleven Jaliscan friars 147 days to cross the gulf to Loreto. Earlier, for another group of passengers, the same voyage had taken just eleven days. A little while later, it took only four days for the boat carrying the exiled Jesuits to make it from Loreto to San Blas.

Elizondo may have appreciated the gulf's dark comedy, but he didn't need its uncertainty. Defying Gálvez, he gathered 180 troops and began to march overland to Sonora on January 14, 1768. A Queretaran, the lean and haughty Antonio de los Reyes, went along as his chaplain.[5] Five months after arriving at Tepic, at least one College of Santa Cruz friar was finally on the road to the Sonoran mission field. Soon Reyes's brethren would wish they were marching alongside him.

Elizondo had left orders that as soon as the *San Carlos* was repaired the Queretarans, along with the 150 members of the mountain fusiliers, were to sail for Guaymas on it and a smaller ship called the *Lauretana*. The repairs were done quickly, for on January 17, 1768, just three days after Elizondo left on foot for Sonora, the Queretarans traveled the twenty miles from Tepic down to San Blas, where the rank air carried the stench of decaying vegetable matter.[6] There the missionaries divided into two groups. Buena and the first group, consisting of six friars in total, set sail on the *San Carlos* on January 20. The second group, consisting of seven friars, left the same day on the *Lauretana*. One friar was left behind to serve as the chaplain of the packetboat *El Príncipe*, not scheduled to sail for Guaymas until March.

We do not know which group Garcés was with, but we do know he suffered through another terrible sailing experience. Neither the *San Carlos* nor the *Lauretena* got beyond Mazatlán, 170 miles from San Blas, without mishap. The *San Carlos* was once again forced to turn back to San Blas for repairs, and the *Lauretana* discharged six of its seven friars in Mazatlán. All had gotten so sick that they decided to follow in Elizondo's footsteps and walk to Sonora. Among this group of six was Father Gil, who, perhaps recalling his brush with death a few years earlier on that reef near the Yucatán, had surely had enough of sailing.

By the end of March the *San Carlos* was again on its way to Guaymas. Also on its way was *El Príncipe* with the last friar. That ship arrived in Guaymas, along with the *Lauretana*, sometime in late April. The *San Carlos* finally arrived with Father Buena and his five companions on May 9. It had been nine months since the Queretarans had left their colegio. Had they traveled the thousand miles by foot, they would have had to average less than four miles per day to arrive at Guaymas in the same amount of time. So much for the advantages of travel by sea.

In Guaymas was another group of priests: the Jesuits of the northern frontier who had been cast into exile by Charles III. Fifty of them—two had already died—had been held as prisoners for eight months while they waited for a ship to arrive and transport them to San Blas. The conditions in which they lived were described by Jesuit historian Peter Masten Dunne as "a ramshackle barracks of mud and straw without window, door, chair, or table" that "was ill-smelling, rat-infested, hot."[7] The food they received was tainted, the water warm and salty. Scurvy had begun to take hold. The Jesuits' communication with the outside world had been cut off completely, a decision justified by the authorities on the grounds that they had tried, or would try, to sow discord among their Yaqui friends.[8]

Were the Queretarans aware of the scandalously horrid conditions in which their Black Robe brethren were being held, or even of the Jesuits' presence? None of the Franciscans mention anything about the exiles in their letters or diaries, nor does Father Juan Domingo Arricivita, the College of Santa Cruz's official chronicler.[9] Whether that silence reflects ignorance or a prudent reticence is impossible to say. In any case, what a lost opportunity, not only for the Franciscans to offer consolation to the Jesuits but also for them to learn firsthand something about the unique region they were about to enter.[10]

It was a region that at first lifted their spirits. Having rested at Guaymas for four days, Father Buena led his group of friars inland toward Horcasitas, where he was to meet with Sonora's well-educated, grossly overweight governor, Juan Claudio de Pineda, to discuss, among other things, each friar's particular mission assignment.[11] Traveling northeast along relatively verdant rivers through the long-settled Yaqui country, Buena and his companions were impressed by the size and prosperity of the settlements they encountered. But as they journeyed farther into the Pimería,

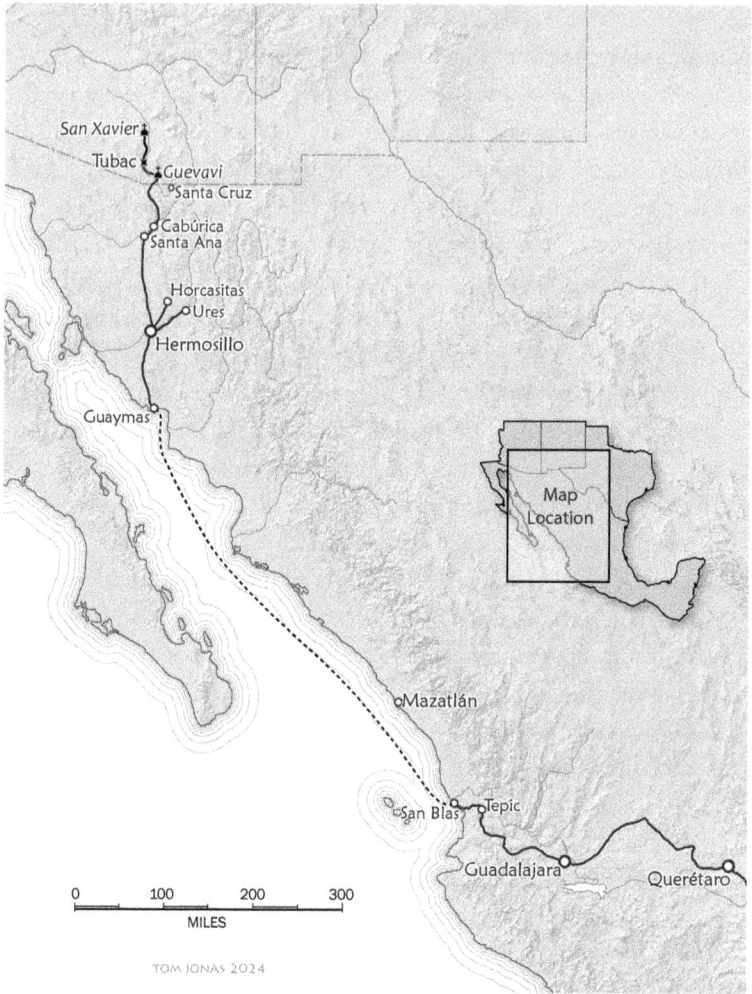

Route taken by the College of Santa Cruz missionaries from Querétaro to Guaymas and beyond, including their individual mission stations, many of which lay farther north. *Map by Tom Jonas, based on maps by Don Bufkin in McCarty,* A Spanish Frontier in the Enlightened Age, *26–27, 38.*

they became more and more dejected. The natives were scattered, there was little if any prosperity, the land seemed infertile, and the climate was unbelievably torrid. As they traveled, they received a letter from Governor Pineda, who informed Buena of the appointments he had already temporarily made (Gil and the rest of the friars traveling overland had long since arrived) and requested that Buena take into account physical strength and health when he made his permanent appointments. This was a tough land.

Along the way, the group of friars divided. Garcés went east with five others to the run-down mission of San Miguel de los Ures, where Father Esteban de Salazar had already taken up residence, while Buena and the rest continued north to their appointment with Pineda. At Ures, Garcés and his companions tarried for a little over a week, provisioning themselves for their journeys to their missions, gathering their strength, and no doubt discussing how they would go about their work in such an inhospitable place. (Salazar was happy to be temporarily reunited with his brothers but sorry to see them take so much of his scanty stores.) Soon Buena sent the padres word of their assignments.[12] With what supplies or pack animals the friars traveled to meet up with their father-president one last time at the mission of San Ignacio de Cabúrica, 150 miles to the north of Ures, we are not told. Surely they were meager, for the Pimería Alta was poor. It was not hard, here, for a Franciscan to keep his vow of poverty.

By mid-June 1768 all the Queretarans were at or on their way to their posts. In light of Pineda's instructions, it is a testimony to Garcés's physical and mental fortitude that Buena assigned him to the northernmost mission in Sonora, the most isolated mission in all of New Spain: a place called San Xavier del Bac.

✳ ✳ ✳

San Xavier lay 115 miles directly north of Cabúrica, an outpost that must have already felt far beyond anything a European would call civilization. Garcés likely traveled roughly half that distance with Father Francisco Roch, who had been assigned to the mission of Santa María de Suamca in today's Santa Cruz, Sonora, just a few miles south of today's international border to the east of modern Nogales. From there it was another thirty miles to the mission of Los Santos Ángeles de Guevavi, just north of Nogales, where Francisco's oldest friend in New Spain, Father Gil, had been posted. Their relative proximity must have made both men happy. Guevavi was the closest mission to San Xavier del Bac, although that didn't make it "close" in any objective sense of the term. Both missions lay along the north-flowing Río Santa Cruz, one of the very few perennial streams in this part of Sonora, but Guevavi was still more than fifty miles south of San Xavier.

Though we do not know for certain that Garcés stopped to see Father Gil as he journeyed north, we do know that he stopped at the presidio of Tubac, twenty miles north of Guevavi in the same river valley. There, on June 30, he was hosted by the wife of the garrison's commander, Captain Juan Bautista de Anza, as we learn from a letter Garcés wrote a month later to Anza—the earliest Garcés letter we have.[13] The letter implies that as Garcés traveled north the two men had met somewhere near Pitic, where Anza was in command of a detachment in Colonel Elizondo's campaign against Pima and Seri warriors. Garcés had immediately been impressed by Anza's sophistication and manners. No wonder: with his intelligent eyes; thick, black pointed beard lined with threads of white; and broad moustache that swept in an arc from his nose to his ears, Anza looked every bit the part of a dignified commander.

Indeed, Anza had been born to the life he was now living. His father of the same name had been a captain in the army, ultimately commanding the Sonoran presidio at Fronteras and gaining renown as an effective Indian fighter. Anza the younger had been born at Fronteras in 1735. At the age of sixteen he entered the king's service as a cadet at that lonely post. Three years later, in 1755, he made lieutenant.[14] Haughty, hard, and brave, Anza, like his father, was military through and through. While at

Presidio of Tubac's Captain Juan Bautista de Anza as painted by a Fray Orsi in Mexico City in 1774. *From the California Historical Society Collection at the University of Southern California.*

Fronteras, he led multiple campaigns against the Apaches and killed, according to his own account, several dozen of their warriors. In 1760 he was made captain and commander of the Tubac presidio. Ever since, Anza had been tasked not only with keeping the Apaches from penetrating the Sonoran interior but also with assisting in fighting the rebel Pimas and Seris to the south. He had even quelled, and received an arrowhead wound in, a Papago uprising that had flared briefly in 1760.[15] By 1768 it was clear that New Spain had few frontier officers more competent or dedicated than Juan Bautista de Anza.

On the last day of June 1768, when Señora Anza entertained the greenhorn missionary at her Tubac home, Garcés learned that he was entering especially dangerous territory. Señora Anza, born Ana María Pérez Serrano, had herself been raised in the Sonoran mission town of Arizpe—her brother had been a secular priest there—and had married Anza in 1761. Doubtless she took time to inform Garcés about life on this farflung frontier—what the natives were like, the condition of the mission at San Xavier del Bac, the moods of the Apaches and the Papagos and the Pimas, the program and legacy of the Jesuits whom she and her husband had known so well, the morale of the soldiers and (the very few) settlers. Judging from the content of Garcés's letter, written on July 29, in their earlier conversation the captain had covered much the same conversational territory.[16]

When he wrote that July 29 letter Garcés had been at San Xavier del Bac for only a month, but his aptitude for missionary life was already revealing itself. First of all, he was "very happy."[17] The Jesuits who preceded him had found the post an extraordinarily hard one, "even with their cattle, horses, and fields." "Armed only with my royal stipend, which they had as well, I have not found it so," he reported to Anza, one of the few examples we have of a Garcés boast. The many flies and mosquitoes constituted the only hardship he had yet endured. Anza must have been pleased to hear that the two soldiers who lived at the mission not only were behaving themselves well but were also "very faithful in calling the people to Christian instruction." The natives at San Xavier needed such instruction badly, in Garcés's estimation, for they showed "no sign of knowing Christian teachings—even in their own language," despite the mission's seventy-plus-year history.[18] Nevertheless, they were welcoming and friendly. Garcés believed that the Indians at his mission would undertake a campaign against the Apaches, their much-feared enemies, whenever he gave the command. He was especially impressed by the Indians who lived at the satellite mission station—called a *visita*— of Tucson a few miles to the north. They had built him "a tiny brush hut" and were relieved by his promise that, unlike his Jesuit predecessors, not to mention other Spaniards, he would not— indeed, according to the new regulations, *could* not—ask them to work for him in the fields. "I have visited them three times and have promised that I will live there a week or two during August, since they are just as much my children as the people here at San Xavier. They are quite pleased at this," reported Garcés. Things were off to a good start.

The Jesuits, as Garcés noted in his letter, had held a much more negative view of this post and its location at the *Ende der Christenheit*, as one of their number, Father Gottfried Bernhardt Middendorff, had phrased it.[19] Father Eusebio Kino had first visited the village of Bac—or Wa:K, in the O'odham language—in 1692, showing its people a map of the world and regaling them with a brief history of Christianity, Spain, and New Spain.[20] Situated in a broad flat valley punctuated by hills rising abruptly from the desert floor, and with an estimated population of eight hundred, Bac was perhaps the largest Indian village in the Pimería Alta at the time, and Kino gave the prospective mission site as much attention as his too-busy schedule allowed, visiting six times prior to April 1700, when he stayed for a week and laid the foundations for a church and a house. Kino had great affection for Bac and its people; it was because of proofs given him by Indians gathered there that he became convinced that California was not, as was commonly believed, an island but rather a peninsula.[21] But Kino never lived at Bac, and his church was never finished.[22]

For almost sixty years, despite their consistent belief in its strategic importance, the Jesuits failed to gain a real foothold at Bac. At the turn of the eighteenth century, Father Francisco Gonzalvo lived at Bac for a year or two; he left because of illness and died in 1702.[23] Not until 1732, with the arrival of forty-three-year-old Swiss Jesuit Philipp Segesser, did the San Xavier mission get its second resident priest. Gonzalvo's time at Bac had left such little mark that Segesser believed himself to be the first.[24] As the son of a wealthy, close-knit, noble family from Lucerne, Segesser had given up more than most to come to the New World. Stirred by the exploits of Saint Francis Xavier, he had cherished a dream of becoming both a Jesuit and a missionary since he was ten years old.[25] He ended up serving in Sonora for thirty-one years. They were not easy ones for a sensitive, naïve patrician used to an urban existence. It wasn't every missionary who wrote home to ask for a sawmill wheel, roasting spit, waffle iron, pastry tube, butter churn, gingerbread molds, pie plates, carnation seeds, and pocket-watch cases—to name just a few of the dozens of items requested by Segesser shortly after his arrival in the Pimería Alta.[26] But, then again, life on the Río Santa Cruz wouldn't have been easy for anyone. In his letters back to his family Segesser complained about the heat (it was so hot that "one cannot travel by day"), gnats, flies, scorpions, snakes, spiders, mice, rats, even "toads as big as a fully grown king's hare," one of which startled him when it hopped onto the altar during Mass.[27] The mission's Indians, he added, were nearly impossible to manage, "too lazy to work," and ignorant of "what good and bad are,"[28] which was not so surprising in light of the fact that in their nighttime dances they regularly communed with Satan.[29]

When he arrived at San Xavier, Segesser could, like Garcés some thirty-six years later, find among the mission's residents "no single sign of Christianity aside from the names they received in baptism."[30] He found it difficult to make much spiritual headway. His successor, Father Francisco Paver, fared little better. When Father Jacobo Sedelmayr visited San Xavier in 1751, he lamented that it was "still very backward, without a catechist, without obedience, and without any church other than a ramada and a wretched house."[31]

At this point the authorities finally had the good sense, or perhaps the good luck, to veer away from the discipline-minded German Jesuits who had so spectacularly failed to connect successfully with the O'odham living at and around Bac. Twenty-six-year-old Father Alonso Espinosa, a Canary Islander born to a military family, arrived at San Xavier in 1756. Over the years his crops and herds were continually decimated by Apache, Seri, and Pima raids. The number of mission residents consequently diminished. He was profoundly troubled by religious scruples. But the dogged Espinosa stayed the course. Soon after his arrival, he prevailed upon the O'odham to help construct a rectangular

110- by 22-foot-wide church, the narrow width necessitated by the region's relatively short trees. The building's sun-dried adobe-brick walls, rising to a height of ten feet, were just over twelve inches wide and mortared with mud.[32] The flat ceiling's beams, supported by posts running down the middle of the nave, were made from mesquite, its laths from saguaro cactus ribs. These were covered by a thick layer of mud and cow manure. Two side chapels and a sacristy completed the structure. All in all, it was a rather typical Jesuit church for this area and time, a church not at all built for the ages but considerably better than nothing.[33]

When Garcés took formal possession of San Xavier in July 1768, the leaky Espinosa church still stood. Little came with it. The civil commissioners and Indians alike had despoiled the missions of their stores during the interim between Jesuit and Franciscan supervision.[34] On top of that, the new regulations meant that a mission came with comparatively little, anyway. Formerly, a missionary would have been entrusted not just with a church and its appurtenances but also with a mission's livestock, stores of grain, agricultural implements, and everything else that went into running the combined economic, governmental, and ecclesial institution that, in the traditional sense, constituted a mission—including, crucially, the labor of the mission's neophytes, or baptized Indians, of whom there were at San Xavier 166 in 1768, a relatively large number on this part of the frontier.[35] All that was now by the boards. The Indians, in theory, owned all nonreligious goods at a mission; in reality, their use was managed by a civil commissioner. The missionary was supposed to pay for his own food, for native help, for the maintenance of the church and his house, and for anything else out of the measly three hundred pesos provided annually by the crown. Unscrupulous commissioners, many of whom lived fifty or a hundred miles distant, could make life even more miserable by, for example, refusing to provide animals for transportation. Governor Pineda himself, who strictly enforced the new policy, not coincidentally ran a store in which he price-gouged his customers, including the friars.[36]

The baptismal font at San Xavier del Bac. The copper font on top of this stand was inherited by Garcés when he took over at San Xavier del Bac in 1768. It remains in the baptistery there today. *Photo by author.*

According to the formal inventory signed by both Garcés and San Xavier's civil commissioner, Andrés Grijalva, and witnessed by the mission's O'odham gobernador Ignacio and its O'odham alcalde Manuel, on June 30, 1768, the items that conveyed with the mission of San Xavier del Bac included some sticks of wooden furniture; a few vestments; a handful of silver liturgical vessels; a hodgepodge of altar ornaments in "very poor" shape; a couple of statues; paintings of Saint Francis Xavier, the Virgin Mary, and Saint Joseph; eight engraved prints; and a copper baptismal font.[37] Visitors to the famously beautiful church that stands at San Xavier today—a structure that was not started until 1783— can still see the font in the baptistery.[38] It may be the only item from the Garcés era to have survived to the present.

For better or worse, San Xavier did come with the visita in Tucson, which had acquired that status by 1737 and where, at the time of Garcés's arrival on the scene, there were, he estimated, no more than twenty families.[39] During the Jesuit period, Tucson for a brief while had a resident missionary in the person of

Gottfried Middendorff, who arrived on January 5, 1757, with the charge of making Tucson into a full-blown mission of its own. For four months the Westphalian priest slept under the open sky or in a brush hut built for him by the Tucson natives. He said Mass under a ramada, and he did what he could to teach Christian doctrine and European ways to those Indians who would submit to instruction, but his stay in Tucson lasted only until May, when a massive force of Apache warriors drove him and many others back to San Xavier. It would be a couple of generations before San Agustín del Tucson—the station's formal name—again had a resident priest.[40] Thanks to the Apaches, the post was nearly uninhabitable for the O'odham, let alone what the Spaniards snobbishly referred to as *gente de razón*, persons of at least partial European descent or others who had become Hispanicized.[41]

To Garcés, contemplating his new mission obligations in the summer of 1768, so much must have seemed not just dangerous but utterly foreign. He was familiar with the wheat, corn, and other crops grown in the relatively fertile, flat irrigated fields that bordered the narrow, silvery Río Santa Cruz as it threaded its way northward toward Tucson and beyond. But the tall, rugged mountains that ranged to the mission's east—the Santa Rosas, the Rincons, and the Santa Catalinas, as they are known now— were studded with giant saguaro, cholla, ocotillo, palo verde, and dozens of other mysterious plants. The O'odham language with its guttural speech was difficult to learn.[42] The summer air was at times unbearably hot, much hotter than anything Garcés had known in Aragón or Querétaro. Stranger yet were his Indian companions' ways—ways that, as the long, brilliantly sunny days passed, he would try his best to comprehend. Many of his predecessors at San Xavier del Bac, not exactly weak men, had been overwhelmed by the situation. Garcés—liberated, perhaps, by the limitation of his authority to spiritual matters alone—seems, by contrast, to have reveled in it. He also kept his eyes open for an opportunity to explore.

✳ ✳ ✳

In the weeks after his arrival at San Xavier, Garcés wrote Governor Pineda for a few things (a chest that would keep his Mass vestments and vessels out of reach of the rats, a kettle, a small inkwell with which he could travel, a razor case, and a few other practical items), oriented himself to his new surroundings, and did what he could to ingratiate himself with the Indians who lived near San Xavier and Tucson.[43] His primary duty was to educate them in the basics of the Christian faith. But it was a hard duty to fulfill. Among the sixty or so families that he was able to identify at San Xavier (far fewer, he sighed, than was implied by the 1,108 baptisms listed in the mission's register since 1755, even accounting for the 213 listed deaths), he lamented to Governor Pineda that he was able to discover no knowledge of Christian doctrine whatsoever. Nor was there much interest among the O'odham residents in receiving Christian instruction or attending Mass. They were more interested—as Garcés realized was only rational—in tending their corn patches.[44]

To the corn patches, therefore, Garcés went. In the first few weeks after his arrival, he reports having made two such visits. He issued no jeremiads, exerted no pressure, as he talked with the O'odham people caring for the precious crops they had planted in the desert arroyos. Garcés was willing to listen, teach, and persuade as patiently as was necessary. Given time, he thought, the beauty and power of the Christian message would win the natives' hearts. "I trust in God that it will be possible to catechize them, whatever the means," he wrote Pineda.[45]

We should not read into this approach the presence of a proto-modern attitude, much less some kind of growing internal conflict between Garcés's "Catholic conscience" and his "personal tendency to identify with these Native Americans," a tendency that soon had him fearing the loss of his own "allegiance to his Order and culture," as has been implausibly speculated by one modern scholar.[46] As he emphasized to Governor Pineda, Garcés had the legal right to ask San Xavier's native governor and *fiscales* to force *baptized* Indians to gather at the mission. Though he was "not inclined to be rigorous" with the adults, he did "threaten the children" and even began "to spank them so that they should not play hooky," a measure to which the governor raised objections, such that Garcés had to "quiet" the governor's "scruples."[47] Garcés probably did not realize that the use of corporal punishment as a method of correction was foreign to O'odham ways.

By the standards of his era Garcés was kind and patient. But he was still an eighteenth-century, paternalistic Spanish priest who accepted his traditionally defined duties, not Bing Crosby's Father O'Malley in *Going My Way*. Over time he would become kinder, more patient, more separated from his peers in these respects. But in his first couple years on the frontier he was, like other Franciscans, in principle open to using force with baptized natives—although other than the aforementioned spankings he never reports having employed violent means with his flock.[48] In any case, in the summer of 1768 his comparatively gentle methods helped win the affection, or at least the respect, of the San Xavier Indians. Soon some of them, especially the children and younger, unmarried persons, began to attend religious instruction at the mission.

At the visita of Tucson, too, he made a good impression. He listened with sympathy to the natives' complaints that, although they were on the very front lines of the Apache frontier, and therefore suffered frequently from Apache attacks, the Spaniards neglected to provide them with a mission of their own (and, by implication, the soldier escorts that came with a mission). Garcés promised to divide his time between Tucson and Bac. He asked for a hut to be built in which he could stay during his visits, a request to which his O'odham flock happily assented; they designated one of their young men to assist Garcés and care for church matters in his absence.[49] Finally, he assured those at Tucson that the king cared about them, which was truly if only abstractly the case, and that before long they would have their mission, a rash promise that spoke better of Garcés's faith and enthusiasm than his prudence.

Not that he didn't try to keep that promise. By August 13, 1768, Garcés was already pleading in his inimitably circuitous way with Father Guardian Flores at Querétaro for the establishment of additional missions to the north and west of San Xavier, including at Tucson. Faced with receptive O'odham—"I love them and they love me," he exulted to Flores—and intransigent Apaches, Garcés had caught the vision of frontier expansion articulated previously by Kino, Sedelmayr, and many others. The natural next step for the Spanish, he thought, was to expand northward to the Gila River—where Garcés had been told there was a large population, cultivated land, and baptized, if uninstructed, Christians—and westward to the Colorado River.[50] Indeed, although it had never been fulfilled, an advance to the confluence of the Gila and Colorado had been commanded by the Spanish crown as long ago as 1744.[51]

Garcés was eager to contribute to the knowledge base necessary for making that expansion a reality. The day before he wrote Flores, two Papago headmen came to San Xavier and invited him to visit their villages to the west.[52] For Garcés, this was an opportunity too good to be missed. Recalling that along with the instruction of his mission Indians another of his duties was to discover what lay beyond San Xavier—to "reconnoiter the neighboring lands and tribes," as he put it—he gladly accepted the chiefs' invitation. He was ready to make his first *entrada*—that is, to enter into an unfamiliar world, a world unmapped, unknown, uncertain. Who lived there, and what would they be like? Would they be friendly or unfriendly, docile or devilish? What would they wear? What kind of language would they speak? What would they customarily eat? And what would the land itself be like? Would it be a green land of shady trees and flowing streams or a brown land of thorny cactuses and dry washes? Local Indians could often answer some of these questions, but not always. For them, too, there were worlds *beyond*. To say that the New

World was indeed new is not merely to acquiesce to European ethnocentrism.

Garcés kept a diary of this first prolonged visit beyond the borders of his mission.[53] That diary appears to have long been lost, but in another document Garcés prepared seven years later we have his brief summary of its most important contents. The Papago chiefs were very friendly, he writes there, and Garcés, who realized that few if any missionaries had visited the region west and north of San Xavier since the Pima Revolt of 1751, spoke to them about his desire to visit their territory and "tell them some things" about the two "majesties" he served: God and the Spanish king. That was fine with the Papagos, who asked only that he travel without military escort. Were the O'odham chiefs testing Garcés's sincerity, or were their intentions malevolent?

Prior to Garcés, the list of missionaries who had reported visiting the Indian settlements west and north of San Xavier is a short one, consisting only of the Jesuit fathers Kino, Keller, and Sedelmayr.[54] Brave as they were, these fathers had typically, if not always, traveled with soldiers by their side. But if Garcés hesitated to accept the Papago chiefs' conditions, he gives no indication of it in his narrative. Others were less sanguine. Garcés writes that an unnamed "officer," almost certainly Anza, "learning of my determination, wished to prevent" Garcés's journey, claiming that the Papagos "were in revolt." Garcés dismissed such warnings as "manifest deception."[55] Soon, four Papagos arrived at San Xavier to accompany Garcés and one of the San Xavier Indians, who apparently knew Spanish and could serve as an interpreter, on the trip. On August 29, 1768, Garcés saddled up and went on his way. He took with him only his Mass vestments, some jerked beef and pinole, and some sugar to share with the O'odham children.

As soon as Garcés left San Xavier he found himself in country that was, for him, terra incognita. He almost certainly had no map, and at this point he appears to have had no familiarity with the written accounts of Jesuits who had traveled in the area.[56] He

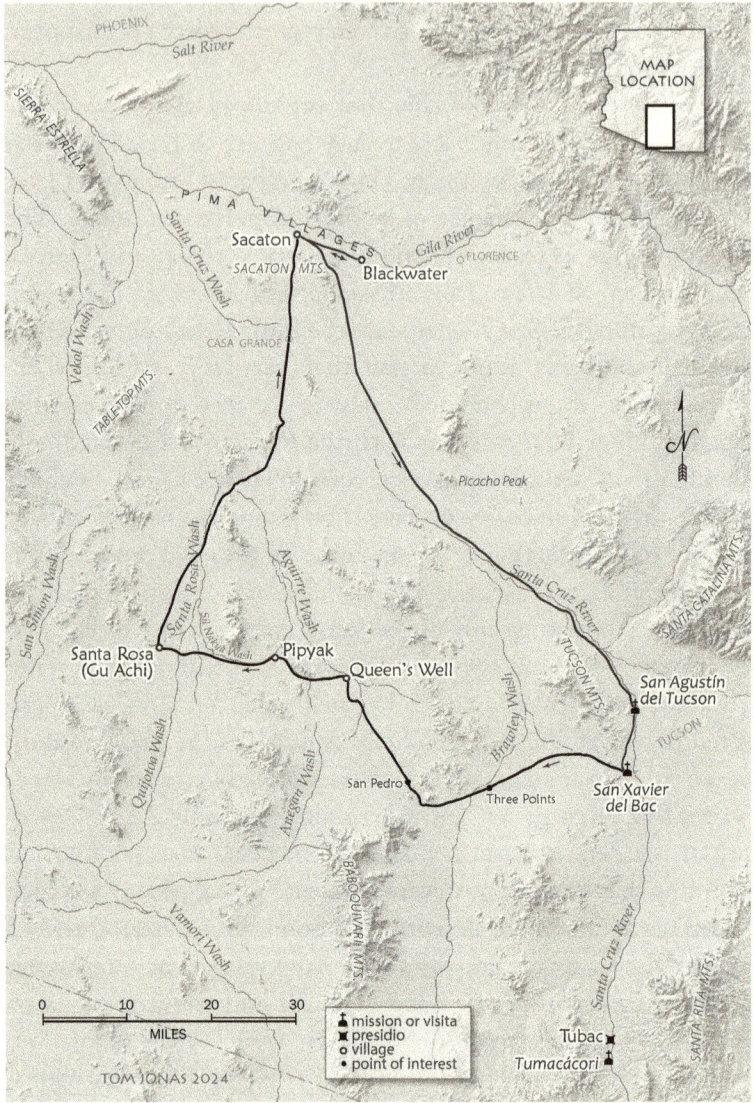

Route Garcés likely took to the Gila River and back in
August and September 1768. *Map by Tom Jonas.*

tells us that he went "about eighty leagues to the west, north, and southeast," which would constitute a roughly two-hundred-mile circuit.[57] He also says that it took the party two days to reach the first village, so the first leg of his journey was at least fifty miles, probably west through saguaro-studded foothills toward Kitt Peak, then down the broad Aguirre Valley through the villages of Queen's Well and Pipyak (Garcés called it Pipian) to modern Santa Rosa or Gu Achi (Garcés called it Ati) in the Santa Rosa Valley.[58] Because this was late summer in the heart of the Sonoran Desert, conditions were doubtlessly hot, dry, and difficult. In terms of his physical stature, Garcés was unremarkable.[59] But it is one indication of his stoic toughness that he makes no mention of heat, dust, bugs, or any other of nature's annoyances.

While he was at Gu Achi, Garcés took a moment to write a letter to missions president Father Buena informing him about his trip—sending the letter via a Papago messenger, and prudently writing after his entrada was a fait accompli, for as Buena later wrote he never would have consented to such a dangerous journey had Garcés asked for permission first—and the pleasure with which he had been greeted by both the Papagos and Pimas.[60] Indeed, every village Garcés visited treated him hospitably, no trace of that rumored Papago "revolt" present anywhere. "The Indians of one *ranchería* escorted me to the next," Garcés recalled in 1775, and if they did not greet him with arches and bowers as they had Father Kino, "everywhere they gave of what they had to the [San Xavier] interpreter and me." Their generosity made a deep impression on Garcés. "Such gifts, and from such people, and at a time when I was so poor, were extremely gratifying," he recalled.[61] For their part, the O'odham seemed touched by Garcés's evident poverty and impressed by his courage in traveling without soldiers or any other Spaniard—or perhaps they carefully gave that impression in order to establish access to whatever material and spiritual goods Garcés could provide, and to buttress his confidence that soldiers were unnecessary. Regardless of O'odham motives, as word about Garcés spread, leaders from the

Pima villages on the Gila River traveled south to ask Garcés to
visit their settlements as well, to which request he complied. Garcés mentions in his diary that among the multiple settlements he
visited was a populous ranchería somewhere on the Gila River,
probably near today's Sacaton, Arizona.[62]

The Pima villages of the Gila River were flourishing at the
time of Garcés's 1768 visit. Their population had been swelled by
migration from the south. Village authority had been clarified
through consolidation under one headman. Large, well-irrigated
fields of wheat had come to supplement the staple crop of corn.[63]
The Gileños looked healthy and sturdy. Fray Pedro Font, who
would come through this region with the second Anza expedition
in 1775, has left us a memorable description of their appearance:

> The Gila Indians ... are quite fat and strong.... They attempt to
> clothe themselves in their cotton cloaks that they process and weave
> themselves, and with some coarse cloth that they acquire through the
> trade they have ... and they use the coarse cloth to make their clouts
> with. Those who have no breeches replace them with a folded, tied-
> up blanket, and the women cover themselves with deerskins. The hair
> styling they employ is an unusual one, since they take a thin woolen
> cord ... and bunching it up they insert it through their hair and tie it all
> together with a long cord and wind it around their head from the left
> side to the right. Then they fasten it with the leftover end, giving one
> or two turns around their head, and a projection like a sort of wreath,
> is left atop it where those who possess any feathers put in some, along
> with little sticks, and ornaments. The women wear their hair dangling
> over their shoulders and ears and cut it off in front as far as their eyes
> or their eyebrows.[64]

Garcés, unlike his Jesuit predecessors, and unlike the members of the second Anza expedition, had no gifts to distribute to
the O'odham in 1768. But he did have good talk and the strange
ceremony of the Mass, and those intangible gifts were apparently appreciated. In whatever ranchería Garcés found himself in the evening, he would first say Mass and then summon
the elderly Indians for talk around the fire, which conversation

would last from nightfall until around two o'clock in the morning. The missionary spoke to them "of the divine mysteries" and of Charles III—the traditional Franciscan approach.[65] Perhaps because they could make little sense of the former, his auditors appear to have been more interested in the latter. What was the king like? they asked. And what was Garcés himself doing here? How did he cross the sea? What was he looking for? Or was he just curious? The questions reported by Garcés are so natural that it is easy to believe they were asked.

As was the case with his adventurous missionary predecessors, uppermost on Garcés's mind were two questions of his own. How well disposed were these natives toward the Spaniards? Would they like missions to be planted among them? The answers Garcés consistently received to these queries were "very well" and "yes," accompanied by frequent requests to baptize infants and disappointment when Garcés reluctantly refused to do so. (He did baptize four sick children, but since the Catholic Church taught that baptism conferred not only the possibility of eternal life but also an obligation to live in a Christian manner, missionaries typically did not baptize natives whom they did not believe they or others could instruct in that way of living, unless they were very ill.) Although such a disposition among the Indians obviously nestled conveniently within the interests and desires of the Spanish authorities, there is reason to believe Garcés's report was accurate here, too, for the O'odham were not blind to the pros and cons of mission life.

There were material advantages to be obtained, first of all. Garcés mentions how on this entrada his "sandals and robe" provoked admiration among his hosts. So would, as the missionaries discovered, many other articles, including pieces of cloth, metal implements, eyeglasses, guns, and horses. European technology fascinated and attracted New Spain's natives. Missions also brought food advantages. The extent to which the O'odham had adapted, culinarily, to the exigencies of desert dwelling was remarkable. From Emory oak acorns to agave hearts, staghorn cholla buds to wolfberries, saguaro fruit to amaranth greens, the Sonoran Desert provided the O'odham with more than four hundred plants with edible components. These were supplemented with the staple crops of corn, squash, and tepary beans, which the O'odham planted along stream banks and at the mouths of desert washes.[66] But especially in such an inhospitable environment, innovative adaptation went only so far. The rains were highly unpredictable, and as one scholar reminds us O'odham life was "far from utopian. Food supplies were often precarious and there were surely times of starvation. Life expectancy was probably short. And it is also some measure of the quality of [O'odham] existence when one takes into account their ready acceptance of many plants, animals, and artifacts" brought by the Spanish.[67] Wheat, in particular, filled a gap in the O'odham agricultural cycle, and other seeds introduced by Spanish missionaries ultimately doubled the number of plants and fruits under O'odham cultivation.[68]

Having a mission nearby meant more than a more regular and varied food supply. It also meant the presence of Spanish soldiers—and hence greater protection against the chief O'odham adversaries, the Apaches. To the native peoples of the Pimería Alta, the Apaches were, like the Spaniards, johnny-come-latelies, having arrived on their doorstep only a century or two before the Spanish had first marched through the land.[69] The presence of both groups complicated matters for the O'odham, but at least the Europeans provided new foodstuffs and technologies. Proximity to the Apaches came with no such advantages. Their warriors acquired status by raiding, and lately, thanks in part to the 1762 abandonment of Sobaípuri Pima villages on the San Pedro River that ran to the east of the Santa Cruz, villages that had once acted as a welcome front line of defense for the Pimería Alta's interior, the Apaches had become even more daring.[70]

Having promised the Pimas on the Gila, as he had the people at Tucson, that they would soon receive resident missionaries, Garcés returned after a few weeks to San Xavier. He was elated at the success with which he had scratched this first itch to wander and preach, and he was thrilled by the new relationships he had built, especially with the Pimas who lived on the Gila River, the natives who impressed and attracted him the most. As he wrote Father Buena, the opportunity to expand the reach of Christendom was obvious.[71]

But on this rugged frontier nothing was easy. As the United States would later find out, the Apaches had no wish to live under anyone's control but their own. They were simply biding their time.

In 1768, with the Sobaípuri Pimas out of the way and the Spanish military's campaign against the Pima and Seri rebels dragging on, the Apaches saw an opening. Ordinarily, fifty men were posted at presidios like the one at Tubac. That was none too many for so vast a country—New Spain's military frontier was perpetually short on manpower. But the campaign in southern Sonora meant that by 1768 the Tubac presidio's force had been reduced by about half—and with Captain Anza gone it was without its energetic commander. Even in the best of times the garrison at Tubac offered little in the way of a real-time defense of San Xavier del Bac, since it was some forty miles distant. Yet at least the Apaches knew that if they did attack the mission a punitive expedition would be swiftly mounted by a commander, in Anza, who had no compunctions about exacting a high price in consequence. With Anza and 50 percent of the presidio's soldiers missing, the calculus changed.

Thus, on October 2, 1768, between eight and nine o'clock in the morning, Apache warriors descended on the San Xavier del Bac mission. Caught by surprise, the two soldiers posted at the mission, as well as its native governor and those of the village's male warriors who were present (as the Apaches knew, many were out picking wild berries in the hills), were initially helpless to prevent the Apaches from capturing much of the mission's cattle and horse herd. After gathering themselves, the mission's defenders gave chase, just as the Apaches knew they would. At today's

Redington Pass, forty miles east of Tucson between the Santa Catalina and Rincon Mountains, another group of Apaches ambushed the Spanish soldiers and O'odham warriors, capturing the former and killing some of the latter, including Bac's native governor.[72]

By good fortune—or perhaps, from the Apache point of view, by design—Garcés was convalescing in Guevavi when the Apaches attacked. For soon after his return to San Xavier from the Gila River, he had found himself on the cusp of death.

The nature of Garcés's illness is unclear. Fevers (including yellow fever), muscle spasms, and those sicknesses our ancestors once called "agues" were not uncommon in the Pimería Alta among missionaries.[73] The disease that befell Garcés immediately after his return to San Xavier was probably the same that overcame several other friars in the summer of 1768, including Father Buena.[74] Garcés's case seems to have been particularly severe, for he was "seized by an apoplectic fit, which deprived him of his mental and speech faculties for over twenty-four hours and ended in very painful chills."[75] Someone reported Garcés's alarming condition to Father Gil. Soon Garcés's old friend had come to San Xavier to minister to and remove him to Guevavi so that he could remain in his care. Garcés was too weak to resist. As Father Buena later reflected, his absence from San Xavier that October 1768 could be seen—through the eyes of faith—as an act of divine providence.[76]

CHAPTER 4

Are You a Woman or a Man?
1769–1770

Unlike several of his predecessors, Francisco Garcés would not be driven from his post by illness, even one so dangerous and disabling as the one he suffered in the autumn of 1768. By early 1769 he had returned to Bac. His right arm was still ailing enough that he would ever after find writing an even more terrible chore—at this point his handwriting becomes truly wretched—but otherwise his health had been restored. Now was his chance to settle as best he could into the routine of mission life, something the previous year's expedition and his subsequent sickness had denied him. The Apaches had other ideas. At about 8:30 in the morning on February 20, 1769, approximately thirty of their warriors swept into the San Xavier mission from the east.

As always, the Apaches timed their attack strategically. On that crisp winter morning nearly all the residents of both Tucson and San Xavier were in the mountains to the west gathering agave.[1] The raiders could therefore proceed at an almost leisurely pace.

Those on horseback rounded up as many horses and cattle as they could, while the handful who were on foot kept at bay Garcés, the two resident Spanish soldiers, and the few Bac natives who were present by launching arrows into the buildings where they had sought protection. Just one Pima was wounded, but by the time the Apaches finished their work the mission had been devastated. San Xavier was left with only a few riding horses, a handful of colts, twenty mares, and thirty or so head of cattle. The Apache braves paused, before leaving, to shoot a hail of arrows into the church's door and to draw three circles in the sand, indicating that in three moons—the time of the next agave harvest—they would be back to do it all again.[2]

As he took stock of San Xavier's losses, Garcés fumed. He immediately asked the soldiers at Tubac presidio to retaliate. Yet he knew that even if such a campaign took place it would be too little, too late. Given the malnourished condition of the remaining horses, and with Anza and many of his soldiers still absent from the presidio, "we simply do not have the forces needed for effective control of the Apaches here." His mission and visita at Tucson were ridiculously exposed. "Now you know, Sir, something of the seriousness of the situation," he wrote to Governor Pineda. His only hope was that José de Gálvez, the king's visitor-general, would "provide a definitive remedy to this problem."

It was a hope to which many of the frontier's Franciscans clung. King Charles III had sent Gálvez to New Spain in 1765 with the mission of finding ways to strengthen the treasury and military. Charles was boring, unintellectual, and homely; he and his wife María Amalia, daughter of the king of Poland, made "the ugliest couple in the world," in the opinion of Britain's envoy to Spain. But he was also a genial, hard-working, intelligent administrator.[3] His biggest geopolitical mistake, to date, had been to ally with France against England in the conflict that became known as the Seven Years' War (or, in America, as the French and Indian War). That war, won by the English in 1763, had cost Spain dearly. Charles had been forced to cede to England the territory of Florida and to pay a huge sum to regain the key Spanish ports of Havana and Manila. If he were to avenge these losses—an opportunity that by 1765 he sensed was on the horizon, given the troubles the British were experiencing with their North American colonists—he needed to replenish his treasury.[4] Fortunately, his reforms in Spain were already leading to increased revenues at home. Gálvez was by 1769 well on his way to achieving the same end in New Spain.[5]

Gálvez had shown little sentimentality in carrying out Charles's order to expel the Jesuits. As a highly ambitious aristocrat who knew which way the royal wind was blowing, Gálvez was committed to the implementation of the king's centralizing and rationalizing Enlightenment convictions.[6] Such a man in another country might be a sworn enemy of clerics. But whatever else Gálvez was—and he was often punitive and petty—he was apparently a committed Catholic, and his rectitude and energy were highly regarded by the Franciscans.[7] They loved that he was a man of action. Having rid New Spain of the Society of Jesus and organized the expedition to put down the Pima and Seri rebellion, in February 1769 Gálvez was in the midst of overseeing final arrangements for the occupation of Alta California. This was the so-called Sacred Expedition that would lead to the founding of a mission in San Diego that July by Father Junípero Serra.[8] Gálvez, in other words, was focused not only on securing but also on expanding the Spanish frontier. Francisco Garcés was about to reveal to him how both ends might be accomplished on the Gila.

※ ※ ※

In March 1769, after another Apache attack on San Xavier, the ensign commanding the Tubac presidio in Anza's absence decided to go on the offensive into the Apache-controlled territory to the garrison's east and northeast. Garcés, as chaplain, accompanied the expedition, which included ten soldiers, fifteen settlers, and forty auxiliary Pima warriors. After a few days the group found the Apaches in camp. The ensign had expected no such success; as so often happened on the frontier, the strategy he decided upon was an immediate retreat. When confronting Apaches, few Spanish soldiers had the courage of an Anza.[9]

From a military perspective this expedition was fruitless. But it did allow Garcés to see for the first time, on the San Pedro River, the deserted Sobaípuri villages. They were a depressing reminder of how the frontier was getting closer to, rather than farther from, his own post at San Xavier. Garcés also made notes about the terrain and, no doubt influenced by the knowledge and views of the soldiers with whom he rode, he reflected on how a military alliance with the Gileño Pimas might either inflict a crushing military defeat on the Apaches or else push them so far eastward that they would no longer be a problem. Garcés sent his thoughts to Father Buena, who showed them to a curious José de Gálvez.[10]

During the late eighteenth century, the Gran Apachería, as the Spaniards called the territory inhabited by Apache bands, spanned 750 miles east to west, from about the 98th to the 111th meridian, and 550 miles north to south, from roughly the 38th to the 30th parallel; think of a massive rectangle containing most of Texas, all of New Mexico, southern Kansas and Colorado, southeastern Utah, and the eastern third of Arizona.[11] From this large territorial base bands of Apaches raided deep into what are now the northern states of Mexico: Nuevo León, Coahuila, Chihuahua, and Sonora.[12] Such raids were foremost on frontier Spaniards' minds, thanks not only to the property losses they inflicted but also because of the depredations accompanying them. It was widely reported, for example, that Apaches "tore off and ate the living flesh of Spaniards who fell into their hands and slashed the bodies of pregnant women, pulled out the unborn infants, and beat them to death."[13] Father Antonio de los Reyes claimed that an Apache band had stolen three children; when the littlest child began to cry, the warriors grabbed him by the legs and smashed his brains out against a boulder while his siblings watched in horror.[14]

A modern historian writes that although torture "had long been a common practice among the Apaches ... they practiced it on the Spanish with a vengeance." A chief of the Aravaipa Apaches once bragged that he had buried a captive alive up to his neck and then watched the ants devour his head. Prisoners were often staked out on anthills with their mouths propped open to allow ravenous insects easy entry. Men were tied naked to cactus or thorn-laden trees and then skewered with lance and arrow. Teamsters were tied upside down to their wagon wheels with hot coals placed under their heads. Men were flayed alive until they slowly bled to death. Female relations of slain warriors were given captives to torture to help assuage their grief. They proved particularly ingenious at this work, often ornamenting the mouths of male victims with their own penises.[15]

The circulation of such stories tended to inhibit the achievement of sympathetic interethnic understanding. So did other Apache characteristics. For example, the Apaches of Garcés's time generally did not have settled communities. They preferred a semisedentary existence in which for much of their sustenance they preyed on animals raised by others, especially horses and mules, whose meat they savored.[16] These Apaches also maintained a different, less hierarchical kind of social organization than did most of their native neighbors. The affiliation of families with bands was fluid, and there was little if anything in the way of universally recognized Apache leadership. This kind of structure made it impossible for the Spanish to broker a peace deal with the Apaches as a whole. Form a treaty or pact with one band and, not only did that leave all the other bands free, but the band with which you had made a treaty might use the safe harbor you had given them to raid a Spanish presidio, mission, or pueblo somewhere else.[17] To yield such an outcome from peacemaking efforts was, to the Spaniards, maddening. But from the Apache perspective, the Spanish were but another aspect of the usable environment in which they lived, and to whom they recognized no ethical obligations.

Any notions Garcés may have entertained about peaceful coexistence with the Apaches were entirely abandoned by the summer of 1769. That spring, on April 3, San Xavier was for the fourth time in less than a year sacked by Apache raiders, despite the fact that Anza had detailed two additional soldiers to live at the mission.[18] Most of the mission's livestock was again stolen. At least San Xavier's few buildings still stood. The mission of Santa María de Suamca, thirty miles southeast of Guevavi, was not so lucky. On April 11 it was burned by attacking Apaches. For neither raid were the Apache warriors punished by Spanish or Pima forces. Three months later, on July 3, 1769, the Apaches were back at Bac, stealing more livestock but, fortunately, failing to inflict additional damage. More threats—and frightening rumors of a large-scale attack—reached San Xavier in the days that followed.[19]

By this point Garcés was doing little more than managing an Apache-owned ranch. "I ask you," he wrote Governor Pineda on July 23, "who owns the livestock of the west, as well as that of Santa María, Guevavi, and San Xavier? I say the Apaches."[20] The people of both San Xavier and Tucson lived in terror of their enemies, at whom they had become disinclined to throw a counterpunch. Garcés himself, who almost never admitted to being scared of anything, confessed that he was too frightened to travel to Tucson, or even into the desert where the O'odham were harvesting saguaro fruit, without a soldier escort. Both places, he lamented to Pineda, could easily soon "go the way of Santa María"—that is, be burned to the ground. His only solace came in the knowledge he had gained through the grapevine that his proposal to build new missions on the Gila—and to ally with the Pimas there in waging a common defense against, and when possible an offensive war upon, the Apaches—had been passed on to Visitor-General Gálvez and met with his enthusiastic support.[21]

Gálvez had arrived at Los Alamos in Sonora on May 11, 1769. His mission on the northern frontier was not only to effect the final subjugation of the rebellious Seris and Pimas but also to institute whatever legal and military reforms were necessary to make this war-torn, troublesome region an asset rather than a burden on the royal treasury.[22] Naturally, Gálvez requested information and counsel from the Franciscans who had been serving in the region during the previous year. At a meeting with Father Buena, the visitor-general was shown Garcés's reports of his entradas into the Papaguería and Apachería. Here, Gálvez concluded, was a path forward. By redirecting the military northward, by planting missions among the friendly Papagos and Gileños, and by allying with these groups to crush the Apaches, New Spain's territory could be enlarged and a troublesome enemy defeated. Not only that, but Sonora and Alta California could be connected via the Gila River corridor—even if the precise route by which such a connection might be effected was not yet known. Further discussions with Father Buena and other Sonora-based friars followed, during which, one historian has reasonably speculated, Garcés's "exploits and dreams for the future must have been one of the principal items of table talk."[23] Gálvez therefore decided to pay a personal visit to the Santa Cruz and Gila Rivers regions.

Buena and the rest of the Franciscan missionaries from Querétaro were elated. The most powerful man in New Spain was four-square behind their enterprise, which now promised to be covered in glory. New missions would be established, more souls would be won for Christ, and peace would reign on New Spain's northwestern boundary.

It was not to be—at least not yet. First the Seri and Pima rebels unexpectedly rejected Gálvez's terms of peace and stubbornly defied Spanish efforts to bring them to heel. Then Gálvez lost his mind. He had been sick all summer. The fathers speculated that the extreme heat was getting to him, and perhaps it was, but it seems likely from this and later episodes that Gálvez suffered from a mental illness that today would be diagnosed as bipolar disorder.[24] By October 14 he was severely manic. Saint Francis of Assisi, he reported, had told him that the Spanish officers were completely incompetent. Gálvez would win the war by putting six hundred apes—yes, apes—from Guatemala in uniform and unleashing them on the enemy in his fastnesses. The next day Gálvez visited his soldiers in their barracks and promised them all the money they wanted. Any officer who interfered with his orders, he announced, would be put to death.

Finally, Gálvez's secretaries contrived to confine him in his room, where his sufferings continued unabated for forty days— not least, perhaps, because he was bled three times by the expedition's surgeon. After a brief recovery in December, in February 1770 Gálvez's madness returned. At one moment he was the king of Prussia, at another the king of Sweden, at another the Eternal Father himself. Viceroy Croix had no choice but to recall him to Mexico City. There Gálvez partially recovered. The next year he returned to Spain, where a position on the Council of the Indies awaited him. For the moment, the plan for new missions on the Gila had stalled.[25]

✳ ✳ ✳

As Gálvez's psychiatric drama played out to his south, Garcés built up his mission the best he could. He could be consoled, at least, by Gálvez's rescindment of the regulations limiting missionaries' authority to the spiritual realm alone. The visitor-general's discussions with Father Buena had persuaded him that the frontier was not yet ripe for this reform; Gálvez had come to the same conclusion in California in discussions with Serra.[26] Temporal authority—complete control of the missions and all their properties, including the labor of neophytes—was restored to the Sonoran missionaries on June 3, 1769.[27] They could henceforth operate their missions in closer adherence to the traditional model. Let us draw from a thorough report prepared at about this time by Father Reyes, as well as from the work of modern scholars, to describe that model's most typical elements.[28]

The mission's day began at sunrise, when the church's bells were rung to call the residents to Mass.[29] As the bells chimed, native officials—called the *mador* and the *fiscales*—would walk through the village calling all the children and unmarried adults to church.[30] After Mass, the friar would lead those present in reciting various prayers (e.g., the Our Father, the Hail Mary, the Salve Regina, and the Apostle's Creed) and parts of the catechism in Spanish.[31] At sunset, the same persons were to gather in front of the church to again recite prayers and doctrines before saying the rosary and singing a hymn, typically the Salve Regina or the Alabado. The latter hymn was a particular favorite among New Spain's Franciscans. It took its name from the first word of the first verse: *Alabado y ensalzado sea el Divino Sacramento, en quien Dios oculto asiste de las almas el sustento*—"Praised and exalted be the Divine Sacrament, in whom the hidden God provides sustenance to souls." Finally, regardless of the time of day, neophytes at Queretaran missions were taught to greet others with the words "Hail Mary!," to which the correct reply was "Conceived in grace!"[32]

On Sundays and feast days the same routine was followed, except that everyone—married and unmarried, adult and child— was required to attend Mass. Mission residents were expected to do so "bathed, hair combed, and with clothing poor but clean," as Reyes put it.[33] On these days Mass was sung with the assistance of native women and whatever musical accompaniment could be rounded up (probably very little at an out-of-the-way place like San Xavier del Bac). During Lent, Mass and the recitation of prayers were daily requirements for all the neophytes, and on Sunday afternoons there was teaching about the Four Last Things: Death, Judgment, Heaven, and Hell. Holy Week was the most liturgically intensive time of the year. The church normally required all baptized Catholics to receive communion at Easter, but only if a baseline level of doctrinal understanding had been achieved and a good confession had been made. Getting their neophytes to this stage was a major priority for all the missionaries. Thanks to the cultural and language barriers standing in their way, not to mention the passive resistance often offered by their pupils, it was a difficult task. It was precisely because of this challenge that the friars emphasized the importance of liturgical participation and moral formation—a religion of the senses and of the heart, more stereotypically medieval than modern, that would help generate deeper understanding over time.[34] They would have followed much the same strategy if they had been assigned to a community of peasants near Mexico City.

Major feast days, especially the Marian feasts, were truly festive, mission resources allowing. Besides Mass and the usual ancillary liturgical activities, a large meal would be served and native games and dances permitted, so long as the missionary believed, or at least pretended to believe, that such diversions had no rival religious meaning. Here the personality of the missionary obviously played a large role, with the more authoritarian clamping down on native traditions and the more tolerant allowing them to go on much as they had before—although few if any missionaries countenanced open drunkenness or sexual licentiousness. Night dances that included both men and women were particularly frowned upon.[35]

The friars' paternalistic regulation of daily existence—physically enforced not only by native officials but also by the missions' handful of soldiers—extended beyond religious worship. Agricultural development was the next-highest priority on a missionary's list. In this area the Franciscan missionaries in Sonora generally tried to practice persuasion, explaining to residents, where necessary, the advantages of sowing a multiplicity of crops and vegetables, raising stock, storing surpluses, and so on. Gaining consensus on these matters among the Pimas was not usually difficult, although compromises often had to be reached that allowed natives to leave their fields to gather nuts, seeds, berries, or wild plants elsewhere.[36] Difficulties arose if the missionaries or the native overseers to whom they outsourced much of the day-to-day management in the fields overworked the mission's Indians (as had famously been among the causes of the Pima Revolt of 1751). Indians also occasionally registered complaints about the literally communist nature of arrangements; much of a mission's land, and hence much of its produce, was held in common, which could lead to predictable resentments.

Finally, clerical paternalism implied the right—indeed, the moral necessity—of punishing wrongdoing. For several years the extent of the Queretaran friars' authority in this area over their neophytes was unclear, but in 1773 it was officially granted them by the viceroy.[37] This authority included preventing baptized Indians from leaving the mission without permission, as well as the right to forcibly retrieve those who fled, making each neophyte something like a "spiritual debt peon."[38] As draconian and repressive as this rule was, it is worth noting that, even among non-Indians, Spanish authorities discouraged mobility. It was royal policy to create stable populations in frontier villages, and those who moved about from place to place were considered vagabonds.[39] Spanish paternalism was transethnic.

In practice, the missionaries of the Pimería Alta tended to demand less work on communal projects, and to allow converts more time to work on their own plots, than did their peers in the Californias. They also gave their flocks more freedom to search for labor when necessary. As a result, there tended to be less overt resistance to missionization in the Pimería Alta, and less abuse.[40] Nonetheless, most missionaries did not hesitate to have the native alcaldes whip noncompliant Indians, nor did they refrain from ordering them put in wooden stocks or shackled in irons.[41] Although work quotas were surprisingly humane, "missionaries or their Indian assistants routinely flogged or beat neophytes who skipped Mass, shirked assigned labor, engaged in premarital sex, committed adultery, or ran from the missions."[42] Even when in doing so the priests thought they were acting in loco parentis, and therefore appropriately, to the O'odham, who rarely if ever employed corporal punishment with their own children, such measures were perceived as shockingly brutal.[43] The ability to inflict violence was frequently accompanied by intimidation and psychological coercion. Among neophytes, poor health, despair, and resentment were more often the fruits of this approach to evangelization than was an interior embrace of the missionaries' faith.[44]

※ ※ ※

In the province of Sonora the Franciscan mission ideal was almost never strictly implemented, especially at underdeveloped outlying missions like San Xavier. It was an ideal perhaps rendered more attractive—or, at least, less unattractive—to the O'odham than to others because even prior to the arrival of the missionaries they were a provident agricultural people who liked to sing and whose culture taught the virtues of modesty and self-restraint.[45]

When Garcés first encountered the O'odham he was spared the embarrassment that completely naked Indians caused Serra and the Fernandino Franciscans to the west, for the O'odham wore at least some clothing, thanks to the cotton grown, spun, and woven by the Gileños.[46] Not that they wore much. O'odham women went topless, with a one-piece skirt that hung to their knees and was made of either cotton cloth or buckskin. Men wore breechcloths of the same materials. Both men and women wore sandals made of skin from bighorn sheep, a practice that made good sense in a desert filled with sharp cactus spines, thorns, and rocks but was considered so odd in the wider world that Indians to the north called them Sandal People.[47]

Both sexes wore their hair long and adorned their ears with large rings, often made of turquoise. The young O'odham men considered the most handsome boasted flowing hair (often worn high in a knot) and low-dangling earrings that nearly touched the shoulders. Women augmented their beauty by tattooing their faces with blue lines running from the corners of their mouths to the bottoms of their chins on both sides. For special occasions, both sexes painted their torsos with red, yellow, and white paint made out of clay, the women going so far as to paint designs of animals

The O'odham encountered by Garcés would not have looked very different than the four "Pimos Indians" depicted in this ca. 1875 photograph. *From the Smithsonian American Art Museum.*

like birds or butterflies, or perhaps stalks of corn, on themselves.[48] Some priests, like Garcés's Queretaran counterpart Father Pedro Font, sought to discourage these body-painting practices.[49]

For shelter the O'odham bent rods across four rafters to form a kind of dome. Over this frame they first tied bundles of sticks and grass and then placed a layer of earth. This *kí* or *olas kí* was the round "brush hut" mentioned by both Garcés and Middendorff. Although it had no windows and a door big enough only to crawl through, it more or less effectively kept out the weather.[50] Prized possessions were stored in these houses' roofs.[51] Outside was an open-air ramada, or *vato*, supported by posts made from saguaro ribs or ocotillo branches; the latter sometimes took root and leafed and flowered in season. Cooking, cleaning, and other chores took place under the vato, on which hung ollas of water or perhaps pinole (roasted corn meal).[52] Other huts stored tools and food. A group of dwellings and their associated outbuildings constituted a village, or what the Spaniards called a ranchería. With each house placed at a respectful distance from the others, an O'odham ranchería was arranged nothing like what a Spaniard considered a proper town.[53] Somewhere in the midst of these structures was a brush building where O'odham men held nightly council meetings. This building was maintained by the village's headman, who obtained his position through a consensus of adult males.[54]

In their fields, planted in the spring and tended until October, when they moved to the mountains, the Tohono O'odham planted not only corn but also beans and squash. From the Spanish they obtained wheat and legumes, which the O'odham planted in the winter, giving them two growing seasons instead of one, as well as various other fruits and vegetables. They had also procured the welcome innovations of oxen and wooden plows from Father Kino. Cultivated crops were supplemented by hunting—bighorn sheep, peccary, deer, rabbits—and the gathering of cactus fruits, cholla buds, roots and stalks (e.g., the stalk of the century plant), and wild greens.[55]

Frame that supports the brush hut, or *ki*, the typical O'odham
dwelling, ca. 1900. *From the California Historical Society
Collection at the University of Southern California.*

The O'odham's most advanced cultural inventions were string
bags they made to carry venison; nets that O'odham women
used to carry large loads of wood on their heads and backs, one
of their chief duties; waterproof black-and-white coiled baskets made from willow, yucca, and devil's claw seedpods; hard,
woven yucca mats used as mattresses; coarse clay water jars;
rough cooking pots; and painted seed vessels.[56] The O'odham
had no written language, of course. Children were taught to
count to ten, using their fingers, but no higher. Indeed, before
the arrival of Spaniards they probably had no words for numbers greater than ten, for they had felt no need to count so high.
The O'odham did keep a kind of chronology of their people
by using a long "calendar stick" made of cactus ribs on which

Coiled food trays made by O'odham women, ca. 1900. *From the Califor-nia Historical Society Collection at the University of Southern California.*

special marks were made to remind the old man who kept it of various important events.[57]

The O'odham family was patrilineal and patriarchal. Women were subordinate to men, and young men were subordinate to old. Girls had little to no say with respect to whom they became married. From the time they were toddlers young O'odham boys and girls heard their grandparents teach them, over and over, about how hard they must work. Running, farming, and the art of war were emphasized for boys; providing cool water and food for their families, as well as other domestic chores, were empha-sized for girls.[58] Both genders were taught to be quiet in the pres-ence of elders. Direct opposition and frank self-expression were discouraged.[59] Many of the patriarchal traditions and hierarchi-cal doctrines of the Catholic Church resonated with O'odham values and practices.

One idea that *was* difficult to accept was the Catholic doctrine of monogamous and indissoluble marriage. O'odham men often had more than one wife. Indeed, if he was a good husband, the parents of a man's first wife would often present him with a younger sister. Marriage ceremonies consisted solely in the man coming to the woman's house and staying there for four nights. Divorce was even easier; the couple simply separated, the woman returning to her father's house with the small children, while older boys might stay with their father.[60] Such practices caused wonder, and often consternation, among the Catholic missionaries who sought the natives' conversion. For a native man to accept the need for baptism was one thing. For him to accept that he must put away one or more of his "extra" wives was quite another. Father Segesser reported that when he counseled some Pima men on the need for monogamy they replied: "Do you not see that the rooster has more than one hen, a stallion more than one mare?" He does not say how he responded.[61]

As for religion, the O'odham told an origins story in which Earthmaker had made the whole world out of a ball of dirt. Another god, Itoi, emerged soon thereafter. Coyote also helped put the world into shape. People were eventually created, but they were not the right kind and so the gods destroyed them via a great flood. Itoi was the first to emerge from hiding after this flood and thus became the elder brother to Coyote. He, Itoi, made the new people and taught them everything. After a while, however, the people turned on him and killed him—these people were the ancients, said the O'odham, who had built Casa Grande. Itoi later returned, bringing with him the O'odham, whom he had found underground, and helping them drive away those who had murdered him. He gave the O'odham the desert as their own and taught them the ceremonies they must use to obtain rain, food, and health.[62] Of course, the consistency with which this story was told to outsiders, and the extent to which missionaries came to grasp it, tended to vary. What was clear to friars like Garcés was that O'odham religion, unlike Christianity, purported to be neither metaphysical nor historical. Nor was there reference to anything like conscience or interior belief.

Then again, to speak about O'odham "religion" at all is to speak in misleading terms. For Native Americans, there was typically no separate sphere of life marked out as "religion." What Westerners would label religious ideas and ideals were in fact a frame that encompassed—everything. Action. Thinking. Being. There was no eating that was nonreligious. No dreaming that was nonreligious. No war-making that was nonreligious. No love-making that was nonreligious. No festivity that was nonreligious. The idea that some parts of life might be labeled and cordoned off as "religious" is arguably a peculiarly Western, even Christian, concept.[63] It was certainly foreign to the O'odham, who spoke instead of the Piman Way, or *himdag*.[64]

❋ ❋ ❋

During the Queretaran Franciscan era, most O'odham in the Pimería Alta did not accept Christianity; there were fewer than one thousand baptisms there between 1768 and 1795.[65] Even among those O'odham who did accept baptism, there would have been a good deal of what one scholar has called "protective ingratiation," which kept the priests from interfering too much in their lives, and native dances and rituals often continued to be practiced in clandestine fashion.[66] Surely some of those O'odham who accepted Christianity came to regret their choice. But it is just as certain that many did not, even among those who continued to have affection for, and to some extent practice, O'odham *himdag*. Besides the material and security benefits that accompanied life at a Catholic mission, there were two other advantages that may be worth mentioning.

For one, as had been the case in the first centuries of Christianity, the socially unfortunate could stake a claim to full membership in a Christian community. It was the unquestioned and unquestionable duty of the friars to arrange for the care of those who could not care for themselves. "Each of the sick receives the food and nourishment called for by his illness," Father Reyes reported. "Help is given to widows, the aged, and the disabled insofar as the abundance or scarcity of the produce and goods from the common store of the Mission permits, and the Father Missionary shelters and takes care of all orphans."[67] There is evidence that this was not just talk. When he arrived at Tubutama, Father Buena discovered that he had inherited the responsibility of caring for five children who had been captured or bought from other tribes. Within a year, he had also taken over the care of five Pima children whose abandonment had forced them to beg for food from house to house. Some of the community's sick and aged were also neglected, reported Father Buena, as were some widows with children. He did all he could for them.[68]

Such practices, even if they were not always perfectly implemented, reflected a new, or at least more expansive, ideal of charity for Sonora's natives—just as they had for ancient Romans.[69] The Jesuit Joseph Och emphasized the disadvantages suffered by women among the natives of Sonora. He surely exaggerated in saying that "parents do not esteem their daughters and give them little care." It is uncertain whether, as he maintained, young teenage girls were pressured against their wills into marrying old men. It is definitely the case that the Indian women of northern Sonora were not only expected to perform an incredible amount of domestic work but that they could also be easily divorced, exchanged for another man's wife, or given to an honored visitor for sex.[70] Among some groups, native women, when traveling, were supposed to yield to any shaman who wanted to have intercourse with them, whether they were married or not.[71] Women have not historically viewed such practices as empowering.[72]

A second advantage of Christianity was that it may have helped dispel fear. We have no firsthand or even secondhand accounts from O'odham Christian converts until much later than Garcés's time. But later memoirs like that by Anna Moore Shaw, a twentieth-century proud Pima activist and fervent Christian who knew her people's history well, emphasize the consolations and hope found in the new faith.[73] Indeed, it is clear from anthropological accounts that fear was ever-present in the traditional world of the O'odham, as it was among many peoples: fear of ghosts, fear of breaking taboos, fear of animals, fear of enemies, fear of the *hechiceros* (whose witchcraft might be used to kill as well as cure), and especially fear of the dead. It was O'odham practice to bury the deceased as quickly as possible and to never mention their names again, for they were fearful that the dead would try to take them with them. In the burial place, they placed the dead's weapons, tools, and four days' worth of food, enough to nourish the deceased as they made their journey to the next world. They then burned the dead person's house—which made it impossible for him or her to return.[74] Often the community then moved to a different place.[75]

In short, it is not difficult to believe that as it became better understood Christianity exerted some attraction because it promised relief from an atmosphere of fear. Today, in fact, in the Tohono O'odham lands that were known to Garcés as part of the Papaguería, small adobe shrines containing statues of Jesus, Mary, Saint Francis Xavier, or other Christian saints dot the roadsides. At the Gu Achi Trading Post—a convenience station, essentially—a cross adorns the wall behind the cash register, another wall features a large shadow box containing a figurine of Saint Michael the Archangel (protector against demons and the devil), and many sacred candles are for sale. North of the village of Gu Vo there is a shrine to Our Lady of Guadalupe on the north face of a rocky outcropping. A mile or two to the south one finds another shrine, this one created by a Gu Vo youth organization in 1976 and dedicated to the Sacred Heart of Jesus. Christianity still exerts attraction among the O'odham, in other words, and surely much of this appeal has to do with the triumph it purports to offer over fear and death.[76]

※ ※ ※

In April 1770, almost two years after Garcés had invited him to come stay in the mission's "captain's room," Juan Bautista de Anza finally found time to visit San Xavier. At Governor Pineda's command, he had just ridden north with sixty soldiers through the Papaguería, where the unrest that appeared to infect more and more of Sonora seemed now to be spreading. Having made a show of force among the Papagos, and procuring new professions of loyalty from them, Anza, clad in the navy blue and bright red uniform of a captain in the king's service, swung through Bac.[77] There he listened to Garcés's report on the security challenges he and the mission's residents faced—and began to implement a plan to help.[78]

Anza's first task was to convince those few O'odham still living at Tucson to stay where they were. His second was to persuade others to return. To his military mind, Tucson needed as many bodies as it could get. Next, Anza ordered the construction of an earthen, fortified corral, including gunports, in the middle of the Tucson ranchería. By May 10, this project was coming along well, but the Tucsonans pointed out that their safety could be reasonably assured only if a church was planted among them. When they had asked for one before, they had never been promised any food as recompense for their building efforts, so they had demurred from undertaking such a difficult task. Garcés saw their point. He promised ten bushels of wheat and half the next harvest at the San Xavier mission as wages for building the church, a deal the Tucson natives readily accepted.

Finally, Anza procured the Gileños' agreement that the Sobaípuri Pimas who used to live along the San Pedro would be returned to Tucson, where the Spanish had originally moved them, now that they could better defend themselves against the Apaches there, and now that they actually liked and trusted the missionary who served that station. As promised, the Tucsonans constructed a permanent adobe church after the fall 1770 harvest. It was finished by February 1, 1771, when Apaches again attacked. This time, thanks to the fortifications that surrounded the building, the residents were able to repel the raiders.[79]

Apaches, alas, were not the only deadly enemy the O'odham in the Pimería Alta faced in these years. In the autumn of 1770 an epidemic of measles and cholera broke out.[80] Like the unrest recently experienced in the Papaguería, the epidemic arrived from the south; Father Gil, as Garcés probably heard, was forced to bury eight of Guevavi's Indians in a single week.[81] When the sickness hit San Xavier, Garcés ministered to its residents as best he could. Nevertheless, many died. Soon the epidemic spread westward and northward. The O'odham living on the Gila River—out of a fear of Hell, a desire to go to Heaven, a notion that Christian baptism might effect a cure where the hechiceros had failed, or all three—sent messengers to San Xavier asking Garcés to come baptize their sick, one of whom was a married Christian woman who had fled San Xavier some time earlier.[82] That detail helped seal Garcés's decision. On October 19, at nine in the morning, with a single horse and in the company of four natives from San Xavier, but with no soldiers or any other European, he began his second major entrada.[83]

Garcés began by riding northwest along the Santa Cruz, the same route he had traveled back from the Gila in 1768.[84] He passed by three Papago villages where, because there was more fear that he would bring rather than save them from death, he was unable to gather the people together. At nightfall he arrived and slept at a village he called Quitoa. The next morning he visited three more rancherías, baptizing before her death a very old woman before spending the night at a place called El Aquitum, or Aquituni. On the third day, October 21, Garcés rode north over a waterless stretch of desert, skirting westward of the *"casas grandes,"* the impressive ruins at today's Casa Grande National Monument. As he neared the Gila, he met on the trail the chief of the village of Pitaique, whom Garcés had met in 1768. This man

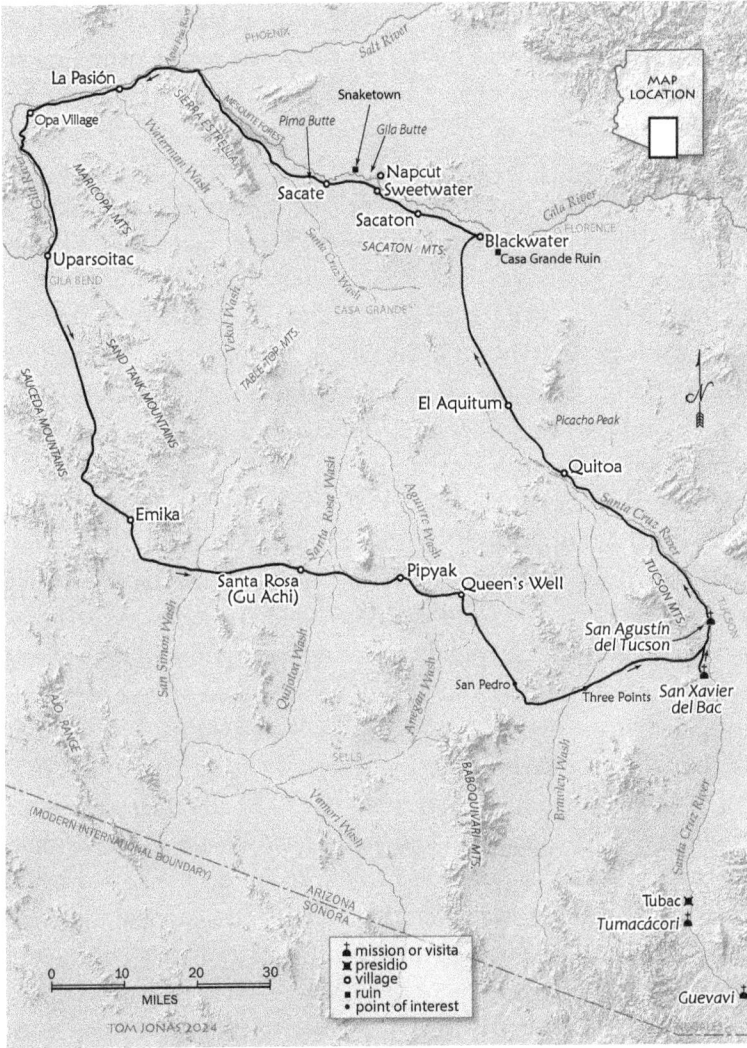

Garcés's second entrada to the Gila River, made in
October and November 1770. *Map by Tom Jonas.*

requested that Garcés head farther east on the river to a place
called Pitac, thought to be today's Blackwater, to be the first to
minister to the people there (Pitac was apparently also governed
by the Pitaique chief).[85] Garcés happily complied, arriving at
Pitac that evening. At this point in Garcés's diary of his journey,
we find the first piece of evidence that he had become familiar
with the Jesuit writings on this region, for he speculates—incorrectly, as it turns out—that Pitac was the place Kino had called
San Andrés.

As soon as he arrived Garcés began to undertake the grisly if
theologically gratifying chore of baptizing dying sick children,
maintaining strict protocol by refusing to baptize those who
were healthy. He then stayed up late into the night talking with
the village's men around the fire. Typically Garcés tried to focus
such discussions around religion. But on this night the Gileños
had news to share. Far to the west, close by the ocean that surely
none of these villagers had ever seen, soldiers had arrived. Their
presence had aroused trepidation among the tribes in that far-off
place, "since it was not known whether they were good people or
bad," and, when they had tried to get natives to come close in order
to "give them a piece of paper," none would do so for fear of being
captured. The O'odham indicated that this had taken place in or
about June 1769. Clearly, as Garcés understood, these soldiers had
been part of the Sacred Expedition to Monterey. The news had
been so momentous that it spread eastward from people to people
and village to village. Whether to the natives it was considered
good news or bad the Gileños did not say—or, at least, Garcés did
not report. But obviously there was an established land route from
the Pacific coast to the Gila.[86]

The next morning, as was his custom, Garcés said Mass and
preached through an interpreter to all those present. He then
headed downstream (west) to Pitaique—probably at or near
today's Sacaton. He was greeted warmly by the chief but was
immediately presented with a request that caused a crisis of conscience. In baptizing the sick children at Pitac, Garcés had acted

only as would have any friar courageous enough to leave his mission. But the natives of Pitaique pleaded with him to baptize not only their sick children but also their healthy ones. Even many adults, perhaps only slightly ill, begged for baptism. The governor advanced cogent arguments for why Garcés should accommodate these wishes. Wouldn't the healthy likely soon get sick themselves? Hadn't he promised them in 1768 that there would soon be a mission established there? Weren't his people good?

Garcés was an obedient priest. He was not, as some writers have anachronistically suggested, a maverick, eighteenth-century anticipation of the type of post–Vatican II hippie friar who distrusts the church's hierarchy and takes satisfaction in flouting its rules. But he was definitely kindhearted, and if he could help it he did not wish to see any of these people consigned to eternal perdition. He had conceived a special affection for them. In fact, having learned on his 1768 visit that the Pimas at Pitaique diverted water from the Gila to their fields via a weir that was periodically destroyed by floods, he had thought to bring with him on this journey three axes he knew they would find useful (he gave one of these precious axes to the Gileños as a gift, and the others as a loan).[87] He therefore decided to probe the Pimas' religious beliefs further. With relief he "ascertained that they know there is a God, whom they invoke when they plant grain and hunt." He was further heartened to see that, when he explained fundamental Christian doctrine to them as well as he could, it "pleased them greatly to hear the truths of our faith." They seemed as well disposed toward it as they had been when visited by Father Kino some seventy years earlier, assuring Garcés they would accept a missionary as soon as one was assigned there.[88] Believing that with Gálvez's support such a day was not far off, and perhaps reasoning that he could help hurry it along, "as a matter of justice" Garcés finally consented to baptize "a goodly number" of healthy children. He remains silent as to whether he also baptized any of the "slightly ill" adults, but in his diary he notes that he afterward learned that "almost all" the children he baptized soon died, which confirmed to his satisfaction that he had made the right decision.

With some difficulty, for his friends did not wish him to leave, Garcés continued down the Gila the next day, October 23. Soon he encountered two rancherías near today's Sweetwater; he named them San Juan Capistrano.[89] He was impressed by what he found. The natives here "had beautiful, large fields of wheat, growing well and already well out of the ground, so punctual are those Indians in their planting." After spending a little time with the Indians in these prosperous villages, he crossed the Gila and found on its northern bank a larger village he called Napcut, which must have been located near the ruins of Snaketown. Here Garcés met some "very old men who remembered well Father Kino." If so, they must have been nearly one hundred years old. Surprisingly, that is not entirely implausible, for both missionaries and later O'odham memoirists claimed it was not infrequent for O'odham to live that long or longer.[90] Garcés preached to them, per usual. He also told them it was his intention to continue downstream to visit the Opas, a people he knew had not been visited by a missionary for decades. The Gileños apparently did not wish to share with the Opas the friendship and resources of the Spanish, for that night, around the fire, they introduced an Opa who did all he could to discourage Garcés from going to his people. By this time Garcés was coming to understand intertribal dynamics: a given group nearly always wished to monopolize a padre's friendship, resources, and spiritual power. He dismissed the Opa's words as a "deluge of lies" and continued on his way the next morning.

It would not be with the four San Xavier Indians who had accompanied him thus far. They "had not the courage," Garcés reports, to visit the Opas, who unlike the Gileños were not Piman-speaking relatives but instead spoke a Yuman language. Before arriving among them Garcés, led by a Gileño guide and accompanied by three other Gileños, including the governor's son, encountered a final group of three Pima rancherías called

Sutaquisón—probably where Sacate is today. On this desert plain ten miles or so north of modern Maricopa the residents had been blessed with an abundance of water, relatively speaking, in part thanks to nature (the Santa Cruz and other washes run northward through this area) and in part because of their shrewd use of dams.[91] Garcés was happy to find not only that the epidemic had not yet spread here—one wonders whether he and his companions unintentionally brought it with them—but also that these Indians were "much given to work, are very docile, [and] are attracted by what is good." Not only that, but they often successfully, and aggressively, defended themselves against the Apaches, even if the latter had scored a damaging victory against Sutaquisón's warriors the previous year.

The Sutaquisón residents asked Garcés to stay the night, but he wanted to keep moving. Already it was the sixth day of his journey and he had intended to be gone for only five. There was still much to see. He had no time to linger anywhere, especially since he refused to take shortcuts. From Sutaquisón Garcés's guide tried to take a cross-country course southwest, away from the Gila and around the southern tip of the Sierra Estrella. But when Garcés discovered his intentions he insisted they turn northwest, keeping the Estrella to their left. He didn't want to miss the Opa villages he knew were in that direction along the Gila. And so the little group made their way northwest through swampy, salty land until they made camp at nightfall.

Early the next morning, October 25, Garcés was up and going. The way led through a giant, marshy mesquite thicket along the eastern flank of the Estrellas.[92] Eventually the group made contact again with the river, which, alas, was too muddy and salty to drink. The Pimas obtained water for the men and their horse by digging a well on the river's bank. Then, to get the lay of the land, the party clambered up one of the Estrella peaks, the highest of which rise more than three thousand feet above the desert floor. From this vantage point Garcés could see many miles to the east and north. Nearby he could see the tree-lined bed of the Salt River (the Río Salado, as he knew it; it was already shedding its previous Spanish-given name, the Asunción) as it made its way westward to intersect with the Gila. A mile or two west of this confluence he could see a line of trees marking the course of another river, this one dry and coursing from the north. Garcés had sighted the Agua Fria.[93]

Returning to the path by the Gila, at nightfall Garcés arrived at the first Opa ranchería, which the residents called Tugabi and he called de la Pasión. Given the way news traveled on the native frontier, these Opas had no doubt heard about Garcés, but they may have never before seen a missionary, and many had probably never seen a European (except for Kino, the only one we know previously to have traveled in this area was Father Sedelmayr in 1744, though of course some Opas would likely have encountered Europeans in their trading travels). They "received me joyfully," wrote Garcés, and even though they spoke an entirely different language than did the Pimas, thanks to the services of an Opa woman who understood the Piman tongue they were able to understand Garcés well enough.[94] They generously fed the no-doubt hungry friar and his Gileño friends (Garcés notes that with only one horse between them his Gileño companions had brought little in the way of food) and gave them gifts.[95] They were stunned that Garcés dared travel alone to their country, and his long gray habit, unlike anything they had ever seen, fascinated them. Are you a woman or a man? they asked him. Are you married? Such were just two of the many questions "natural to their uncivilized state" with which they peppered the friar. They had a talent, as one ethnologist would later note, for "good-humored obscenity."[96]

With these Opas, Garcés and the others spent the night. He observed that they were less technologically advanced than the Pimas. They did not practice irrigation.[97] A lower proportion wore clothes woven from cotton than among the O'odham. Many of the men went about completely naked; the women wore aprons made from strips of dangling, supple willow bark. Still, they raised wheat, corn, and legumes, like the Pimas, and were becoming better fighters, he was told, under the Pimas' tutelage.[98] Most interesting, some had Hopi blankets, which they obtained through intermediate Indian traders like the Yavapais, who lived to their north.

From this point, Garcés wished to leave the river, which turns south, and continue west. Just why he wanted to do this he does not say. He reports that when he had "pointed out the direction in which I desired to go," the Opas "thought I was going to the Moqui" to visit the Hopis and sought to dissuade him from doing so.[99] Garcés does not say that such was *not* his intention. Perhaps it was, especially since the Spanish generally believed the Hopis' home to be farther south, and sometimes farther west, than its actual location.[100] In any case, the Opas persuaded him to visit their tribal leaders at a village downriver instead. Garcés writes that he saw many Hopi blankets when he arrived there, as well as a desperately sick and loudly wailing infant, whom he was able to baptize before it died. Among these Opas were those who spoke the Piman language, meaning that Garcés could communicate easily with them through his companions. The Opas wished to take Garcés to visit some rancherías—"friends of theirs"—that were not located along the Gila. Who these friends were, and where they were located, we are not told, but the Gileños who were with Garcés flatly refused to go along if he went to see them, and so the proposed side trip was scotched.

On October 27, Garcés continued south along the Gila, noting the whitewater that formed along the river where it narrowed between two mountain ranges, almost certainly the spot where Gillespie Dam stands today. Along the route he passed through rancherías wherein he found Pimas who had intermarried with Opas. From these natives he gathered information that once again reveal what was on Garcés's mind, beyond the baptism of sick children; for example, he reports learning that the Colorado

River was three days distant, and that the Hopi people lived near the Colorado. Evidently Garcés had, or was forming, a vision not only for how the Pimería Alta could be connected with Alta California via the Gila and Colorado but also for how both Sonora and Alta California could be connected with New Mexico, for it was well known that Moqui was not far from the latter.

Garcés arrived at the village of Uparsoitac, which he named San Simón y Judas, on October 28. This was at or near modern Gila Bend. Garcés tells us he "stopped in the house of a baptized Pima, where many people gathered from all sides to see me." In the crowd were four very tall, very naked young men—"strong young fellows"—evidently from a different tribe. They gave Garcés some gifts, and he discovered that they lived farther downstream, were enemies of the Yumas who lived on the Colorado (Garcés noted that several female Yuman captives were present in the village), and were called the Cocomaricopas. Father Segesser had thought this people "so wild and big that they frighten[ed]" him "terribly."[101] Garcés, who was made of sterner stuff, promised to come visit them as soon as he could (a little while later he received word that they had made him a little room, which he supposed was made "of sticks and earth"). Garcés baptized a sick boy but summoned enough resolve to deny baptism to those who were well. Then, having already explored the unmapped north for much longer than the five days he had intended, he decided he must return to San Xavier, and by the quickest route possible, which meant forswearing the Gila to travel directly southeast across the dry desert.[102]

For more than three days, Garcés and his Gileño companions, who did not know the country, made their way "half lost" across the Papaguería. One of them became seriously ill, "but he implored God to aid him because of the goodness of his heart and the service he was doing" for Garcés, recorded the friar, "and was heard apparently by Him Who is the Father of mercy, for he recovered immediately."[103] Finally, on his fourth day out from Uparsoitac, Garcés ran into the San Xavier guides whom he had left some days ago along the Gila. A day later, November 1, 1770, he arrived back at his Tucson visita feeling strong and energized.[104] Many Indians had gathered there and at San Xavier while he was gone, doubtless in the pursuit of medical attention. Some looked like "skeletons." Garcés nursed them while pondering how the country he was now coming to know better could ultimately be conquered for Christ and king.

CHAPTER 5

El Camino del Diablo

1770–1771

*G*arcés's 1770 journey down the Gila made him the first
European to follow that river for an extended distance
since the Jesuit Jacobo Sedelmayr had done so from near
Casa Grande to the Colorado in 1744. The journey has historical
importance for contemporary scholars. It is thanks to Garcés
that we know most if not all of what we know about the Opas.
Few travelers left behind a better description of a visit to the Gila
River Pimas. And no one prior to the mid-nineteenth century
had inventoried Gileño settlements so well.[1] When it came to
people, unlike flora and fauna, Garcés was a keen observer.

For the Spanish authorities of his time, the value of the intelligence provided by Garcés was utilitarian rather than academic.
Now that Visitor-General Gálvez had shown interest in placing presidios and missions on the Gila, Garcés's journey had
considerable strategic importance—and the friar knew it. Soon
after his return to San Xavier in late 1770, Garcés traveled south
to Tumacácori, where his friend Father Gil was now based.

Together they put Garcés's trip notes into shape, and on Garcés's behalf Gil drafted a long letter describing what Garcés had seen and learned to Querétaro's new Father Guardian, Father Joseph Miguel de Araujo.[2]

Father Gil had not undertaken the daring travels of his fellow Aragonese, but he had certainly encountered his share of difficulties since arriving in the Pimería Alta. His mission of Guevavi and its three visitas of Tumacácori, Calabazas, and Sonoita comprised only fifty Pima families, and their numbers were declining, thanks largely to disease.[3] In the low, adobe- and mud-brick buildings and brush *kí* at Guevavi, Gil administered last rites to a tragically high number of natives. So unhealthful was life at Tumacácori that those born at the mission between 1775 and 1825 lived to a mean age of just fifteen.[4] Of 123 children born at the mission between 1773 and 1825, 93 percent died before the age of ten.[5]

Gil had more success at Tubac, another settlement of low-slung adobes, where he served as chaplain and was warmly welcomed by most of the Spaniards and other gente de razón, especially the women, who appreciated his imposing a little moral discipline on the five hundred people living there.[6] But the garrison at Tubac was depressingly ineffective in providing defense against the Apaches, especially during Captain Anza's absences. In July 1770, a few months prior to Garcés's arrival at Tumacácori, Apaches slaughtered nineteen native residents, including eleven children, at Sonoita. A little earlier Calabazas had also been attacked; the number of O'odham killed had been seven. Father Gil decided it would be prudent to move his headquarters from Guevavi to Tumacácori, which was close enough to Tubac that even that presidio's sluggish soldiers might conceivably be of help when the next, inevitable raid occurred.[7]

In short, if there was one thing the padres must have discussed at some length as they put Garcés's travel notes in order for their superior at Querétaro, it was the infuriating Apache problem. By the autumn of 1770 it was a dilemma whose solution had been high on King Charles III's list of priorities for at least six years. As he had surveyed his dominions after the end of the Seven Years' War, the king had become distressed. Not only had expansion on New Spain's northern frontier ceased, it was actually being pushed backward, thanks to the staunch resistance of—indeed, the aggressive warfare waged by—the Apaches, Seris, and some of the Pimas.[8] By 1764, Charles had had enough. He ordered a final reconquest of the frontier so that he could redeploy resources toward what he felt would soon be another European war.[9] Gálvez had been sent to New Spain in part to facilitate this end. So had another nobleman: the Marqués de Rubí. His brief was to overhaul the military organization of the frontier while Gálvez focused on reforming the viceroyalty's administrative and financial operations.[10]

From 1766 to 1768, Rubí and his party surveyed New Spain's northern front. Among the marqués's findings—besides inadequate supplies and poorly trained soldiers—were that the gaps between Spanish garrisons were too large and their placement too far north.[11] Those flaws made it easy for Apache bands to sweep south of or through the Spaniards' notional line of defense. Tubac was one of the presidios, Rubí believed, that ought to be moved, especially since, he argued, the settlement there was large enough to defend itself. (Whether the settlers were brave enough, or supplied well enough, to defend themselves Rubí did not say.)

To the marqués's mind, it was time to consolidate. Rubí's final report, which he submitted to the minister of the Indies in 1768, recommended moving the Tubac presidio to the southwest.[12] The presidio at Altar would be moved southwest of Caborca, near the Gulf of California. Sonora's two other frontier garrisons, Terrenate and Fronteras, would also be moved, and the presidios of Horcasitas and Buenavista would be eliminated.[13] It all made good military sense. But for San Xavier del Bac and the Queretaran friars' dream of extending their missionary work northward, implementing the Rubí recommendations would be a disaster.

✳ ✳ ✳

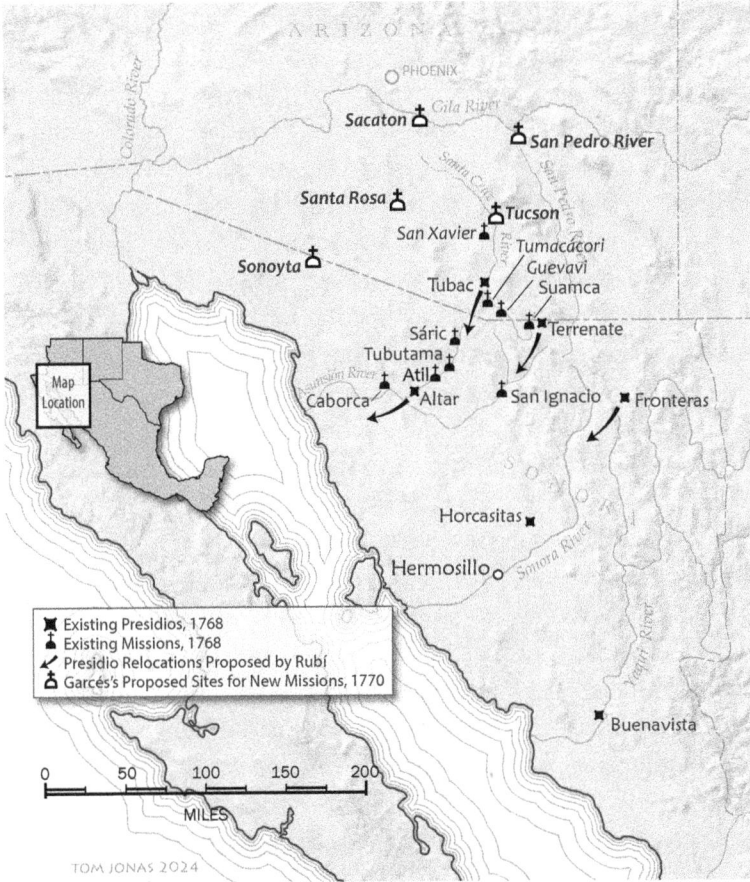

Locations of presidios in the Pimería Alta as of 1768, when
Rubí completed his recommendations, as well as Garcés's
proposed new locations for missions and garrisons as outlined
in his proposals of 1770 and 1771. *Map by Tom Jonas.*

As he pondered the possibilities glimpsed during his autumn
1770 entrada, Fray Garcés was not thinking about Rubí; that
would come later. But he *was* thinking, deeply, about the same
challenges. He was also thinking about Gálvez, and about what
information and advice he might provide the great and powerful

man in order to persuade him to continue to support the Franciscans' mission expansion plan.

Upon its completion, Garcés's 1770 travel diary was sent to Father Buena. The missions president, still fired with enthusiasm for expansion by the strong relationship he had built with Gálvez, thought it so important that he rushed it to the College of Santa Cruz. The colegio showed it to Gálvez, who had not yet been recalled to Spain, before sending the diary along to Viceroy Croix, along with a cover letter asking for funds to establish five new missions to the north—for that was the number requested by Garcés in his late November 1770 letter to Araujo.[14]

Garcés already had sites in mind for these missions. One would be placed where the Sobaípuri Pimas used to live along the San Pedro, near the intersection of that stream with the Gila. Garcés had visited the spot in 1769, when he rode with the military's expedition into the Apachería, and he understood well its strategic value. Another would be placed at Tucson, which, although only a few miles north of San Xavier, had a large population and was essential to keeping communication open with the Gila; besides, it was continually harassed by the Apaches and might otherwise be abandoned.[15] A third proposed mission site was at Pitaique, today's Sacaton. Garcés called it San Andrés and had formed a special bond with the friendly Pimas living there during his visits of 1768 and 1770. A fourth site was at Sonoita—not Father Gil's visita but another village of the same name that is today spelled "Sonoyta" and is in Sonora just south of the international border opposite Lukeville, Arizona. It had a brief mission history under Father Kino and later Jesuits and was regarded by Garcés as close enough to the Colorado River to be of use in influencing that territory. The final new mission was to be placed at Santa Rosa del Ati, most likely today's Santa Rosa, Arizona, halfway between Sonoita and San Xavier. As we have seen, Garcés had probably visited Santa Rosa in 1768, if not at other times since then.[16]

In short, Garcés suggested placing missions in five places he knew at least fairly well. Gálvez was in his corner, for in an

April 13, 1771, letter to Croix he advised that the viceroy go forward with the establishment of five new missions in the Gila River region.[17]

Of course, Garcés did not know this. He kept pondering what could be done to protect the possibility of bringing within the Christian—and Spanish—family the Indians to whom he had been sent. It was no idle question, for two more Apache attacks had brought Garcés to the brink of total exasperation—and his mission to the brink of annihilation. Thus, in February 1771, Garcés wrote Father Buena expanding upon his vision for extending the rim of Christendom northward.[18]

Apache warriors had attacked the visita of Tucson on the afternoon of February 1, Garcés reported to his missions' president. They were unable to do serious damage thanks to the fortified enclosure the residents had recently built there at Anza and Garcés's request (Garcés notes as an aside that it took the O'odham three hundred workdays to build the complex). When he heard about the attack, Garcés feared that the Apaches would soon target San Xavier. So he sent for help to the Tubac presidio, which responded by sending all of four soldiers to supplement the two who lived at the mission. It did not take long for Garcés's fears to be realized. Apaches attacked San Xavier on the morning of Tuesday, February 12—one day prior to the beginning of Lent. And though the soldiers kept them at bay, the Apaches nevertheless killed two boys who "had gone out to get the horses," then "came to the pueblo and jeered at us" and pointed at the horses "as if challenging us." The Apaches proceeded to run off all the mission's horses and cattle and to kill 350 sheep and goats, leaving the mission with only forty. The devastation of stock was perhaps not as depressing for Garcés as the realization that there was nothing that could be done to stop it from happening again, and again, and again. San Xavier and Tucson would soon be destroyed "if strong and prompt measures are not taken."[19] And if San Xavier and Tucson were destroyed, Spanish access to the Gila would be cut off for good.

Garcés proposed that Spain take a radically new course of action by going on the offensive in a serious, sustained, strategic way. He mused on the possibilities of a Gálvez-led expedition through and north of the Apachería that would lead to new diplomatic alliances, drive a wedge between the Apaches and the Yavapais, and ultimately surround the enemy from all directions. But Garcés's primary suggestion was to extend the line of presidios and missions. He now imagined a permanent garrison placed as far north as the Verde River.[20] "Oh, what advantages this would bring," exclaimed Garcés, "especially if regular troops were stationed there! For then we would see commerce" between New Mexico, the Pimería, and the tribes living along the Verde and Colorado, even Moqui. "This alone would conquer more land and more people than would compose three or four Pimerías." More immediately, a garrison on the Verde would prohibit the Apaches from allying themselves with the tribes who lived on that river and the Colorado. For, in Garcés's mind, that was precisely the major danger facing Spanish policy on the frontier—the threat of an alliance of the Apaches with the Yumas and others against the Pimas, Opas, and Cocomaricopas, which could ultimately mean Apache dominance from New Mexico to Alta California.[21] The possibility gave Garcés chills. It was the nightmare scenario for the Spanish northern frontier.

To push the Apaches back to the north and east ought therefore to be the strategic objective. And to do that meant securing the area between the San Xavier mission and the Gila, a gate now totally uninhabited and unpoliced, and thus completely open for the Apaches to use as they pleased. Presidios and missions should therefore not be moved south, as Rubí proposed, but north—right to the Gila, wrote Garcés, where there ought to be at least four new missions, backstopped by three more in the Papaguería and "and afterwards many others" serving the Opas, Cocomaricopas, and the Yumas. Would anyone listen to his ideas? Garcés was doubtful, but he would nevertheless speak his mind "frankly, because when one sees that his house is burning, he doesn't dwell on trifles," as he wrote a fellow Queretaran friar who had recently removed to Rome. "I can't do any more now than cry out to God and my superiors," sighed Garcés. "And that I have already done."[22]

No one could accuse Garcés of sycophancy. Nor could he be accused of not having a grand vision—indeed, his was every bit as large as Junípero Serra's. Were it not for the unremitting hostility of the unconquerable Apaches, it might also, like Serra's, have been realized.

Serra was, in fact, very much on Garcés's mind when he made these recommendations. Both Garcés and Captain Anza were quite aware of the interest and enthusiasm that had been aroused in Mexico City by Serra's founding of missions at San Diego and Monterey. Why not connect that aborning mission chain with this one? Anza had told Garcés that he wanted to find a way to Monterey through the Gila-Colorado region. "The proposition is not repugnant to me," wrote Garcés to Buena, "nor does it seem to me very difficult if proper provision is made for everything." In fact, if the superiors at Querétaro could send another friar to care for San Xavier in his absence, he hoped to see if he could "acquire some information or see more in that direction." Garcés was acutely aware that neither he nor any other Spaniard actually knew firsthand much of the terrain he was so lightly discussing. It was time for another entrada.

✳ ✳ ✳

It pleased Garcés, as he toiled at San Xavier during the winter and spring of 1771, to know that accounts of his 1770 entrada had reached the highest levels of New Spain's government.[23] His notes and recommendations had caused excitement among ecclesiastical, military, and civil officials alike. Captain Juan Bautista de Anza was one of them. To this point he had been more irritated with than impressed by the headstrong missionary of San Xavier del Bac. Not only had Garcés annoyed him by taking off on explorations without his permission and by going over his head to offer unsolicited military suggestions to Anza's superiors; the two men had also argued about things like who should pay for the support of the soldiers at San Xavier.[24] Garcés seemed always to be causing difficulties. But he was undoubtedly courageous, and his 1770 entrada had given the friar information about the land and its peoples that Anza did not possess. Thus, after Garcés's return from that 1770 journey, Anza thoroughly debriefed the padre. It was during this meeting that he informed Garcés that he too wanted to connect Sonora to California via the Gila and Colorado, a desire that Anza had nursed since Alta California had been colonized the previous year.[25] As we have seen, Garcés laconically replied that to do so did not seem to him particularly difficult.[26]

Of course, thinking it and proving it were different things. By the summer of 1771 the new missions Garcés had requested had been approved by Viceroy Croix—or so the friar thought. The next logical step was to reconnoiter the ground and more carefully discern precisely where and among whom the new missions should be placed.[27] Then, if an opportunity should present itself to travel beyond the Gila and Colorado, perhaps as far as the new missions of Alta California or even to New Mexico, Garcés resolved to remain open to those possibilities. He never had trouble convincing himself to go *más allá*.

As the summer sun scorched San Xavier, Garcés made his preparations.[28] He did not know how long he would be gone, so he would need a priest to take his place, at least temporarily, at his mission. The College of Santa Cruz, fully supportive of Garcés's plans, sent one of its friars to San Xavier to fill this purpose, and on August 8, 1771, Garcés set out westward on horseback, taking with him a mule and three Indians from San Xavier. It was noon—"The sun was at its zenith," he tells us in his diary.[29] Soon he would be riding somewhere in the unknown.

It would be difficult to overstate the hardships inherent to such a trek. "To sleep on the bare earth under open sky; to use your boots for a pillow; . . . to hump along on a horse all day under a

Garcés's third entrada, to the Colorado River and beyond, made in August–November 1771. *Map by Tom Jonas.*

burning sun; to be on the alert at every instant for savages; then, to sleep without supper; to rise and depart without breakfast; to suffer torture by mosquito." Paul Horgan's catalogue of the miseries undergone by one of the Southwest's later intrepid clerical travelers, Santa Fe archbishop Jean-Baptiste Lamy, applies fully to Garcés, who had the additional challenge of rarely knowing where he was.[30] Garcés tried to convey the anxiety he felt in starting this journey in what was for him a rather poetic passage, placed at the beginning of his full diary of the excursion. He knew he would be alone, he writes,

> Alone among the Yumas—better alone than in bad company. . . .
> Alone. It could not be otherwise, because some of the people of the
>   lands which I saw are hostile to one another. . . .
> Alone, supported by the prop of divine providence. . . .

At least for the first few days of this 1771 entrada, Garcés could draw comfort from traveling in familiar territory.[31] On August 10 he arrived at the place he now called Pipia—probably, as we have seen, the tiny O'odham village of Pipyak on today's maps—where he was received with the usual generous hospitality. He told the Papagos there, who lived but a short day's travel from Santa Rosa del Ati (today's Santa Rosa or Gu Achi), one of his proposed new mission sites, that padres would soon come to live among them. They were somewhat surprised, since even more than most O'odham they suffered from a shortage of water. Garcés assured them this could be remedied by Spanish irrigation techniques and the digging of more wells.[32] (One wonders what these experienced irrigators and water-finders thought about such confidence.) The next two days Garcés spent at Santa Rosa, in his opinion "the most beautiful site" in all of Papaguería. It had been a wet monsoon season, and Santa Rosa was blessed with thriving corn fields. Along with some infants, Garcés baptized "a very old woman, who was most anxious to receive it." And as at Pipia he reported to the residents that "in view of their good disposition" a mission would soon be established there.

On August 13, Garcés set out to the southwest.[33] He was now traveling beyond the bounds of his previously documented travels. With every step his horse took, the land became a little drier, the heat a little more intense. Probably his route took him along the path of today's Indian Highway 15 to Covered Wells (Maish Vaya), for he mentions drinking from a very deep well on this day. Late that night Garcés arrived at a village whose "governor," as Garcés usually called the headman of native villages, had fomented recent troubles in the Papaguería—perhaps the unrest put down by Anza in 1770.[34] This man told Garcés he was now on good terms with Anza and otherwise "comported himself well" with the padre, who took the opportunity to emphasize the power of the Spanish king and the necessity of banding together against the Apaches. Everywhere on this trip Garcés would do what he could to align the region's natives with Spanish strategy.

The next day, at a place called Cubba (today's Kupk, it seems), Garcés was welcomed not only with the usual graciousness but also with interesting information.[35] These Indians were friends with the Yumas on the Colorado, and they gladly told the visiting priest what they could about the Yumas' constituent bands, enemies, and alliances. As they spoke, Garcés's excitement rose. It had not been in his plans to visit the Yumas. He had intended to go on to his proposed mission site of Sonoita before heading north to see his beloved Gileños. But here was providence intervening to open a way to the land of the Yumas—and thus to the Colorado, the great river of the north—by way of their allies. If he were ever to visit the region of the Colorado-Gila junction, clearly this was the best path to take.

The governor of Sonoita met Garcés in Cubba. On August 15, they threaded their way through low, narrow mountain ranges through an unusually fertile area dotted with rancherías and fields until they arrived at the O'odham chief's villages. Garcés made note of the ruins of the Jesuit church that had stood there until the Pima Revolt of 1751, an uprising in which the Jesuit priest Enrique Ruhen had been killed.[36] Father Kino had built the first church at Sonoita in 1701, and Father Sedelmayr had visited on a handful of occasions. Garcés must have taken satisfaction in thinking that on his recommendation a mission in Sonoita would soon be reestablished. (He probably did not know that Father Sedelmayr's attempts to do just that in 1756 had been rebuffed by the village's residents.)

It was a suitable spot. Rebel Indians often took refuge in Sonoita, a practice that would be discouraged by the presence of a mission. There was surprisingly ample water, pasturage, and cropland. Moreover, the unnamed native governor impressed Garcés with his "very fine qualities." Garcés was grateful when this chief helped disentangle Garcés from his people, who attempted to raise "insurmountable objections" to Garcés's going to the Yumas. On August 17, the governor provided Garcés with two guides—necessary not only because they knew the country but also because Garcés's San Xavier Indians would go no farther—and sent him on his way. That evening, camp was in all likelihood made at or close to Quitobaquito Spring, an ancient oasis on the edge of today's Organ Pipe Cactus National Monument well known to the Indians of the region.[37]

The objections to Garcés's proposed journey to the Yumas raised by the Papagos at Sonoita may have been self-serving, but they were not entirely unjustified. The road ahead was exceedingly dangerous. Garcés and his guides arose on the 18th and continued west down the Río Sonoyta, stopping to water at a place called El Carrizal. A little later they encountered a parched family coming from the opposite direction. The father in this group warned them to turn back. There "was neither water, nor grass, nor road, nor people" ahead, he said. Yet somehow Garcés and his companions prevailed upon him to turn around and help them find the way. What help this exhausted man might be able to provide that the Sonoita guides couldn't is unclear. In any case, Garcés soon learned that his new companion was telling the truth, even as he was annoyed by what he regarded as the loquacious man's exaggerations. Leaving the Río Sonoyta to turn northwest, the party did not drink again until nine o'clock that night. It was the first of many days on this trip during which Garcés would be forced to contend with the awful feeling of profound thirst—and the awful anxiety of not knowing when it might be quenched.

On the next day, continuing to travel west, the party began to pass by outcrops of the great Pinacate Volcanic Field that sits like a great black circle on the desert between today's Puerto Peñasco and the international border. The dark, lifeless rocks reminded Garcés of Hell, so he decided to pass the time by preaching on that subject to the Indian man whom he believed had been telling him a string of lies. On this day the travelers were lucky; they found two water holes. There is no mention of water on the next day, August 20, on which the massive sand dunes of the Desierto de Altar came into sight. Garcés knew from the old Jesuit accounts that the Colorado could, in theory, be reached by trudging straight west across them. He knew from the same accounts that such a route was highly inadvisable. So did his guides. The party veered again to the northwest. It was not much less desolate than the dunes: "no birds, no grass, no mesquites," wrote Garcés.

It was an utterly grueling road, as Kino and a handful of other Europeans had discovered. Garcés and his companions were on El Camino del Diablo.[38] The name was not then in use, but it is no less apt for that. Garcés and his companions had entered a magnificently empty land, too dry to support much visible plant life other than dusty creosote and saltbush, and broken at intervals by stringy mountain ranges bending from northwest to southeast as if buffeted perpetually by a strong southwestern gale. Today's travelers are discouraged from using El Camino del Diablo, especially in the deadly summer, just as Garcés had been by the very first man he met as he rode from Sonoita into the shimmering desert light.

On the 21st the Garcés party rose early to avoid the day's heat. Riding northwest, they rejoiced when one of the guides found water in the mountains at a place now called Coyote Water. At midday they encountered a ranchería—the first they had seen since leaving Sonoita, almost one hundred miles ago. There was water here, and some pasturage, although it was difficult to access. The native children brought to the haggard and emaciated horse and mule baskets of water from small wells on the rocky mountainside. Garcés and his Indian guides were grateful for the food the natives shared with their customary generosity. Though they spoke the Piman language, their women wore deerskin skirts, Garcés noted. They were surely representatives of the hardy Hia Ced O'odham, who made this harsh country their home.[39] To Garcés they resembled Yumas, with whom they were in fact friendly. He was getting closer to the object of his search.

Garcés asked his hosts to guide him to the Gila-Colorado junction, where he knew the Yumas were based, but they insisted that he travel first to the Gila. Judging that it was best to stay in everyone's good graces, Garcés acceded to their wishes.[40] Two more days of northward travel along El Camino del Diablo brought him to the Gila, somewhere between today's Ligurta and Wellton.[41] Garcés was farther downstream than he had ever been, but he recognized the "sierra of the Opas"—the Gila Bend Mountains—in the eastern distance. Climbing a mountain, he saw that to the west the Gila turned sharply south. That was strange; the Jesuit explorers had not mentioned a southern turn of the Gila in this region. But perhaps they had never been to this spot. Garcés did not realize he was looking at the south-running Colorado, that the Gila ended not many miles from where he stood. Confusion was piling upon confusion. Here began a misconception that would bedevil Garcés until the end of his journey.

The Indians at the Gila, especially grateful for his gifts of tobacco, greeted Garcés warmly and guided him downstream to a large ranchería. That evening, August 23, Garcés met another Indian chief who would become a friend and key Spanish ally—a man who would also, ten years later, indirectly cause his death.

*   *   *

Garcés awoke on the morning of August 24, 1771, believing he was near the junction of the Gila and Colorado. He was. But what he did not know was that the "governor" he had met the previous evening was a Yuma, not a Pima, as Garcés believed him to be, and that he was therefore now among those he had been seeking.[42] Because of his own entirely understandable confusion, Garcés's diaries at this point begin to involve us in insuperable difficulties of comprehension. Exactly where he was, and with whom, and what Garcés was thinking at the time are not easy to decipher. Yet until his return to Sonoita on October 23, 1771, the essential points of Garcés's journey are clear enough. We know that he explored the lower Colorado River more thoroughly than had any European before him; that he successfully crossed the unforgiving sandy desert to the river's west and spied a route that would have taken him to San Diego, if only he had been given the opportunity; and that he sowed the seeds of a history-altering relationship with the Indian leader who greeted him on August 23, a man known among his own people as Olleyquote-quiebe—"The One Who Wheezes."

The asthmatic Olleyquotequiebe was known as Salvador Palma to the Spaniards living in the nearest Sonoran settlements, which he visited from time to time.[43] In the parlance of the Yumas, or Quechans, he was a *kwoxot*, a man who had risen to authority among his people by virtue of both the power given him in dreams—the *icama* experience—and the acceptance of the people themselves. "When a man knew he had the power to be a good leader, he told his dreams," explained a Quechan man born a century after Garcés made contact with the tribe. "If his dreams were good, his plans would be followed." If those plans led to negative results, that was proof his power had deserted him. A kwoxot had continually to renew his authority, and fend off rivals, by the appeal of his talk and the wisdom of his actions, or else be abandoned for someone else.[44]

Palma was nothing if not articulate and wise, but because of the nature of Quechan leadership his authority was circumscribed

Edward S. Curtis
photo of a Quechan
woman from ca. 1908.
*Courtesy of the J. Paul
Getty Museum.*

and uncertain. To maintain and grow that power, and no doubt
as a strategy to serve his people well, he was disposed to culti-
vate friendly relations with the powerful Spaniards who lived
to his southeast—and now also to his west. He had taken the
name Palma from an overseer with that name at the mission of
Caborca, and he had won the respect of the commander of the
presidio at Altar, Captain Bernardo de Urrea.[45] He must have
figured that friendship with a friar like the intrepid one who had
just arrived at his doorstep could not fail to be useful.

It was not inevitable that a Quechan kwoxot would make such
a calculation. Father Eusebio Kino led parties to the Colorado
River each year from 1699 to 1702 and was greeted warmly by

the Yumas he met there.[46] But that was not the case with the most recent clerical visitor, Jacobo Sedelmayr, who from his post at Tubutama had made multiple explorations—with a soldier escort—into the Papaguería a generation prior to Garcés's arrival.[47] On a 1749 trip to the Colorado, the Yumas stole stock from and verbally challenged the Jesuit's large party, after which the Sedelmayr group quickly made its exit. Things went worse in 1750. An unfriendly reception from the Yumas led to a battle in which thirteen Yumas were killed and many others wounded. Nevertheless, Sedelmayr concluded that both Spain and the church's interests could be effectively promoted by the placement of missions along the Gila and Colorado.[48]

Garcés knew this history. Father Sedelmayr's reports gave him much of the little information he had about the Gila-Colorado region. They likely played a sizable role in forming his conviction that traveling with soldiers was a mistake unless absolutely necessary—that traveling with natives alone gave the missionary more freedom to act in whatever ways he thought necessary while also spurring him to behave in a manner that was "less conceited, more charitable, and more humble, qualities that seem more suited for undertakings of such caliber."[49] Garcés picked up further information about Father Jacobo as he approached the Gila-Colorado junction and began to meet natives who certainly remembered the Black Robe who had visited them a generation earlier. Garcés may well have wished they hadn't.

Fortunately, thanks in part to his choice to travel without European accompaniment of any kind, and in part to the strategy Palma had decided to follow, Garcés's own reception was very different. On the night of his arrival on August 23, Palma gave him a gift of corn and the Quechans held a great feast. Garcés says he "was received with great joy, which they manifested by their songs, dances, etc."[50] That was encouraging. But he was confused about his whereabouts. Garcés would later explain that, because it had been an extremely rainy summer, the Gila was so full that the Colorado, which he knew was supposed to be much bigger, did not appear to him any larger.[51] In addition, the junction of the two rivers was not obvious because of the tangled web of marshes, islands, and channels that surrounded it. Twice Garcés asked Palma to take him to the Colorado, and twice Palma obliged. Both times Garcés thought he was being deceived. He knew the great river had to be close, but he had seen no junction and this river looked the same as the Gila. When Palma refused to continue to guide him downstream, he thought it was because he was afraid of the Yumas farther on. The real reason, as Garcés later learned, was that the Quechans' enemies, the Halyikwamais and the Cocopahs, lived downriver.

A long period of fruitless wandering commenced. Garcés kept making attempts to make his way downstream to the Yumas of the Colorado, and he kept getting lost. He finally procured a guide on September 8, but the Indian tried to break the friar's spirit by smashing the gourd that held their water (unintentionally, as he pretended) and saying they must now turn back. Garcés's response was to say he would henceforth always ride within close range of the river. The next day the Indian disappeared with one of the mounts. Alone once again, Garcés continued to ride south on the only horse he had left.

On September 11 he encountered a new group—Halyikwamais, as Garcés only later learned. If anything they were even more welcoming than the rest. Garcés continued on his way in the "great heat" of the lower Colorado summer. On the 14th, having been forced to veer away from the river by various lagoons and mud holes, he found himself trapped on all sides by brush. There were no trees, and what water he found was salty. Clearly he was near the sea. But still he had not found the Colorado. More pressing, he was carrying no water and there was none to drink anywhere in sight. Garcés's darkening mood was not lifted by the corpse he encountered—with mummified skin still stretched out "on the face, hands, feet, and skull"—as he searched through the night in increasing desperation for a potable pool. Finally, at daybreak, he rested—and his horse, half-crazed by hunger and thirst, seized the opportunity to flee. Soon, Garcés reflected, he would be a skeleton himself.

On September 15, sustained only by the little bit of corn he carried with him, Garcés turned north toward the rancherías he had passed a few days earlier. All day, under the searing sun, he trudged forward. Somewhere along the way he must have found drinkable water. Then, after nightfall, he was thrilled to cross paths with his horse. As he wrote in his diary, perhaps he was not yet "destined to be ruined."[52] Whether he felt so sanguine at the time may be doubted, for there was still the problem of hunger to be solved.

Fortunately for Garcés, it was solved quickly. The next morning he stumbled onto a melon patch. Then, as he was saying morning prayer, a group of fourteen armed warriors came into view. Yumas! thought Garcés. In fact they were Kohuanas, or Cajuenches, a people who lived downriver from the Yumas, and they were so "astonished" to see this lone, strangely dressed, bearded white man in their country that they approached only after Garcés coaxed them to do so.[53] Soon they were sharing their fish and taking the friar to where three dozen of their companions were fishing on the river. A "good meal" was prepared, and Garcés's heart was warmed by the "humanity, politeness, and attention" they showed him. They then made two rafts with which to ferry Garcés, his bags, and his horse across the broad stream.[54] They swam across themselves, pushing and pulling the rafts along as they went. As Garcés could see, they were expert swimmers. Not him. The peasant lad from arid Aragón had never learned to swim.

It was a sleepless night, for at their village on the other side of the river—the river, keep in mind, that Garcés believed to be the Gila but which was actually the Colorado—the Kohuanas whom Garcés thought were Yumas held a great, noisy feast that did not end until less than an hour before daybreak. It was an amazingly fertile country, thought Garcés, especially when juxtaposed with the surrounding desert. Yet he could not get a guide to lead him west. The people instead kept trying to persuade him to let them take him back to the missions.

Despite their entreaties, Garcés would not be deterred. For the next ten days he wandered from ranchería to ranchería on the western side of the lower Colorado, somewhere south of today's international border on the east side of the Cocopah Mountains. He was warmly welcomed and well fed in those brushy lowlands, confusingly crisscrossed by dozens of the Colorado delta's over-flow channels, but where was the Colorado? Was it this large lagoon (Lake Jululu, speculated Herbert Bolton), even though it seemed to have no current and no clear banks with groves of trees, as rivers here normally had?[55] It didn't seem likely, but Gar-cés could not be sure. The wise thing, he figured, was to keep going west as best he could. But the Indians, even though they seemed to understand his objective, kept trying to guide him in other directions.

Then, on September 25, having forced his way westward as far as he could, Garcés came to a village whose people had seen his like before. "As soon as I arrived there they began to tell me—touch-ing my habit, my boots, and my bandana—that in the west, both above and below, were fathers like me; that they were seven days away." Two of the young men had seen the priests there with their own eyes. They showed familiarity with compasses and magnify-ing glasses. Shells worn in the ears of this people testified further to their traffic with the coast. What an opportunity! Garcés had himself seen two gaps in the mountains to the west and concluded that getting to the coast probably wouldn't be very hard. He also saw in the western distance a "great blue sierra" that he figured was the eastern side of the high range that the Serra-led Francis-cans had kept to their east as they traveled north along the coast.[56] Garcés asked his Indian hosts if they would take him there. They said they would. But on the next day, for reasons he could not make out, they recanted. Garcés kept traveling west, alone, toward the Colorado that had to be close but somehow never was.

The Indians had warned him there was no water to the west. It didn't take long for Garcés to discover that, once again, they had told the truth. For eleven days he tried to find the river to the west, but a mountain range—the Cocopahs that begin a little to the south of today's Calexico—and sand dunes kept getting in his way, and the waterless desert kept forcing him to retreat.[57] Furthermore, the Indians of the region were of little help, friendly but full of tales that his long absence from the Pimería was causing discord, it being rumored that he had been killed or captured by the Yumas. They therefore kept trying to steer Garcés back east. On October 7, having made repeated fruitless attempts to find the Colorado, Garcés and his horse slaked their nearly maddening thirst at the only freshwater well he had been able to discover in that "horrible country." The friar took stock of the situation and reluctantly determined it was time to head back. He did not know that he had already crossed the Colorado; that he had ridden some fifty miles west of Yuma to within 125 miles— perhaps four long days of travel—of Father Junípero Serra's mission of San Diego de Álcala; or that he had crossed a desert that no European on record had ever traversed. He simply thought he had failed.

❊ ❊ ❊

Four days later, on October 11, Garcés found himself weeping with two hundred natives inside a very large, square hut at a ranchería near the Gila-Colorado junction.[58] Several days earlier the people there—Yumas, of course—had been involved in a battle with the Opas, Cocomaricopas, and Gileño Pimas who lived to the east. Garcés, moved by the mourners' emotion, could not help but cry along with them. This was difficult for the Quechans to understand. Was the padre sad over the death of *their* relatives, they asked, through the translation services of an elderly Pima Indian who lived among them. Of course, Garcés replied. Had he not shown that he loved them by traveling to their land without soldiers? Did he not give gifts to all? Did he not preach to all? Did he not baptize every dying child, man, and woman he encountered? He deeply regretted that the peoples of the Gila made war on each other, because he "cherished all the nations with all my heart." This notion of human solidarity, Garcés later reported, was hard to make his hearers understand. In any case, he told his audience that the perpetual conflict between different peoples would have to stop when the fathers came to live among them, for if it didn't the king would send soldiers to chastise them.[59] "This talk impressed them greatly," Garcés believed, "for apostolic works even among the most barbarous are well understood."

Whatever the Quechans made of Garcés's claims, the Spanish military had already gotten their attention. Garcés had now been absent from San Xavier for more than two months, and rumors had reached Anza that he had been killed. The Quechans were anxious to prove their innocence, lest they soon be confronted by a combined force of Spaniards, Pimas, and Papagos. Garcés was at this point still toying with the idea of making his way to Zuñi—the westernmost Franciscan outpost in New Mexico— but when he came to understand the great anxiety he was causing among all parties, he reluctantly decided to head back to San Xavier.

It was his ardent wish to avoid returning by way of the horrifyingly difficult Camino del Diablo. If he could not go to Zuñi, Garcés wanted at least to return to his mission by way of the Gila and Santa Cruz, which would allow him to visit both old friends and future mission sites. But to go by that enemy-territory route now would be taken by the Yumas as a grave insult, thanks to the recent battle. Besides, Garcés needed to show his face to the Spanish authorities as quickly as possible, in order to assure everyone of his well-being and thereby keep the peace. Thus, on October 12, Garcés began to make his way southward along the Colorado. On the 14th, he struck southeast across the Yuma desert's sand dunes, apparently rejoining his outbound trail on October 17 on the Gila River near the head of the Gila Mountains. Bolton marvels that in crossing these dunes Garcés "had accomplished a feat which Kino had three times tried in vain."[60] Indeed, it was a feat that no European on record had achieved.

On October 23, Garcés rode into the Papago village of Sonoita, having discovered a couple of new water tanks along the way. The people of Sonoita were "overjoyed" to see him, writes Garcés, so sure were they that he was dead. Three days later, having taken a circuitous route that allowed him to visit additional Papago rancherías, in which he was given presents of pitahayas—fruit of the organ pipe cactus—Garcés arrived at Caborca, and five days after that, on October 31, 1771, Garcés rode into Tubutama. "When I set out on my journey I was sick," recalled Garcés in one of his diaries. But by the time he got to Caborca he was, unlike his skin-and-bones horse, entirely healthy—in fact, he was "fat, happy, and very content," in the words of Father Esteban de Salazar, who gleefully greeted him at Tubutama. Eighty days in one of North America's hottest and most arid deserts.[61] Three hundred leagues ("without counting the detours"), or roughly eight hundred miles, traveled, by Garcés's own estimation. Miles not infrequently traveled without water or food, miles in which Garcés was often tortured by mosquitoes, miles that found him sometimes entirely alone and almost always sleeping in the open air on cold desert nights—this regimen resulted in Garcés becoming "fat, happy, and very content."

At Caborca, Garcés came into contact with three retired soldiers who had accompanied Father Sedelmayr on his 1750 journey to the Yumas. When Garcés told them about his *entrada* and his failure to locate the Colorado, the soldiers insisted that he had been on the Colorado virtually the whole time—that the Colorado was the river he had crossed on rafts, and that the Indians who had at times guided him were Yumas. At first doubtful, Garcés soon concluded they were right. He had made many "blunders and errors," but in his central task he hadn't failed after all. If the river he had crossed and explored was in fact the Colorado, the way from Sonora to Alta California was now clear.[62] Given the "many favors," "great fidelity," "respect," and "courtesy" shown Garcés by the peoples of the Colorado, it was also clear that both his own plan for new missions and the

Rubí plan for the placement of frontier presidios needed to be rethought.

As he recuperated at Salazar's mission of Tubutama, Garcés told his brother friar all about his journey. He emphasized the overwhelming hospitality of the Indians he had met, saying that they were "very kind and liberal to excess," and that at times two to three hundred of them accompanied him as he traveled from village to village. He raved about their food: their "ears of maize, calabashes, melons, and watermelons are delicious; their *atole*, bread of maize and seeds exquisite; their fish, mice, and lizards of rare types. Of birds, roots from the ground, and fruits from wild trees, I had more than I needed." Their generosity with amaranth greens and mesquite seeds had restored his health. "When I set out on this trip, my legs were swollen," he would later write, "and I was considering going away to be cured. Now . . . I am well, without any inflammation large or small."[63]

Garcés told Father Salazar that he would have gone to see the new missions in California had the Indians not been so frightened by the Spaniards' demands that he be immediately delivered. And he enthusiastically informed Salazar that the Yumas traded with people from Moqui, for they had told him so and he had seen their woolen blankets. He had learned that this land of the Hopis, as well as Zuñi, were but nine days' journey from the Gila-Colorado junction (a significant underestimate for anyone who traveled fewer than fifty miles per day, as he would later come to know firsthand).

The momentousness of his journey had now fully dawned on Garcés. Rather than simply finding sites for new missions, he had discovered new routes, new peoples, new possibilities, new worlds. He asked Salazar to help him convert his notes—which, his handwriting now being so bad, he himself could barely make out—into a readable diary. This the two Franciscans set out to do. But on November 3 a messenger arrived from Tumacácori. Father Gil was once again very sick, and Father Juan José Agorreta, who had gone to minister to him, had now become ill himself and was in bed with chills and a high fever (not to mention a bad case of hemorrhoids).[64] Garcés did not wish to delay in going to help them—especially, one suspects, his dear friend Father Gil. So that evening, right after dinner, he set out from Tubutama to do what he could. Salazar, in reporting on all this to Father Buena on November 13, could barely suppress his admiration for this priest and his seemingly supernatural energy.[65]

CHAPTER 6

ℕot Impossible

1771–1773

*F*rancisco Garcés arrived back at his mission of San Xavier del Bac in late 1771 brimming with hope. The natives he had met on the Colorado had been unfailingly kind. Their lands were fertile—especially in comparison to the all-but-waterless desert of the Papaguería. His good friend Father Gil was recovering his health—and, as it turned out, would soon be made president of the Queretaran missions in upper Sonora. Gil's replacement at Tumacácori, another Aragonese named Father Francisco Sánchez Zúñiga, was an old friend from Garcés's student days in Calatayud.[1] It seemed clear that new conquests for the kingdoms of God and Spain were in the offing. Missionary life had its hardships, but for Garcés it was amply rewarding.

That was true even on a purely human level. Garcés was nearly always enchanted by the natives he met on his travels. The Indians on the Colorado, no less than those on the Gila and in the desert interior, had treated him with courtesy, respect, and generosity.

They had unfailingly led and cared for his horse, provided guides (so long as there "was not great danger"), and given him "to eat of the best they had." To a typical Spaniard, their fare may not have seemed like much, but Garcés was amazed "to see the means God gives to His creatures for subsisting on various roots, seeds, and other wild fruits which I would not have believed were so healthful if I had not learned it by experience." He was equally amazed at the offers he received from native men to sleep with their women; on one occasion, some women even made the offer themselves. Amazed—but not shocked, nor even particularly troubled. He chalked such suggestions up to their innocence. "O, what simple women! And what simple people!" When the friar had indicated he could not accept such a gift, his hosts had "inquired of me through ugly motions whether I did not have relations with women as their men did." (One can only chuckle at imagining what those "ugly motions" consisted of.) Garcés responded by raising his crucifix skyward as a way of communicating "that in this respect I did not live like them." This display of chastity, he believed, not only caused wonder among his hosts but also inspired "greater affection."[2]

Not much shocked this peasant from Aragón. Garcés had always lived in close contact with the land. The earthy lives of the Quechans and other southwestern Indians were not so different, in their essence, from the one he had known in Spain. To hunt, fish, farm, forage, and sit around a fire for hours telling stories— there was nothing so alien in that for a man with his background and sensibilities.

Garcés wove reflections on the Colorado River Indians into the entrada diary he was preparing for the new viceroy, Antonio María Bucareli y Ursúa, who had replaced the Marqués de Croix in Mexico City on September 23, 1771. It was slow, painful work given the padre's dyslexia and the difficulties he had with fine motor skills in his right arm. But it was important. As Garcés must have learned soon after his return to San Xavier, if not earlier, the new missions he thought had been approved for the Gila and Colorado were, in fact, still under review. Viceroy Croix had been recalled to Spain before giving them his imprimatur, and in best Spanish fashion it was thought prudent to wait for the new viceroy to arrive and settle in before proceeding. The Queretaran friars thought—it may be better to say they hoped—that Bucareli's approval of a scheme endorsed by no less a figure than the illustrious José de Gálvez was a mere formality. But one could never be sure.

Garcés had already produced a rough diary of the trip. That version, along with a summarizing cover letter by Father Esteban de Salazar, had been forwarded to Viceroy Bucareli by Sonora's intendant, Pedro Corbalán, on January 21, 1772.[3] It was a difficult document to understand, especially for a reader unfamiliar with the particularities of the northern frontier, but it captured Bucareli's attention. Bucareli forwarded the documents to Julián de Arriaga, the minister of the Indies in Madrid, on March 25, 1772. He noted that he had already asked both Corbalán and Sonora's new governor, Don Matheo Sastre, to communicate to him any further news or information that might be gathered about the region Garcés had explored, and to do everything in their power to maintain good relations with the natives there.[4]

Hard as it was for Garcés to write, it was even harder for him to stop thinking about the future. In support of the Indians who lived at his visita of Tucson, Indians to whom he had made many promises yet unfulfilled, he spent much of his time in 1772 overseeing the construction of an adobe church.[5] That was one way in which he hoped to bring about the mission expansion plan that was now his fondest hope. He also politicked. In a letter written sometime in 1772 to his superiors at Querétaro, he noted that because Tucson's population was now considerably larger than that at San Xavier it should at least get its own permanent padre, if not status as a full-blown mission. He restated his original recommendations for establishing five new missions in the Pimería Alta and the Papaguería. Indeed, he went further, proposing an alternative scheme that would see four missions placed directly on the Gila and a presidio among or near the Yumas on the Colorado. The total number of missions, at minimum, that could be profitably founded in this region was now nine, argued Garcés. This would be too much for the colegio at Querétaro to staff by itself, he conceded, but the Indians, the land, and the strategic need all justified such a project.[6]

Garcés had a very definite idea on how to proceed—a method quite different than that which had heretofore been the norm. In its fullest form, that norm was the so-called Texas method, which called for congregating natives into a physical mission complex and exerting as much control as possible over their lives. It had not only prevailed in Texas but was also coming to characterize the California missions at the time Garcés wrote.[7] Two missionaries, he wrote, one based in Caborca and one in San Xavier (he was evidently proposing himself), ought to enter the Gila-Colorado region and stay in a proposed mission site for fifteen to twenty days, "establishing themselves little by little as God enables them, and instructing the Indians in the things of God." They should be patient, subtle, and nonthreatening, "not talking about great harvests nor of the baptism of adults nor of bringing into subjection others than the children." Rather than by projecting grand designs—Garcés drew from his own and others' experience here—"let them speak by their deeds, notice no annoyance," and ask for no service. This way of proceeding, Garcés thought, would be far the wisest course of action; indeed, he had written along the same lines to Father Araujo as early as November 1770.[8] Repeat this approach over and over, "and it will be seen how the thing will insensibly be accomplished." On the other hand, were missions to be founded with a great show of force and demands for work, it was certain that resistance would be encountered. "As for work and subjection to an orderly life, it is necessary to see what [the Indians] offer of themselves; the important point is that they should admit the minister or ministers, and this, with or without difficulty, will everywhere be accomplished by means of humility."

This was indeed a radical idea. It not only anticipated the way in which missionaries in later centuries would tend to go about their work; it also reflected a kind of humanity and wisdom not characteristic of every missionary, or even of Garcés himself when he first arrived at San Xavier del Bac. Evidently his encounters with the Pimas, Papagos, Opas, Yumas, and other native peoples had given Garcés a new point of view. Perhaps, too, he had been influenced by conversations with Anza. Sometime in 1771 the captain had cautioned Garcés that in his explorations he should stop telling Indians that missions would one day be established among them. As Anza complained bitterly to Bucareli at the end of 1772, whatever the friars might say, the prospect of being "reduced" (the Spanish term for gathering natives at missions) to a mission repulsed many of the Pimería Alta's natives. The missions' rules and philosophy concerning work drove them away and kept them from becoming useful to the crown. Anza was in favor of major reforms, some of which would begin to be implemented on the Colorado River a few years later. Apparently, to some extent, so was Garcés.[9]

Garcés's recommendations for the placement of presidios and missions contradicted those of the Marqués de Rubí, whose own recommendations—in the so-called Reglamento—were finally codified by the crown in September 1772. Rubí, it will be recalled, had argued for a *retreat* in the presidial line, one that would have moved the frontier south, not north, and would have left San Xavier and Tucson completely exposed. But when Garcés heard about Rubí's ideas he was unfazed. He wrote Father Buena that the Reglamento had been read to him and he thought it "splendid." It "fits our desires exactly," he said, for in ordering the presidio at Altar to be moved to a place "near the sea having good soil and pasturage," Rubí was effectively recommending that it be placed near the convergence of the Gila and Colorado. And that meant that the new missions Garcés had proposed would have the protection they needed. Nor did he see any problem with moving the presidios of Tubac, Terrenate, and Fronteras to new positions that would put them at a more sensible distance from one another.[10]

It was a reading of the Reglamento that was idiosyncratic, if not perverse, for Garcés interpreted Rubí as calling for, or at least as allowing for, the advance of the presidio line, not its retreat. Garcés imagined the Tubac presidio being moved northward to the Gila, with Altar moved also to the Gila some forty miles or so west, near where the Opas lived. Put one more presidio on the western side of the Colorado, near its junction with the Gila, wrote Garcés, and communication with the Spanish communities in both Monterey and New Mexico would be possible. Conversions among the peoples of the Gila and Colorado would be made. The Apaches would be effectively surrounded. Garcés, now thoroughly fired by enthusiasm, asked Buena for permission to go see Commandant-Inspector Hugo O'Conor, who had been charged with implementing the Reglamento, and relate his vision of the new plan and its advantages for the purposes of both defense and evangelization.[11] Garcés would argue for spacing the presidios as Rubí intended, but with the line moved northward to the Gila–San Pedro–Colorado river system, thereby defending the territory in which Garcés's envisioned new missions would be placed. Was this not an improvement on the inspector's plan?[12]

* * *

The man in whose hands all such decisions now rested more than any other's, save those of King Charles, was Antonio María Bucareli y Ursúa, forty-sixth viceroy of New Spain. Bucareli had arrived in Veracruz on August 23, 1771, to assume his new duties. Despite the viceroyalty's prestige, it was not an appointment about which he was enthusiastic. Yet it would prove to be one in which he excelled.

Born in Seville on January 24, 1717, Bucareli was a nobleman. His father was a marqués, his mother a condesa. At five, through a special dispensation given his family, he had become a member

Portrait of Antonio
María Bucareli y
Ursúa, whose term
as New Spain's
viceroy lasted from
1771 to 1779. *From
Museo Nacional del
Virreinato, Tepotzot-
lán, Mexico, and the
Instituto Nacional
de Antropología e
Historia, Mexico City.*

of the San Juan de Jerusalem military order. At fifteen he had
been made a cadet in the Royal Carabineers brigade, leading to a
lifetime career in the military. Before being named governor and
captain-general of Cuba in 1766, he had reorganized the Spanish
cavalry. Prior to that he had fought with distinction during campaigns in Italy and Portugal.[13] A contemporary portrait of the man
indicates well the personality he brought to the viceroyalty.[14] It

shows Bucareli with a large, aquiline nose, receding hairline, high cheekbones, and serious yet not unfriendly countenance, a countenance that betrays hints of both weariness and wariness. Lines crease Bucareli's face from nose to lips. He has a distinctly aristocratic mien. In fact, in a number of ways Bucareli represented the Spanish aristocracy at its best. Unmarried, pious, and diligent, Bucareli was no visionary, but he was an efficient executive and a fine navigator of bureaucratic and interpersonal dynamics. He was temperamentally conservative but not completely resistant to change. In many ways he was the perfect person to oversee the implementation of the Gálvez reforms, for he had the instincts to proceed with prudence.[15] As they would soon discover, Garcés and the other friars working on New Spain's northern frontier could hardly have asked for a better friend.

Numerous problems—revenue shortfalls, inadequate militia, impoverished veterans—confronted Bucareli upon his arrival in Mexico City. Nor was Bucareli helped by Croix's failing to bring him completely up to speed before hastening back to Spain. For some time, Bucareli did not even know how California, Sonora, and Sinaloa were governed, much less how they were financed.[16] How to address the northern provinces effectively, he confided to his friend General Alejandro O'Reilly, was his biggest dilemma.[17] By the time Bucareli came to grips with the strategic challenges there, they could be boiled down to three: the problem of transportation and settlement; the problem of foreign incursion; and the problem of hostile Indians, primarily Apaches.[18] The discoveries made by Garcés during his 1771 entrada, coupled with a proposal sent to the new viceroy by none other than Juan Bautista de Anza, presented Bucareli with a plausible strategy for solving the first two, and potentially all three.

The problem of transportation and settlement was primarily a California problem. The Sacred Expedition of 1769 approved and planned by Visitor-General Gálvez and led, in its ecclesiastical component, by Father Junípero Serra had by 1772 brought seven settlements to Alta California: presidios at San Diego and

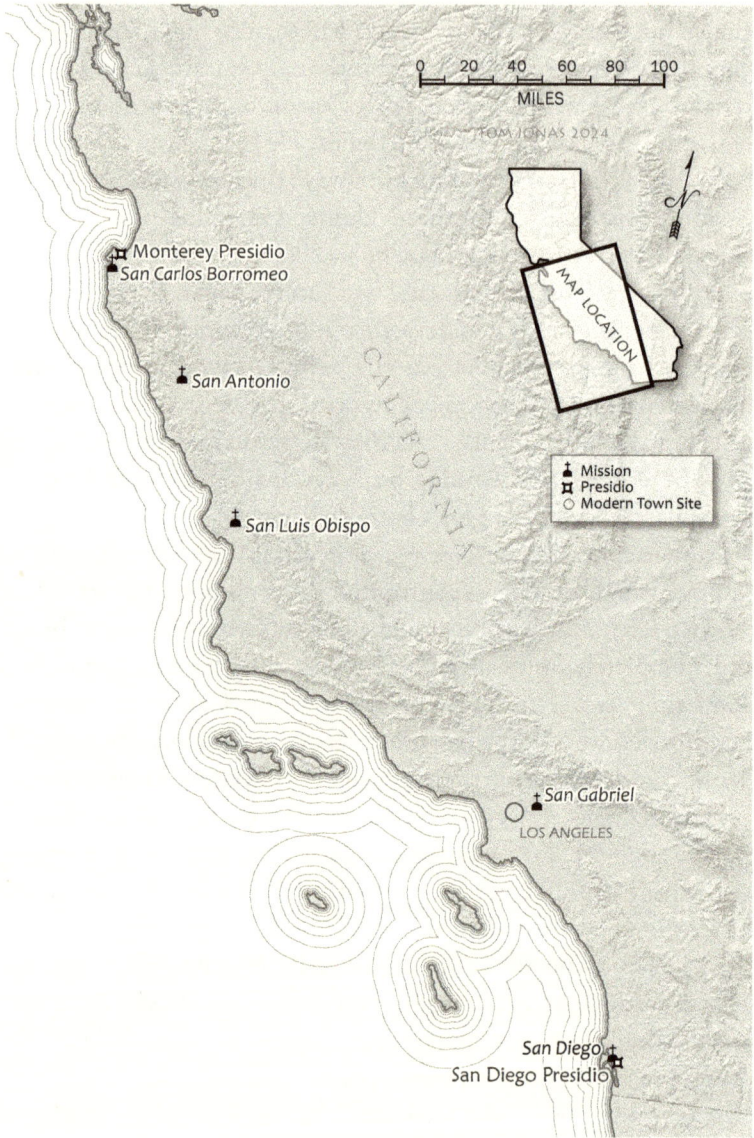

Missions and presidios that had been established in Alta California as of 1772. No overland connection had as yet been established with the missions, presidios, or towns of the Pimería Alta. *Map by Tom Jonas.*

Monterey and missions at San Diego, San Gabriel, San Luis Obispo, San Antonio, and San Carlos Borromeo (Carmel), with many more already envisioned by the fervent Serra. The problem came in feeding their residents. Already the Spaniards living at San Diego and Monterey had come close to starving, saved only by the last-minute—and as far as the friars were concerned, miraculous—arrival of a supply ship in the case of San Diego and a desperate bear hunt in the case of Monterey.[19] Native agriculture was of little help, for it was relatively rudimentary (from the Spaniards' perspective) in Alta California, and with respect to much of what the Diegueños (Kumeyaay), Channel Indians (Chumash), Gabrielinos (Tongvas), and other tribes did eat—well, few if any Spaniards could be expected to be as flexible in their dietary requirements as was Francisco Garcés. Furthermore, the land in Baja California was so poor that the more established missions there could offer little help.[20]

The problem of food was therefore tied up with the problem of supply—supply of seeds, animals, tools, and, most crucially, Spanish settlers. The challenge here was not one of resources so much as it was of route. Everything that made its way to Alta California must be transported by sea, either by ship from horrid San Blas across the Gulf of California to Baja California, and thence by pack train northward through the long desert peninsula to San Diego and beyond, or else, as was almost always preferred, by ship from San Blas directly to either San Diego or Monterey. Neither option was attractive. The former was considered too expensive and time-consuming to be practical. The latter was uncertain and undependable. Only a few vessels plied the route, and they were often blown off course, in need of repairs, or manned by crews ultimately afflicted by scurvy. They also had limited capacity. Settlers who could grow things and make things, and a route by which they could arrive overland, were badly needed.

Settlers would address the second problem, too: the problem of foreign incursion. The crown had authorized the move into Alta California partly out of fear that if it did not Russia might well extend its own settlements from Alaska down the Pacific coast. Or perhaps the British would move in; their trading ships had been seen in increasing numbers along the coast of the North Pacific, where it was presumed they were looking for the inland strait that all parties, including mapmakers, could not help but believe existed. Bucareli understood well these geostrategic considerations and was therefore on the lookout for means by which the Spanish hold on Alta California could be strengthened.[21]

The rough account Bucareli had, in early 1772, of Garcés's 1771 journey had already inclined him to believe that, had he found willing guides, the friar would have blazed a trail from the Colorado River to San Diego. But could it really be done? And if so, how difficult would it be? Bucareli, like everyone else in Mexico City, had no real idea of the distances involved, of the terrain, or of the region's inhabitants, save what he had learned from the compressed and confusing Garcés report he had only recently received. As he awaited the arrival of Garcés's definitive diary, the viceroy received an unexpected missive from Captain Anza.

⁕ ⁕ ⁕

As befitted his no-nonsense, military personality, Anza's letter to the viceroy came right to the point.[22] He sought permission, should it be "granted to anyone," to "make the necessary efforts to see if we can open communication between the port of Monterey and the province of Sonora." This had always been considered "impossible or very difficult," wrote Anza, but that opinion was based on the shakiest of foundations. In fact, he had reason to believe that the opening of such a route might now "be effected at slight cost, although with some effort on our part." This was the right bait, for Bucareli was not just in the market for a solution to his California problem; he was in the market for a *cheap* solution.

Anza recounted that he had been told in 1769 by Pimas living on the Gila that they had heard about Spaniards traveling somewhere to the west of the Colorado. Father Garcés, he noted, had heard the same tale when visiting the Gileños. This was clear evidence that the peoples of that region communicated with one another, which meant there was a regular route of travel between them.[23] After Garcés had returned from his 1771 entrada, Anza had interviewed him. Garcés had told the captain that Indians in the Colorado-Gila region had volunteered, without his asking (an important detail, since it indicated that the natives were not just telling Garcés what they thought he wanted to hear), "that at no great distance from them there were white people. Those who had chanced to see them begged him by signs, which was the common language, that he should show them the compass, the glass for making fire, and other instruments which we use but which the father did not have, and which, if they had not seen them in that country, they could not have known about." These natives had also given Garcés "to understand that to the north and east of them were also people of our kind, distinct from those whom they indicated to the west, and that some of their relatives maintained communication with the Indians who lived in the Pueblos near to those of the Spaniards. These we judge must be those who live in New Mexico."

The third piece of evidence adduced by Anza was that Garcés had spied from the Colorado River, to the distant west, "a great mountain chain of blue color, and although he did not cross it he thinks that it may be the one which our troops skirted when they went to Monterey." This observation was significant because, as Anza the frontiersman knew, where there are mountains there is water, meaning that the country seen by the friar was almost certainly passable. Up until now, no one had reported to Anza the existence of these mountains.

Having discussed the matter with Garcés, wrote Anza, both men were "convinced that the distance from here to Monterey [could not] be so great as formerly has been estimated, and that it [would] not be impossible to overcome any obstacles encountered on the way." They were ready to find the route that had eluded New Spain for nearly a century. All Bucareli had to do, concluded the captain, was ask the Queretaran missions president to allow Garcés to accompany him on an expedition. Anza was ready to leave that October, and he would bear all expenses for the journey personally if he were only given twenty to twenty-five soldiers to accompany him.

It was a tempting offer, but the government of Spain was not structured for rapid decision-making, and in any case Bucareli was a man of circumspection. Bucareli therefore consulted with Miguel Costansó, an engineer who had accompanied the Sacred Expedition of 1769. Costansó framed the issue in terms of three key questions: How far is it from Anza's home base of Tubac to San Diego? Is it possible that the Pima Indians had heard of the new California settlements? And would it be both possible and useful for Anza to open up communication between Sonora and those far-flung establishments?[24]

On the first question, Costansó estimated that it was 180 leagues from Tubac to San Diego. This turned out to be remarkably accurate; it is about 430 miles. To the second, Costansó answered that it was very possible. He had noticed himself that the Indians living along the Santa Barbara Channel possessed items made by Spaniards in New Mexico—wrought silver, knives, manufactured iron, and so on. His time on the frontier had taught him that both goods and news traveled easily from Indian neighbor to Indian neighbor. Costansó was right about this, as well. An extensive and long-established trading network bound together the tribes of California, Arizona, New Mexico, and points beyond in a complex economic relationship.[25]

On the third question, Costansó observed that thanks to Garcés and others the route to the Colorado was now already known, so it was really only a question of getting from there to the Pacific, or what Costansó and his contemporaries called the South Sea. When he was in California he had noticed that the mountains to the east were "wide and rough." Yet it was also clear that the Indians traversed them. Spaniards should be able to do the same, as long as they carried the right equipment, and he had seen some openings in the mountains that suggested potential routes. Most important, the road from Loreto, in Baja California, to San Diego was terrible and long, and the sea voyage from San Blas to San Diego was treacherous and used ships too small to carry families—facts Bucareli already knew only too well. The upshot was that "the men whom we have left there and at Monterey are condemned to perpetual and involuntary celibacy," which was not exactly a good recruiting pitch (nor did it help in maintaining strong Indian relations, as the situation tempted some soldiers to assault native women sexually, as Father Serra would soon complain to Bucareli). Sonora, by contrast, was a relatively fruitful province. A route from there to San Diego would allow supplies to be sent from where they currently existed, and families could go from there to help settle the land.

In sum, the distance between Tubac and San Diego was not too great, a route surely existed between them, and that route was just as surely needed. The question was how best to make an exploration. Costansó wisely suggested that two soldiers from San Diego be ordered to accompany Anza, so that if and when the officer and his men got to the coast they would know where they were and wouldn't waste time wandering around. José Antonio de Areche, the king's fiscal in Mexico City, wrote Bucareli a month after Costansó and also gave his unqualified support for the plan.[26] The time had come, thought the viceroy, to call a council of war.

By the time the Council of War and Royal Exchequer met to consider Anza's petition, it was already October 17, 1772, about the time Anza had hoped to leave. But due diligence took time, and Bucareli was not disposed to rush things. Utlimately, the council decided that before approving the plan it would be wise to gather more information.

First, what did Fray Francisco Garcés think—and where was his long-awaited diary? The council resolved that "the very reverend father minister of the mission of San Xavier del Bac, Fray Francisco Garcés, be requested and charged to report what might occur to him in the affair [that is, with respect to the proposed expedition], . . . and at the same time he be asked to send the diary which so many times his Excellency has requested him to send." Second, the council resolved to ask Matheo Sastre, the new governor of Sonora, for his opinion, especially with respect to whether an Anza expedition might upset the natives through whose lands he would travel. Bucareli didn't want another war on his hands. Third, Anza was charged with inquiring "of the intelligent and experienced persons whom he may find, whether the exploration or opening of communication by land from the presidio in his charge to Monterey will have any drawback which may disturb the peace of those provinces, and . . . propose . . . the means which there may be to prevent it." Anza was to make a report back to the viceroy about what he discovered.

On October 28, 1772, certified copies of the council's discussion and resolutions were sent to the interested parties. From Anza and Garcés's perspective, it was so far so good. Even if they did not yet have the full approval they sought, they did have the attention of New Spain's highest authorities.[27]

❋ ❋ ❋

Bucareli's letter bringing news of the council's discussion and questions reached Anza on January 22, 1773, in a military field camp near today's San Bernardino National Wildlife Refuge, more than one hundred miles east of Tubac. Anza was engaged, as usual, in fighting Apaches. But California was a higher priority. He wrote the viceroy back immediately, saying he would ask Governor Sastre for a furlough so he could return to Tubac to consult his papers and begin to speak with "persons experienced in the country," as Bucareli had requested.[28] In truth, as Anza would later tell Bucareli, there were exceedingly few such people with whom he might speak. The most important and most experienced by far was the pastor at San Xavier del Bac, Francisco Garcés.

In the meantime, more information was filtering into Bucareli's office. By coincidence, just as the council of war was meeting, Sastre had written Bucareli a long letter from his seat at Horcasitas, two hundred miles south of Tubac, about Garcés's 1771 entrada and the broader situation in upper Sonora.[29] It reinforced all Bucareli had learned from Salazar about Garcés's journey while adding certain flourishes—for example, that the natives had, in imitation of the missionary, taken Garcés's crucifix "into their hands" and venerated it. Sastre also took the occasion to endorse the idea of placing new missions in the region; like Garcés (he had perhaps consulted with the friar), he thought the right number was no longer five but at least eight. And he revealed that Garcés had already asked the new missions president, Father Gil, for permission to make another journey aimed at opening communication between the Pimería Alta and Monterey. In this and other letters Sastre thus offered his own full support for the Anza plan.[30]

Then, at long last, Garcés's diary arrived at Bucareli's office.[31] Father Romualdo de Cartagena, guardian of the College of Santa Cruz, forwarded it to Bucareli on January 29, 1773, with apologies for its infelicitous style.[32] Garcés may have labored long on the text, but he was more wanderer than writer. "Your Excellency will remember that the simplicity and artlessness of that father is great," warned Cartagena, who wished to prepare Bucareli not just for the style but the raw content of the diary, for Garcés did not always report "any excess which he noted among the heathen with respect to lasciviousness" with the usual tactful euphemisms. Cartagena closed by noting that the College of Santa Cruz stood ready to provide more friars for the new missions of upper Sonora. The colegio's interests lay more in the establishment of these new missions than it did in the opening of new roads.

Bucareli was a kind man, but he could not help but agree with Cartagena about the quality of Garcés's prose. On April 26, 1773, he sent a copy of Garcés's diary to Julián de Arriaga in Madrid.[33] Earlier, he had written Arriaga that the "zealous spirit and apostolic labors of Father Garcés are . . . worthy of praise,"[34] but he now had to admit that the "language of this document is very difficult to understand, and I doubt whether it will serve as a

guide for making a decision in council concerning the enterprise." Fortunately, the further information Bucareli and the
council had requested the previous fall was on its way to Mexico
City. When Anza had gotten back to Tubac in late February
1773, he had immediately sent for Garcés to join him. They must
plot a coordinated response to the council. By March, long letters by both men were making their arduous way southward to
New Spain's capital.

Anza's letter was of course the better organized and written.[35]
He began by assuring the viceroy that for years he had been
gathering what information he could from soldiers who had
accompanied the Jesuit fathers on their expeditions to the Gila-
Colorado region, and that he had done so again in accordance
with Bucareli's request. Unfortunately, these men remembered
little in the way of detail, and what they did claim to recall was
confused and contradictory. Anza had tried to go to the Gila-
Colorado junction himself in 1756, but the soldiers who were to
guide him "raised so many objections that the plan was given up."
It was now clear to him that they had exaggerated the difficulty,
since "a poor friar, with only an inferior horse and what he carried in his saddle bags, was able to make the journey in a very
few days, and lived among those tribes long enough to learn that
those unhappy people, although they are so numerous, are inca-
pable of doing any evil if they are treated with the kindness which
is due their simplicity." One senses Anza's disgust with both the
cowardice and tactlessness of his region's soldiers, although one
also wonders if the positive reception given Garcés owed more to
his own charismatic personality than it did the failings of others.

Anza pointed out that, unlike the Jesuits, Garcés did not tell
the natives on the Colorado that, if Spaniards came, the Indians
would have to plant crops and labor on their behalf—a prospect
that did not appeal to them, "as is to be expected from any free
tribe that is indolent by nature. Although it is necessary to correct this defect in all Indians, it is also necessary to take time for
it, for it if is done otherwise it will be an entire failure." (Here is

more evidence that, with respect to mission administration and development, Anza and Garcés were at this point on the same page.) Another reason Garcés had succeeded where others had failed was that he did not try to strike the Colorado so close to its mouth, where it was guarded by terrible sand dunes. Nor was he burdened in his explorations by the heavy apparatus of a large expedition. In short, Anza had come to put little stock in either the old reports of the Jesuits or those of the soldiers who went with them, whereas, knowing "the religious integrity" of Garcés, he was "convinced . . . that his reports are the most reliable concerning the affair." The captain added that the Indians along the way were so docile that, not only would they not be troubled by the expedition, they might not even necessitate the establishment of new presidios in the region. Smaller guards attached to missions might do the trick. This prediction would prove to be tragically wrong.

Anza concluded by assuring Bucareli of Garcés's "honest, apostolic zeal" and by saying that, if the expedition were approved, he would "not spare any labor to succeed," to the point of sacrificing his life for the enterprise. He did ask for three favors: that he answer directly to Bucareli; that Bucareli order Sastre to furnish Anza with the few necessary supplies (Anza would pay out of his own pocket for presents for the natives); and that after his return he be permitted to report to Bucareli in person about what he had seen and observed. The ambitious Anza knew the ways of politicians, and he had little interest in letting others minimize, distort, or take credit for his accomplishments.

Garcés, in his letter, returned Anza's praise: the captain was upright, generous, honorable, and well liked by the Indians.[36] Given the information he, Garcés, had gathered about the natives in the region and the fact that in 1771 he was able to undertake much of the journey on his own, he saw no reason why it couldn't be done by well-supplied soldiers. In fact, the danger lay not in proceeding but in *not* doing so. For if the Spanish did not subdue the Colorado territory, it was possible that future rebels would find succor there or that the Yumas and others who lived along

the river would ally with the Apaches. Indeed, from that perspective, "Oh! How much better it would have been if missionaries
had been placed in the whole of Pimería and on the rivers sixty
years ago."

As for the road, Garcés suggested that to go to Monterey it
would probably be best to go by a more northern route, avoid-
ing the Quechans altogether and cutting northwest toward the
Colorado River from the area of today's Phoenix or Gila Bend,
whereas to go to San Diego it would be best to avoid the road he
had taken from Sonoita to Yuma—that is, El Camino del Diablo.
That "very bad road" had made an indelible impression on the
friar. Whatever the route, the expedition should include interpreters and presents, especially tobacco, for the Indians. And
"above all, they should be notified in advance, and if necessary
I will go ahead. They should be told only that the king is sending the captain to visit them because they are good people, . . .
and whatever else is necessary to enable us to gain their affection,
not giving them the slightest cause to fear that it may be to their
disadvantage." In other words, there must be no language of conquest or "service" or anything else that would make proud hearts
recoil. As grateful as Bucareli must have been for Garcés's advice,
he may have been more thankful that for this letter the father
had used an amanuensis. Garcés realized that "because of my bad
handwriting" his diaries had "not met the greatest appreciation"
at the colegio, "and perhaps they have not been able to understand them." The friar was nothing if not self-aware.[37]

✳ ✳ ✳

The additional information and arguments provided by Anza and
Garcés, and the concurring opinion of Sastre, inclined Bucareli to
approve Anza's plan. But he was still uncertain when a short, sore-
legged friar arrived in Mexico City to bend the viceroy's ear about
the host of problems he and his brother padres were experiencing in Alta California. Viceroy Bucareli had never met Junípero

Serra, but whether because Bucareli shared the padre's passion for converting the natives of California or because he perceived in Serra high levels of intelligence and competence, Bucareli soon found himself asking for, and inclined to defer to, Serra's opinions.

The trip to Mexico City had nearly killed Serra. Having left San Diego on October 20, 1772, he had twice fallen seriously ill, even receiving last rites as he lay abed at the College of Santa Cruz in Querétaro. He had finally arrived in the capital on February 6, 1773.[38] Now, in early March, Serra made his way to the Palacio Nacional for an interview with Bucareli, during which he introduced his case for replacing the ineffective (in Serra's opinion) Pedro Fages as military commandant of Alta California; for settling farmers, blacksmiths, and carpenters; for bringing doctors into the region; and for much else. Serra stressed the need for married couples, in particular. Not only would the presence of women help forestall the problem of soldiers' sexually assaulting Indians, they would also serve to persuade the natives that the Spanish were not, in fact, the offspring of she-mules, as had become the prevailing opinion.[39] The bill of particulars, or *representación*, that Serra drew up for Bucareli's formal consideration after their initial meeting included thirty-two points. Serra presented it on March 15.

Bucareli listened with interest to Serra during their March meetings; it was not every day that he could discuss in person the situation in Alta California with someone intimately familiar with that faraway territory's challenges and possibilities. Naturally, he asked Serra his opinion of the Anza proposal. Serra told Bucareli that the expedition could and should be undertaken. A road between Monterey and Sonora would be of inestimable value, for traffic in settlers and supplies alike. In fact, Serra argued, a road between Monterey and New Mexico ought also to be explored by an officer moving westward from Santa Fe.[40] After he had received the more detailed responses to his questions penned by Anza and Garcés in March, Bucareli consulted again with Serra, since the friar knew the country and its needs

better than anyone else.⁴¹ Serra's feedback opened Bucareli's eyes
to additional advantages of sending Anza to Monterey. Anza
could explore the coast north of Monterey once he arrived there,
suggested Serra, thereby helping Bucareli determine to what
extent the Russians really were a threat on that coast, and the settlers brought by Anza would help Spain defend the area against
whatever threat there was now or might be in the future.

Buoyed by Serra's input, on September 9, 1773, Bucareli convened
another meeting of the Council of War and Royal Exchequer. It
was quickly "agreed by common accord that the exploration of a
road by way of the Gila and Colorado Rivers to the new establishments of San Diego and Monterey, on the terms proposed by
Captain Juan Baptista de Anza, would be useful and desirable."⁴²
All that was left was to set things in motion. Anza was apprised of
the decision. Fernando Rivera y Moncada, who thanks to Serra's
complaints had just been made commandant of Monterey in place
of Pedro Fages, was told to cooperate with Anza when he arrived.⁴³
Most important, the crown, which Bucareli had been keeping in
the loop as well as he could, was informed that the expedition
was going forward. The dutiful viceroy must have been relieved
when sometime in the late spring or summer of 1774 he received
a letter from Minister Arriaga relaying Charles III's approval of
the decision.⁴⁴ For by that time the glorious deed had been done,
and Bucareli's thoughts were concentrated on how best to leverage
what seemed to be a kingdom-altering achievement.

✳ ✳ ✳

News of the council's approval of their proposal reached Captain
Anza and Father Garcés in or around October 1773. The decree
directed Anza to take with him twenty soldiers; Garcés, from
whom he was expected to "take counsel in cases which may arise
for the success of the expedition"; and another friar selected by
Garcés. There was to be no conflict with the natives, insofar as
it could be helped, and no settlements established. Everything

was to be recorded "in great detail," and, just as he had requested, Captain Anza was expected to report to Viceroy Bucareli in person after the journey had been completed.[45] Bucareli sent the decree northward to Anza via a soldier named Juan Bautista Valdés, who was to go on the expedition as well; having accompanied Serra's Sacred Expedition in 1769, Valdés was familiar with Alta California and its roads.[46]

When he received news of the council's decision, Garcés was in low spirits. Not only had he been sick and depressed by what he felt was a lack of support for his plans, he was still mourning the death of his friend Father Gil, who had been killed by rebel Tiburón Indians that March.[47] Though he had been ambushed and pounded to death with rocks, it "was the friars more than the Indians who crucified and martyred him," wrote Garcés, referring to the spiritual sufferings caused by the many intraclerical conflicts Gil had been forced to deal with as missions president.[48] The theoretical possibility of martyrdom on the Sonoran frontier had, for one Queretaran, finally become a reality. But when he read the viceroy's orders Garcés did not hesitate to spring into action. By early January 1774, he and Anza were ready to go. Or so they thought.

The plan was for the captain to gather men, animals, and provisions at Tubac before marching northward along the Santa Cruz to pick up Garcés at San Xavier del Bac. They would then continue along the now-familiar road to the Gila River, which they would follow westward to its junction with the Colorado.[49] From there, instead of attempting to find a route through the dangerous and confusing sand dunes and marshes west of the junction, they would move north along the Colorado, gathering geographic information from the natives and ultimately, at some promising point, striking out west-northwest for Monterey. Father Garcés was especially keen on this plan. He was plenty familiar with the desolate country west of the Gila-Colorado junction thanks to his 1771 journey. It was not an acquaintance he wished to renew.

By New Year's Day, at Tubac Anza had gathered Valdés, twenty
volunteer soldiers, and Father Juan Díaz, Garcés's fellow Queretaran whose post was at the northern Sonora mission town of
Caborca.[50] Garcés had entered the colegio with Díaz in 1763 and
come with him to the frontier in 1768. A native of Andalusia, Díaz
had become a priest at the age of twenty-seven. Now thirty-seven,
he had distinguished himself both at Querétaro and in the field by
his close observance of the Franciscan rule, his genuine piety, and
his preaching.[51] His handwriting was legible, too, another characteristic that made him the ideal second cleric to include on the
expedition. Also gathered for the journey were two of Anza's servants; five muleteers; a Pima Indian from Tubac expected to serve
as the expedition's carpenter; another Pima who, it was hoped,
could serve as an interpreter (it was believed, incorrectly, that the
languages spoken in California were related to the Piman tongue);
and, perhaps providentially, an Indian whom the Spanish called
Sebastián Taraval.

Taraval was a native of Baja California, from the area around
the mission of Santa Gertrudis, which had been founded by the
Jesuits in 1752 and was about halfway up the peninsula near the
gulf side. It is at that place he first comes into historical view,
for it was at Santa Gertrudis that in 1769 Taraval joined Father
Junípero Serra and the Sacred Expedition en route to Alta
California. He was one of eight Baja California natives in camp
when the mission of San Diego de Alcalá was founded by Serra
on July 14 of that year. He must have helped attend to the sick
men who had been brought ashore from the *San Antonio* and *San
Carlos.* He also presumably served as a translator and cultural
interpreter for the Spaniards in their contacts with the southern
California tribes.[52]

Sometime later Taraval came to live at the mission of San
Gabriel, founded ten miles east of modern Los Angeles in 1771.
It was not a satisfactory situation. He may have missed his native
land and kin. He may have been pressured or forced to join the
Sacred Expedition in the first place. He simply may not have liked

San Gabriel, where his freedom was restricted, food was scarce, and tension between the natives and Spaniards high. Whatever the reason, he, his wife, and her brother decided to leave—or, rather, to escape; apparently all three were baptized Christians or neophytes and therefore considered by the authorities to be subject to the missionaries' rule and discipline. The three Indians struck out southeastward across the desert. Were they trying to circle back, undetected, to Baja California? Or were they trying to make the Colorado? We do not know. We know only that Sebastián was the sole member of the trio to emerge from the desert alive. The Quechans found him on the banks of the Colorado. Salvador Palma, perhaps because he did not wish to have a mission escapee on his hands, perhaps because he hoped for a reward, or perhaps because he simply wished to continue to gain esteem from the Spanish contacts he was cultivating, promptly took Taraval to the military authorities at Altar, arriving on December 26, 1773.[53]

For Anza, Taraval's appearance at Altar—to which Anza was summoned after Taraval's surprise arrival there—was a gift from Heaven. Much as the commander may have trusted Garcés to help lead the way to the Colorado, Garcés's account of the country beyond the river was confusing. Taraval had just crossed that region, and since in leaving San Gabriel without permission he had broken the law, Anza felt justified in pressing him into service as another guide. Only weeks earlier Taraval had been made a widower by the forbidding desert that guarded the eastern flank of the Sierra Nevada. Now he was being forced to cross it again. What he felt about this piece of luck we can only guess. Palma's presence at Altar was also a blessing. Anza learned from Palma not only that he had met Garcés in 1771 but that he was disposed to be friendly toward the Spaniards and that he and his people would welcome the expedition upon its arrival at the junction of the Colorado and Gila.[54]

All was in order, it seemed—except for that implacable force of frontier disorder known as the Apaches. On January 2, no doubt having watched the goings-on at Tubac with a growing sense of opportunity, an Apache band raided the presidio and rode off with 130 good Spanish horses. Anza was faced with a choice: send soldiers south to search for replacements, which would mean delaying the expedition, or change his route to a southerly one that went through the presidio of Altar, where new mounts would be available, and leave on time. Anza chose the latter course of action. Delay might mean returning from California during the searingly hot and dry early summer, and no one wanted that. He also figured that were he to open a road from Altar to Monterey the route would be both more direct as well as safer than the Gila River option, since Apaches did not harass the Spaniards so close to the Gulf of California coast.[55]

It was an entirely reasonable decision, but upon learning of it Garcés was disappointed. He had told his Gileño Pima friends that the expedition would be coming through their lands and had arranged for some of them to accompany the expedition as guides. Mindful of the many as yet unfulfilled assurances he had made about missions being established among the Gileños, another broken promise was the last thing Garcés needed. Worse, as Garcés knew better than anyone, the new route meant traveling to the Colorado by way of the horrible Camino del Diablo and "the sand dunes and bad stretches" he had encountered in 1771.[56] Reluctantly, Garcés told the Gileños about the change and, for what it was worth, gave it his blessing upon his arrival on Tubac on January 6.[57] The important thing was to be on the move.

CHAPTER 7

A Vast Heathendom

1774

The first Anza expedition left Tubac on January 8, 1774. The captain and both friars left diaries of the journey, some in multiple versions. The entrada was discussed at length in various official reports and letters. Herbert Bolton followed the trail by automobile, horse, and foot in the late 1920s, as have others since. We know with quite a bit of precision what happened, and when, on this journey of exploration. It did not lack for excitement.[1]

That January day began, as would become the norm, with Mass—said "with all the ceremony which the country permits," as Anza wryly observed. The liturgy was concelebrated by a group of five friars that included not only Garcés and Díaz but also Fray Gaspar Francisco de Clemente and Fray José Matías Moreno, both resident at Tumacácori, and the tall, ruddy-faced Juan Gorgoll, Garcés's temporary fill-in at San Xavier.[2] By one o'clock, Anza's group of thirty-four men was on the move. Besides its personnel it comprised an unknown number of horses; thirty-five

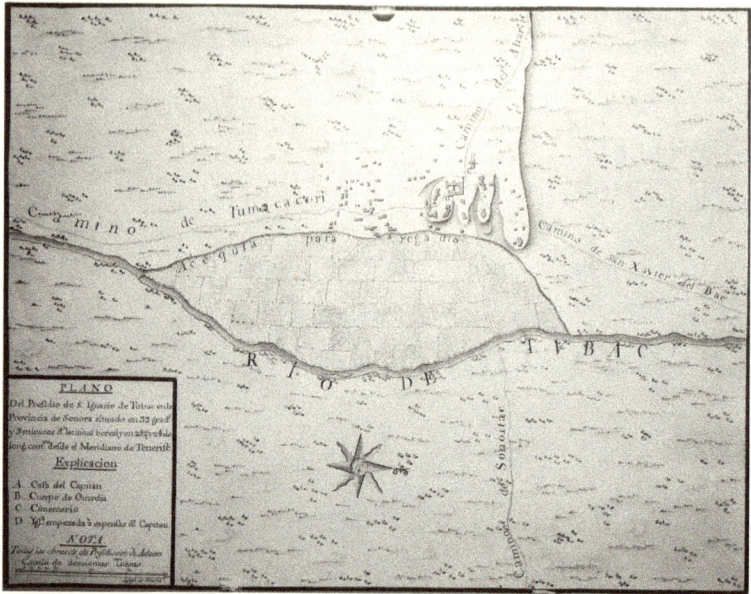

Map of Tubac made circa 1766–67 (the top of the map is facing west).
Image courtesy of Tubac Presidio State Historic Park.

muleloads of provisions, including shovels, picks, tents, cooking
utensils, ammunition, gifts for the Indians, and food enough to
last, it was hoped, for four months; and sixty-five head of cattle
to be slaughtered and eaten along the way.[3] One soldier brought
a violin. Since arriving in the Pimería Alta, Garcés had never
traveled with so large a company, and one perceives from the tone
of the entries in his diary that he was not as comfortable, or as
happy, as when he traveled with only one or two guides.

The expedition's route went north, at first, in order to skirt the
northern end of the low, terracotta-tinted Tumacácori Mountains that rose in the west.[4] Ahead and to the right loomed the
considerably higher pine-topped, snowcapped range known both
then and today as the Santa Rita Mountains. The light was thin,
the air crisp. Although it was winter, bright yellow leaves still

At 7,730 feet, Baboquivari Peak, sacred to the Tohono
O'odham, is visible for many miles in the region the
Spanish called the Papaguería. *Photo by author.*

fringed the tops of the cottonwoods that stretched along the Río
Santa Cruz, which paralleled the road to its east.

After nine miles, Anza and his men turned west to enter the
Arivaca Valley along a well-known trail that ran southwest to
Altar. Along the way were old, abandoned mining settlements,
casualties of the Pima Revolt of 1751 and other Indian wars. Birds
of prey circled overhead as the party marched over rolling hills
through tall, golden grasses and past lush, permanent springs—
grasses and springs that would soon be nothing but cruelly tanta-
lizing memories for both man and beast. The O'odham's sacred
peak, dusty-orange Baboquivari, the region's most noticeable
landmark, seemed ever-present on the western horizon.

The weather was much less pleasant than the landscape. On
January 10 it began to snow, then rain, without pause. For two

days the expeditioners waited out the precipitation in camp at a place called Agua Escondida, located on the southern slope of the mountains that straddle today's international border some ten miles east of Sasabe. Finally, when the skies cleared on January 13, the expedition resumed its march southward, passing near the place—called Arizonac or Arizona—where massive slabs of pure silver had once been found lying on the ground. That night the party arrived at the mission town of Sáric. It was beautiful and fertile—forty O'odham families lived there—but it was also as harassed by the Apaches as any place in the Pimería Alta, according to Anza.[5]

For the next four days the party moved southwest over broken ground dotted with mesquite, catclaw acacia, palo verde, saguaro, and organ pipe cactus through small towns familiar to most of them: Tubutama, Santa Teresa, San Francisco del Ati (or Atil), Oquitoa. Each settlement was materially poor, but both water and pasturage remained plentiful. At the presidio of Altar, on January 17, Anza acquired some new saddle animals from its commandant, Captain Bernardo de Urrea. Here the party turned west-northwest, angling toward the great desert of the Papaguería through the town of Pitic (today's Pitiquito) to Father Díaz's home base of Caborca, where it arrived on January 20.

At Caborca, Anza could take some satisfaction in seeing settled, more or less peacefully, some of those O'odham who had joined with the Seris in revolting against the Spaniards a few years earlier. Whatever pleasure he took from this situation was dashed, however, when he was presented with the mules he had requested, animals the settlers were bound by government orders to provide. Instead of mules, quipped the captain, "I saw only stacks of bones which the animals torpidly moved." Only two of these beasts did he deem healthy enough to take on the journey. Three others were acquired from surrounding missions. With these five animals, sighed Anza, "I remained in almost the same need as before." But there was nothing to be done about it. On

Guided in part by Garcés, and following largely in his footsteps of 1771, the Anza expedition of January–May 1774 successfully connected the Pimería Alta to Alta California. Map by Tom Jonas.

January 22 the march continued. The hard part—the *first* hard
part—was about to begin.

* * *

Garcés knew what lay ahead. He had come through Caborca on
his return journey from the Colorado River in 1771.[6] He knew
that from here until the Gila River the expedition would be traveling through the heart of the Papaguería. Water and food for
the animals would be distressingly scarce. In the hope of finding
more of both, Garcés advised Anza to take a more roundabout
way than that by which the friar had returned from the Colorado
three years earlier. The expedition did so, but camp on the evening of January 22 was still dry. Thirst began to thrust itself into
the forefront of the men's minds.

It was a good twenty to twenty-five miles the next day before
the party, which now included about two hundred animals,
arrived at a place called Arivaipa. Here, by "digging in the sand"
of an arroyo, "the water seeps out so that with some labor the
animals can drink," explained Garcés. Even so, there was little
to no fodder for the animals. Anza shook his head at the Franciscans' inability to induce many of the Papagos to settle at the
missions, given that the Indians' land was to his way of thinking
"one of the most unfortunate regions that can be imagined, for
even water necessary for their support is very scarce, and they
are never sure of having any." Nor did the area have either "shade
trees" or "roof timber." Surely, he thought, a mission system that
could not attract people living in such circumstances should be
reformed. On the other hand, as Anza also noted, epidemics had
greatly diminished the native population in recent years. It wasn't
clear to him or anyone else what missions could do about that.[7]

Fortunately, it had been a rainy January in the Papaguería.
Despite the increasingly forbidding appearance of the desert
through which the Anza party marched—at a place called San
Juan de Matha, Garcés recalled that it was there where a snake

had bitten his worn-out horse in 1771—the land continued to provide enough wells and grass to nourish the expedition's members. The water was increasingly muddy or alkaline. But it was there.

The expedition reached the oasis of Quitobac, a place with a few springs—and the only running water the men had seen since Caborca—on January 26. The next day, as the party approached the old Jesuit mission town of Sonoita, Garcés could not help but observe, with just a touch of sarcasm, that the clearly visible Baboquivari to the east indicated "how short and direct is the road from here to the presidio of Tubac," which is to say, how maddeningly circuitous the expedition's route had been. Nothing mattered now, though, except to get the route right going forward. Already the animals were starting to suffer. For them, camp on this day was dry.

The following day, at Sonoita, both men and animals ate and drank their fill. But it was still well over one hundred miles to the Gila, and there were only a few known watering spots along the way, none of which were guaranteed, or even likely, to have enough water for the entire expedition. Perhaps that was why Garcés persuaded Anza to hire "the Indian official" at Sonoita, "the most experienced in the road to the rivers," as a guide.[8] They were now well and truly about to travel that "very bad road" of Garcés's 1771 entrada: El Camino del Diablo.

On January 29 the expedition moved west along the south side of the Río Sonoyta past the marsh called El Carrizal to a camp near present-day Agua Salada. The name indicates the quality of water found along the way, but it was the best that could be had; despite the water, there was almost nothing for the animals to eat. To the west there were good wells all the way to the Gulf of California coast, the party's natives said—but also massive sand dunes that had frustrated the ambitions of more than one Spanish explorer. It was therefore necessary to stay on the road that would ultimately turn northwest toward the Gila. Garcés was anxious to obtain information about watering holes along the way. Several times he queried the Indian guide Taraval about them, and each time Garcés was disappointed that none were mentioned except those he had seen in 1771 on his way back from the Colorado. The friar could not see how the road could support such a large party, for grass was nearly nonexistent and the water often trapped in virtually inaccessible mountain tanks. But Taraval insisted that El Camino del Diablo was the best way, and in truth Garcés knew of none better.

The next known source of water was at El Aguaje Empinado in the Sierra Pinta Mountains, today called Heart Tank because of its shape. Father Kino had made use of this *tinaja* several generations earlier, as had Garcés in 1771. It was one of the places to which the friar had hoped there was an alternative, for it was not very big. Knowing all this, Anza decided to proceed with prudence. Dividing the party in two, on January 30 he left the pack train at Agua Salada and set out with a small party northwest along the mostly flat but exceedingly rough road. After going through a low pass in the O'Neill Hills, Anza reached a valley in the Tule Desert, which Garcés reported had "little or no water"[9] and Anza himself said had "no pasturage, . . . as was true of all the country traveled over this afternoon." But the animals needed rest. Another dry camp was made.

At 7:30 the next morning the parched men drove the even more parched animals another fifteen or so miles along a road of bare rock. The march was made all the more difficult, wrote Father Díaz, by "the little spirit which the saddle animals" now displayed.[10] Finally the travelers reached the canyon where Heart Tank was located. To say it was difficult to reach would be an understatement. Anza rode as near to it as he could before dismounting to hike. The hike then became a scramble. A panting Anza finally arrived at the water "rather more on my hands than on my feet," only to encounter disappointment. "I saw at once that there was not enough water for all our animals, and that if it were given to all of those which I was taking ahead, it would leave the pack train exposed to death," he wrote. "For this reason I decided to go on to the next watering place and leave this one free." The men in his division surely slaked their terrible thirst here, but their increasingly desperate animals went unwatered.

Having moved forward another ten miles, the party spent a second consecutive thirsty night among some small, rocky hills in which a little pasturage was found. The next place where there might be water in this terrible desert, if the rains had been heavy enough, was a series of six tanks, arranged by the forces of nature one above the other, stairstep style, in the Cabeza Prieta range approximately ten miles to the northwest. Sleep on that cold desert night was troubled not just by thirst but by fear. If those tanks should turn out to be dry, all the creatures on this journey were in serious trouble.

On the morning of Tuesday, February 1, bedraggled men and exhausted animals arrived to find the Cabeza Prieta tanks filled to the brim. We can only imagine their joy. Men and animals drank their fill, with plenty left for the pack train that followed behind. Anza named the place Aguaje de la Purificación. The site was special to the Papagos, he noted, not only for its water but also because in these mountains they hunted bighorn sheep. A large pile of their horns, which Anza was told by the party's Indians were left there "to prevent the Air from leaving the place," was present near the water holes.[11]

It was two more days before the pack train arrived at this place, "completely worn out."[12] The next day, February 4, Anza continued the march. Fifteen miles later another set of desert wells (today's Coyote Water) was reached; once again luck was on the party's side, for when Anza had them dug out enough water ran to provide plenty for all. On February 5 the party marched through Tinajas Pass and northward along the west side of the Gila Mountains before turning up today's Arroyo San Albino. Some hard, long digging in the sand once again brought enough water to serve horses and mules, but not cattle. Anza could only hope to water them early the next morning.

As the men and animals rested here, a Papago family came into camp. The father's name was Luis. He was a Christian and was returning to Sonoita from the Yumas' village at the Gila-Colorado junction. He had left early in order to warn Anza that the Indians there, especially those who lived upstream, intended to kill the Spaniards and steal their possessions. Palma and two other headmen, said Luis, were trying their best to dissuade them from acting so deviously—or, from another perspective, so boldly.[13]

Although Luis said that the Indians were particularly interested in killing "the fathers," Garcés did not think the threat was genuine. The Indians who lived upstream from the Yumas on the Gila were the Cocomaricopas, the Yumas' hereditary enemies but friends of the Gileño Pimas. Most likely either they or the Yumas were simply trying to stir up trouble against the other. Garcés offered to go alone to the river to "see both the good and the bad, and talk with them concerning our coming."[14]

Anza deemed that plan imprudent. Taking Luis's warning seriously, he promised him a horse and presents if he would return to the river and bring back Palma for a tête-à-tête. On this mission Luis left the next morning, February 6. A few hours later Anza got his party on the move; it was once again necessary to find not just water for the cattle but nutrition for all the animals. Moving slowly, the party was in the middle of a sand dune some seven or eight miles from the Gila on February 7 when they encountered Luis, a Quechan headman, and eight other Quechans and O'odham, all mounted. Palma was out hunting at the moment, said the chief, who was naked except for the firebrand he held in his hand, but he assured Anza that the Spaniards would be treated with warmth and hospitality. Anza believed him. "As soon as he had finished his speech I answered him tenderly, telling him to dispatch one of his followers to tell his people to come to see me, with the assurance that I loved them all, and that I would neither injure nor incommode anybody. He did so at once, although in truth it was not necessary, for from here forward all the country swarmed with people, most of them unarmed."[15]

By the time Anza and his men reached the Gila River, they were being followed "by a company of more than two hundred men, all of them overjoyed at our coming, which they celebrated with cheers and smiles, at the same time throwing up fistfuls of earth into the air and with other demonstrations expressing the greatest guilelessness and friendship." When the party, now moving west down the Gila toward its mouth, finally halted at about three o'clock for the animals to eat, drink, and rest, the crowd grew even larger. Men and women pressed in upon the Spaniards. "The longer they looked at our persons, our clothes, and other things used by us, the more they marveled," wrote Anza.[16] It was both flattering and disconcerting, for the curious Quechans wished to touch everything. Nor did they necessarily stop at touching. Garcés found their ability to steal objects with their feet simultaneously comical and astonishing.

Palma, with sixty retainers at his side, arrived a couple hours later. He embraced Anza and was soon assuring him of the Yumas' friendship. The people who were causing unrest were not his but another people who lived upriver—the Cocomaricopas, it would seem.[17] Palma renewed his friendship with Garcés, proudly reporting that, except for the Cocomaricopas, he had kept his promise to the friar to remain at peace with all the peoples around him. Palma's charm and apparent sincerity dispelled any suspicions the Spaniards might still have harbored about the Quechans' intentions. As Father Díaz wrote, Palma "manifested such capacity and loyalty that he caused us no little admiration to see such talent in the midst of such barbarism."[18]

Anza in turn assured Palma that his people were "just like my children and my friends, for such they were, since he was." Then, in a shrewd stroke of diplomacy, he asked Palma to gather all his people near Anza's tent. Anza asked them if they recognized Palma as their chief. When they said yes, he announced that in the name of the king he was confirming Palma as their superior. This conferral of royal authority he symbolized by hanging around Palma's neck a red ribbon bearing a coin with the king's likeness. Just as Anza had hoped, Palma appeared to be deeply moved by this ceremony, and the people "marveled at the gift" and expressed their pleasure at it "with unbounded joy."[19]

There could hardly be a better time, thought the captain, for a big speech explaining just what the Spaniards were doing here. There was one God, who had made everything there was, explained Anza to Palma after the ceremony was finished, with some help from Fathers Garcés and Díaz. That God had given this land and others to the Spanish king. And that king loved not only his Spanish subjects but all the Indians who lived in his lands. He had sent Anza to this region to give the people who lived there "peace in his name, without injuring anybody, and in order through my report to learn about them." Furthermore,

> the king does not ask from them any other thing than that they return the love which he feels for them, by rendering him vassalage and obedience, and living without killing one another; that God also commands this; and since we are all children of both God and the king, and just as none of them like to have their children killed, and if any of them should die the father would grieve, just so it is with God and the king. I told them that I was saying all this to him so that he might tell it to his people. To everything he listened attentively, saying that he had never heard any words more welcome, and that he would make them known to all who were under his rule.

Anza's words expressed well not only the chauvinism but also the idealism that lay at the heart of the Spanish enterprise—as it was understood by people like him and the missionaries who served on the frontier.

Palma took the cue. Taking Anza's cane, he again gathered his people and spoke to them for over an hour, repeating (he said to Anza) what Anza had told him. He then assured Anza that he would do the same not only in the other Quechan villages but also in those of the Quechans' allies. Thus was a friendly relationship established that would last more than seven years—and might have lasted much longer, had circumstances allowed Palma and Anza to keep their promises.

✳ ✳ ✳

In the days that followed, both sides did what they could to prevent, through acts of generosity, the development of ill feeling. Guided by Palma, on February 8 the Anza party moved down the southern bank of the Gila River for a mile or two to a ford where the water was only four feet deep. Anza ordered the cargo unloaded from the animals' backs so they could swim the 125 yards across. Palma suggested that the strongest and tallest Quechans—they were an exceptionally tall people—carry the cargo across on their heads; both Quechan men and women were superb swimmers. Uncertain whether this was a trick, Anza accepted Palma's offer but first crossed the river with half his soldiers. The Quechan men then brought the cargo over without mishap. They also brought over Francisco Garcés. Unwilling to cross over on horseback, in case he should fall off, the otherwise intrepid friar was carried over in the arms of natives.

Anza now found himself on a beautiful island formed by two branches of the Colorado River as it swept southward to meet the Gila. Here was the site of Palma's village. It included, by the captain's estimation, more than six hundred people, virtually all of whom, Garcés noted with some satisfaction, recognized him from his previous journey. The milling crowd of Quechans gathered around the Spaniards to touch them and ask them questions, "for which reason the utmost patience and tolerance" was required, in Anza's telling. "Everything caused them wonderment, and they examined with their hands what they saw with their eyes," wrote Father Díaz. To satisfy their curiosity, Anza arranged the natives in a row, then moved down the long line giving beads and tobacco to all present. The Quechans, for their part, gave the Spaniards beans and calabashes from their fertile fields. This formal exchange of gifts won the Spaniards some peace by nightfall.

The next day brought another river fording and another day of intercourse between the Spaniards and hundreds of inquisitive

Indians. It was also a day of important information-gathering. Guided again by Palma and the helpful Quechans, the party crossed the surprisingly swift Colorado at a wide (two hundred yards) but shallow (three feet deep) ford, Garcés once again making the crossing in the arms of a Quechan warrior. As it was the first time the great Colorado had been crossed by Spanish arms, Anza marked the occasion "by firing off some rockets." The Yumas appreciated this display, he wrote, "although the roar frightened them so that on hearing it they threw themselves on the ground."[20] Anza noted that the two rivers, immediately after uniting, formed the largest stream he had ever seen. It then passed through two small hills. This passage he and the friars named the Puerto de la Purísima Concepción.[21] The view from the top of the nine-hundred-foot volcanic hill on the west side of the Colorado was, especially to a desert dweller, lovely, with thick groves of willows and cottonwoods bordering both the Gila and Colorado as far as could be seen—trees, Anza happily noted, that are actually "useful for beams because they are so straight."[22] One could envision a Spanish settlement here.

Later in the day Anza was told that he was not, in fact, very far from the settlement the Spanish had established at San Diego. It was only a five-day journey from the river to the coast—but to reach it, added the natives ominously, "there was a scarcity of water even in the rainy season."[23] Anza was also told that El Moqui—Hopi blankets were everywhere present among the Quechans, thanks to their trade with the middlemen Mohaves—was a twelve-day journey to the north. Thanks to this information and the reports he had received from Garcés and Taraval, the geography of this mysterious part of the frontier was starting to take shape in Anza's mind.

Questions of culture no less than of geography occupied the Spaniards' minds. Fray Díaz examined the Quechans with the eyes of a missionary. That they were "agricultural and little devoted to the chase" augured well for the prospect of establishing a mission among them. So too did the fact they were "docile and friendly."[24] Garcés and Anza made special note of the exten-sive fields of wheat, maize, melons, and other crops. Anza was impressed by the Quechans' height (Díaz measured one of them at six feet three inches), robust physicality, and "festive, affection-ate, and generous" temperament.[25] On the other hand, challenges would be posed by the Quechans' habits of body painting, naked-ness (Quechan women wore willow-bark skirts, but the men considered clothing "womanish," reported Anza), homosexual-ity and transgenderism, and frequent wars with their neighbors along the river, habitual violence that none of the Spanish diarists failed to mention.[26]

Now safely on the western side of the Colorado, Anza had a decision to make. The plan he had formed with Garcés was to advance northward along the Colorado before heading west to Monterey. Once they made contact with a people who had direct communication with the Indians of New Mexico, or at least the Hopis, Garcés planned to send a letter to the nearest New Mexico missionary and wait for a response as a way of judging the distance. He had been charged to do so by Father Cartagena, the guardian of the College of Santa Cruz, who had been asked by Viceroy Bucareli to investigate whether communication was possible between Monterey and Santa Fe.[27] Garcés quite sensibly wanted to send this letter from somewhere upstream, nearer to a straight line between those two places. And, of course, the letter must be couriered by natives he believed he could trust.

The testimony of a Mohave Indian present at Palma's village offered hope that both the desired northern route to Monterey and a viable way to send the letter might exist. This man gave Garcés to understand that his people communicated with both the Hopis and the Pueblo Indians of New Mexico. He also seemed to say there was a large river to the north that might empty into the western sea, so far as he or any of his people knew. But when Anza interviewed another Mohave he was warned about limited pasturage and an immense and possibly impassable sierra to the west of the Mohaves' homeland. Garcés thought this second Mohave meant to deceive the captain, but Anza found him credible. Should the plan be changed?

There was more risk in going north and then west than south and then west. (Imposing sand dunes made going directly west unthinkable.)[28] After all, the friendly Yumas' territory stretched southward rather than northward, and the one person who definitely knew the way to a California settlement was Sebastián Taraval, who had come to the Colorado via the mission at San Gabriel, not Monterey. Taking such considerations into account, Anza changed the plan. He would have Taraval guide him to San Gabriel by way of the southern route. It was the second time Anza had decided to trust the experience of Taraval over that of Garcés, and it was a nearly fatal mistake.

※ ※ ※

On February 10, the Spaniards proceeded. Palma and a crowd of six hundred Quechans led them down the western side of the Colorado, clearing the trail and helping to drive the animals. For two days the party traveled downstream, finally angling a few miles west of the river to the end of Quechan territory, a couple miles south of today's international border, all the while in an area familiar to Garcés. This was the beginning of the land of the Kohuanas, on the western side of the river, and that of the Halyikwamais on the east. Because they had reached the region of the Quechans' enemies, Palma and his people left them— Palma "raining tears," as each of our three diarists testify. Camp was made at a place called Santa Olalla, thought to have been near the Pescadero Dam on an overflow channel later called the Bee River.[29]

From here Anza would attempt to strike west for the Cocopah Mountains and thence the great Sierra Madre. From here began ten days of continuous trials.

There was, as Garcés and Taraval knew better than anyone, little to no potable water or pasturage on this even sandier side of the Colorado. Without any Quechans to use as interpreters, it was impossible to understand, except by signs, the Kohuanas and other Indians they encountered (mostly Cocopahs). And after their Kohuana guides, having reached the limit of their territory, left them on February 14, the landscape in which the Spaniards traveled became even less legible. Garcés recognized a couple places from his 1771 entrada. Taraval was supposed to know the route, but in this flat, all but landmark-less delta he became none too sure of it. Worse, the expedition's animals, only barely recovered from their ordeal on El Camino del Diablo, were again showing signs of exhaustion.

Before they left, the Kohuana guides pointed out in the far distance a mountain—Signal Mountain, just west of today's Mexicali on the southern side of the border—at which the next water could be found. So Anza pressed westward through the sand and brush until, on February 15, he was forced to leave most of the pack train at a little well so that it might recover. Ten miles later, he found himself standing, entirely lost, in a trailless sea of treacherous, wind-blown dunes, wondering what to do. Taraval was not as reliable a guide as Anza had hoped.

For Anza, the sensible thing was to send half the animals and men, as well as one of the friars, back to the Colorado. There they could recuperate in safety while he pressed as quickly as he could with the healthier half of his party toward San Gabriel and then Monterey. There was no way many of the animals, not to mention the soldiers, could afford to wander around much longer looking for a trail to the ocean coast. But when the captain presented this plan, Garcés vigorously dissented. Like his acquaintance Father Serra, it was not in his nature ever to turn back. In addition, splitting up meant the expedition would have to return by a southerly route in order to meet up with the group that was left behind, and he was still hoping to blaze a northerly road from Monterey to Tubac. Finally, he sensed an opportunity to prove his value. Thus did Francisco Garcés make a nearly fatal mistake of his own.

There was a village a few leagues to the south, said Garcés, which on his 1771 journey he had named San Xacome.[30] It was one of the few places with adequate water and grass for the animals, and he knew the way. Anza, recalling the high standing Garcés had with the Spanish authorities, reluctantly decided to trust him. Trudging forward across the shifting dunes as best they could, many of the soldiers on foot because their horses were now too fatigued to carry them, the party reached the location of San Xacome just after sunset—only to find that San Xacome was not there. There was no sign of it. Certain that it could not be far off, Garcés went with two soldiers in search of it. But there was no trace of the village that had treated him so hospitably in 1771. Returning to camp with the soldiers, he set out a final time on his own. After midnight the friar returned, as humiliated as he was perplexed. Neither San Xacome nor water was to be found anywhere.

The situation was dire. Had Anza not allowed Garcés to talk him out of his plan to divide the party in two he might be able to risk going forward. Now, having taken this long, pointless detour, he was in danger of losing everything and everyone. The only rational thing to do was to attempt to return to the last place where there had been enough food and drink for survival: Santa Olalla. Thus, after a waterless night, on February 16 he and the others, traveling by short stages and strung out in various groups, wearily began to retrace their steps, slaking their terrible thirst as best they could at the little well—now called by the soldiers Pozo de las Angustias, the Well of Tribulations—and other scanty, salty watering holes that lay along the way. Not until midnight on the 23rd—a full week later—was the entire party, less the horses and mules who had died somewhere among the dunes, back at the slough where Palma had left them. Ten days of extraordinarily arduous travel had gotten the Spaniards nowhere. As Anza confided to his diary, things were in a "generally disastrous condition."[31]

Among the few animals and men who were not yet exhausted was, as usual, Father Garcés. Immediately he asked Anza for permission to take a scouting trip downriver. However abashed he may have felt about his wild goose chase, it was clear to Garcés that "we could not be guided through those lands by the California Indian"—that is, Taraval—"who lost his way and was almost dead from hunger and thirst."[32] Perhaps he could learn from the Indians downstream how best to cross the foreboding desert to their west. Anza assented, with the stipulation that Garcés be back by March 1, when the commander intended to resume the journey.

Garcés set out on February 24 on horseback with three Indian guides, some beads, and a little tobacco. A palpable sense of contentment reenters his diary. He is full of interest in the lives of the natives he meets, including what they eat (he mentions, for example, the tornillo bean, "shaped like a screw") and the words they use as greetings. He makes note of the different villages and their chiefs, one of whom he had met in 1771. And he records the changing width and depth of the river, which, as a nonswimmer, he crossed twice on a raft made for the purpose by the natives. Strangely, nowhere does he report asking about routes or watering places. This is the diary of an insatiably curious traveler more than a scout.

While Garcés wandered, Anza pondered. The plan Garcés had rejected on February 15 seemed the right one. If Anza was to make San Gabriel or some other Spanish settlement without loss of life, he needed to travel nimbly and lightly. That meant leaving men, animals, and goods here at the Colorado in Palma's care. But could this pagan chief be trusted? Anza interviewed him at length, searching for reasons to be skeptical. He could find none. Palma seemed utterly sincere in his affection for the Europeans, even if it was the material advantages offered by their friendship that he most truly coveted. Then, too, if while Anza was gone Palma absconded with anything or hurt anyone, one of the friendly O'odham that frequently visited the Quechans would report the matter to the Spanish. Palma had incentive to act well.

Besides, were the Indians really so different from Anza's men? Hundreds of Yumas, Kohuanas, and Halyikwamais gathered around camp every night. Curious about everything they heard and saw, they learned to make the sign of the cross and to say "¡Ave María! ¡Viva Dios y el Rey!" as a greeting. They loved to hear the violin, and the native women learned Spanish dance steps with astonishing quickness. The interethnic comity was remarkable. And yet ... one day the Spaniards discovered that two of their mules were missing. Some Quechans volunteered to bring them back. One of them—a man of high status whom the Spaniards called Pablo—soon returned with one of the animals, smiling. A Halyikwamai from across the river had stolen the animals, he said. He had been unable to apprehend him, and one of the mules had already been killed, but he had found the thief's wife. So, to avenge the wrong, he had killed her by shooting an arrow through her heart. Anza was aghast. "He showed me the arrow and even wished me to take it in my hands," recorded Anza in his diary. "The deed was repugnant to me, and I disapproved it as its barbarity deserved." Pablo, expecting approbation, was offended by this scorn. "As soon as I turned my back he said very serenely that one life was of little consequence," wrote Anza, "and that as for the one which he took, he was only sorry that I did not approve it."[33]

Between Quechans and Spaniards there might be friendliness. But underneath, as both sides could readily perceive, there was a chasm in understanding.

❊ ❊ ❊

Garcés returned to the expedition's camp at midday on March 1, making Anza's deadline only by walking all night and all morning to get there, his horse having become too tired to carry him.[34] He had discovered no news of value downriver, so Anza decided to go forward with his new light-travel plan. Most of the expedition's cargo, many animals, three soldiers, three muleteers, one of Anza's servants, and two Pima interpreters—but neither of the stubborn friars, as Anza had originally intended—would be left behind with Palma and the Yumas. The next day, reduced to a total of twenty-five men, the expedition was again on its way, carrying but a month's worth of supplies on the backs of its ten remaining mules.

This time Anza went farther downriver before cutting west toward the Cocopah Mountains. This more southerly road was easier, passing by many willow and cottonwood groves and taking the men through Kohuana lands in which Garcés had traveled in 1771. The padre was recognized, some of the natives greeting the party with cries of "Jesús, María," as Garcés had taught them in 1771. "They handed over to us four idols and without regret they saw me break three in pieces," Garcés later recalled, "but the fourth escaped my hands because the soldiers took it."[35] The road also took the expedition through the former site of San Xacome. Garcés was gratified to learn from the Kohuanas that he had not been wrong about its location after all, but that it had been abandoned when the well there had dried up.

On the morning of March 6, having completed an exceedingly difficult march by crossing the barren Cocopah Mountains— the Cerro Impossible, the men called it—and camping along the northwestern tip of Laguna Salada, in which they found hundreds of stranded saltwater fish, the Spaniards awoke to find that their guide had fled. Fortunately, on the previous day the Kohuana man had indicated the location of the next available water. Hoping against hope that he had not lied, Anza sent a corporal and six other soldiers ahead to find it. They did, and at the springs they also found a Kumeyaay (Diegueño) Indian boy, whom they seized and kept—apparently with the idea of forcing him into service as a guide—until his father, descending from the mountains, begged for his release.[36] Anza records the episode with some embarrassment, for he had "always impressed upon the minds of all the soldiers . . . that they must not use force upon any heathen, even in minor matters, except in cases of extreme necessity, in order that we may not acquire a bad name at first sight."[37] Yet the following day the same corporal found and held hostage six other Kumeyaay until they led him to water.[38] High ideals eroded quickly in the presence of biological necessity.

The next day, March 8, the expedition, heading north through the Yuha Desert and its millions of fossilized oysters and barnacles, came to a spring the men called Santa Rosa of the Flat Rocks. It was at or near modern Yuha Well in extreme south-central California.[39] Water and pasturage were abundant. Here Garcés recognized the spot, a little to the east, where he had turned around in 1771; that was also the spot where he had looked northwest and seen two gaps in the mountains. More important, here Sebastián Taraval finally found himself in familiar territory. A few leagues to the north was a watering place where he, his wife, and his brother-in-law had emerged from the great mountain chain to the west. Drooping spirits lifted. The route to San Gabriel was now clear.

On March 10, the Spaniards arrived at a place they called, in honor of Taraval, San Sebastián, near today's Harper's Well. At Santa Rosa, Anza had noted they were but two days' journey from the Colorado, had they known the route. Here at San Sebastián, the natives told them of wells directly to the east that could be used in making that journey. They also spoke of other soldiers having been there before. Garcés speculated that this had been Captain Pedro Fages, who was based in Monterey but had crossed the mountains east of San Diego in 1772 in search of deserters and ultimately reemerged on the coast at San Luis Obispo.[40] If Fages had been here, Garcés wrote in his diary, then not only was the road to San Diego known but so also was an interior, more northerly route to San Luis Obispo. By arriving at this spot from Sonora, the expedition had now decisively linked that province with Alta California. The deed was as good as done, and Garcés the missionary could not help but express his emotions: "Oh, what a vast heathendom! Oh! what lands so suitable for missions! Oh! what a heathendom so docile! How fine it would be if the wise and pious Don Carlos III might see these lands! . . . because, indeed, seeing a thing is very different from hearing about it!"

Over the next week, guided once again by natives, Anza and his men made their way through the strangely carved, fossil-filled

desert that now bears his name—the Anza-Borrego Desert—up
the Borrego Valley, then the Coahuila Valley, before ascending
the southwestern flank of the San Jacinto Mountains through
San Carlos Pass and descending to the Santa Ana River near
today's Riverside.[41] No European, save Fages and his soldiers,
had ever traveled in this land. With water now present at regular intervals, the journey seemed less a matter of survival than of
adventure and exploration.

There were new peoples to be met and described. The friendly
if somewhat timid ones living at the mouth of the Borrego Valley wore fiber sandals and used a curved throwing stick called a
macana to kill rabbits and deer.[42] Their women, the friars happily
recorded, never failed to cover themselves with skirts, even the
infants. Upvalley a new group of Indians was met, smaller and
less friendly. They had a distinctive manner of communicating
that Garcés could not help but find humorous. When speaking
"they move their feet, raising them high behind, and wave the
arms as though complaining and grumbling," wrote Garcés, "and
they likewise raise their voices, speaking in tones like some little
crows which abound in this region. It certainly is laughable."[43]
This group, to whom the Spaniards perhaps appeared just as
comical, would come to be called by the Spanish Los Danzarines—The Dancers.[44]

There were new plants and foods to be described, too, as the
elevation got higher, the climate colder and wetter, and the landscape greener: A "sour cane" that the Indians called *sotole*. A
"little palm which bears dates which are not like those of Spain,
but very different." A "countless multitude of white geese." A
species of grass that "bears a seed very much like rye." At the
higher elevations, besides conifers and bears, there were rose-
mary, sage, and other herbs in abundance. By the time the "most
beautiful and broad valley" of the Santa Ana River was reached
on March 20, it was not difficult for Garcés and everyone else on
the expedition to behold in their mind's eyes a flourishing land
of Spanish pueblos and missions.[45] Indeed, the vibrant fertility

of California struck these highly practical travelers as so lovely they could not fail to mention it. "Looking toward the South Sea and toward our new establishments on its coasts, all the view is most beautiful," wrote Anza on March 15, who also remarked upon the "beauty" of a valley on March 18, and a "most beautiful lake" on the 19th.[46] "Beauty" was a word seldom used by the Spanish to describe the desert. They had entered upon a friendlier world. Even the light and the air were different. The former was less sharp and more diffuse, the latter softer, seeming rather to bathe than attack.

From the Santa Ana River northwest to Mission San Gabriel was but forty-five miles. The only difficulty now was hunger. Food supplies were distressingly short. Dozens of deer and a few bears were spotted here and there, but unlike later American pioneers Spanish soldiers were not typically enthusiastic hunters, and so game animals were left undisturbed. As the men marched toward San Gabriel, they were sustained as much by the delightful scenery—the variously colored wildflowers, the thick stands of grass, the tall cottonwoods and sycamores—as by the tiny rations to which they had been reduced. Plentiful food, the men figured, would be available at the mission.

Finally, at sunset on March 22, the expedition arrived at isolated San Gabriel. It was completely unexpected, as far as the soldiers and four priests—Father Antonio Paterna, the mission's pastor, and Fathers Antonio Cruzado, Juan Figuer, and Fermín Francisco de Lasuén—posted there were concerned. Anza was deeply gratified by the "unrestrained jubilation and demonstrations of joy" with which he and his men were received. "Even though the friars and the soldiers saw us, they could hardly believe that people could have come from Sonora," reported Anza, "and they kept repeatedly asking me if it were true, tears springing to their eyes, caused by the joy and pleasure at seeing this expedition accomplished, and at knowing how close at hand Sonora was and how easy the transit from it."[47] Needless to say, nothing about the journey had been "easy."

A celebration ensued. The missions' bells were tolled, a solemn Te Deum chanted, Mass said.[48] The happiness gradually dissipated, however, as it was discovered that San Gabriel was a deeply *un*happy place. The most pressing problem concerned sustenance. Somehow, back on the Colorado, Anza had badly miscalculated. Garcés tells us (as Anza does not) that the expedition had just run out of food when it arrived. Furthermore, and quite contrary to the expeditioners' expectations, things were little better at the mission—despite the fact that, as Garcés perceived, it had "everything to make it one of the best in these provinces."[49] Father Paterna told Anza that the soldiers there were surviving on a daily ration of three corn tortillas and whatever wild herbs they could collect. The corn for the tortillas, he added, would run out in less than a month. Poverty had met poverty.

Both sides were embarrassed by their inability to relieve the others' needs. We know from a grateful Father Lasuén that Garcés did what little he could to help. Born in 1736, the black- and curly-haired, thick-bearded Lasuén was a proud Basque who had come to New Spain in 1759.[50] In later years—from 1785 to 1803—he would succeed Father Serra as president of the California missions and become famous among travelers for his gracious manners, keen intelligence, and able administration. Such a future would have been unimaginable to Lasuén in March 1774. At that time, having served his ten years in the mission fields, he wanted nothing more than to retire to the College of San Fernando or even to return to Spain, where his ailing parents were in dire straits. It didn't help that he was dressed in rags, a situation that profoundly mortified the well-bred priest. Lasuén had neither underwear nor sandals, and the habit he had worn every day for five years was now tattered beyond recognition. "I have done what I could to keep the clothes in repair," he wrote his college around this time. "But they no longer can be repaired, partly because there is nothing to repair, and partly because there is nothing with which to repair them." In another letter he dryly remarked, "It was because of my very necessities that the Indians became so devoted to me, for if 'like attracts like' I resemble them closely in scantiness of attire." Garcés and Díaz took pity on Lasuén, whom they had met at Tepic in 1768, giving him a habit, cowl, tunic, and pair of sandals. Garcés also gave a cloak to another of the underclothed friars.[51]

Like Lasuén, Fathers Paterna and Cruzado had petitioned the College of San Fernando to return to Mexico. They were not just starving; they had also failed to build friendly relations with the area's inhabitants. San Gabriel had been founded on the slopes of the Montebello Hills overlooking the San Gabriel Valley in 1771. With its cool breezes, the unmistakable sense of the sea in the air, the wild blackberry canes and grapevines that adorned the countryside, and the green pines that clothed the imposing mountain range to its north, the mission was prettily situated. And things had started well enough. When the first Franciscans arrived at the location where they intended to found San Gabriel, they showed the standoffish Indians they encountered an image of Mary. The natives were fascinated. To the Spanish, they seemed to think the image, so unlike anything they had ever seen, was alive—or perhaps, like one of their idols, was a god. They "came bearing various seeds," reported one missionary, "which they placed at the feet of the Most Blessed Lady, thinking she would consume them as other humans did." Something similar had happened when the Spanish founded the mission of San Diego, Fray Francisco Palóu reported. When the Kumeyaay there "were shown another painting of the Virgin Mary, Our Lord, with the Infant Jesus in her arms, and the news was spread to nearby villages, the natives came in to see it. And since they could not come into the enclosure because of the stockade, they called the fathers and they stuck their breasts in between the posts of the enclosure, meanwhile signifying in a vivid manner that they came to give milk to that tender and beautiful Child in possession of the fathers."[52]

Aside from that promising beginning, the San Gabriel padres had made little material or spiritual headway with the Gabrielinos (today known as the Tongva, or the Gabrielino-Tongva), despite the Gabrielinos' impressive material culture, which included well-made baskets, relatively sophisticated tools and jewelry, and permanent villages.[53] This failure was thanks, the priests claimed, to the grave sins of some of the soldiers who had been stationed there. In 1771, one soldier sexually assaulted a Gabrielino chief's wife. Later, groups of six or more would ride out from the mission to outlying villages, lasso Gabrielino women as they would calves, and rape them. If any of the native men dared to intervene, they would be shot.[54] These were the sorts of ugly crimes which, weighing heavily upon his spirit, Father Serra had traveled to Mexico to complain about.

Three years later, the residents of San Gabriel were living on the edge of starvation. Fortunately, a solution had just come to hand. The *Nueva Galicia*, carrying Serra and supplies from Mexico to Monterey, had been forced to dock at San Diego on March 13, 1774.[55] The friars at San Gabriel had received this news just three days before Anza's arrival on March 22. Paterna offered to share the mission's scanty food supply with Anza and his men until they could reprovision themselves from the ship that a beneficent providence—or blind luck—had just brought ashore down the coast.

Anza had no choice but to try to do just that. He immediately wrote the authorities at San Diego requesting fresh animals and provisions. The hope—doubtless pressed by Garcés more than anyone—was to obtain enough food, horses, and mules to allow the entire expedition, not just the advance guard currently at San Gabriel, to continue to Monterey. That would allow the party to find a route back from Monterey that bypassed the coastal camino real to emerge on the Colorado well north of Yuma. Garcés continued to believe such a route must exist, and that a trail from there to the Gila also must be more direct and better than the arid and treacherous road of which he had had more than enough experience.

Paterna offered Anza pack animals with which to go to San Diego to get the needed supplies. On March 25, as a constant rain watered San Gabriel's fields, a grateful Anza sent the always reliable Valdés, two other soldiers, and fifteen mules to San Diego over the muddy royal road to procure them. Two days later, Palm Sunday, Garcés decided, with Anza's blessing, to go down to San Diego to assist. He would also attempt to bring Father Serra himself to San Gabriel, so that Anza and the head of the California missions could exchange information face to face. Father Paterna soon went down to San Diego as well.

Serra was writing his superior at the College of San Fernando on March 27 when, to his great joy, messengers arrived from San Gabriel with letters from Garcés, Díaz, and Anza, followed three days letter by Garcés himself. The expedition that Serra had helped persuade Viceroy Bucareli to approve had succeeded! Garcés told Serra all about it—the Apaches running off the horse herd, the terrible ordeal experienced by Taraval (whom Serra knew well), and, with a bit of self-pity, how Taraval had replaced Garcés as Anza's preferred guide. He also impressed upon Serra the desperateness of their and San Gabriel's situations. The mission had little food, the expedition had none, and the animals that had traveled from Sonora were so worn out that Anza's men had arrived at San Gabriel on foot. Anza had written the sergeant at San Diego, the *Nueva Galicia*'s Captain Don Juan Pérez, and Serra begging for as much food and as many mules, saddle animals, and soldiers as could be spared for the king's service. Garcés attested personally to the legitimacy of the commander's requests.

Serra had been in favor of the expedition, but he had expected it to relieve his California missions, not burden them. Anza's requests were "the same as to wish that at the expense of what supplies we have, we should make an expedition, more difficult, more doubtful, and more costly than his," he complained in his letter to San Fernando's guardian. He decided that after the important liturgies of Holy Week had concluded he would go to San Gabriel to have a chat with Anza and figure out how the commander could instead send to the Colorado for the animals, men, and supplies he had left there. Still and all, Anza's expedition was "very welcome," wrote Serra, for now the road from San Gabriel to Caborca was known, and it was said to be but a twenty-day journey—with the distance from Sonora to San Diego being even shorter. Serra's missions could henceforth be supplied via this road, "and our conquests shall be extended in these directions to the ends of the earth," for Viceroy Bucareli had told him that with the opening of an overland supply route Serra might establish his long-desired new missions at San Francisco and Santa Clara.[56] Anza, in particular, inspired confidence. He was a "devoted friend of the College of Santa Cruz, a distinguished benefactor, and a source of great encouragement to the missionaries of the Pimería," wrote Father Lasuén to the College of San Fernando. Fathers Garcés and Díaz must have spoken highly of the captain. Because of him, "everyone is already convinced that in a short time the enterprise will lead to much progress in this new territory."[57]

For the next week, Garcés and Paterna remained at a wet and dreary San Diego with Serra, helping to assist with the sacred liturgies, baptizing ten Indians on Easter, and arranging for the needed supplies. With his fellow friars' help, Garcés wrote a preliminary, brief diary for Bucareli, to be sent to Mexico City by extraordinary courier. Alas, San Diego could not provide any fresh animals for Anza, nor did it have much to offer in the way of food. What little could be spared was sent to San Gabriel on April 1.

On April 6 the three priests, along with Serra's servant Juan Evangelista, left San Diego for San Gabriel. The waterlogged roads made the going slow, and the party did not reach San Gabriel until April 11. By that time Anza was gone.[58]

* * *

When Anza received the provisions from San Diego on April 5, he quickly realized he needed a new plan. Captain Pérez, who had been instructed after resupplying Monterey to explore the northern Pacific coast as far north as modern Alaska, had sent Anza only nine bushels of corn, half of which was spoiled; some jerked meat, all of which was spoiled; three bushels of beans, all but useless on the road due to a lack of cooking pots; and a little flour. Here were starvation rations indeed. Not only was there no longer any possibility of taking the entire expedition to Monterey, there was not even the possibility of taking all those who had come to San Gabriel. Anza therefore decided to ride as quickly as possible to Monterey with just six men (four of his own, and two from the mission to serve as guides). Díaz, Garcés, and the others were instructed to return to Yuma, where they should await Anza's arrival—except for Valdés, who was commanded to continue to Mexico in order to convey to Bucareli the diaries of Anza, Garcés, and Díaz, "so that as soon as possible he may get the news that it has been accomplished in the main."[59] Opening a better, more direct road from Monterey to Tubac would have to wait for another time.[60]

Garcés, who knew how pitiful the San Diego provisions had been, took the commander's decision to proceed without him in stride.[61] Given how fast the commander intended to travel, he doubted he would have wanted to accompany him anyway. He watched Serra present the impoverished San Gabriel padres with a painting of San Gabriel the Archangel for their altar—they had been reduced to tearing "a page out of a missal containing a print of the Archangel Gabriel" and placing it on the altar instead— and took counsel with Díaz.[62] As the more mechanically inclined of the two, Father Juan, with two soldier escorts, would stay behind at San Gabriel to take observations with an astrolabe. Garcés would lead the rest of the men back to Yuma.[63]

The return to the Colorado River began on April 13. The trip was full of wrong turns, mucky paths, and hunger pangs. The men shot and killed a bear. The Danzarines killed one of the expedition's horses, an act Garcés believed was undertaken out of desperation for its meat rather than out of hostility—and which the Spaniards prudently ignored.[64] Other natives did things the men could not understand, such as the "very droll Indian" who sang "a lively tune and with measured tread. Then, keeping the step, and taking the posture of one sitting on a low bench, he ended the song. All out of breath, he continued in plaintive key, still keeping the step, amusing us greatly." Another Indian danced "as if in great distress, cried out, moving his arms and legs wildly and acting like a maniac, while a crouching woman made turns around him, and beckoned with her hands like our Spanish women."[65] With his unquenchable interest in people, Garcés recorded it all as best he could. Indeed, he recorded it with more detail than he did the return route back to the Colorado, which, once out of the Borrego Valley, seems to have run through the middle of the dry Imperial Valley to the northeast of the outbound path, saving men and animals about fifty miles.

On April 24, the Garcés-led party arrived back at Santa Olalla. Palma's village near the junction of the Colorado and Gila was reached on the 26th. The men who had been left there, having heard reports that Anza and the rest of the advance guard had been killed, had gone back to Caborca, taking most of the animals and provisions with them. Sixteen cattle and a few other supplies had been left in Palma's faithful care, however (apparently the men had hedged their bet on the veracity of the report), and with these provisions Garcés and his companions settled down to await Anza while Valdés rushed off to Mexico City with the diaries for Bucareli.[66] It had been done "with impossible equipment, and over bad roads," wrote Garcés in his diary, but thanks to God, and thanks to its wise and patient commander, the expedition had been not only successful but also peaceful.[67]

Anza reached Monterey on April 18 and found it even more impoverished than San Gabriel; in light of their suffering, he was amazed that any friars and troops remained there. On his return south, he crossed paths with a northbound Father Serra somewhere along the Santa Barbara Channel. He bowed to Serra's request to spend the night there in order to tell him about the new road to Sonora. On May 1, Anza arrived back at San Gabriel. After a brief rest, on May 3, he left, now with Father Díaz in tow, for the Colorado. Guided by notes Garcés had left along the way, one of which was carved into the trunk of a willow, Anza reached

Palma's village on May 10—taking a week to travel what had previously taken him forty-one days.[68] The Spaniards were greeted
by the Quechans with their customary friendliness and courtesy.
Anza was particularly gratified by their cries, in Spanish, of such
words as "Capitán," "Señor," "Soldados," and "Compañeros." By
that afternoon the Spaniards had been ferried across the river
on a large raft and reunited with the Garcés group. "I have never
crossed a river with greater assurance," wrote Anza, "since even
though the craft had been wrecked I had close at hand more than
five hundred persons ready to rescue me."[69]

Palma, said Anza, had displayed to him and all the Spaniards
nothing but fidelity and generosity—"his equal is not to be found
amongst his kind," Anza wrote with appreciation in his diary.[70] Yet
there was also a flicker of hostility, a sign of some growing division
among the peoples of the Colorado. Anza had brought with him
six soldiers from Monterey so they could learn the road to Yuma.
Quechans from the village the Spaniards called San Pablo, downriver from Palma's village, regarded these men from enemy territory as enemies themselves and attempted to steal their horses and
cattle.[71] It was only thanks to Palma's intervention that these men
and their animals were safely conducted out of the area and put
back on the road to San Gabriel and Monterey (for which service
Anza left Palma four cows). The situation was tense enough to
cause Father Díaz to reflect: "I have formed the opinion that passage through these lands will not be easy unless our nation estab-
lishes itself at some points on these rivers." For if the Indians there
"should come to be discontented, and disinclined to cooperate in
the crossing with their aid, and on the contrary should attempt to
impede it, a large force of arms would be necessary to vanquish so
numerous although so uncivilized a heathendom."[72]

Father Díaz was describing the very dynamic that would lead
to his and his friend Father Garcés's deaths.

CHAPTER 8

An Indian Himself

1774–1775

After all they had been through, there was no possibility of Anza and his men returning to Sonora in that spring of 1774 by way of El Camino del Diablo. They would travel by way of the Gila River instead. The route might be somewhat circuitous, but except for the Apache threat it was considerably less dangerous.

From Yuma the party advanced by easy stages upriver into the region visited by Garcés in 1770, a region inhabited by Cocomaricopas, Opas, and Pimas. By May 21 they were in what is now Gila Bend, and by May 26, having gratified the Gileño O'odham by traveling through their villages, Anza and his men were passing through San Xavier del Bac. San Xavier's pastor was not among them. Neither the rigors of five months on the trail nor the trauma of having nearly experienced death by dehydration was enough to dampen Francisco Garcés's ardor for exploration. He was now off on a solo expedition of his own.

Garcés simply wasn't satisfied with the expedition's accomplishments. From his perspective the failure to explore the region north of the Colorado-Gila junction was significant. It may have been God's will that the expedition did not find such a route: "The leaves on the trees don't move unless it is God's will that they do so," he reflected in one letter.[1] Even so, there had to be a better road to Monterey. And not just to Monterey, but to New Mexico as well. As he reminded Father Díaz, he had been asked by their colegio's Father Guardian to try to communicate with New Mexico, and he had yet to fulfill that request. So Garcés parted from the expedition at Gila Bend, saying he wanted to see if he could send a letter to the friars of New Mexico via the tribe from whom the Pimas and others procured red hematite—the Yavapais, as he would come to know them.[2] They lived north of the Gila and east of the Colorado and were known to be friendly with the Hopis and Apaches. What he did not confess to his brother friar was that he hoped not just to send a letter to New Mexico by way of the natives but to travel there himself. Díaz blessed his brother priest's designs with some misgiving. He pleaded with Garcés not to do anything too dangerous. Anza was also concerned. He offered Garcés a soldier escort, but the padre would not have it. Only with reluctance did Garcés accept the companionship of one of Anza's servants, who, as the friar put it, "invited himself to stay."[3]

Garcés's plan was to ride directly into the territory of the Yavapais.[4] Their enemies, the Opas and Pimas living on the Gila, persuaded him this was unwise. He should go back downriver to Agua Caliente, whose residents might be able to get the letter to the Yavapais on his behalf. The natives of Agua Caliente, it turned out, had no wish to be part of the effort. But they suggested that the Halchidhomas (Jalchedunes, in Garcés's writings) who lived on the Colorado north of the Yumas, and who carried on trade with the Yavapais and Hopis, might be game. Two Halchidhomas happened to be present at Agua Caliente. Garcés spoke with them through a Pima interpreter, and seeing

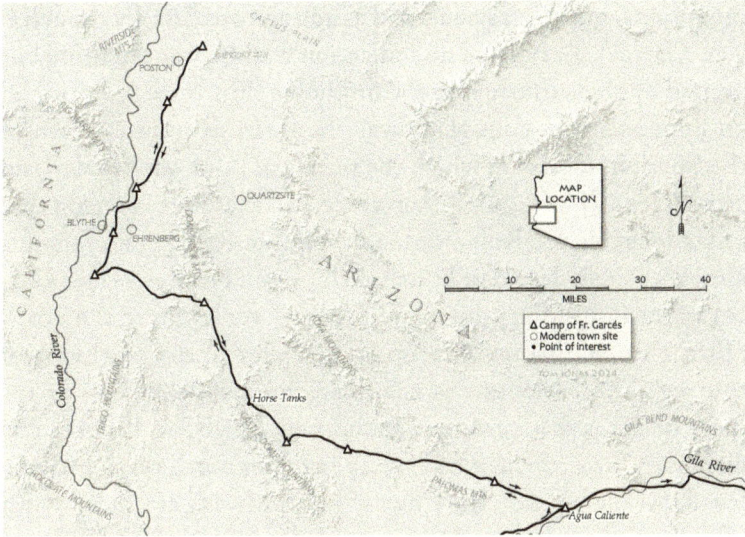

Garcés's explorations northward from the Gila River and along the Colorado, after he left the first Anza expedition's main body in May 1774. Note that Blythe, California, is closer to the western bank of the Colorado River today than it was in the late eighteenth century, when the river was several miles farther east. *Map by Tom Jonas.*

that they "manifested great affection" for him, not to mention that he had at least since 1770 wished to visit their homeland, he decided to go back with them to the Colorado. Anza's servant— "because he would serve me rather than as a burden than as an advantage, he being so timid and pusillanimous, and since I was carrying nothing to eat"—was left behind.[5] This would be no journey for the faint of heart—although, it might be added, one man's timidity was another man's ordinary prudence. What sort of man rode into the unmapped desert, the servant must have wondered, without any food?

With his two Halchidhoma guides, Garcés broke camp at Agua Caliente at noon on May 24. Travel was to the west-northwest. Among Europeans, only Father Sedelmayr, in 1744, had ever rode through this sienna-and-umber country of red-and-black volcanic mountains, gravelly bajadas, and sandy arroyos.[6] Risky though it was, Garcés's diary gives no indication that he was anything but excited by this venture into the unknown. His route led through an unpopulated—*despoblado* was the Spanish term—region of the Sonoran Desert in which the principal flora was brittlebush, creosote, ocotillo, saguaro, palo verde, and mesquite, a region that today includes the Kofa National Wildlife Refuge and remains almost entirely devoid of human habitation. From the clues Garcés leaves in his diary, his route probably took him to the north of the Palomas Mountains, up King Valley to the southwest of the jagged Kofa Mountains, then west through Felipe Pass (in his diary he notes that he named a mountain range San Felipe, so he may have left a toponymical legacy here) on today's dusty Cibola Road. He emerged on the Colorado about five to ten miles south of modern Ehrenberg, Arizona, on May 28, after a journey of some ninety miles.[7]

He would not have emerged anywhere—not alive, anyway—were it not for the charity of his Halchidhoma guides, who of course were traveling on foot. It was an extremely difficult journey, even by the friar's standards, and Garcés was deeply touched by "the pleasure and willingness with which the two Halchidhomas served me on the way and the attention with which they cared for me, giving me of what they carried for their sustenance and saving the water so that I might not lack, the patience with which they beat the horse in order to hurry him up, and the care with which they made stops in order that I might eat." God would one day reward them, he believed, and "show His mercy with these people."[8]

At the Halchidhoma villages Garcés was received with the usual celebrations. He spent the next three days making his way upstream, stopping to visit at the rancherías he encountered and making note of those places that might serve as suitable mission sites. There would be advantages to placing a mission here, he thought. The material culture and beliefs of the Halchidhomas were very similar to the Quechans'. But unlike the Quechans they wore blue cloth and blankets procured from the Hopis and Gileños and built, to his mind, better, larger houses. They also made a tasty bread out of a grain they cultivated. The padre was impressed.[9]

On the 31st of May, Garcés encountered four Yavapais. He asked them to take him to their lands in exchange for a pair of spurs and some scissors. To this bargain they cheerfully assented, but the Halchidhomas argued strenuously against it. They persuaded Garcés that his horse was too worn out to chance a journey into the dry and mountainous interior. Fine, thought Garcés. From here, he would send his letter to the priests in New Mexico, and in it he would ask them to send a neophyte to guide him to their missions; he would wait here on the Colorado for their response. But he soon sensed that this effort was unlikely to be successful. He decided instead to leave the letter with an old Halchidhoma man, who promised to send it to New Mexico "when the mesquite pods were ripe," but he would not wait for a reply.[10] (A good thing, for as far as is known the letter was never received.)

Letter or no letter, the Yavapai men added much to Garcés's understanding of the geography of and peoples living in the area that is now central and northern Arizona. Already Garcés could see that there was no great mountain barrier on the western side of the river. Now he learned from the Yavapais that it was still at least a five-day journey to Moqui, and seven or eight days to the nearest New Mexico mission. Furthermore, in talking to these men he began to sort out the differences between the Yavapais, Apaches, Mohaves, Hopis, and Havasupais, as well as the relationships among them and the places where each people lived.

Although he had given up on the idea of traveling to New Mexico, Garcés was not yet ready to turn around. On June 2 he decided to continue upstream to see the Mohaves, from whom sometime earlier he had received a message that he would be well received. Perhaps he would also visit the Havasupais who lived upriver. On this trip he would travel completely alone, for since the Mohaves were their enemies the Halchidhomas opposed it as much as they did Garcés's going with the Yavapais, and they would therefore not supply guides.

Garcés went north along the eastern side of the Colorado as far as he could until, at sunset, he ascended a hill—today's Mesquite Mountain, about seven miles south of Parker, Arizona—to get his bearings. He got a good look at the V-shaped Riverside Mountains on the California side of the river.[11] On this height, with no food, no water, and an exhausted horse, his conscience pricked him. "Father Juan had ordered me not to put myself in manifest danger," he recalled in his diary, "and not being accompanied by Indians it is very doubtful if I lacked this." There was no need "for doing any more foolish things than those already done," he concluded. And so he turned back to the Halchidhomas.[12]

Garcés rested for a while with his new friends, refreshing himself with the plentiful food they provided and observing with interest their agriculture, customs, and alliances. When he was ready to return to Agua Caliente, he was offered several youths to accompany him—"but I chose only one, knowing the hardships they must face on the painful journey and that I had nothing with which to reward them."[13] This young Halchidhoma man served him with even more kindness than had the padre's original two guides. "He carried a firebrand in one hand all the way, and it did not go out," Garcés marveled. (By passing such a firebrand from one hand to the other the unclothed Halchidhomas managed to warm their bodies, a practice that Spanish observers had noticed among lower Colorado River natives as early as 1538.) "In the other hand he carried a stick with which to drive the horse, which could not hurry for lack of shoes, especially where there were stones. And besides all this he carried a jug of water on his head, enduring thirst in order that I might not suffer, and all this with a smiling face." Not only that, but the young man served as cook, making *atole* for the pair of men when they stopped to eat. All this amid the searing heat and baking sun of the Sonoran Desert summer. "Who will say that this Indian is a savage?" asked Garcés in his diary. "And who will not praise a service of such qualities?"[14] The friar's experiences were revealing that qualities the Spanish associated with "civilization" could be present within other, very different cultures.

Garcés and his horse, now too tired to be ridden, were back on the Gila River on or around June 18, where he exchanged mounts with the kind Cocomaricopas. He had been absent from San Xavier for five and a half months, but still he was in no hurry. Until July 8 he followed the Gila eastward at a leisurely pace, regaining his strength, renewing acquaintances, and happily taking advantage of the hospitality offered by those he encountered. At Uturituc—modern Sweetwater—Garcés was invited to rest for a week; he was so tired that he accepted.[15] Before leaving he concluded that no village more deserved a presidio and mission than this one. Not only was it strategically located and situated among fertile fields, but its people made an "urgent offering of their children for baptism," just as they had been doing since he had first met them six years earlier.[16]

Finally, on July 10, 1774, Garcés arrived back at San Xavier del Bac. He had just missed an official visitation by Father Antonio Ramos, who found that the baptized populations of San Xavier and Tucson were now 160 and 239, respectively—all of them O'odham, and all displaying to Ramos little if any comprehension of Christian doctrine. Tucson had added one hundred residents since 1766, thanks in part to its new fortifications and church. But San Xavier had seen growth in neither Christian understanding nor numbers; in 1766 its population had been 187. This stagnation wasn't entirely the fault of Garcés and his substitutes. Thanks to a lack of water, Ramos complained, the neophytes of San Xavier and Tucson tended to "wander" in search of food, and as a consequence it was difficult to instruct them effectively.[17] (What Ramos called "wandering" was the O'odham's typical and quite deliberate pattern of seasonal food-gathering.)

Of course, Garcés had done little to prevent such "wandering." He was inclined toward patient acceptance—to play the long game once a mission had been established. Garcés never claimed to have had success in growing the church at San Xavier, nor to have helped the mission make material advances. While in residence he seems rather to have succored his flock the best he could, and otherwise to have focused his energies on helping New Spain create and implement a strategy that would give all the Pimería Alta's missions a fighting chance to flourish.

In any case, Garcés spent just a couple of weeks reacquainting himself with his charges before riding upstream along the Santa Cruz to Tumacácori, where he asked Fathers Clemente and Moreno to make a clean copy of his otherwise all but illegible diary.[18] He had concluded that report with no expressions of weariness, no reflections on what he had accomplished, no delight at being reunited with his neophytes after an absence of more than six months. He was preoccupied with one fundamental question: how to find a better road to Monterey.

✳ ✳ ✳

A better route from Sonora to Monterey was one of the issues occupying the minds of many Spanish officials in 1774 and 1775. It was linked in those minds with other pressing matters: How could the Spanish presence on the Pacific coast be secured? How could more missions be established there and elsewhere on the frontier? How could communication and commerce with New Mexico be achieved? And how could the Apaches finally be, if not conquered, at least subdued?

Viceroy Bucareli was among those pondering these questions. New possibilities came into view as, sitting at his desk in the magnificent royal palace, he received and reflected on the field reports he received from Juan Bautista Anza, Father Juan Díaz, Father Francisco Garcés, and Juan Bautista Valdés on the progress of their journey to distant Monterey.

Valdés was the first of their company to arrive in Mexico City. On June 14, 1774, he gave Bucareli the diaries he was couriering as well as a formal personal statement on the expedition's warm reception by Salvador Palma at the Colorado-Gila junction, its terrible difficulties in crossing the desert, its successful arrival at San Gabriel, its gathering of fresh provisions at San Diego, and Captain Anza's lightning ride to Monterey.[19] As more details filtered in from the field (including supplemental diaries from Díaz and Garcés), Bucareli became increasingly enthusiastic about the expedition's success. "There is no longer any doubt," he exulted, "that the presidios of Sonora and Monterey can join hands more easily" now than formerly.[20] He was convinced of the expedition's significance; indeed, there was "no project of greater importance in this province today."[21] He was equally impressed with the qualities of the men to whom he had entrusted this mission. He asked Julián de Arriaga at the Council of the Indies in Madrid to promote Anza to lieutenant-colonel of cavalry. He also requested that each of the soldiers who accompanied Anza be given an extra *escudo*—a gold coin worth eight pesos—every month for the rest of their lives.[22] Then Bucareli began formulating a strategy for building upon the new, quite amazing fact that there was now a usable road from the settlements of Sonora to the missions of Alta California.[23]

By the time Anza arrived in Mexico City that autumn—to Bucareli's great annoyance, he was detained for several months by a frontier military official who was blithely unaware of how badly the viceroy wanted to see him—Bucareli had conceived the captain's next assignment. The recently discovered port of San Francisco, although it needed to be much more thoroughly explored (was the rumor true, for instance, that a great river flowed into it from the east?), clearly had strategic significance. A presidio ought to be established there. So, too, according to Father Junípero Serra, should missions—two of them, in fact, for which Serra had ready and willing pastors-in-waiting with him at Mission San Carlos Borromeo in Carmel. But soldiers were needed to staff that new presidio. And California also needed *settlers* so that it could begin to produce its own food and supplies and thus relieve the royal treasury of the burden of its support.

Another Anza-led expedition could solve both problems, thought Bucareli. Let him take to California thirty married soldiers, their families, and plentiful animals and supplies. The men would staff the new presidio at San Francisco. Their women and children would begin to fill the land with Spaniards. And the presence of wives would offer protection for the native women.

In the meantime, everything possible should be done to ensure that Salvador Palma and his Quechans remained friendly to the Spaniards. Bucareli directed the commander at Altar, Bernardo de Urrea, and the governor of Sonora, Don Francisco Antonio Crespo, to provide the Quechans with clothes, presents, everything except arms in order to maintain their friendship. For Bucareli's plan to work, the road through Yuma must remain open.

Anza responded with eager willingness to Bucareli's request that he lead a second expedition. He had traveled through the towns of Culiacán, Sinaloa, and El Fuerte on his way to Mexico City and had noticed that most of their residents were "submerged in the direst poverty and misery."[24] He had no doubt that a sufficient number "would most willingly and gladly embrace" the opportunity to emigrate to San Francisco.[25] He would merely need to make soldiers of these recruits, which he proposed to do by selecting five veteran military men from among the presidios of Sonora to serve as their officers. As escort, he wished to take along ten of those men who had proved their mettle on his last expedition. The new recruits and their families would need to be supplied for the journey with, quite literally, everything—"from shoes to hair ribbons," as Anza put it.[26] Finally, he would need many cattle, good saddle animals, and colorful beads and tobacco for the Indians (see the Appendix for a full list). This would be a massive undertaking.

On November 28, 1774, Bucareli agreed to everything Anza had requested, asking only that the captain present to his court a detailed estimate of expenses, and adding that "it appears desirable that Father Garcés or another companion should go with the expedition as far as the Colorado River," where it was expected that the friar would solidify relations with the Quechans until Anza returned from Monterey.[27] Anza was willing—if not particularly happy—to travel with Garcés again. Because the latitudinal coordinates of various places along the route were of great interest to everyone involved, he also accepted the proposed inclusion of Father Pedro Font, a Franciscan based in Sonora who was both capable of taking geographic measurements and a good draftsman and writer. For those reasons, among others, Font had been proposed by the College of Santa Cruz as an appropriate participant in the project.[28]

By December 5, Anza and an official named José de Echeveste had drafted an itemized memorandum of necessary supplies, along with an estimate of their cost: 21,927 pesos. The inventory provides a fascinating glimpse into the lives and customs of Sonoran *paisanos* in the latter part of the eighteenth century. One notes, for example, that Anza and Echeveste assumed both an average of six children per couple and that the families (doubtless the mothers) would make the children's clothing themselves.[29] A Council of War and Royal Exchequer held on December 16, 1774, approved it all. The second Anza expedition was officially a go.

※ ※ ※

Garcés was with Father Díaz at the Sonora town of Ures in March 1775 when he received a letter from Bucareli dated January 2. Therein he learned of his assigned role in the second expedition. He was no less eager than Anza to serve his country. But he was left with questions: Why was he supposed to go only as far as the Colorado? And why was he to wait there until Anza's return? Bucareli's letter was silent on these matters. The viceroy said simply, and vaguely, that he wished for Garcés to remain at the Colorado "in order to do that which it appears to me may be of interest to the service," adding that "in this interim your Reverence may be free to examine the sites, treat with the neighboring tribes, and to ascertain the spirit and disposition of the natives toward the catechism and toward vassalage to our sovereign."[30]

Bucareli's letter found Garcés in Ures because, apparently unbeknownst to the viceroy, Garcés was at that moment en route to see him. Thanks to the groundwork laid by Garcés's explorations, the College of Santa Cruz had divested itself of its missions in the mostly tamed Pimería Baja in order to focus its resources on the Pimería Alta.[31] Its authorities had asked Garcés to make the long trip to Querétaro for a conference. From there, it was thought, he would proceed to Mexico City, where he would present Bucareli his reflections on the frontier's conditions and peoples, as well as the colegio's ideas on where to found new missions and, by extension, presidios.

This was not a journey Garcés was keen to take. "If truth be told," he had written the colegio's guardian on January 12 of that year, "I can find out more regarding the rivers than anyone else because I have been here so long and have interacted [successfully] with the Indians."[32] But he was apparently on his way when the viceroy's letter changed his travel plans. Allegedly because he was "suffering from some indisposition," as Díaz put it, but possibly because he remained reluctant to make the long trip, Garcés decided not to continue to Mexico City. Instead, with Díaz's quasi-coauthorship, he decided instead to reply to Bucareli's letter.[33]

In his response to the viceroy, Garcés shared his opinions with customary boldness. A better road to Monterey than the one followed in 1774 badly had to be found, he began, but Anza would be in no position to do so with two-hundred-odd settlers in his train. A separate expedition therefore should also be sent, "on the express business of inspecting the country and assuring the road, not only to the River of San Francisco, but also to New Mexico."[34] The man to do that, proposed Garcés, was Sonora's Governor Crespo—with whom, as Garcés does not mention in his letter, he had met in the fall of 1774.[35] Furthermore, rather than pull back the presidial line and expose Tubac, Tumacácori, San Xavier, and Tucson to ruin at the hands of the Apaches, as had been ordered by the Spanish crown in the Reglamento of 1772, the garrisons should be pushed forward to the Gila.

In other words, Garcés had not forgotten the scheme he had outlined in 1772. He had simply refined it. The Tubac presidio should be moved northeast, near the Gila–San Pedro junction. The Terrenate presidio should be moved to the Santa Cruz. And the Altar presidio should be placed on the Colorado, eighty or so miles north of its junction with the Gila (in or near the Halchidhoma homeland). The advantages of this plan were numerous: the fight could be taken more effectively to the Apaches; new missions could be placed safely on the Gila and Colorado; the way to Monterey would be more effectively secured; and the edge of the Sonoran frontier would be pushed that much closer to New Mexico. Garcés even enclosed a diagram showing where everything ought, ideally, to be placed.[36]

The long Garcés-Díaz letter included many additional details and arguments pertaining to the eagerness of the Gileño Pimas for ministers, ways to mitigate costs, military tactics that could be used against the Apaches, and other items.[37] In truth, it was not at all a bad plan. Crespo, for one, bought in entirely when he met with Garcés in September 1774; he had himself already written Bucareli to much the same effect. To Bucareli's credit, he took the friars seriously. "I at once recognized that this project was well thought out," he reported to Minister Arriaga, and so he requested his commandant-inspector, Hugo O'Conor, both to consider the padres' arguments and to speak to Crespo and Urrea about them.[38]

In the meantime, the second expedition, which Bucareli hoped would shed more light on the subject of garrison placement, would proceed as planned.[39] To Garcés's objection that his remaining alone on the Colorado would accomplish little or nothing, the viceroy replied that the friar did not have to go on the expedition at all. Since this was an even worse outcome, Garcés backed down, assuring Bucareli that he had been misunderstood; he absolutely wanted to be part of the expedition and was "happy

to cooperate in everything I am assigned."[40] Fortunately, the viceroy did accede to Garcés's request that four soldiers (even though,
wrote the friar, ten or twelve would be more appropriate), two
interpreters, two servants, and two muleteers remain with him
on the Colorado River.[41] He also provided, at Garcés's request, a
companion in Father Tomás Eixarch, a short, black-eyed, zealous
missionary born near Valencia and now resident at Tumacácori.
Eixarch could stay put at the Gila-Colorado junction while Garcés explored.[42]

Bucareli also made it clear, at Anza's instigation, that the friars
were to be subordinate to the captain's command; the proud and
sensitive Anza had too often felt second-guessed by Garcés and
Díaz in 1774.[43] "Must they interfere in everything as happened on
the last expedition?" he inquired plaintively of Bucareli, especially
given that, as Spanish-born priests, they were "of a different class"
and "do not have the experience or knowledge that I have?"[44]

Friars may have seemed mere encumbrances to Anza but, if
exploration was what the viceroy wanted, Garcés was destined
not to disappoint him.[45]

✳ ✳ ✳

Thanks in large part to the wonderful diary kept by Father Font,
the second Anza expedition is even better documented than the
first. It has also been studied more intensively. Its diaries have
been published, sometimes in multiple translations.[46] Several
books have told its story.[47] Its campsites have been located.[48]
There is a National Historic Trail, maintained by the National
Park Service, that follows the route as closely as possible along
major Arizona and California highways. Descendants of the settlers who made the journey can join a group called Los Californianos.[49] There is also an organization of volunteers, the Anza
Trail Color Guard, which from time to time reenacts portions
of the expedition. Yet, despite all this, and despite the fact that
it led directly to the founding of a great American city in San

Francisco and indirectly to the founding of another great American city in Los Angeles, the Anza expedition of 1775–76 is not a journey with which most Americans are even remotely familiar. That is even truer, of course, with respect to Garcés's improvised branch of the expedition, an eight-month, two-thousand-mile trek unparalleled in the annals of American exploration.

As the year 1775 proceeded, Anza concentrated on the daunting tasks of recruiting settlers, finding good animals, and gathering adequate supplies. Remarkably, by May the newly commissioned lieutentant-colonel had his group of soldiers and settlers on the move. His starting point was Culiacán. From there he marched through the towns of Sinaloa and El Fuerte, gathering what recruits and animals he could, a task he found more difficult than expected, thanks to the fears large families had of embarking on so risky a journey.[50] From El Fuerte he continued to Horcasitas, where a final rendezvous of all persons and provisions was to be effected. His plan was to leave Horcasitas for Tubac in early to mid-September, after the end of the rainy season. To beat the weather—the cold chill of the desert nights, especially—it was important to stay on schedule.

Father Pedro Font met the group on May 23, when Anza passed through the friar's mission of San José de Pimas. Font had come to New Spain in 1763 on the same ship as Garcés, but unlike Garcés he had until very recently remained stationed at the College of Santa Cruz. The pale, somewhat chunky friar's talents were more academic, even artistic, than they were physical. Font had the persnickety temperament of a librarian and the sensitive soul of a musician, and his service to the college—which included arranging and copying music for the choir, and probably also organizing its archives—had reflected those qualities.[51] It must have been believed that he did more good for the colegio's cause in such positions than he could have on the wild frontier.

Yet finally his time had come. Font had recently been assigned to the relatively benign Piméria Baja. Now, with the Queretarans about to give up their missions in that region, the colegio nominated him to the viceroy as the perfect friar to accompany Anza. Font could take measurements with myriad instruments, he was an excellent draftsman who could make accurate maps, and he was a wonderful writer whose diary would surely excel that of any other, especially that of the good Father Garcés. Font also had a heavy pastoral touch, not to mention a compulsive need to be critical, but no missionary was perfect. In any case, Font the bookish nerd and Anza the square-jawed soldier would prove to make for an awkward combination.

In May 1775 that awkwardness had not yet manifested itself. After greeting the slow-moving party as it marched through San José, Font let it go on its way, not catching up to it until August 2, when he met the expedition at Horcasitas. Here there was a long delay while Anza finished gathering the needed animals and supplies. On September 13 the commander was nearly ready to go when—maddeningly, unbelievably, yet all too predictably—a messenger from Tubac arrived saying that Apache raiders had swept through the presidio and relieved it of its entire remuda: five hundred horses. It was December 1773 all over again. After Anza had managed to resupply himself with some mounts, a stampede robbed him of yet more animals. An unspecified sickness also led to the death of three recruits.[52] Then there was another reason for delay. In an unguarded moment—of which he had many—Font confessed to a friend of Anza's wife that it would be ideal if the party could delay leaving until September 29, the Feast of Saint Michael, one of the expedition's patron saints. That was just what Señora Anza, who was looking for any reason to postpone her husband's departure, wanted to hear. An exasperated Anza grudgingly assented to what he was told to be Font's dearest wish, and the seeds of discord were effectively sown.[53]

The group that finally left Horcasitas on September 29 included 302 head of cattle, 140 pack mules, 450 saddle animals, and 277 men, women, and children; the oldest settler was but forty-seven; ninety-two were under the age of twelve. Font took care, during that morning's Mass, to exhort his companions "to

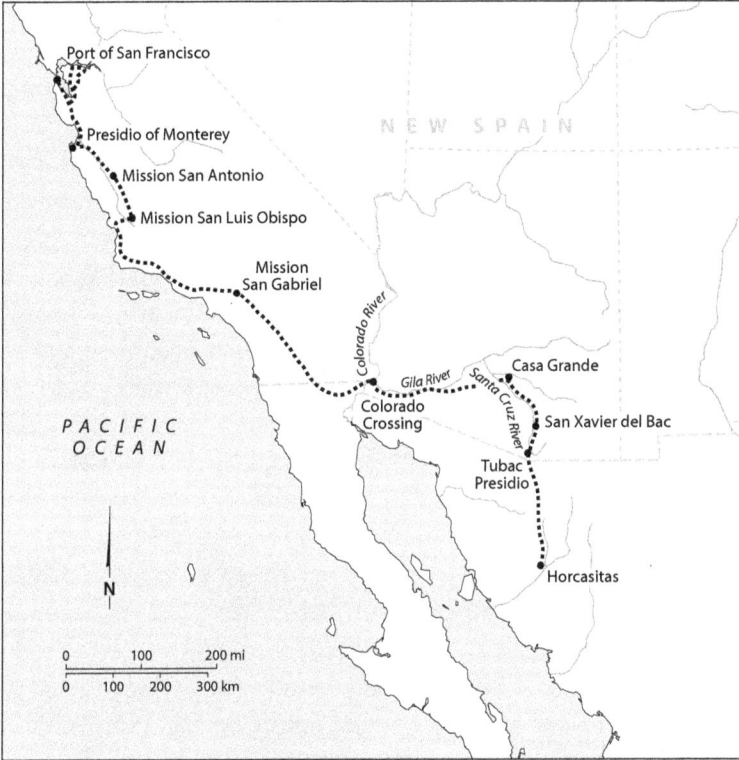

Route taken, September 1775 to March 1776, by the second Anza expedition, from Horcasitas to Monterey and San Francisco. Garcés accompanied the expedition only as far as the junction of the Gila and Colorado rivers at today's Yuma, Arizona, marked as "Colorado Crossing" on this map. *Map by Bill Nelson. From Kittle,* Franciscan Frontiersmen, *109. Used by permission of the University of Oklahoma Press.*

endurance during the hardships of traveling, and above all to the fact that they must give a good example to the gentiles, so as not to shock them in any way."[54] Such a large party was prone to stretching along the trail for dangerously long distances, which made Anza anxious. For good reason: Apaches stole four mares one day, a mule on another, and had a history of harassing the

Sonoran ranches through which the expedition marched. Font, in the meantime, quickly proved to be a high-maintenance sort, repeatedly requesting the commander for a servant and generally acting like one utterly inexperienced in frontier life.

When the party reached the presidio of Tubac on October 15, 1775, Anza could exhale, at least for a while. One of the most dangerous parts of the journey had been successfully traversed. Here the commander was met, as promised, by Garcés and Eixarch, as well as by Father Pedro Arrequíbar, minister at nearby Tumacácori, and by Father Félix Gamarra, who had been assigned to serve as Garcés's new substitute at San Xavier. A week passed as Anza got everything in order for what would now be a journey into genuine wilderness. Font spent most of it in bed with diarrhea. Taking pity on the padre, Anza relented and assigned him a personal servant. By Sunday, October 22, at a Mass he concelebrated with Garcés, Font had recovered enough to deliver another stem-winding homily in which he compared the expeditioners to the Israelites on the road to Canaan.

The next day the full expedition would finally be on its way. With Father Font around, it would not be boring. Nor would it be lightly chronicled.

✳ ✳ ✳

Francisco Garcés had spent much of the fifteen months between his return to San Xavier in July 1774 and his departure for Tubac in October 1775 lobbying for frontier expansion. That was something both Anza and Garcés wanted. But with respect to how it might be achieved, they did not always see eye to eye. In his official correspondence, such as his diaries, Garcés nearly always spoke highly of Anza and his abilities. But privately, mistrust had grown between the two men. From Anza's point of view, Garcés remained too much of a wild card. He resented the friar's opinionated independence. From Garcés's point of view, Anza was a touchy and unreliable ally. He probably knew that Anza had viciously criticized the missions in 1772. Anza did not share Garcés's passion for finding a more northerly route to or from Monterey. And although Anza had sworn, upon his return from the 1774 expedition, that he favored the founding of seven or eight new missions and would say as much to his superiors, Garcés had concluded that Anza "says something different in different company." He had not trusted Anza personally to convey his, Garcés's, views on the new missions to Bucareli when Anza left the frontier for Mexico City in August 1774, sending instead his own private letter for the viceroy. Anza resented that, and relations became further strained.[55]

Garcés's suspicions were well founded. Anza had told Bucareli in January 1775 that he supported the placement of four new missions on the Colorado, to be protected by unusually strong garrisons, but not missions on the Gila, which he thought would be too exposed to Apache raids and violence. Anza added that Garcés was the ideal missionary for the proposed Colorado River missions, thanks to "his great devotion, spirit, and natural genius" for the delicate job at hand.[56] Was Anza being honest, or was he seizing a golden opportunity to transfer a troublesome priest to an outpost far away from Tubac? Perhaps a little of both. In any case, before returning to San Xavier from Ures, Garcés had argued to the College of Santa Cruz's Father Guardian for the necessity of building Spanish settlements, not just missions, on the Colorado if that gateway to Alta California were to be held over the long term—a prescient and rather extraordinary suggestion for a frontier missionary at this time, when the general idea was to keep neophytes as far away from frontier Spaniards as possible. Garcés had also proactively deflected a rumor about his being made president of the new missions, suggesting Díaz for the post instead. After all, he remarked, how could he be the missions' president when he could hardly write his own letters?[57]

Upon his return to San Xavier from Ures, Garcés had also composed a summary of his entradas from 1768 through 1774.[58] Soon, Father Gamarra had arrived to serve as Garcés's temporary replacement.[59] Then, on August 20, 1775, Garcés had witnessed the formal (but not yet material) transfer of the presidio of Tubac to Tucson by Commandant-Inspector O'Conor, a variant implementation of the Reglamento that to Garcés's mind was much better than that originally planned, since it represented what he most desired: a forward advance of the presidial line. Still, it also represented a lost opportunity to place a presidio even farther north, on the Gila.

O'Conor had been none too pleased to hear from Bucareli that Garcés and Díaz had proferred their own thoughts on where garrisons should be placed, preposterously accusing them of making suggestions based on theory rather than practical knowledge of the terrain. So when they met, Garcés laid on the charm, praising O'Conor's choice of Tucson and promising him that until permanent residences were built at Tucson for the presidial troops the O'odham there would erect temporary shelters for them.[60] As irritated as O'Conor may have been when he first heard Garcés's thoughts on presidios, he ultimately agreed with his main points, moving Terrenate forward to the San Pedro River, as the friar had suggested, and Fronteras forward to the San Bernardino Valley.[61]

One thing Garcés had learned on his travels was that, given the language barriers separating Spaniards from Indians, and often enough Indians from Indians, pictures and images offered a surer way to communicate than did words; the crucifix he wore around his neck, for example, seemed always to be of great interest. And so, thinking perhaps of the homiletic stratagem employed by Father Antonio Garcés back in their native Aragón, during this interim period at San Xavier he acquired, or had made, a painted canvas banner that had on one side an image of the Madonna and Child, and on the other an image of a man suffering the torments of Hell. He thought the canvas would come in handy in the explorations he intended to undertake after leaving the Anza expedition on the Colorado. He wasn't wrong.

On October 23, 1775, the Colorado was still more than a month's march away. And though no more horses were stolen, the expedition's first days out from Tubac were inauspicious. After a windy, dusty march, the group had just stopped for the first night's camp, about fourteen miles north of Tubac at a place on the Santa Cruz called La Canoa, when one of the women, María Ignacia Manuela Piñuelas, began to suffer labor pains. A hospital tent was hastily erected, and at nine o'clock that night the woman gave birth to a "very lusty boy," in Anza's words. Then trouble set in. The baby had been born feet first, the afterbirth could not be removed, complications continued to arise, and in the middle of the night, having received the last rites from Garcés, Eixarch, and Font, the young mother died. The next morning Garcés and four soldiers rode ahead to San Xavier del Bac with the corpse. Garcés said a funeral Mass on the morning of the 25th, and that afternoon Father Eixarch baptized the baby boy. How the bereft husband and new father handled this tragedy is left unstated by the expedition's diarists.[62]

While Garcés was away, four couples approached Font and asked to be married. Font examined them and found three of the pairs eligible for the sacrament. (He found the woman in the fourth pair to have broken off a previous engagement without her fiancé's consent and therefore refused to oblige her and her beau; Font was about the last priest to bend a canonical regulation.) The three couples were married by Font before Mass on the morning of Thursday, October 26, in the leaky church at San Xavier del Bac, which helped reintroduce some cheer to the journey.[63] No one could say that the leg from Tubac to San Xavier had been uneventful.

By 8:30 that morning the expedition was again moving forward. It is worth pausing here to note what was necessary, each day, to get the party on its way. First, the horses and mules had to be brought in from wherever they were grazing. Then each family had to retrieve its own animals. Tents—for those few who had them; there were only thirteen on the trip—had to be broken down, supplies packed, horses and mules saddled and loaded. While all this was happening, one or more of the priests typically said Mass. Font tells us how things went from there:

> When the pack trains were ready to set out, our commander would say ¡Vayan subiendo!, "Start mounting up!," and we all got on horseback and the march at once began, forming into a line in the following fashion. Four soldiers went in front scouting out the way; our commander rode on point in the vanguard; then came myself; and behind me followed the people—men, women, and children—along with the soldiers escorting and watching over their families, and the line was closed by the lieutenant in the rear guard; afterward usually came the pack trains, then the loose mounts, and the livestock last of all: all of which together formed a very long line.[64]

Where Garcés and Eixarch fit into this formation Font does not say. Presumably they were not as concerned as he about their position.

At the beginning and end of the day's march Font would chant the Alabado, the people—he hoped—responding as appropriate. At night each family prayed the rosary (such, at least, was Font's claim) and ended its prayer with the Alabado or Salve Regina or perhaps "some other thing, each group in its own fashion, so that, what with the variety of sound, it was a pleasant thing to hear," at least to a cleric concerned about the salvation of the settlers' souls.

Given the large number of people involved, camp was rarely quiet. Nor, despite the grime and dust, was it gray. With the material Anza had provided and whatever they had brought from home, the people did their best to dress in the colorful style of the time. Red and navy blue were the dominant shades. The soldiers wore blue trousers, short blue jackets with gilt buttons and red collars, and blue cloaks.[65] Anza had also provided each settler with a hat, round and stiff with silver piping, if possible, as trim. It was often decorated with a ribbon. The long hair underneath was tied close to the head or braided in a plait. The men must have felt blessed to also have been given three pairs of underwear, three pairs of shoes (probably open-toed), two pairs of buckskin boots, two pairs of hose, two pairs of pants, two jackets that reached just below the hip, two blankets, and a cape.[66] The women had been outfitted with three chemises, three petticoats, two skirts, one underskirt, two pairs of stockings and hose, two shawls (*rebozos*), and a hat, as well as six Spanish yards (*varas*, about thirty-three inches in length) of ribbon and two Spanish yards of linen with which to make their own jackets. Their skirts were worn long, with a blouse that ended at the waist and closed at the neck. Their hair was, like that of their menfolk, usually worn braided. Ribbons were worn therein, with the rebozo as a head covering. Both sexes, as well as children over ten years old, smoked *cigarros* (akin to cigarettes) or *puros* (more like cigars) to the extent supplies allowed.[67]

Camp on the night of October 26 was made just a little beyond the visita of Tucson—the last vestige of Spanish civilization, noted Anza, that they would encounter until they reached the California missions. Anza was nervous about the next several days' marches. It was necessary now to leave the Santa Cruz and its abundant grasses and golden-leaved trees, and there would be no water until they hit the Gila, more than fifty miles distant. That was three days away. In addition, the expedition was about to ride as close to Apache territory as it would get—and, as Font pointed out, the soldiers, who often rode carrying two or three of their young ones in their arms, were not exactly always ready to fight. Camp on the evening of the 27th was apparently dry, but fortunately the expedition encountered plentiful pools of water on the 28th.

In the meantime, there was more drama. Two muleteers deserted the party on the 27th. They were quickly apprehended by Pima Indians with whom Anza entrusted the task, and like the Indian who killed one of his horses in 1774 they were soundly whipped; in such matters Anza's administration of justice was evenhanded. Garcés had his own run-in with the commander. He had been promised some saddle animals, but now Anza, who was not above such pettiness, told him he had none to give, in response to which "Father Garcés spoke to him rather plainly, which the commander showed that he resented very much," recorded Font.[68]

On the 29th, Anza ensured that everyone attended Mass, at which he proclaimed the penalties that would be imposed upon "anyone who should violate women, especially heathen, or steal their goods." By this point, thanks to the punishment given the muleteers, it must have been clear to all that the commander was deadly serious. "Under the same penalties," reported Anza in his diary, "I forbade anyone to raise arms against the heathen in the country through which we pass, except in a case of necessity for the defense of life, or at my orders, and likewise against anyone who should spread any report which might withdraw these heathen from the true religion and the dominion of his majesty." The Gileños had been nothing but friendly to the Spanish and Christianity. Anza, no less than Garcés, who thought the commander's speech manifested Anza's "sure sense of what was fitting," aimed to keep it that way.[69] To everyone's relief, the Gila was reached without incident on the 30th.

The Gileños received the expedition with their customary graciousness. They presented as gifts the scalps of two Apaches they had recently killed, and they made their usual inquiries as to when they would receive padres to live with them and baptize their children. On the 31st, while the main body of the expedition rested, the Gileños led Anza, the friars, and some of the soldiers on a side trip to see the Casa Grande—or the Casa de Moctezuma, as the Spaniards frequently called it. Font made a signal contribution to anthropology by recording the stories the Gileños told about the structure's origins and the fate of the people who had constructed it. Much later, after he had visited the Hopis, Garcés concluded that it was the Hopis' forebears, not the ancient Aztecs, who had built the huge structure on the Gila, for their own houses looked not dissimilar, and their pottery resembled some of the shards found at Casa Grande. We now know that Garcés's thesis was closer to the truth than was the commonly received notion about the Aztecs.[70]

Garcés's disposition allowed him to appreciate the accomplishments and virtues of the O'odham who lived on the Gila more fully than could someone like Font, who, at least at first, saw "nothing worth praising in this entire country." Even when he was impressed by the natives he met, as he was at the Gila River ranchería the Spaniards entered on November 1 (today's Sweetwater), Font could not help but note how "ugly" and "foul-smelling" they were.[71] If Garcés's perceptions were the same, he gave them no voice. At this village the Spaniards were greeted much as Father Kino had often been. About a thousand men and women lined up in two lines, separated by sex, below a ramada they had constructed for the purpose and in front of which they had planted a large cross. Each greeted the commander and fathers by shaking their hands and saying, in a blend of Spanish and their native O'odham tongue, "God favor you all."[72] They carried water from the river for the Spaniards and slaughtered some of their sheep for a feast. Garcés was equal parts amazed at their charity and distressed at his inability to offer them the baptism for which they asked. All the Spaniards could do was give them some tobacco, beads, and hope that they would soon return on a permanent basis. Since it was the same as the one spoken at San Xavier, Garcés was able to preach to them in their own language. Indeed, for all his difficulties with writing, he was one of the very few priests on the Sonoran frontier with the linguistic ability to do that. He also displayed his new canvas painting of Mary and the Damned Man. He did the same the next day at the village of Sutaquisón (Sacate).

To avoid the river's detour to the north, and because he had been told there was water along the way, Anza led the expedition cross-country toward what later became Gila Bend on Friday, November 3. It was a short, flat trek of only five or six miles to the reported pools. It was also a rainy and slippery march, which

Anza says was especially annoying to the women of the party. But at least there was water, and soon camp was made for the night.

The expedition was now just a few miles south of the future Phoenix metropolitan area.[73] The low South Mountain range lay to its north, with the much higher pointed peaks of the Sierra Estrella to the west. Garcés had sung Mass—Font accompanying him on his psaltery, a small harplike instrument—and Anza had just given the order to raise camp on Saturday the 4th when a soldier rushed up. His wife was gravely ill and unable to travel. Anza sincerely wished to avoid any further loss of life, so he reversed his order and had the woman attended to as well as possible. To mollify the people, and since it was the feast of the king's namesake, Saint Charles, he distributed to each person a pint of fruit brandy (*aguardiente*). The resulting drunkenness, though it was mild, deeply troubled Font (Garcés, predictably, took no notice of the episode).

The woman was still sick the next day. Anza was waiting as patiently as he could for her to recover when another woman suddenly went into labor. Her "violent child-bearing pains" were such "that it was thought she would die."[74] She too was given what medicine was available. With two women now seriously sick, Monday the 6th was again spent in camp. Some folks were now calling the place Las Lagunas del Hospital. Not a little had gone wrong since the expedition had left Tubac—or since its horse herd had been stolen, for that matter. To Font and surely many others, this scrubby part of the Sonoran Desert was "quite an ugly country" to boot.[75]

On the 7th, Anza decided that although the women were faring no better the expedition had no choice but to forge ahead. The water at Las Lagunas was too saline for the people to drink (for that purpose water had to be carried from the Gila), and now it was making the horses sick, too. Two of them died on that day's march through the almost level, creosote-dotted desert, during which the "sufferings of the sick women continued."[76]

On November 8, Gila Bend was finally reached. At least now the expedition was back on the river.

As was becoming his habit, Garcés preached and presented his canvas to the mixed group of Opas and Pimas living at Gila Bend, after which he "asked them if they wished with all their hearts to be Christians and to admit the missionary priests to their lands and they answered, with great pleasure, yes."[77] His images, reflected the friar, were serving well the ends of evangelization. Font meanwhile continued to record with disarming frankness his reactions to the unusual customs of the Indians he met. The body and face painting of the Opas and Cocomaricopas living at Gila Bend drew his attention, as did their nose and ear piercings. Nor could he help but notice that their mesquite-bean-heavy diet led to flatulence. When they gathered together to receive beads and tobacco from Anza, there was "no small stink from their windiness, which they let go without reserve," he reported.[78] The expedition would later observe this same freedom on the Colorado, when a Quechan man "let out a formidable fart, and although the commander told him that was not something that was done, he kept smiling quite undisturbed."[79] Junípero Serra, too, had been caught by surprise when traveling in Baja California on the way to found San Diego in 1769. His party had encountered a lone old man, and Serra had begun to talk to him about the faith and other matters, when, in Serra's words, "while he was standing there in the midst of our circle conversing with us, he squatted and, since he was untrammeled by clothes, he straightway relieved nature while he continued to speak to us."[80] It was hard for Europeans to get used to that sort of thing.

Anza remained at Gila Bend for three days. There was too much sickness within the group to be in any kind of hurry. The woman who had suffered the miscarriage was still very ill, as were several other members of the party; a soldier had suffered some kind of stroke; Father Font continued to suffer intermittently from diarrhea, chills, and vomiting; and Father Eixarch was battling a fever. On the 14th the group arrived at Agua Caliente, the place from which Garcés had departed with the Halchidhomas the year previous. The party remained there the next day, the families washing their clothes in the river, the soldiers doing some scouting, and Anza and the friars treating with the two hundred Cocomaricopas who arrived to greet them. It was getting cold. The hot water that emerged from the springs quickly became chilly in the people's water bags, and with nighttime temperatures dropping below freezing expeditioners awoke in the morning with teeth chattering. Regardless, the Cocomaricopas, who had of course met Garcés in his previous travels, were friendly and stayed up well into the night "singing their own kind of music, quite a mournful one."[81] Anza and Garcés were happy to learn they had made peace with the Yumas, Garcés noting with satisfaction that so long as the peace lasted it would prevent many deaths.

Here at Agua Caliente, Garcés gave a sermon on basic Christian teachings and was told by his audience that a mission and padres would be welcomed. In that case, he and Anza thought it well to appoint, in the name of the king, one of the Cocomaricopas as the people's governor and another as its alcalde, as Anza had done in villages farther up the Gila. But unlike Christian theology, this attempt to establish Spanish law raised questions. "Look here," said an old man to Garcés. "A magistrate's duty is to punish evil, and as we are not bad, why the magistrate? You Spaniards have already seen that we are not thievish, nor quarrelsome, and even if we are near a woman we do nothing wrong." Garcés smiled at this riposte. "My faith in their goodness does not extend so far," he wrote in his diary, "although this . . . nation is quite as worthy as the Pima."[82] Anza went ahead with the appointments and the accompanying instructions. Whatever they made of all this talk, the man who was appointed governor took his new duties so seriously that, apparently out of fright, "for more than an hour he did not cease to tremble so hard that he appeared to be shivering from the severest chill."[83] So claimed Anza.

They were now only ninety miles from the Colorado. On the 16th, Anza raised camp. He also sent four scouts ahead to apprise Salvador Palma of their impending arrival and to see if they could find a better road to the place called San Sebastián, the first place beyond the Colorado that the Spanish knew to be a halfway decent watering spot. For the next eleven days the expedition plodded downriver through the sandy, yellow soil and gray-green brush, its members doing their best to avoid choking on the immense clouds of dust raised by their great train. Garcés's painted canvas saw little use, since no one lived on this part of the Gila, a sort of no-man's-land that provided ample separation between the Quechans and their erstwhile Cocomaricopa enemies. On the 18th of November some of the latter rode into camp in order to join Anza in going to the Yumas and having their peace with them ratified in the commander's presence. In the early morning hours of the 19th, the woman who had suffered labor pains back at Las Lagunas del Hospital went into labor and gave birth to a baby boy, the fourth child born since the expedition had left Culiacán and the second since it had left Tubac on October 23. He was given the name Diego Pascual and baptized the next day by Father Font. To allow his mother to recover, Anza stayed put until the 22nd.[84]

They were no longer in danger from Apaches or dehydration, but here in one of North America's hottest deserts it was bitterly cold, much colder than is typically the case today, thanks to the Little Ice Age, a global cooling phenomenon that would not reach its end until the next century. Six animals had died from exposure, wrote Anza, and on the 23rd many of the party's cows became entangled in the mesquite thickets that lined the river, necessitating another day's delay. Then another pregnant woman began to go into labor prematurely, and to prevent another miscarriage and nurse her back to health Anza stayed in camp yet a day longer. Nothing about this expedition seemed to be easy. On November 27, soon after Anza had made camp at a spot about fifteen miles east of the Colorado-Gila junction, Palma and thirty of his warriors rode into camp. The Spaniards had finally reached the land of the Yumas.

✳ ✳ ✳

It did not take long for Palma to show that his disposition toward the Christians had not changed. He embraced the expedition's leaders warmly and made a present of *yorimuni* beans to the commander, with whom it was not long until he was engaged in a deep and wide-ranging conversation. Palma had much he wished to say.[85]

He wished for the Spanish to come live in the Quechans' territory, he began, indeed had wished it for several years now, and in attempting to show themselves worthy of the favor he and his people had done everything that the Spaniards had requested. They had taken steps toward clothing themselves in ways the Spanish considered modest. Many of the men had cast off all but one of their wives. As best they could they had attempted to memorize the words the padres had taught them, like "Ave María," "for they wished to embrace all the laws of our religion, of which they had some information."[86] And, crucially, they had kept peace with the surrounding peoples—all, said the savvy Palma, except those who lived in the mountains to his west, for he had heard about the theft and murder they had committed at one of the nearby missions.

That was at Mission San Diego, where there had been a bloody uprising several weeks earlier, while the Anza expedition was stuck in neutral at its muddy camp of Las Lagunas del Hospital. On the night of November 4, six hundred Kumeyaay, fed up with the Spanish soldiery's violent sexual assaults on their women and theft of their land, had attacked and set fire to the sparsely occupied mission's buildings. Father Luis Jayme had been clubbed to death. Two other Spaniards had also been slain. Father Vicente Fuster was wounded—and traumatized—but survived.[87]

How much of this tale Palma knew, or told Anza, is unclear. Anza passes over the matter lightly in this day's diary entry. It was almost certainly the first time he had heard the terrible news. He does not seem to have comprehended the scale of the tragedy. Perhaps he thought Palma was exaggerating an event of small importance in order to portray his enemies in a bad light (although the Kumeyaay were traditional allies of the Quechans). Perhaps he simply did not find Palma credible. Or perhaps he did not want to spread fear among his people. Anza certainly seems to have made no mention of Palma's report to the friars, for none of them say anything about it until January 1, when, as the expedition approached San Gabriel, they were informed by a distressed corporal about the San Diego rebellion and its consequences.

Anza told Palma that he could not, just yet, say when Spanish settlements would be established among the Yumas, but he assured Palma that it would happen in due course. To this vague reply The One Who Wheezes made another request, which was to be taken to Mexico in order to make his case directly to the viceroy. Clearly Palma was not a man who allowed others to derail his ambitions easily. To this surprising appeal Anza just as surprisingly assented. Months later the commander would discover that Palma was entirely serious.

Anza's conversation with Palma went a long way toward putting the commander's mind at ease. The crossing at Yuma could not, it seemed, be in friendlier hands. Nor need he worry about leaving Garcés and Eixarch here, with appropriate provisions, as he continued on his way to Alta California. That night Anza was made to feel even better by a long speech given by another Quechan headman. Anza recognized him as the homely man the Spanish called both Pablo and El Capitán Feo. It was he who had killed either a mule or its thief in 1774. And it was he who on Anza's return from Monterey had threatened the soldiers who had come with him. It was a huge relief, therefore, when Pablo instructed his people neither to steal from nor do any harm to the Spaniards, whom he now considered their friends. Pablo was, like Palma, an impressive orator and intelligent man. It was important to have him on the Spaniards' side.[88]

The next day, Tuesday the 28th, was another marked by important ceremonies and conversations. It began with the expedition marching downriver for four hours until it reached a ford at which all could cross to the Gila's northern bank. There, a couple miles east of the river's junction with the Colorado, the Quechans had constructed a large ramada to accommodate the Spaniards' camp. More demonstrations of their friendliness—and agricultural ability—followed, including gifts of food in abundance: beans, gourds, corn, wheat, and more than three thousand watermelons that the natives had carefully preserved in dry sand since their harvest some months earlier. It was more than the Spaniards could eat, wrote Anza. In gratitude he had the soldiers fire a salvo of musket shots, to which the Quechans responded "with a great cheering and hubbub."[89]

The next order of business was the confirmation of peace between the Indians of the Gila and the Quechans, during which Pablo made another long speech in which he announced that, as had been requested by Anza and the friars, all wars would henceforth cease, and all other peoples were henceforth to be considered the Quechans' fellow countrymen. That is how Pablo's speech was explained to the Spaniards, anyhow. However sincere it may have been, it was certainly impressive. Font gave Garcés the credit for laying the seeds for peace in his prior visits to the Yumas.

For his part, Font, with typical interpersonal clumsiness, went after sunset with an interpreter to have a private conversation with Palma and Pablo. He wanted to stress to them that if friars came to live there the Yumas would have to learn Christian doctrine. Not only that, they would "have to learn masonry, carpentry, tilling the fields and toiling, and so forth. And they would have to live together in a pueblo that the people would build in order to live there together in their houses, not scattered about as they do now, and that a house must be built for the Father as well as a church." To this poor diplomacy—precisely the sort both Garcés and Anza thought should be avoided—Palma and Pablo cheerfully agreed, reported Font. And so he made things worse by promising them that, if they remained on good terms with the Spanish, "the king next year would doubtless tell us to return and live here with them."[90] Garcés was among those who would later pay a high price for this sort of reckless talk.

Anza's chief problem now became finding a way for his huge party to cross the Colorado. Even though the river was low, the Quechans said they did not know of a ford, and when Anza raised the possibility of towing people, animals, and supplies across on rafts they objected that the water was too cold for them to swim while also toting such heavy loads. (Anza's people were not keen on the raft idea anyway; they were terrified of falling into the chilly water.) Here was a dilemma. Fortunately, by doing his own reconnaissance with a soldier and a Quechan, Anza found nearby a high but suitable ford on the afternoon of the 29th. The rest of the day was spent clearing a road through the dense thicket that lay between the river and the expedition's camp. Once again Anza was reminded that nothing on this trip would be easy.

The laborious crossing was made the next morning—a crossing that was really three crossings since the river was here split into multiple branches. The deep water reached to the knees of riders on even the tallest horses, which were sometimes forced to swim. To quell fears (probably very few of the expeditioners knew how to swim) and protect against mishaps, at each crossing a little distance downstream Anza stationed ten men on horseback; they could rescue anyone who should fall. As it happened, this occurred to only one man and his child, and they were swiftly rescued. It took three hours—taken together, the Colorado's branches were estimated to be as wide as three football fields—but with the eager help of the Quechans everyone came across safely. Garcés crossed the river in a unique manner. He must have been afraid to attempt the task on horseback, and so instead "three Yumas carried Father Garcés across on their shoulders, two of them at his head and one at his feet, stretched out face upward like a dead man."[91] Father Font is the source of this wonderful portrait, for Garcés declined to record it.

Having reached the far side of the Colorado, Anza wasted no time with celebrations. Immediately he went with Garcés and

Eixarch less than a mile downstream to scout the area around Palma's house, near which the fathers intended to build the hut that would shelter them as they awaited the commander's return. Building commenced the next morning, December 1, and was finished on December 3. During this interval, a group of three or four Halchidhomas came to report to Garcés that, because he had requested it of them, they too would make peace with the Quechans. Their news brought the friar great pleasure.[92] Meanwhile, Palma paraded himself in a suit that included a yellow jacket of suede, a blue cape of cloth, and a black cap of velvet topped by a palm-leafed plume, which Anza had presented him as a gift from the viceroy. Anza used the time for his company, which now included two extremely ill persons, to rest up for the difficult desert crossing on which they would soon embark. He also carved out of the expedition's provisions those that would be needed by Garcés, Eixarch, and the seven others—three interpreters, two servants, a young boy, and an Indian "lent" to the fathers by Captain Bernardo Urrea—who would be remaining on the Colorado with them.[93] One of those interpreters was Sebastián Taraval, who had not been returned to San Gabriel in 1774 after all. It is not until this point in his diary that Garcés mentions the presence of the man who had caused him such irritation on the previous expedition.

In his diary, Garcés makes no complaints about how all this was handled, but Font makes plenty. He pouted that Anza had presented the clothing to Palma without the friars being present, that he had distributed beads and tobacco to the rest of the Quechans rather than allowing the priests to perform this task, that he insisted on being present when Font made his astronomical observations and would not give him free use of the expedition's quadrant, and that although he had asked Font to bring it along he never seemed to ask the friar to play his psaltery. One wonders if Anza regretted not leaving the whiny Font instead of the amiable Garcés on the Colorado.

Personality defects aside, Font did his best to look out for his fellow Queretarans' interests. By this point he had learned that "Father Garcés is so well suited to getting along with the Indians and going among them that he seems to be very much like an Indian himself."[94] That did not mean he and Father Eixarch were not entitled to protection. Font queried Anza on why no soldier guard was being left to ensure their safety. To this question Anza responded bitterly that in building the fathers a hut he was already doing more than was required. He regarded Garcés, at least, as a mere volunteer to whom he owed nothing. He reasoned that the viceroy had not ordered the friar to come on the journey at all but rather had simply given him permission to do so as far as the Colorado. Clearly the two strong-willed men had not cleared up their differences. Just as clearly, Anza was tired of being second-guessed by Font. In his own diary Garcés gives no indication that relations between him and Anza had become so poor. But then, unlike Font he was the sort of man who would minimize or ignore that fact.

In the end, Font thought Anza treated his brother friars poorly not only in failing to leave any soldiers with them—which indeed they had very clearly requested before starting out from Tubac, and which would have been a prudent and not terribly costly precaution—but also in shorting them on provisions. Here Font was a little unfair. Anza gave the friars and their small party 125 pounds (a *tercio*) of tobacco and two boxes of beads for distribution to Indians; 25 pounds (an *arroba*) each of chocolate, sugar, and lard; 375 pounds of dried meat; five cows; a couple hundred pounds of beans; and various amounts of flour, chickpeas, cake, ham, and cheese, along with a frying pan, a griddle, an axe, twelve cakes of soap, and twelve candles and a jug of wine for Mass. Along with the food that the friendly Quechans would surely provide, this does not seem to have been exceptionally stingy. Font himself reports that Garcés and Eixarch were "sufficiently content" with what Anza provided, although Garcés was forced to have "some polite discussions" with Anza "over why he was not leaving him the animals that had been promised him for his journeys," a conversation that resulted in Anza leaving thirteen mounts with the friars and their servants.[95] This largesse notwithstanding, certain goods *would* run short very soon after Anza's departure.

Garcés, at any rate, worried little about the question of supplies. For, as soon as the expedition departed, he would be moving on himself.

CHAPTER 9

We Now Are Brothers

1775–1776

*T*he entrada for which Francisco Garcés now began to prepare would secure his legacy. Garcés's epic—no other adjective will do—1775–76 journey saw him travel an estimated two thousand miles over a ten-month period. For perhaps four hundred miles of that stretch, at most, he was accompanied by soldiers or fellow Spaniards. For only a few weeks was he present at even the most ragged outpost of European civilization. After he left the main body of the Anza expedition in December 1775, he never again traveled in the company of another Spaniard. Most of the time he was accompanied only by two or three native guides. Sometimes he was completely alone. His supplies were limited to what he could carry on his mount. For food he depended mostly upon the generosity of the people he met. He carried no arms.

It is difficult to find anything comparable in the annals of American exploration. Father Eusebio Kino rode throughout Sonora and much of today's southern Arizona, but he never traveled as far or for as long as Garcés did in 1775–76, and he seems always to have traveled with a sizable retinue. The Lewis and Clark expedition of 1804–6 went much farther than Garcés—eight thousand miles—but it also included something like forty-five comparatively well-supplied members. The Jesuit Jacques Marquette's 1673–74 expedition with Louis Jolliet is perhaps the most apt comparison. That journey started in St. Ignace, Michigan, and followed waterways down the Mississippi to a point near the current Arkansas-Louisiana border. But even the Jolliet-Marquette expedition included seven Europeans. The famed mountain men and trappers operating in the American interior made impressive journeys. They also had guns, and unlike Garcés's journey, their travels did not tend to contribute much to our ethnological documentation.

In 1775–76, Garcés would become the first European to make contact with or provide substantial descriptions of the Mohaves, Hualapais, Havasupais, and Chemehuevis, among others. He added considerably to our knowledge of several other California groups, and few scholarly discussions of the tribes of the lower Colorado River basin as they existed before 1800 fail to mention Garcés. What he lacked in scientific methodology he made up for with genuine interest. When he left Yuma—or San Dionisio, the name the Spanish gave to the Quechan villages at the junction of the Gila and Colorado—it was in the hope that he would make a lasting contribution to the prosperity of the Spanish empire and the expansion of Christendom. Our contributions are rarely what we intend. The lasting lessons of Garcés's final entrada have to do with how certain qualities can help close the gap, if only partly, between vastly different cultures.

✳ ✳ ✳

Having rested and resupplied for a few short days, Captain Anza and the expeditioners departed from Yuma on December 4, 1775, to continue their journey to Monterey. Father Eixarch knew that his clerical companion intended to do his own exploring in their absence. He probably didn't expect Garcés to leave the very next day. But that is what Garcés did, traveling on horseback and taking with him Sebastián Taraval and the two other native interpreters left in his care by Anza. Before exploring northward, where the bitingly cold weather would be unfavorable, Garcés decided to head downstream to assess the disposition of the lower Colorado's natives toward missions. Things got off to a good start when, among Quechans he encountered some fifteen miles below Yuma, Garcés unfurled his canvas and was told that "that Lady was good and the damned soul very bad; that they were not so foolish as not to know that the good people are up in Heaven, and down inside the earth are the bad people, dogs, and horrible wild beasts." The Pimas had relayed this theology to them, the Quechans told the friar. And although they weren't conscious of wanting or needing any further information about the afterlife, they would be happy for padres to come live among them, for then "they would have meat and a means of covering their nakedness."[1]

The Kohuanas whom Garcés encountered two days later reacted to his canvas in similar fashion. "Showing them the portrayals of Mary Most Holy and the Damned Man, I gave them to hear of the things of God, at which they showed great rejoicing, crying to the Divine Lady that all was very good; but the Damned Man so filled them with horror that they shouted their unwillingness to look at it, and they would make me turn the painting around." Here, at the lagoon the Spanish called Santa Olalla, Garcés caught up with the expedition, which the Kohuanas were liberally provisioning with fish, corn, beans, squash, and watermelons. Father Font was amazed at Garcés's ability to connect with these natives, as he had with so many others. "He acts stolid in everything, like an Indian," wrote Font in his diary.

Journey Garcés began in December 1775 from Yuma, first down then up the Colorado River, west through the Mojave Desert to Mission San Gabriel, northwest into California's great Central Valley, and east to Oraibi Village in Hopiland, before retracing his steps to the Colorado and making his way back to San Xavier del Bac, which he reached in September 1776. *Map by Tom Jonas.*

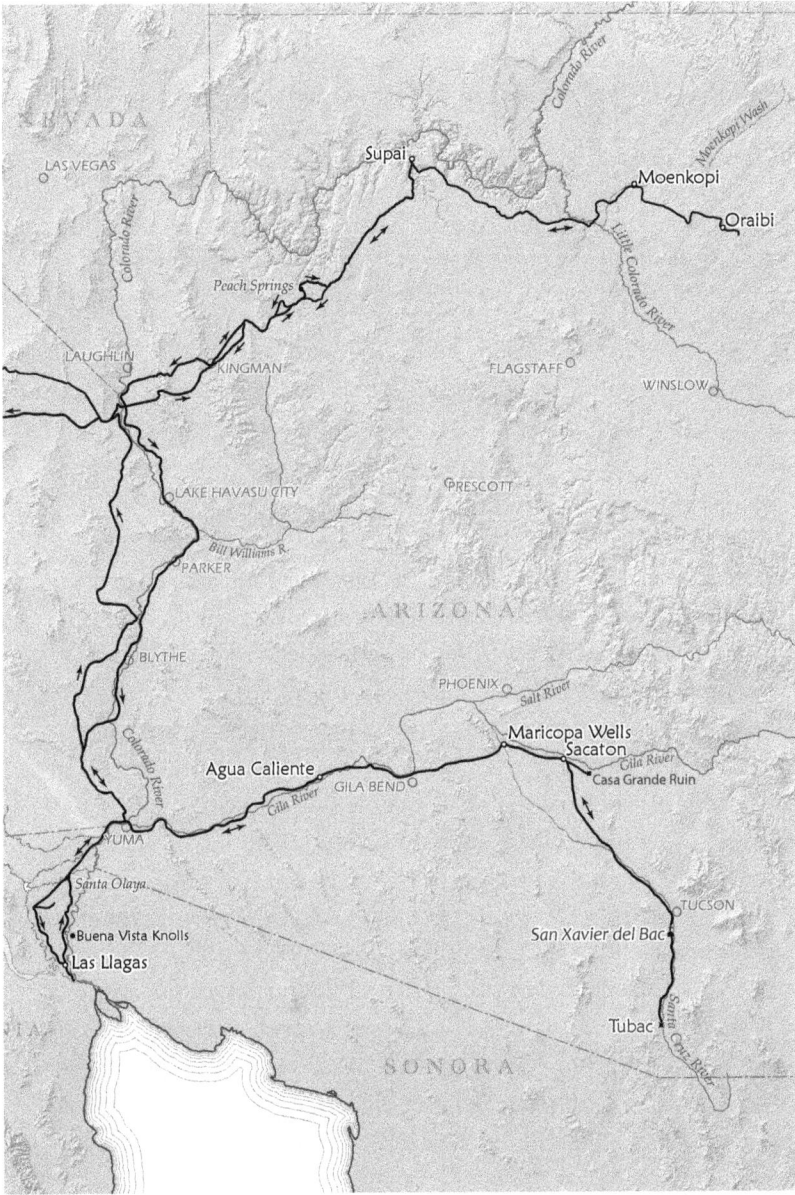

He sits with them in a ring or at night around the fire with his legs crossed and will stay spellbound that way for two or three hours or more, thinking of nothing, chatting very calmly and slowly with them. And even though the Indians' foods are so disgusting and dirty, as unclean as they themselves are, the Father eats them gladly and says they are good for the stomach and quite delicious. In sum, as I see it, God has created him wholly suited to seek out these unfortunate, ignorant, and rustic people.[2]

With respect to his God-given task, Garcés probably agreed. In any case, his reunion with Font, Anza, and the rest of the party was brief, for the next day, December 9, he continued with his small party downriver on its western side.

Garcés had been here before, of course. It was gratifying to see what a difference his previous journeys had made. Thanks largely to his efforts, the Kohuanas were now at peace with the Quechans. As a result, their crops and agricultural activities had been undisturbed, and they were enjoying abundant harvests. As he traveled along, Garcés was given a hero's greeting, the Kohuanas "showing their joy with big dances and much shouting." In fact, "so great was the crush of people upon me whenever I left my shelter," wrote Garcés, "that I was obliged to stay inside it."

As much progress as had been made toward peace, Garcés would learn the next day, December 12, that interethnic violence was not so easy to extirpate.[3] Hearing a great disturbance, he emerged from his hut to learn that a Halyikwamai had speared a Kohuana man in the chest.[4] Garcés baptized the injured man, who later died, and he prevented the Kohuanas from killing the, or at least *a*, Halyikwamai in retribution. Even so, it wasn't long before a "free-for-all fight began" between the two groups. Garcés was able to convince them to stop before anyone was killed, but the episode disconcerted his companions. On December 17, two of his interpreters turned back. Only Taraval was brave enough to continue.

It wasn't long before Garcés and Taraval were met by a group of Cocopahs traveling upriver to greet them. The Cocopahs were culturally similar to the Quechans, from their language (they spoke a Yuman dialect) to the agriculture they practiced, to the importance they placed on dreams, to the centrality of formalized warfare in their cultural patterns and practices, to the creation stories they told.[5] Garcés had been among them in 1771, and they were happy to see both him and his effects, for they found fascinating both the pictures in his breviary and the compass with the astonishing needle. Garcés took advantage of his good standing to implore the Cocopahs to live at peace with those upstream, whom he predicted would no longer launch attacks against them. One woman, he discovered, "seemed unwilling to believe what I said to her." Her skepticism was rooted in sorrow. Garcés had baptized her son in 1771, she reminded the friar. Both he and another infant Garcés had christened had subsequently died. Garcés could only attempt to console her by "telling her that her son was now in Heaven." The episode showed how, from a cultural if not a divine perspective, baptism was a dangerous game.

The Cocopahs told Garcés that the Gulf of California—the "sea," as Garcés referred to it—was near, and three days later Garcés confirmed their statement. On the crisp evening of December 21, having ridden across "a very wide treeless and grassless flat" about fifteen miles long, Garcés and Taraval came upon a body of water that was partly salty and had high waves. It stretched both east "as well as south as far as one could see." It was clear that Garcés had finally and certainly reached the mouth of the Colorado River—one of the first Europeans ever to have done so via land. That night, back at the nearest Cocopah ranchería, Garcés could hear "the great murmur of waters" caused by the incoming tide as he stared up at the cold, bright stars of the winter solstice. To him alone, among those of European ancestry, the Colorado River below its junction with the Gila was no longer a mystery.

The next day he returned to the river's mouth and assured himself that, as long as it was not in flood, the great Colorado could be crossed at this point to reach either the missions of Baja

California or the one at San Diego. This opinion was confirmed when, in the evening, natives visiting the Cocopah ranchería from the mountains to the west asked Garcés if he would be going on to one of those places. Garcés was filled with both pity and affection for these Indians (probably eastern Kumeyaay).[6] On the one hand, they were "very poor, very ugly, and in poor health." On the other, they were "very agreeable" and amusing. For his entertainment they brought to him "a little girl about ten years old, who, covering only the absolute minimum, threw her right leg over her left shoulder, took a stick in her hand, and in this fashion danced, hopped, and ran about, afterward repeating with the left leg. This brought great shouts of laughter from the mountain Indians and the Cucapás [Cocopahs] of the ranchería where I was staying."

The mirth aroused by such a performance crossed all cultural barriers. But the conceptual chasm that separated these natives from the Spanish was even wider than with the natives of the Colorado River. It was jarring, for example, to both Garcés and Taraval when the mountain folk greeted the missionary's mules "as if they were persons." It was surprising when "on two or three different nights they compassionately removed the mules' hobbles and took them to another ranchería to eat squash." And it was astonishing, even inspiring, when, after one of the mules got bogged down in mud, "they all ran to help him, took him out in their arms, and carried him to the fire to get warm." Converting such warm-hearted people to the religion of Christ, Garcés must have thought, could surely not be difficult.

※ ※ ※

Two weeks later, at about seven o'clock in the evening on January 3, 1776, Garcés arrived back at Palma's village, where a lonely Father Eixarch was delighted to see him.[7] The Anza expedition was at the moment camped about eight miles east of Mission San Gabriel, its members immensely grateful for the pleasantly green, flowery, well-watered surroundings in which they now found themselves. The last month had brought them considerable trials, including perilous sand dunes, nearly inaccessible wells, thick clouds of fine dust, bone-chilling winds, cattle-killing snows, and horse-stealing natives. The group's fortunes seemed to improve only after the birth, minutes before midnight on Christmas Eve, of a healthy baby boy; aptly enough, he was named Salvador.[8] Garcés had surely worried about the discomfort the unusually icy winter had caused the settlers—the temperature had fallen below freezing most nights along the lower Colorado, too, although Garcés does not mention it—but about the particulars of their tribulations both he and Eixarch were ignorant. Eixarch had been treated with exceptional hospitality by Palma, Pablo, and the other Quechans, to the extent that the friar felt almost suffocated at times. The Quechans could do nothing about the bitingly cold weather, but they conscientiously provided the friar with plenty of food and water, and they even listened attentively to Eixarch's explanations of Christian doctrine.

Despite such fruitful conversations, Eixarch had suffered spiritually in Garcés's absence. He morosely reflected, on being offered an opportunity to purchase a young Apache captive from an elderly Quechan man, that this slave trade, in which frontier Spaniards complacently participated, was "altogether contrary to law" and ignored "the fact that the Indians were born free."[9] He had been left only twelve wax candles for saying Mass, and, what was worse, the wine Anza had provided looked and tasted like muddy water. Three or four times Eixarch had attempted to celebrate Mass with it; each time he had vomited. As he awaited new supplies, Christmas Eve and day passed. It was probably the first Christmas in his life on which he had neither attended nor celebrated Mass. The holiday was made even more depressing when Eixarch was informed, on the 24th, that Garcés and Taraval had been attacked by the Cocopahs and left destitute and naked. Not until the 29th did Eixarch discover that this report was a fabrication, and that a well-treated Garcés was on his way back.

He sure was taking his sweet time, though—"moving very slowly among his Indians," as Eixarch put it. On January 1, 1776, with neither Garcés nor the new provisions yet arrived, Eixarch resolved to take action. He would go to the mission town of Caborca himself to get what he needed, including a few days of Spanish companionship. The next day he discovered that what Garcés made look so easy was anything but. Eixarch's Indian guide abandoned him, and not being sure of the way, or where to find water, Eixarch did what anyone not named Francisco Garcés would do: he turned back. Eixarch returned to his house among the Quechans on the afternoon of the 3rd, just a few hours before Garcés made his entrance. Together, the two friars sat around the fire long into the night, bringing each other up to date and reveling in the pleasures of friendship—for missionaries like them, one of the frontier's rarest commodities.

❉ ❉ ❉

For the next month and a half Garcés tarried at Yuma with Eixarch. It remained strangely cold, and Fray Eixarch was sometimes annoyed by what he regarded as the Quechans' impertinence ("they make such a hubbub [and] are filthy and have no shame whatever," he wrote in one characteristic passage), but for the sanguine Garcés these were pleasant days.[10] A new, much stronger house, safe from floods, was built for the priests on the hill at El Puerto de la Concepción.[11] Garcés made day trips to baptize the sick and evaluate potential mission sites. Additional supplies finally arrived from Caborca and, thanks to Taraval, Tubutama.[12] Eixarch made a copy of the diary Garcés had kept of his trip down the Colorado. Garcés sat and talked with visiting Indians for long periods of time, "as is his custom," wrote Eixarch in his journal.

The Quechans continued to be extraordinarily friendly and accommodating, with Palma engaging Garcés in theological, even cultural discussions. Yes, said Palma, he had always known there was a God, but the fathers had increased his knowledge. He held to traditional Quechan beliefs about the afterlife—which beliefs held that at death the soul went to a better, deathless place called Anai Matapoi, or Dwelling of the Dead.[13] And he expressed surprise that the Spaniards did not seem as pained by the passing of their relatives as did his own people. Whatever he understood, or thought he understood, about the faith of the Spanish, and whatever his true intentions, Palma continued to participate in their religious ceremonies, putting "many Christians to shame by the reverence with which he followed the Mass, imitating the Catholics in crossing himself, beating his breast, and [displaying] other signs of devotion."[14]

That was an encouraging sign. So was Palma's apparent commitment to peace. "We now are brothers who formerly were enemies," announced Palma to a delegation of visiting Cocomaricopas and Halchidhomas, before making it clear that it was not out of fear but out of respect for Spanish power that he was laying down his arms.[15] (A great leader, after all, has his dignity to protect.) He and Pablo then went downriver to confirm the peace with the Kohuanas and returned "loaded with provisions," in Eixarch's words.[16] Several members of a tribe Garcés called Jequiche, the same that the Spaniards had dubbed the Danzarines on the 1774 expedition, came down from the western mountains and made peace with the Quechans as well. Garcés explained to a group of nine visiting Yavapais the promises of friendship that had now been made among various peoples of the Colorado-Gila region, and they responded that since "all were making peace they too would make peace with all."[17] Little seems to have been brought more happiness to Garcés than such diplomatic successes. Whether he thought that such a general peace could truly hold is doubtful. He was well aware, certainly, that the Spaniards might screw it up—for example, by forcing the Quechans to build the church and priests' house should a mission be established among them.[18] He felt uneasy even in letting the willing Quechans assist in building a hut for the friars. Increasingly, Garcés was wary of anything that smacked of forced labor.

All peace was fragile. That was indicated anew by a report brought by a Kumeyaay from the California interior. Several tribes there had risen up to drive out the Spanish on the coast, he reported, killing one priest and burning a mission. This was a reference to the November 4–5, 1775, revolt at San Diego, but Garcés and Eixarch did not give it much credence—another clue that this was the first they had heard of it. The request of the Kumeyaay alliance was that the Quechans remain neutral should a larger war break out between them and the Spaniards. Garcés does not say how Palma and his fellow tribal leaders responded, but surely they took to heart the lesson that, if necessary, the Spanish could be ejected.

By early February, as the weather turned fair and the great river, swelled by the rising Gila, began to overflow its banks, Garcés became restless. It was time to find that northern road to Monterey and New Mexico with which he had long been obsessed. Time also, therefore, to visit the Mohaves. Having sent the viceroy an interim report and advising him of his plans to explore upstream, on the sunny Saint Valentine's Day of February 14, 1776, Garcés took his leave once again from Father Eixarch, Palma, and his Quechan friends.[19] His small party consisted of Taraval, a visiting Mohave man, and two native interpreters. His supplies were equally limited, the most important being a sheepskin blanket, a magnifying lens for starting fires, a compass, a quadrant lent him by Father Font, a little bit of food, and glass beads and tobacco to distribute as gifts. It would be more than half a year until the adventurous friar returned, by which time both Eixarch and Palma would be long gone themselves.

※ ※ ※

For a week the Garcés company rode northward on the western side of the Colorado through the Mojave Desert, the friar making note of various landmarks—a peak he called Cabeza del Gigante in today's Castle Rock Mountains stood out in the east—and tribal homelands. The party stayed well clear of the river because of ongoing hostilities between the Halchidhomas and Mohaves. Garcés's route took him northwest from Yuma, past the Cargo Muchacho Mountains, to the southwest of the Picacho Peak Wilderness (a peak known to Garcés as the Peñón de la Campana) through a pass in the Chocolate Mountains now threaded by California Highway 78. He then headed north, riding just east of the Chuckwalla Mountains, about where Wileys Well Road is today.[20]

On the 21st, Garcés encountered a group of eighty Mohaves on their way to visit the Quechans. They had with them as captives two young Halchidhoma girls. Garcés begged for their release, finally overcoming their reluctance by offering in trade a horse and some other gifts. A few days later, he sent the girls back to their people with one of his interpreters, whom he enjoined, with more confidence than the facts warranted, to proclaim that the war between the Halchidhomas and Mohaves was now ended. Later that same day the Garcés band came across a group of forty Chemehuevis, whose lands were situated between those of the Halchidhomas and Mohaves to the west of the Colorado River. Garcés is the first European known to have encountered this Shoshonean people, who lived in small family groups that ranged the eastern half of the Mojave Desert in search of game and edible plants.[21] Their "good sense" and extraordinary running ability impressed the padre, who recorded in his diary other ethnographic information for which later scholars would be grateful.

Leaving the Chemehuevis behind, Garcés and his companions continued to thread their way north. Their sandy route took them from spring to spring under the pale blue winter sky, past and occasionally over the taupe and ash-colored, all but lifeless mountains of the Mojave. From roughly the location of today's Rice, on California Highway 62, they seem to have kept to the west of the Turtle Mountains before crossing them near their northern terminus and descending into the broad Chemehuevi Valley. Here they could follow the Chemehuevi Wash northward

Mohave girl
photographed by
Edward S. Curtis
in 1903. *From the*
Edward S. Curtis
Collection at the
Library of Congress.

to the Sacramento Mountains, which they crossed on February 28. Below them was the lush Colorado River valley; across
the river was a mountain range notable for its soaring, distinctive
spires. They arrived at the river that day, probably right at or just
above modern Needles, California.

A Mohave ranchería was located on the eastern side of the
stream, and soon its residents crossed the river to greet Garcés
with much friendliness. The priest, said these Mohaves, was the
first Spaniard they had ever seen.[22] "They had heard that we were
brave," Garcés recorded, "and they showed extraordinary pleasure at being friends of so valiant a people."[23] Garcés was equally
pleased. "I can say in all truth that these Indians are superior in
many things to the Yumas and the rest of the Colorado River
nations," he wrote. "They are less troublesome, and they are not
thievish. They show spirit, and are very obliging; nowhere have I
been better taken care of."

The longer Garcés spent with the Mohaves, the more impressed he became—with the confidence of their headman, the attractiveness of the women, and the health and hardiness all seemed to display. The Mohaves were among the tallest and most athletic of the American West's peoples. Their superior physicality made them fearsome warriors, or *kwanami*, in their Yuman language.[24] They also possessed phenomenal endurance; young Mohave men were known to travel on foot as many as sixty miles per day, with little food or water to sustain them.[25] Garcés soon discovered that his new acquaintances often undertook such journeys in order to trade with the peoples of the Pacific coast. They would be happy to accompany him there. What luck! With supplies running short, Garcés determined to start immediately. Leaving some of his baggage with his hosts, he left their village on March 1, taking with him, besides three Mohave guides, only Taraval.[26] His hope was to emerge at Mission San Luis Obispo, from whence the road to Monterey was well established.

At first, to please his new Mohave friends, he continued upriver, entering—just barely—into modern Nevada. His presence in the region is memorialized by petroglyphs thought to depict him at the head of Grapevine Canyon near Laughlin, Nevada, and in Davis Camp Park in Bullhead City, Arizona, just across the river from the Mohaves' sacred mountain, Avi Kwa' Ame, or Spirit Mountain.[27] By March 4, he was finally on his way west, his guides taking him on an ancient trading route that still exists today as the dirt-track, four-wheel-drive Mojave Road.[28]

So far as he knew, and as far as *we* know, as he rode west Garcés entered a region of the Mojave Desert previously unvisited by any other European, just as he had done in traveling north-northwest from Yuma. In summer it was as hot and dry, and sometimes hotter and drier, than the inhospitable desert that lay between San Xavier del Bac and Yuma. March was a good month for travel in the Mojave, but even after the comparatively wet winter pasturage generally remained scarce. Water was nearly nonexistent. Petroglyphs occasionally provided directions to nearby springs, and

Petroglyphs believed to represent Garcés located in Davis Camp Park in Bullhead City, Arizona (left), and at the head of Grapevine Canyon near Laughlin, Nevada (right). *Photos by Stan Krok. Used with permission.*

Garcés's guides each carried on his back a pack, or *ku'po*, made of cotton or deerskin.[29] He wondered at the natives' ability to survive in such a land; his companions boasted that a Mohave could go four days without either food or water. Garcés believed them.[30]

Eight days of increasingly dry travel on the tightly packed gravel trail somewhat to the north of today's Interstate 40 brought Garcés west to a pass (likely today's Foshay Pass) through the pleasantly pine-topped Providence Mountains (he called this range the Sierra de Santa Coleta, just one of many Garcés-given place names that did not stick).[31] Turning northwest to trudge north of Kelso Wash through tiresome sand, he then turned southwest until, on March 9, he came to a streambed with a trickle of brackish water. This was the Mojave River, which runs from the San Bernardino Mountains to dry Soda Lake in the Mojave Wilderness south of Baxter, California. Garcés called it the Arroyo de los Mártires. He was the first European to report its existence.

Here, more than one hundred miles west of the Colorado, the Mojave River became the group's road.[32] Water was no longer a problem. In fact, too much of it fell from the sky in the form of a driving, frigid rain. On March 11, the Garcés troupe encountered a ranchería of twenty-five very poor, very naked Indians— Beñemés, the friar called them; they are now considered to have been desert-dwelling Serranos, a Uto Aztecan–speaking people who usually lived in single-clan communities.[33] Like the widow of Mark's gospel, they gave generously from their profound poverty to the friar and his companions, although the tule or cattail roots that served as their fare were not very appetizing to the Mohaves.[34] Hardy as they were, neither they nor Taraval nor Garcés could survive on such food, so on the 12th Garcés decided, as he put it, "to have a horse killed to relieve our necessity."[35] Even this extreme measure was not enough to persuade one of the Mohave guides to continue in the midst of such miserably cold and wet weather. He turned back. To the two who remained Garcés gave a woolen shirt and a blanket. Presumably he went without these items himself. For three days the friar acceded to the Mohaves' request to remain in camp, waiting out the rain and gaining what strength their eating of horseflesh might provide. Such had been the men's hunger that "not even the blood was wasted," recorded Garcés in his diary.

On the 17th, Garcés sent Taraval and one of the Mohaves ahead to scout for more rancherías. They returned the next day, having found one that included five Mohaves returning from a trading trip at Mission San Gabriel. They were "well pleased at their treatment by the Fathers, who had given them maize," reported Garcés. He was amused when they "imitated the bleating of the calves" of San Gabriel. At this hospitable Serrano ranchería the friar and his companions were the next day "treated to hares, rabbits, and plenty of acorn gruel, with which we relieved our hunger."[36] But now Garcés realized the river was swinging him too far south. According to the latitudinal measurements he was constantly taking, to reach San Luis Obispo he needed to

continue west, if not somewhat northwest. Alas, the ranchería's
Indians told him that the only route they knew to the coast led
through San Gabriel. Garcés had little choice but to accept their
statement. Once again he had been frustrated in his ambitions.

Four days later, having been greeted with joyful sprinkles of sea-
shells and showers of acorns—the most important food of many
California Indians—at the Serrano villages he encountered along
the way, he stood atop the high, snow-covered San Bernardino
Mountains looking down into the lush valley he had trod with
Anza in 1774.[37] The tree-lined Santa Ana River threaded through
its bottom. To the west he could make out the immense blue ocean.
The view was beautiful. But it was not the one he had wanted.

※ ※ ※

Garcés arrived at Mission San Gabriel on March 24, almost two
years to the day since his arrival with the first Anza expedition.
Fortunately, the situation at the mission had much improved. In
March 1774 he and the captain had found an impoverished settlement whose friars were reduced to begging their visiting brethren for food and clothing. Now, in the warm spring sunshine of
March 1776, San Gabriel was flourishing. It had been moved to
a new, more promising location some two or three miles to the
northwest. There were new buildings, some of adobe, and adequate supplies had been procured from Mexico. Besides the three
priests—Fathers Paterna, Cruzado, and Miguel Sánchez—and
eight soldiers, five hundred more or less friendly Indians were
now resident. Two rivers, the San Gabriel and the Río Hondo,
provided water via an aqueduct that ran between the natives'
huts and the mission structures. The surrounding plains provided ample pasture for the mission's many horses, cows, pigs,
and chickens. Nearby forests provided live oak for timber and
firewood. Wheat, corn, and beans grew in the mission's fields,
and wild watercress, celery, various edible roots, and a multitude
of flowers could be found nearby. Father Paterna, who two years

earlier had pleaded to be returned to Mexico City, now called San Gabriel the "promised land."[38]

Father Pedro Font, from whom we get some of the above information, agreed. It "is a mission that possesses such fine advantages for agriculture and such fine grazing for livestock that nothing better might be wished for. The cows which the mission owns are very fat and yield a great deal of delicious milk with which they make a great number of cheeses and very good butter. . . . The meat was particularly good, and I do not recall having ever eaten richer and finer mutton than this."[39] Such had been among Font's judgments after he and the rest of the expedition straggled into San Gabriel on January 4, 1776. For six weeks the settlers rested and feasted on the mission's produce while their captain, seventeen of the accompanying soldiers, and Father Font rode south to San Diego to help Captain Fernando Rivera y Moncada, military governor of Alta California, restore order there. All this Garcés discovered upon his arrival at San Gabriel.

While he enjoyed the mission fathers' hospitality, Garcés took stock of his own situation. His goal remained the same: to find a more northerly route from the Colorado River to Monterey, and once found, a route from the Colorado River to New Mexico. He had failed to find such a path westward from Mohave territory through Mission San Luis Obispo, so the thing to do, he figured, was to travel the camino real northward to San Luis from San Gabriel, and from there head east toward the Colorado River homeland of the Mohaves. All he needed was a few supplies and a small military escort. To travel with soldiers at his side was most certainly not Garcés's preference. But the camino real was considered quite dangerous at this time by the Spaniards, especially the Santa Barbara Channel section, which ran through the territory of the populous and technologically adept Chumash. Those who traveled through this unguarded area were always on high alert.[40] Given the recent uprising at San Diego, to travel that road without military accompaniment was considered borderline suicidal.

Captain Rivera y Moncada knew that as well as anyone. But at the moment he didn't give a fig about Fray Garcés's safety. Perhaps because he was peeved at the missionaries, Anza, and everyone associated with them (in San Diego, Anza and Rivera had argued heatedly over several matters), Rivera made various excuses for refusing to provide anything to Garcés for his journey. He would not even let the friar accompany him and his troops as they made their way back up the coast. He "had taken it very ill that I had come into these parts, the more since . . . it did not in the least suit him that the Indians of the Colorado should come through to the establishments at Monterey," wrote Garcés in some wonderment. Why Rivera should hold this opinion is unclear. The Indians of the Colorado already knew how to get to the Pacific coast, as their trade proved. And, in any case, was it not a good thing for the crown that the tribes of the interior should be united with those along the ocean by peaceful economic relationships? Rivera apparently did not think so. He claimed that, had he been at San Gabriel when the Mohaves arrived to trade, he would have seized and deported them. Garcés did not understand him. "The King our Sovereign orders that all Indians, even those unbaptized, be admitted into the presidios with displays of goodwill," the friar reflected in a section he later inserted into his diary. "How, then, without thwarting His Majesty's intentions, can orders be given to seize them? The law of nations permits trade between one people and another. What reason, then, can there be to stop the harmless and long-established commerce of the river people with those of the sea, consisting as it does in some white shell-beads? If we preach to the heathen a law of peace and charity, how can we think of sowing discord?"[41]

How indeed. Font, when he came back through San Gabriel with the return of the expedition, was told about this episode. Unlike his fellow friar, he did not let the matter go without confronting Rivera over his flimsy reasoning and uncharitable attitude. At dinner on May 1, 1776, as the mission fathers sat at table with Rivera to enjoy a first course of salad, Rivera volunteered

This entry in Mission San Gabriel's "First Book of Baptisms" records that on April 6, 1776, Garcés baptized a twenty-year-old man. The baptismal name given him was Miguel Garcés. Presumably because Garcés had poor handwriting, Father Antonio Cruzado wrote the entry; Garcés merely signed it. *From the Huntington Library, San Marino, California.*

that Garcés "must have had some real hardships along the route that he took." "Undoubtedly," replied Font. "And, Don Fernando, since you are bringing up this topic in our conversation, I beg you to please tell me what your reason was for denying Father Garcés what he asked for." The viceroy had not ordered him to supply Garcés, said Rivera. Ridiculous, said Font; how could the viceroy anticipate such details? This was a small matter over which Rivera obviously had authority. Rivera replied that he had had no animals or soldiers to spare, and besides, had he given anything to Garcés he would have been responsible for what happened to him. No more responsible than you are now, having given him nothing, Font countered. To this rebuttal Rivera had no coherent answer.[42]

Eventually Garcés did prevail upon Rivera to let him have one of the horses the Anza expedition had left behind. Out of their own stores, the San Gabriel padres provided Garcés with a little food, a few supplies, and some gifts for distribution to natives. After two weeks of rest, during which he left his signature on the San Gabriel register of baptisms and married a soldier to a widow who had come to the mission with the expedition, Garcés was ready to continue his journey without any assistance from the Spanish military.[43] But since he must avoid the camino real, he would again be traveling into the unknown.

※ ※ ※

Garcés left the comforts of San Gabriel on April 9, 1776, taking with him, besides Taraval and the Mohave Indians who had come with him thus far, two Tongvas to serve as interpreters and, when necessary, advocates. These mission Indians lasted one day before deciding to return to San Gabriel. Garcés does not tell us why, but it does not seem to have been because of any hostility the group encountered. Rather, as he traveled west-northwest roughly parallel, but some miles inland from, the coast through the San Fernando Valley along the route of today's Interstate 5, Garcés encountered fear more than any other emotion, thanks to the crimes of the Spanish soldiery. On April 12, for example, when he arrived at one village "the young women hid," thanks to the "many abuses" they said they had suffered at the hands of the presidials.[44] Garcés, like Junípero Serra, would be repeatedly told this heartbreaking and infuriating story.

The next day, one of the Mohaves fell ill. So for the next ten days Garcés remained encamped in today's Santa Clara River valley, glorying in the abundant water and grass, visiting surrounding villages, and taking note of "how mild and approachable" the Tongvas were. At one ranchería he baptized an elderly man who was near death, having first instructed him for several days through what halting translation services Taraval could provide. In such a pleasant country there was no need to hurry.

Raising camp on the 23rd, Garcés turned north and marched a hard twenty-five miles to cross the San Gabriel Mountains. At a Serrano village on the other side, likely near today's Lake Hughes, he could see, from what he was told and from the items left behind, that Captain Pedro Fages had been this way on his roundabout 1772 journey from San Diego to San Luis Obispo. It was important, Garcés would discover as he continued, to constantly dissociate himself from Fages or any of the other Spaniards "from the west," including men he presumed—probably correctly—to have been deserters, for the locals did not hold them in high regard.

Garcés was now in Antelope Valley—the western tip, essentially, of the Mojave Desert. The Mojave fanned out to his east like a triangle lying on its side. To his north appeared a line of high, snow-capped peaks. That was his direction. Somehow he had to cross that range, which he named Sierra de San Marcos. These were the Tehachapi Mountains.

Garcés headed straight for them, striking and ascending Cottonwood Creek almost precisely where the Pacific Crest National Scenic Trail crosses that streambed today.[45] As he climbed, Garcés caught "sight of lofty mountains and of leafy, grassy canyons." Still climbing the Tehachapis' southern flank, on April 26 he reached several clustered Cuabajai rancherías, as Garcés termed them, transliterating as best he could the word used for them by his Mohave guides. The Mohaves were good friends and frequent trading partners with these people, known to modern anthropologists as Kitanemuks.[46] About Spaniards the Kitanemuks were less certain. Not until they saw that Garcés was the lone Spaniard of the company did the young people return to camp, and even then his Mohave companions expended much energy attempting to persuade them that Garcés was from the east, where "all the nations loved [him] dearly because [he] did no harm to anyone," and that they themselves had such affection for Garcés that they considered him almost to be a Mohave.

The material culture of the Kitanemuks was significantly different than any Garcés had yet encountered. The village's residents slept in a very large, square communal house "with arches of willow and a roof of mats made of rushes split and sewn together." The house enclosed a courtyard. The Kitanemuks possessed many shells, which they traded to Garcés in exchange for hearing him chant the Alabado or pray the Corona (a seven-decade rosary). They collected chia seeds, with which one of the women showered Garcés as he prayed. They had baskets, "woven shellwork," and flint knives and bowls with what looked like "inlaid work of mother-of-pearl," which the friar guessed they obtained from peoples living along the Santa Barbara Channel (the Chumash, about whom Garcés had only heard).[47] And they made a stupendously bitter gruel out of water, tobacco, and lime, a mixture that left one of Garcés's Mohave companions retching so violently Garcés thought he would die.[48]

What their cultural artifacts and sacred ceremonies signified to the Kitanemuks themselves Garcés could only surmise. In his diary he gropes for meaning and understanding (the bitter gruel, he thought, was meant to "banish fatigue"), but most of the time he was in the dark. What was clear was the natives' friendliness and interest in the things he said and did, however little *they* understood *him*. Apparently a people of deep religious feeling, they would kiss his crucifix, listen intently to his songs and prayers ("to their wonderment and pleasure," the friar reported), and tell him what he said was good. He could ask for little more.[49]

By the next day, April 27, Garcés had reached the border of this people's country. Because their enemies lay ahead—to the north, the direction Garcés was still generally attempting to travel—they both urged him to stay and refused to provide any guides.[50] Given what was said about how "very bad" were the people they would encounter on the road, even Taraval and the Mohaves decided they had gone far enough. But Garcés had heard such stories before; the peoples with whom a native group were habitually on bad terms were inevitably described in this way. So when an old man who had married into the Kitanemuks but was a member of the "Noches," the name applied by his hosts to their enemies, agreed to serve as the padre's guide, Garcés moved on. Reluctantly leaving Taraval and the Mohaves behind, the friar crossed the Tehachapis via Tejon Canyon and ventured into California's great San Joaquín Valley on April 30.

He would soon find himself again on the receiving end of native generosity. Three Noche men—whatever they actually called themselves, the "Noches" were apparently one of dozens of closely related groups living on the floor of the San Joaquín Valley known collectively today as Yokuts—were encountered on the trail while Garcés and his guide skirted the western side of the Sierra Nevada on their way north.[51] They would not come very close when Garcés beckoned, but each of them threw the priest and his elderly guide two squirrels. Garcés was grateful to have meat for the journey. Then Garcés came upon a "beautiful and crystal-clear" rushing river. It was the Kern, tumbling southwestward from the majestic mountains to the east. His elderly native guide told him it was too fast to cross, so they continued west a little ways, downriver, until Garcés was urged by four Yokuts across the river to swim over.[52] Embarrassed, Garcés made them understand that he did not know how, whereupon he stripped to his underclothes (his modesty restrained him from getting entirely naked) and the men brought him across by, in Garcés's words, "having four swim me, two holding me by the arms and two by the body; and with that opportunity I had a fine bath in that beautiful water. My mule crossed by swimming; my habit and saddle were taken over in baskets."

Among the green, wrinkled hills that stretched from the Kern to the White River, just south of today's Ducor, California, there was a series of hospitable greetings. The people Garcés met were welcoming, clean, and "notably good-looking," thought the friar; Font encountered members of the same group on the expedition's march up the coast and likewise found them "cheerful and sociable."[53] Although the women did not much conceal "their person," they also did not seem to Garcés to act in ways that were "in the slightest degree immodest." The Yokuts managed oak forests for their acorns, flour from which they made tortillas; bark, from which they produced dyes and medicines; and wood, from which they made snowshoes, bows, needles, and support beams for their buildings.[54] The structure in which Garcés showed most interest was their sweat lodge, the use of which, he noted, they shared with the Beñemés.[55] The friar was fascinated by one man

who sported a "beard so long, thick, and white that he looked
like a reverend anchorite, the more so when, having asked me for
my crucifix, he hung it at his breast." And Garcés was especially
happy, on May 3, to meet a native who asked him, in Spanish, for
cigarette paper. This native reported that he was from the coast,
where he had "seen Spaniards in four different places, and that it
was four days since he had arrived." He kissed Garcés's crucifix—
something the missionary habitually invited the natives to do—
but then began to "preach to the others, making signs to represent
a firelock and the act of whipping. It all made me suspect that he
was an Indian who had run away" from one of the missions on
the Pacific. From what Garcés could gather, the Spaniards there
had not made a positive impression. Nevertheless, the padre was
allowed to baptize a small boy in this village who was sick.

There was ample opportunity to continue northward from the
last village the friar reached on May 3.[56] Garcés was told that a
great river—surely the San Joaquín—was only a few days' journey
in that direction. But Garcés decided he had better turn around.
He was afraid that Taraval and his Mohave guides would not
wait for him much longer if he did not return soon. He had run
out of gifts to dole out in appreciation of the hospitality shown
him. More important, from a height he could see to the west the
"very broad plains" that the Spanish knew as the Tulares, bot-
tomland marshes full of reeds. These were known to lie thirty
or forty miles east of San Luis Obispo. Thus, if he could find
his way back from here to the Mohave crossing of the Colorado
River, a northern route to the missions would essentially have
been blazed.[57]

※ ※ ※

Although he had resolved to go no farther, Garcés lingered on
the White River for two more days. The Yokuts, who did not
wish for him to leave, were reluctant to provide a guide. The sick
little boy, furthermore, was dying, and Garcés was fascinated by

the mourning liturgy enacted in the friar's presence. The boy's "parents began to weep," he recorded,

and some old women to lament; and the weeping and lamenting went on by turns. Other women and children of the ranchería came and made a large circle, in the center of which was a big bonfire. The child's parents began to cry again, and the old women accompanied them in a contralto chorus. They stopped, and the captain with the young men in the circle chanted in a mournful tone but in measured time. They got up without using their hands and, bending over, danced in time to the chant, beating the measure with their feet and letting their arms hang limp. Then they would stretch their arms forward, putting their palms together; then draw them back to the chest; then extend them crossed over each other, palm down; then they would raise their arms and clap their hands; then they would suddenly sit down—following the rhythm of the chant in everything. I went to the little boy many times. His mother had put on him all the shell beads she had, and I placed on his breast a little cross and left them my kerchief for use as a shroud.[58]

Perhaps here Garcés remembered what Palma had told him about how the Indians mourned their dead and dying more fulsomely than the Christians.

The ceremony having concluded, on May 5 Garcés resolved to head south, guide or no guide, this time rather east of his northward route. Soon after he left, an Indian caught up with him and led him to the next ranchería, where the chief offered to take him to see a Spaniard who had gone native. This meeting—with a soldier, the friar figured, who had deserted from the coastal missions—did not interest Garcés. But he could convince no one to accompany him (both because it was cold and because there were a great number of bears about, he judged), and so having been put by the Indians of this ranchería on what they said was the right path, he continued his journey with only his mule as a companion. As night fell, the road petered out into a narrow footpath on which his mule could not travel. All around were deep, seemingly untraversable canyons. Now that he was truly alone, and quite lost, Garcés was genuinely fearful. But providence seemed to be on his side. "God willed that I should get down to a large canyon which I thought would lead to one of the rivers" he had crossed a few days earlier, on his way north. "I kept on in the canyon almost all night, winding interminably, and was elated at coming out, when it was day, on the banks" of a river that may have been modern Poso Creek.[59]

After a cold night in camp, Garcés continued to pick his way south as best he could. Soon providence smiled on him again, in the form of four Indians who gave him some roasted squirrels and some unidentifiable meat wrapped inside what looked like a mule hide. Garcés was simultaneously grateful and troubled, for inside the hide was "what looked like a mule head, and it occurred to me that this might be one of my beasts, as Sebastián might have taken a mule to come looking for me." The friar spent the night with these Indians at their village. He was feted in the usual manner, but sleep was difficult, "haunted as I was with visions of some mishap to Sebastián and the mule." In his concern for the man who had once displaced him yet also served him quite faithfully, Garcés's typical thirst for adventure drained away; "all I wanted was relief from my fears."

After ten or so miles of south-bearing travel the next day, May 7, Garcés happily stumbled upon the village along the Kern where he had first crossed that fast-flowing stream. This time, to cross he was shown a narrow footbridge formed by two alder trunks; the natives brought over his mule and baggage. Indians he met on the southern side fed him meat, fish, "and a sort of caramel cake made from sweetish roots that are plentiful hereabout," for which luxury he was most grateful. But they would not kiss his crucifix; one of their elders—another man who had apparently had some experience with the Spanish and their missions along the coast— told them it was no good. "An example of that sort readily explains why, when a mission is first begun, the scene may change suddenly from great joy and docility to woes and unavoidable disasters," Garcés reflected, although he did not ask—at least in print—why so many of the natives he met were negatively disposed toward the institutions Serra had planted on the coast.

Fortunately, here on the southern banks of the Kern were some of those friendly Kitanemuks Garcés had traveled among on his outward journey. Garcés was happy to see them, but the route on which they led him was supremely difficult. It was pocked by what the friar called kangaroo-rat holes. At one point he was thrown from his mule and lost his compass needle.[60] Worse, as he traveled southward there was no sign of Taraval or his Mohave guides. At last, to Garcés's great relief, one of them—known to Garcés as Luis—came into view with two of his mules. Soon Sebastián himself, who had been searching for Garcés along the Kern, arrived as well. On May 10, the party was reunited with the other Mohave guide, called Ventura. The men were then joined by two other Mohaves who had come to the country to trade.

Garcés suggested that the party return to the Colorado by traveling up the Kern, but the Indians knew it was all but impossible to scale the Sierra Nevada. Nineteen more days of arduous, very dry, but largely uneventful travel over the Tehachapis and by way of a slightly more northerly but no better road back to the Colorado followed. On May 30, Garcés reentered the homeland of the Mohaves. "Their joy at seeing me there once more," he wrote in wonder, "would be hard to describe."[61]

Garcés had seen trails, places, and peoples previously unseen by any other European. He doesn't say so, but he had to have been exhausted (his diary entries become extremely short, even by his laconic standards, by the time he gets to the great river). It was intensely hot, and Father Eixarch, Palma, and the comparative comforts of the Quechan villages at Yuma were just a few days' travel downstream. Then a letter was handed to Garcés. It was from Anza, acknowledging the receipt of a letter Garcés had written him from San Gabriel and urging him to return to Yuma as soon as possible so that he might leave the Colorado in Anza's company.[62] Tired as he was, Garcés read it with some dismay, for his mission was, at best, only half completed.[63]

The scene at the Mohave village was so chaotic it was hard to think. Having been alerted to his impending arrival, the Mohaves had invited the Yavapais, the Chemehuevis, the Halchidhomas, and members of what to Garcés was a new group, the Hualapais, to come for a celebration. Thanks to Garcés's encouragement, they were ready to conclude a general peace, which they did later that day in the missionary's presence. "From the running about, the yelling, and the general hubbub of this meeting, and from the great heat, I feared I should fall ill," Garcés wrote in his journal. He had decided to submit to Anza's urging and return to Yuma, but he found the strength to query the friendly, long-haired, buckskin-clad Hualapais, who lived east of the river at these latitudes, about their land and the distance from the river to Moqui and New Mexico.[64] Someday, after all, he would go, and finish what he had started out to do.

That day came quickly. On May 31, a quarrel provided an excuse for Garcés to change his plans. The four tribes had happily talked about peace in general terms the previous day. But it was hard to maintain that commitment when there were scores to settle—and thus a cosmos to put back in order. As the Hualapais packed up to return to their homeland east of the river, they were loudly threatened by some Mohaves whose relatives they had killed in battle some time earlier. Other Mohaves, who did not wish to see the new peace broken so quickly, called in Garcés, who had already begun riding downriver. Sensing that some of the Mohaves, who had a reputation for military courage, were quite angry, and perhaps that providence was once again at work, Garcés decided "on the spur of the moment . . . to accompany" the threatened Hualapais. "No one opposed my resolve, though it is common enough that serious troubles attend such surprise moves." One Hualapai and two friendly Mohaves immediately left to alert the Hualapais living to the east that Garcés was on his way.

Sebastián Taraval had traveled with Garcés well over a thousand miles since December 1775. But no amount of begging from the friar could convince him to go farther. What did this native of Baja California and former mission deserter think of the

Spanish priest? Sharply divided by culture, ethnicity, language, and a hundred other factors, did Taraval and Garcés become, in any sense, close? Did respect, even love, ever blossom between these two men? It is pleasant to believe that it must have, but the evidence suggests otherwise. Eixarch wrote in his diary on February 15, 1776, that Sebastián was "an unregenerate rogue, without shame, and nothing can be trusted in his hands," a judgment that Herbert Bolton justly noted was rather "harsh and ungrateful" in light of the good service Taraval provided the padres.[65] Garcés, who was initially peeved by Sebastián's replacing him as Anza's preferred guide in 1774, was never so unkind. Yet he did report to Father Ximénez, the Father Guardian at Querétaro, in late 1776 that he ultimately "had no confidence" in Sebastián.[66] Of course, we know nothing of Taraval's thoughts. We know only that, except on two occasions, Taraval went wherever Garcés went, often when others recused themselves. He may have been a scoundrel, but if so he was an unusually loyal and useful one.

In any case, Sebastián would not be budged by Garcés's pleading. The friar finally relented and asked Sebastián to go with the Halchidhomas back to their lands, there to await his return. The two men would never see each other again.[67]

✳ ✳ ✳

With keeping the peace as his justification, on June 4, 1776, Fray Garcés set out to find what the Spanish had thus far not found: a route from the Colorado River to New Mexico. As Garcés understood, that route would necessarily have to go through Moqui, or the homeland of the Hopi people. It was there he was now determined to go.[68]

He revealed this objective to the Hualapais and his Mohave guides on June 7, when having crossed the imposing Black Mountains he arrived at the first Hualapai ranchería, around the area of modern Kingman, Arizona, some forty or so miles east of the Mohave crossing.[69] The Mohaves tried to persuade him to abandon such a foolish goal, "because they feared that the Hopi Indians might kill me." The Hualapais were more sanguine; they traded often with the Hopis for blankets, awls, and other tools. The friar listened to everyone—and pressed on.

On June 9, now with two Hualapais and a lone Mohave as guides, he skirted the Cerbat Mountains and found another ranchería, where he was treated as usual with great hospitality—in order "to get me drinking-water, an Indian woman went to the mountains for it two hours before daybreak"—and the headman and his wife offered to accompany him on the journey. The next day Garcés was provided another lesson in charity. The party spotted two children at the foot of a tree. When asked where their father was, they said he would come soon. And he did, about ten o'clock the next morning, with his wife, greeting us with pleasure. "The man, seeing my mule, asked for it, to bring in a buck that he had left dead. It is remarkable how these Indians share whatever they get from hunting; though the amount be small they share it with everyone. On this occasion, before loading the deer on he cut it up and gave half to the captain [of the previous ranchería] who accompanied me. The days I stopped there, they both gave me of their portions." Such behavior must have served to confirm Garcés's Franciscan belief that an innate goodness lay at the core of human nature, even if that nature was also profoundly corrupted by original sin.[70]

The man who had shot the deer was a Yavapai, "who differ only in name from the Hualapais," wrote Garcés, in recognition of the many similarities between the Pais.[71] His relatives, it turned out, had met Garcés back in May and June 1774, when Garcés had visited the Halchidhomas on the Colorado River. Eager to see the padre again, troops of those relatives soon began to arrive. Garcés rested here, high up on the relatively cool Coconino Plateau, in order to see and talk to them. Speeches were made, and finally the Hualapai headman said, "This Father has a good heart; he is on close terms with our friends the Halchidhomas; he has made peace for us with the Mohaves. Now he wants to go to Moqui, and he asks your permission." This permission granted, a married Havasupai couple and another Havasupai man came forward, "saying they were from near Moqui and offering to go there with me." This was another godsend, especially in that Garcés thought their "bearing was superior, and their dress so good that they looked quite civilized."[72] They would be his guides from here forward.

Taking his leave on June 15, Garcés passed through today's Peach Springs, on what would someday be Route 66, where he marveled at the gum-coated mulberry wood buckets used by little girls to carry water.[73] Soon he left behind the Coconino Plateau's windy and dusty golden, red, and brown mesas for the greener, higher country bordering the Grand Canyon. The trail continued northeast through stands of alligator juniper and pinyon pine. He rode within sight of deep, red-rock gorges. The Colorado was very near, he was told. One of his guides—the married Havasupai man—astonished him by chanting the Alabado. He had learned it from the Utes, he said, who lived north of the Grand Canyon, and they had learned it from some Pueblo Indians. New Mexico was indeed getting nearer.

They reached the unmarried Havasupai man's ranchería on June 17. Here, besides giving him another feast, the Indians drew for Garcés a map on the ground, "pointing out all the surrounding nations and the ways to them." Garcés did the same, showing where he had been on his journey and who lived where. "Thus we understood each other," wrote Garcés. Thus were worlds enlarged. Garcés tried to enlarge them further by speaking

> to the people of God and of Heaven, and they showed their acquiescence in all that I said. They kissed the holy crucifix and raised it heavenward, and thus it was passed from hand to hand, even to the smallest children. In this and in other rancherías there was not one maimed, sightless, infirm, or exhausted person who failed to entreat me to lay my hands on him and say some prayers for him. I would recite a little of the Gospel, or the Magnificat; and so I continued to do throughout the land.

At this ranchería was another Havasupai man. He lived in what is today known as the famously beautiful village of Supai, nestled along Havasu Creek between the Grand Canyon's soaring red walls at an elevation of 3,200 feet.[74] It was decided that Garcés must visit this village on his way to the Hopis, perhaps because the Havasupais and Hopis held each other in high esteem, and the friar's establishment of friendship with the former would help him gain acceptance with the latter.[75] And so, on June 20, Garcés became the first European to descend from the Coconino Plateau into the Grand Canyon on its western side, and the first to visit the Havasupai ranchería that remains arguably the most remote town in the continental United States.

Visitors who hike the shockingly narrow, steep trail to Supai today at least have the comfort of knowing that thousands of tourists before them have survived. Garcés lacked that psychological advantage. A different kind of missionary—an intrepid schoolteacher named Flora Gregg Iliff—descended the same trail in 1900 and left a vivid description of her thoughts upon first seeing it from the canyon rim. "I looked down into a giant bowl that was hundreds of feet across and so deep that I could barely see the shadow-shrouded bottom," wrote Iliff in her memoirs.

> Above the red sandstone formation that held the bowl, the white lime-stone of the outer gorge rose three thousand feet in broken, tumbled walls, fashioned by wind, rain, and frost into pinnacles, towers, and mellowed old castles from which knights might have ridden, their colors flying. In the lingering daylight, glowing pinks, soft grays, and cool blues tinted the white limestone and contrasted strangely with the darkness that filled the somber inner gorge. Nothing moved; the absolute stillness was appalling. Clinging to the south rim of the bowl lay a thin white thread—the trail we would follow the next morning! It started out on smooth, firm ground but somewhere it descended that sheer, red wall.[76]

To call the trail "thin" was to engage in massive understatement. As Garcés's mule picked his way down the canyon's sides, the trail became so narrow that finally it was no more than "three handbreadths wide," wrote the friar in his diary. On Garcés's left was the vertical wall of the canyon; on his right "a hideous abyss." Later, most people (although apparently not Garcés) chose to dismount at this point; there was hardly room for a leg on the mule's left side, and it was dangerous to shift too much weight to the right. More than one person, including Iliff and, in 1858, Lieutenant J. C. Ives, chose to crawl.[77]

The width of the trail—called by Garcés "the new Canfran," after the difficult Canfranc Pass at the summit of the Pyrenees in Aragón—was bad enough. "What came next was worse," wrote Garcés, for after a while, in order to reach the next section of the trail it became obligatory to climb down an ancient wooden ladder whose rungs were held together by leather thongs. Ives, nearly a century later, called it "crazy-looking."[78] Mules and horses reached the lower section of the trail by sliding down a rocky slope on their backsides. Happily, the ladder was sturdier than it looked. Garcés and his companions were soon at the Havasupai village.

Supai is today celebrated for its series of sparkling waterfalls and blue-green pools. The aquamarine water contrasts vividly with the surrounding red-rock walls, which rise two thousand feet above the valley floor. Garcés makes no mention of the pools and waterfalls, which are below the village. As always, his principal concern was with the attitudes and lifeways of the people he met, not environmental aesthetics. Thus, he was surprised to see that the Havasupais had horses, cows, and abundant red cloth, all of which they obtained from the Hopis. He was pleased "to see that at daybreak, the husband would go out with his wife and older children to work their fields, taking along the tools they needed such as digging-sticks, hatchets, and grub hoes," all of which again came from their Hopi trading partners. And he was gratified at the "joyous" reception they gave and their willing acceptance of "the peace proposed by me with the Spaniards and the Mohaves." For five days he stayed with his Havasupai hosts, who fed him venison, beef, corn, beans, and other foods they cultivated. It was a profoundly isolated but bewitching place, besides being the best "natural stronghold" the missionary had ever seen. It must have been hard to leave—especially with that frightening trail still on Garcés's mind.

But leave he must, and on June 25, Garcés, with five native companions, set off on a different trail (later known as the Moqui Trail) for the plateau above.[79] It was just as terrifying as the one he had taken down. The ascent was "most painful," its "precipices . . . horrifying," but by the afternoon Garcés had made it to the top. As he continued westward the next day, he could see in the distance, perhaps from today's Point Quetzal, that "a deep passage was cut, steep-sided like a man-made trough, through which the Colorado River enters these lands."[80] He had seen the head of the Grand Canyon; Garcés called it the Puerto de Bucareli. The night was spent in a cool ponderosa pine forest with additional Indian companions who had joined along the way.

On June 28, the party reached northern Arizona's Little Colorado River, then as now an unpotable chocolatey red. A crossing was found, and for another twenty-five miles Garcés rode northward (probably up the Moenkopi Wash) through the strange pink, mauve, and buttercup striated landforms of the Painted Desert before coming to a ranchería at which lived the married Havasupai man who could chant the Alabado, as well as a brother of one of the Havasupai guides in his company. Here too were two Hopi Indians, clad in leather jackets and otherwise "dressed almost like Spaniards." One kissed Garcés's hand but refused a gift of tobacco and shells. The other would neither come near nor kiss Garcés's crucifix when it was offered by his Pai friends.

Since he had left the Colorado River on June 4, Garcés had encountered nothing but friendliness and hospitality. The coolness of these Hopi men foreshadowed that from here forward things would be different.

CHAPTER 10

Promises Delayed

1776–1779

O n July 2, at about ten o'clock in the morning, Francisco Garcés rode slowly into the windswept, mesa-top village of Oraibi, the westernmost Hopi settlement. He had not received a warm welcome from the Hopis he met along the way, and at first only two of the eight Indians traveling in his company dared enter the village with him.[1]

Oraibi was a settlement utterly unlike, and in his mind far superior to, any of those Garcés had encountered in his extensive travels.[2] Not only did the Hopis live in compact villages and build their houses out of adobe; their residences also had multiple stories, "some with more, some with fewer." Garcés made sure to describe their fascinating living arrangements as precisely as he could for his royal and ecclesiastical audiences:

> From the street level a wall rises to a height of about one and one-half *varas*, at which level is the courtyard, reached by a movable wooden ladder.[3] The ladder has no more rungs than are needed for climbing to the courtyard, but its side rails reach to the flat roof. On the level of

the courtyard there are two, three, or four rooms with wooden doors, bolts, and keys. If they keep chickens, the coop is here. The courtyard wall has a stairway leading to the upper stories, which have each a big room in the middle and other rooms on both sides. There is also in the same wall a set of steps leading up to the roof, which commonly connects with the neighboring houses. The noteworthy thing is that all the living-quarters of the houses turn back [from the street] so that no one can see what another is doing indoors unless he climbs up to the roof. The [house] shape is not square, nor is it exactly rounded.

As the friar took in the scene, Hopi women and children watched him silently from the rooftops. The residents of one of these houses were known by an elderly Havasupai who had accompanied Garcés into the village. The two men approached its ladder, but the woman of the house warned the missionary not to come up. Only the Havasupai was welcome, for on hearing that Garcés was on his way Oraibi's chief had announced that on pain of punishment no hospitality was to be given the friar, whose unexpected arrival—and from the west!—aroused suspicion.[4] It was a measure of the Hopis' hostility toward the Spanish and their priests that even their affection for the Havasupais meant little.

Garcés decided to be patient. He made a place for himself in a corner of the plaza. That afternoon and evening he attempted with some success to entice Hopi children to come near him with gifts of white seashells, while his native companions—all eight had now had the courage to enter the town—pled his case to the Hopis. As evening descended men filtered into the pueblo from the surrounding fields carrying hoes, spades, and hatchets. One by one they strolled over to see the white stranger in the dirty gray robe, and though "they showed no dislike for me," wrote Garcés, they would not come close enough to receive any gifts. When night fell, Garcés built a small fire from corncobs and other rubbish he found in the street. He could hear them "talking a great deal" in the houses—presumably about him.

After it was dark, an old man slipped into his campsite. Garcés gave him a gift, and the man kissed the friar's crucifix, saying

George Wharton James's 1898 photograph of the Hopi village of Oraibi, where Garcés spent several uncomfortable days in
July 1776. The village as seen by Garcés more than a century earlier was likely not very different. *From the California Historical
Society Collection at the University of Southern California.*

"*Dios te lo pague*"—"May God reward you"—before quickly
making his leave. Then a young man came up. He was an Acoma
Indian who had come from Zuñi pueblo and spoke Spanish
well; indeed, his Spanish name was Lázaro.[5] He gave Garcés the
lay of the land: the Hopis were "bad" and did not wish to be
baptized, as the missionary at Zuñi had discovered on a recent
visit. At Zuñi, in contrast, "all the people are good and content
with their priest. We know that those who are baptized go to
Heaven." Garcés, said Lázaro, should come with him and his
two Zuñi companions to their pueblo the next day; it was only
three days' travel, at most. He would be most welcome, too, for
it had already been reported to the Zuñis that a brave, bearded
Spaniard had come into the country, "saying there is to be war no

longer." Providence again! A clear and easy path to New Mexico
had been opened.

And yet . . . the more he thought about Lázaro's offer, the stronger Garcés's misgivings became. He might get to New Mexico
without difficulty, but perhaps the Hopis would block his return;
he figured that the Zuñis would escort him back here, but would
he be greeted with even more hostility? And how would he continue west unless his Havasupai or Yavapai friends happened
to be in Moqui? It seemed to him that it was only their presence that gave him any protection at all. There was the option of
returning from New Mexico by way of a path to the north of the
Colorado. He had heard that the Utes who lived in that territory
were friendly with the Spaniards, but he also knew that a route
through their region would be long and require "an escort and
supplies, neither of which did I have." Then, too, perhaps the governor of New Mexico would be as displeased to have him arrive
in that province as had Captain Rivera in California. Perhaps,
like Rivera, he would refuse to give Garcés any aid—"especially,"
the priest reflected, since the viceroy "had not expressly commanded" Garcés to go there. It was indeed only through a most
expansive reading of his brief that Garcés could justify being here
in Moqui, let alone New Mexico.

It must have been a profoundly difficult decision for the determined Garcés to make, but by the morning of July 3 he had
decided not to go to Zuñi. His Pai friends were too intimidated
by the Hopis to accompany him, and, after all, he had done what
needed to be done in finding a path from the Colorado River to
the Hopi villages; the route from there to New Mexico had long
been known. So he decided instead to write a letter to the priest
at Zuñi, whose name he did not know, to tell him where matters
stood.

This letter written ("as laconic as it is unintelligible," lamented
its recipient),[6] Garcés decided on the advice of three of his native
companions to attempt to visit Walpi, the next Hopi village to
the east. The thought was that perhaps he would be greeted with

greater pleasantness there. Garcés's native friends accompanied him as he began to ride down the mesa's slope, but by the time he reached the plain below he found himself quite alone.[7] The path wound past more peach trees than he had ever seen and through the Hopis' corn and beans, but none of those working in the fields greeted him. On top of the next mesa—known today as Second Mesa—two children guarding sheep and a woman gathering wood fled when he came near. A feeling of unease swept over the friar. He became "sensible of the antipathy of all these people" toward him and decided that it would be most prudent to go back to his friends in Oraibi, to which he returned after sundown. For the second night in a row he slept in a corner of the village plaza, ignored by the Hopis and discomfited in his solitude.[8]

As dawn arrived on July 4, 1776, Garcés was awakened by the sound of "singing and dancing along the streets. The dance passed the place where I was and I saw some Indians with feather ornaments on their heads, and other finery, making a din with small sticks on a shallow wooden basin, in company with flutes. Many followed them and stopped here and there to dance. When the sun was up a great throng moved toward me and made me fear for my life." Rarely did Garcés admit to being fearful, but then his presence had never been so thoroughly disdained as it was here at Oraibi. Four men stepped forward from the group and told Garcés in no uncertain terms to leave. His attempts to calm and charm the crowd, to get them to be seated for a friendly conversation, made no headway. The Hopis were insistent that he must go. Within minutes the friar had loaded and mounted his mule. Then, "with a smile on my face, praising their pueblo and their dress, I left, surrounded by all the crowd until I was beyond the houses."[9]

※ ※ ※

Francisco Garcés was not the only friar who in the summer of 1776 was intent on plotting a route between Alta California and

New Mexico. Although Garcés did not know it, the pastor at Zuñi—the man to whom he had written without knowing his name—was consumed by the same dream. Fray Silvestre Vélez de Escalante, an energetic and intelligent Franciscan priest in his mid to late twenties, had been posted to New Mexico in 1774.[10] By January 1775 he was the presiding missionary at Zuñi. Early that year Escalante's provincial, Fray Isidro Murillo, acting at the request of New Mexico's governor, Pedro Fermín de Mendinueta, directed Escalante to find out what he could about the possibility of creating a road between the Californian and New Mexican capitals.[11]

Escalante gave Murillo's order careful thought. His first step was to visit the Hopis, whom he found to be profoundly uninterested in either friendship with the Spanish or hearing friars like him preach.[12] To their west, Escalante was told by his native friends and contacts, there were belligerent cannibals. A route to Monterey in this direction, south of the Colorado River, did not therefore seem as attractive as one that went to the Colorado's north, through modern Utah and Nevada. It would mean traveling through terra incognita, but Escalante thought that a good thing. However successful such an expedition might be—and Escalante was far from confident that it *would* be successful— the facts that an unknown territory would become explored and mapped for the first time, and that new peoples would be encountered and presented with the gospel, were huge factors in its favor.

Soon, Father Escalante had not only persuaded New Mexico missions inspector Father Francisco Atanasio Domínguez that a northern-route expedition to Monterey should be launched, he had convinced Domínguez that they were the ones to do it. The priests' plans came together quickly in the spring of 1776. The intent was to leave Santa Fe on July 4 with eight other men, but a Comanche raid and other circumstances forced them to delay. As they regrouped, the Garcés letter couriered by Lázaro, and forwarded to them by Father Mariano Rosete, who had been left in charge at Zuñi, forced Domínguez and Escalante to reevaluate their plans.

Garcés's letter was short and characteristically elliptical, but it made clear that he had discovered a route from Alta California— he said, exaggerating a little, "as far as the new establishments at Monterey"—to Oraibi.[13] Although the Hopis had received him coolly, wrote Garcés, all the other tribes he had encountered, including those along the Colorado River long rumored to be hostile, had "outdone one another in their attentiveness to me." At least five of them were "well disposed to receive fathers." He would have come on to Zuñi and Santa Fe himself, said Garcés, except that in light of Hopi hostility he felt he would have to return with troops. To obtain such, even if the governor of New Mexico were to provide them, would have meant a long delay. In any case, he concluded, once a presidio had been established on the Colorado, New Mexico would be able to communicate safely with Sonora. A new day had dawned—or was about to.

Garcés's letter was accompanied by a cover letter from Father Rosete. Rosete had questioned Lázaro at length about Garcés and the situation at Oraibi. Among the many additional facts learned by Rosete, and confirmed by Domínguez and Escalante in their own questioning of Lázaro, was that the Hopis were very angry with Garcés for coming there—and with their Havasupai friends for bringing him. They had "said that if they liked the father so much, they should take him back to their land," which the Havasupais were quite happy to do.[14] This development was of keen interest to Domínguez and Escalante, for they had thought, but not known, that the Havasupais were inclined to receive the Christian faith and were therefore planning to come back through their territory on their return from Monterey.

In light of Garcés's achievement, should the padres now scrap their expedition? Domínguez and Escalante thought about it, but they ultimately decided to stick to their plan. If Garcés had discovered a route below the Grand Canyon (a place name that of course they did not use) from California to New Mexico, all the more reason for them to see what could be accomplished via a northern route. The Escalante expedition, as it would become known, left

Santa Fe on July 29, 1776. Throughout the next four months, the fathers would often ask Indians they met whether they had any word of their brother, Father Garcés. These queries have puzzled some later historians, who have speculated that Domínguez and Escalante faked a concern for Garcés's fate in order to explain their wandering and disarm suspicious natives. To some extent that may have been true. But it is more probable that their concern for Garcés was real. Garcés's letter did not say where he was going next, nor was it certain he had given up on reaching New Mexico. Perhaps this wandering friar was now himself seeking a northern route to Santa Fe from the land of the Havasupais? Anything seemed possible—especially when it came to Fray Francisco Garcés—during the thrilling summer of 1776.

* * *

As Domínguez and Escalante finished preparing for their expedition, Garcés began his westward return to the Colorado.[15] After he left Oraibi he wandered alone for some time, trying to find the path by which he had come, before his Pai guides, who were concluding their trade with the Hopis, caught up with him. Thick columns of smoke on the horizon, they said, signified that their enemies were "assembling for war," and so the party rode quickly, making camp on the Little Colorado sometime after dark. It was a short ride the next day to the ranchería at which Garcés had stayed on June 28. He was now ravenously hungry, since the Hopis had refused to give him anything to eat, and so was exceedingly grateful for the beef shared with him.[16] His hosts also gave him some buffalo meat. That, at least, is what Garcés thought it was. He now came to believe that it was a buffalo hide and meat, rather than that of a mule, that he had been given back on May 6 in the San Joaquín Valley. This seems highly unlikely. In both cases, Garcés may have been given elk.

He was eager now to get back to the Colorado, back to Yuma, back to his mission at San Xavier. But Garcés could not help but stop again at Supai, deep in Cataract Canyon. Although to get there was "very toilsome," he tarried in the Havasupais' sylvan home from July 9 to July 15. He was amused and gratified by their interest in his chanting of the Litany of Saints. "To interest them more, when I mentioned Saint Anthony I would say 'Sancte Antoni de Jabesua'; and Saint Peter, 'Sancte Petre Yavipai.' They made much of this, asking me repeatedly 'And I, how?' So I had to assign to each one a saint, from which all learned their names and chanted what they learned."

On July 25, Garcés struck the Colorado River at the northern edge of the Mohaves' territory—probably at about modern Bullhead City, Arizona. The Mohaves were overjoyed to see him, for once again the friar's death had been reported on the Indian grapevine; this time he had been killed by the Hopis. "They never stopped talking and touching me," he wrote. One of the things they talked about was the behavior of Sebastián in the friar's absence. Taraval had broken into the leather chest left in his care, taken out and given away most of the gifts Garcés was keeping there to distribute on his way back to San Xavier, "and made very bad use of them."[17] The meaning of that last clause Garcés leaves to our imagination.

Garcés was disheartened but, given his rather low opinion of Taraval's character, probably not surprised. He urged the Mohaves to keep the peace with the Havasupais and others. Then, battling the intense summer sunshine and tremendous heat, he continued down the river valley. For the next couple weeks he made notes on the rugged landscape, preaching, baptizing the sick and elderly, occasionally appointing native officials in the king's name, and reconfirming the peace deals he had previously helped broker. The wide, tree-lined bed of the Bill Williams River—the Río de Santa María to Garcés—was reached in early August. A few days later he was back among his friends the Halchidhomas. The two little Halchidhoma girls he had ransomed from captivity among the Mohaves greeted him "very joyfully." The older of the two gathered firewood and cooked for him as the padre beamed.

During his absence three Halchidhomas had been killed by Quechans in revenge for some horse-thieving. He was told by the Halchidhomas "that if it were not for the peace they would have gone down to avenge their relatives; but that they no longer wanted war; even though the friends of the dead men asked for vengeance, the rest would not give consent." That was gratifying to hear. But Garcés was not unrealistic: "So limited is their understanding" of Christian teaching and its moral norms, he confided to his diary, "that I cannot vouch for their maintaining the peace." Indeed, he learned at about this time that the Cocomaricopas had killed seven Yavapais, the Quechans' historic allies. A general peace was going to be difficult if not impossible to maintain even when—and it was now most certainly a *when*, in Garcés's mind— the Spaniards established missions along the Gila and Colorado.

Garcés reached El Puerto de la Concepción (Yuma) on August 27, 1776. He was finally back among the Quechans, who like the Mohaves had mourned him for dead. Even Father Font had speculated, when the expedition had come through this place on its return, that Garcés, in not responding to Anza's letter, might have "died or been killed by Indians."[18] Fray Eixarch had left with the returning Anza expedition in mid-May; he had wanted to wait for Garcés to return, but Anza had insisted he leave with his party.[19] Palma was not present, either. He was on his way to Mexico City with Anza.

Garcés enjoined Palma's kinsman Pablo to maintain good relations with the Quechans' neighbors.[20] Before long he was riding up the Gila, renewing his relationships among the Opas and warm-hearted Gileño Pimas.[21] The latter group, having given the friar up for dead, held a great feast in his honor, to which the outlying O'odham rancherías were invited. Since it was the time of the harvest of saguaro fruit, there was much drunkenness. Garcés asked only that they not hold their festivities in his presence. Officially, he could not approve. But he could not help but smile when they would tipsily ask him to stay on forever, or beg him to baptize a child, or when he heard them singing: "We are good, we are happy, we know God, and we are people who can fight the Apaches. We are glad that the old man has come back and that the Apaches have not killed him."

A few days later, on September 17, Garcés finally arrived at his mission of San Xavier del Bac, grateful, and not a little surprised, to have returned from such a long and eventful journey in fine fettle. He had been gone for 327 days.

✳ ✳ ✳

It was to a Spanish frontier in flux that Garcés returned in that fall of 1776. The presidio of Tubac had now moved in fact, and not just on paper, to Tucson. New priests sent by the College of Santa Cruz were arriving at San Xavier. New missions were being prepared. New Indian troubles were arising. Most fateful, the crown was reorganizing the entire region. The northwestern frontier would no longer be ruled by the viceroy at Mexico City. It would instead be ruled as a special administrative unit called the Provincias Internas by a royally appointed commandant-general whose capital would be in the region itself.

On the question of the presidios, Garcés and Díaz had triumphed. Although none had been placed directly on the Gila, not only had Tubac moved forward to Tucson but Hugo O'Conor had also moved Terrenate up to the Río San Pedro and Fronteras forward to the San Bernardino Valley, just as the friars had suggested. Moreover, the authorities had definitely decided to move two other presidios, Horcasitas and Buenavista, to the Colorado and Gila Rivers, precise locations yet to be determined.[22] Even Anza the hard-edged realist was on board with these changes, although he questioned whether the planned Gila River presidio ought to be placed north of Yuma on the Colorado River instead, the better to protect the road from Monterey to Santa Fe that Garcés had shown to be feasible.

There was a problem, though. Far from subduing the Apaches to their north and east, the newly placed garrisons were being absolutely battered by them. The presidio of Tucson, on the east side of the Santa Cruz, wasn't even finished yet. The O'odham who had promised to help build it had stopped cooperating when the government failed to pay them the promised three reales per day. When Captain Pedro de Allande y Saavedra arrived to assume command of the Tucson garrison in early 1777, he was enraged to find not only that its soldiers lacked basic necessities but that two of the fortress's four walls were only three and a half feet high, and the other two were but bare footings. Worse, the building funds had already been spent. This was not what the crown had envisioned.[23]

The College of Santa Cruz was undaunted. That fall the colegio officially transferred its missions in the Pimería Baja to the Franciscan province of Jalisco, making more manpower available for the new missions to be founded on the Colorado and Gila. That was one reason more priests were now hanging around the missions of the northern Pimería Alta. Another was that it had become so dangerous elsewhere in the region. Disgruntled mission Indians, along with other natives and drifting, socially marginalized persons, were assisting Apaches, Seris, and others in making raids and attacks on Spanish settlements.[24]

For example, Father Antonio Ramos had alerted the authorities in January 1776 that the Indians of Sáric were plotting a rebellion. Only a show of force from Governor Crespo and the arrest of the alleged ringleaders had kept them from succeeding.[25] Then, shortly after Garcés's return to San Xavier, Father Font had barely escaped martyrdom himself. His visita of Santa María Magdalena had been attacked on November 16, 1776, immediately after he had said Mass. Only the arrival of a rescue party at the last minute saved him and many women and children, holed up in his house, from being burned alive. The rescuers came too late to help the "pregnant woman whom the enemy had caught and transfixed to the floor with their lances. Her little daughter's intestines were hanging out and she was dying. I confessed her and she died the following night," wrote a badly rattled Font.[26] A week later, the same band of Indians (Piatos, Seris, and Apaches) attacked Sáric and killed eleven people. There followed murderous raids on Altar (December 8), Ocuca (December 10), Santa Ana (December 12), and Cocóspera (December 19). An already depleted Tumacácori was attacked on December 22. Cucurpe was assaulted on December 28. A few months later, on June 10, 1777, the visita at Calabazas was burned.[27] It seemed that nearly all the Indians in the region were unhappy. Even the usually compliant Ópatas had alleged cruelty and nonpayment for labor.[28] Font begged the College of Santa Cruz Father Guardian, Diego Ximénez Pérez, to reassign him away from the frontier. His existence now was "instead of life . . . a prolonged death."[29]

In the midst of this chaos, Garcés did all he could to keep the plan for an advance to the Colorado and Gila Rivers on track. Within days of his return to San Xavier, he traveled to Tubac and Tumacácori to catch up on frontier news. From the latter place he wrote Ximénez on September 24. He told the Father Guardian that he was worried that Anza wouldn't support a presidio or missions on the Gila, and he therefore hoped to speak with O'Conor in person; he also emphasized—yet again—that only with patience and a commitment to peace could these new establishments be founded.[30] On the same day, he wrote Viceroy Bucareli a brief missive alerting him of his return, adding that he would soon send his diary and that the Halchidhomas and Mohaves were more disposed to receive missions than any peoples he had yet met. Wherever Bucareli might establish them, he told the viceroy, the new missions would stand as a "monument" that would "prove to posterity with what great zeal you have worked for the greater glory of both majesties in the conversion of the Indians."[31] The friar was not so artless that he failed to understand the power of flattery.

A few months later Garcés sent Ximénez a long letter summarizing his 1776 travels; his diary, he apologized, was still not ready to send, which fact may have annoyed but by this time could hardly have shocked the authorities.[32] To Ximénez he repeated his now-familiar argument that a mission and presidio—it could contain as few as twenty or twenty-five soldiers, he thought—ought to be placed among the Gileño Pimas, both because the high-character Indians there deserved such protection and because of the importance of that region for defensive purposes. The Apaches had sent peace feelers to the Gileños, he reported. But the Pimas had remained steadfast in their alliance with the Spanish. "The Indians believe so firmly that missions will be founded that they expect the Fathers at the end of this moon," wrote Garcés. It was yet another expectation that would never be met.

The uprising in San Diego had understandably made some Spanish officials concerned about the missions' future, but as far as the peoples of the Colorado were concerned, Garcés assured the viceroy, that tragic incident only proved their goodwill, in that they had displayed fidelity to the Spaniards both before and since. That said, the new missions there should not be founded all at once, but rather first a presidio, then a maximum of two missions, both on the western side of the river for better protection from the Apaches. It was important to proceed with a kind of deliberateness that would not be too threatening, a strategic—and humane—principal Garcés had first conceived and articulated some years earlier.

With the diary still unfinished, Garcés used this letter to provide his impressions of the other tribes he had met on his travels. The Mohaves had impressed him very much, and they had "given the greatest proofs of their affection for me and of their desire to receive Fathers and Spaniards," not least when two of them accompanied him, on foot, to San Gabriel. The Kitanemuks (Cuabajais) had treated him well, but they had also "complained bitterly to me about the outrages of the deserters as well as of other soldiers who went in search of them." A soldier named Camacho was especially hated.[33] The Yokuts had done something about such men. They "told me ... that they had cut to pieces two deserters for going with the women and committing outrages." Garcés was not particularly sorry to hear it. To him those Spaniards had gotten what they deserved. "I told them that even among the Spaniards they hung the criminals."

The head chief among the Halchidhomas had promised he would be baptized should the Spaniards come to live among his people. The Hualapais were grateful for Garcés's intervention on their behalf with the Mohaves—and for the presents he gave them. The Havasupais enchanted Garcés with their farming, their dress, and their possession of cattle, which he believed they kept more for their hides than their meat. Unfortunately, his friendship with Mohaves, Quechans, and Pimas worked against the friar with the Hopis, their enemy. It was partly because these other groups had expressed openness to missions and baptism, he thought, that the Hopis wanted nothing to do with the Christian faith.

In this letter Garcés was reacting to one written by Anza to Bucareli on November 20, 1776. The viceroy had asked the captain to put down his current thoughts on where, in light of his recent heroic expeditions, presidios and missions should be placed. Anza was willing to say that one of the presidios should be on the Gila at Sutaquisón (Sacate) or Uturituc (Sweetwater), but it would be better for it to be placed at the northern edge of the Halchidhomas' territory (around Parker, Arizona), or even among the Mohaves, not only because such a location would better guard the road from Monterey to New Mexico, such as it was, but also because there was a serious scarcity of pasturage among the Gileños. (In his letter to Ximénez, Garcés brushed off this difficulty by arguing that few animals needed to be kept there anyway, with the Tucson presidio so close.) Anza anticipated the founding of seven missions: one at Yuma, one upriver among the Halchidhomas, and five on the Gila, with three of those placed among the Pimas and two among the Opas and Cocomaricopas. The Indians were ready for them, he wrote. The advance should be made.

But the captain also had a warning, one that harkened back to the criticism of the missions he had leveled as early as 1772.[34]

"I judge that the Indians of whom we are speaking will not deviate from the docility and good nature which they have shown us on all occasions," he told the viceroy. But those Indians would remain amiable only if those who governed them, both secular and ecclesiastical, succeeded in

> avoiding the harshness and force which they have practiced in other reductions, in particular in work on the farms and other work which they exact from them at the beginning of their conversion, for this is a sufficient reason to exasperate the first ones and cause them to instill in the minds of their sons the idea that we grow rich by their labor, which idea becomes hereditary among them all, while by using contrary methods we can win them for this same purpose, if we wish, and what is better, for their instruction in Christianity and civilized life.

In this matter Garcés and Anza were of one mind. Anza knew this was another way in which Garcés differed from some of his fellow friars. Far too often, Anza complained, an Indian was punished for something trivial, resentment festered, and a murderous uprising was the result. Let New Spain set up the new missions with this lesson in mind. It was of vital importance that "no one shall be sent" to the new establishments on the Colorado and Gila "with powers to command who lacks knowledge of the management of Indians, and that he shall be disinterested, charitable, and a volunteer." Anza suggested that the priests who manned the new missions be chosen by their father-president in the region, and that this father-president report to the commandant of the new establishments. Querétaro could not have been happy to hear such a suggestion. But the fathers there agreed wholeheartedly with Anza that two new fully staffed presidios would be necessary.

Anza next waded further into the weeds. Hardy, diligent, spirited persons must be selected to serve in the presidios and missions. Workmen from the interior should be sent to instruct the Indians—and do much of the needed work themselves. Some of these workmen could be found among tribes now living in the interior but originally from the Colorado and Gila—that is,

Indians ("Niforas," the Spaniards called them) who had been illegally sold into slavery among the Spaniards. These Indians were now Christians and Castilian speakers, so they would be perfect for the task. (Knowing that Anza had made this suggestion, Garcés made a point of agreeing with it in his own letter.) But Bucareli would have to decree these natives' return and brook no excuses among their owners, "for besides the fact that they were born free, they will be for their country the most promising race that can be established in it." Bucareli should also permit Spanish families to migrate to the rivers, insofar as they volunteered to do so.

Finally, wrote Anza, the viceroy should not count on the Yumas or other Indians to feed everyone who would live at the new establishments. They had enough food for themselves, but not enough for dozens of newcomers. The new Spanish residents should be charged with developing their own agriculture. Until that time a plan must be developed to provision them, no easy task for such faraway places. Anza's was a wise and sensible letter. One wonders what might have happened had virtually any of its recommendations been followed.

⁂

At the moment, the other primary actor in the Colorado River drama that would unfold over the next five years was in Mexico City with Anza, taking such instruction in Christian doctrine as was deemed necessary for his baptism. Just nine days prior to Anza's letter to Bucareli, Salvador Palma had presented a formal petition for the establishment of a mission among his people.[35] Written by Anza, the petition purported to communicate Palma's words and mind faithfully. To a large extent, it must have; Palma had come to Mexico City entirely of his own volition, and he had made amply clear his desire for the Spaniards' friendship—and the material advantages that came with it. Nevertheless, it should be kept in mind that Palma's petition was drafted in response to a thirty-item questionnaire prepared by one of Bucareli's secretaries. It took two days for Palma to answer the questions. What made it into the petition was filtered first by Palma, who understood rather well what his Spanish audience wanted to hear, then by Palma's translators, and finally by Anza and the secretary.[36] It is finally unclear whose voice emerges the loudest in this extraordinary document, which reads like it has been drawn from the pages of a fairy tale. The Queretaran missionaries certainly knew, as their chronicler would put it, that "many of the things expressed in the petition were dictated by policy and not by experience."[37]

Palma's petition begins with background information on the Quechan chief and his people. They live in "several orderly settlements" along the Gila and Colorado and are successful enough in their agriculture that they want not for sustenance. Palma has "supreme command" over his people "by right of primogeniture" from his fathers. This was either a misunderstanding or a plain untruth designed to exaggerate Palma's authority. More exaggerations follow. For example, Palma "regarded witchcraft as the worst of all sins" and had "always had a horror of polygamy." In addition, he had "never had relations with any other woman" than his current wife. Anza is positioned as Palma's spiritual teacher. Prior to the arrival of the captain at his homeland in 1774, Palma had no more "knowledge of the deity than a confused idea of a being superior to any that I know who dwelt above the clouds, creator of all things, whom I called Duchi or Pa, and whose favor I implored in all my needs and perils." But on the very night they had met, Anza had talked to Palma about God "in such a way and which I found so in accord with my way of thinking that from that moment I resolved to be a Christian, even though at the cost of my life." In fact, it was Anza who had bestowed upon the chief the name of Salvador Palma in 1774, after which he had happily "cast aside" the name of Olleyquotequiebe (another embroidery or outright falsehood, in that none of the diarists of the 1774 expedition, including Anza, mention the captain's bestowing upon Palma his Hispanic name, and there is good evidence that he received it in other ways).

On that night in 1774, Anza had also told Palma about the Spanish king. Palma then communicated all he had learned to his people, and they had "unanimously agreed to do whatever I did" with respect to conversion and vassalage. Finally, Anza had confirmed Palma in his leadership role by giving him "a baton in the name of the King."

It was at this time that Palma told Anza he wanted to go to Mexico to petition the viceroy directly "for the establishment of the Catholic religion in my country." But Anza told him this might take at least a year, and so he waited. Finally, the second Anza expedition came through. Once again Palma renewed his petition, whereupon Anza agreed that on his return Palma could accompany him thither, "where I might throw myself at the feet of your Excellency and relieve my heart by explaining my desires myself."

According to Font, Palma had actually not expressed a desire to go to Mexico City until Eixarch told him about the great festival held there in honor of Our Lady of Guadalupe, and Anza had been reluctant to bring him when he discovered the chief's desire in May 1776. Thus, Anza, Eixarch, and Font had together pressed Palma on this matter, explaining how far Mexico City was and asking if he thought he could leave without trouble brewing among the Quechans in his absence. Palma reassured them on all points.[38] The petition acknowledges none of this but rather says only that Palma had proved to Anza his good faith and goodwill by ending wars with neighboring tribes and banishing polygamy among his people, even taking away seven wives from his own brother—all of which Font does not mention.

The only reason Palma wanted a mission, according to his petition, was a pure desire for religion. Even Spanish arms, though they would be helpful, were not necessary in light of his regional military dominance. In return for the promise of a mission, Palma would confirm his and his people's faithfulness to the king. He and his three thousand people would defend the missionaries and other Spaniards among them from any attack. What is more, the Yumas' neighbors would soon also come "into the service of his Majesty." A general alliance of all Indians in the area would likely be formed, keeping the "roads safe and communication open between California, Sonora, San Francisco, and New Mexico."

Palma and the two Quechans with him—one of them was his brother, the other a son of Captain Pablo—all signed their names with a cross at the bottom of this document, in which, it is worth mentioning, there is no mention of Garcés, Díaz, Font, Eixarch, or any other Spaniard; the padres were quite right in thinking Anza was disinclined to share any glory he could capture for himself.

Before receiving this petition, Bucareli had met with Palma and his companions. Anza had presented them at the viceregal palace on October 26, 1777. Palma proudly carried the baton and wore the suit of clothes presented him by Anza in December 1775. Bucareli was thrilled to receive these men, symbolizing as they did the success of the expeditions he had ordered and, more generally, the policy he had pursued on the northwestern frontier. He ordered new clothes made for each of the Indians and assured them King Charles would treat them with generosity and fairness. He also invited them to a palace celebration of the king's birthday, at which the Colorado River Indians, in the words of Herbert Bolton, were "quite the sensation, causing a stir like that occasioned by Pocahontas at the court of wizened King James."[39]

Whatever exaggerations and fabrications it may have contained, Palma's petition confirmed for Bucareli the need to move forward among the Quechans. Saying that he was "disposed to encourage" Palma's "wishes, because they promise the reduction of many tribes, the extension of the dominion of the king in those regions, and the spread of the gospel," Bucareli sent a copy of the petition to Gálvez, who had already conveyed royal approval for the establishment of the new presidios and missions.[40] For their part, Palma and his companions began to be instructed in the

Christian faith. On February 13, 1777, the Quechan men, along with an adventurous Kohuana boy who had also come on the journey after being inspired to do so by his conversations with Garcés, were baptized in the great Metropolitan Cathedral, Juan Bautista de Anza standing as Salvador Palma's godfather.[41] Palaces, cathedrals, bright new clothing—it is impossible to think that Palma was anything but amazed at Spanish wealth and power.[42] Down here in the viceregal capital, a world away from the impoverished and turbulent frontier, everything was shaping up nicely.

✳ ✳ ✳

While Palma was pursuing his petition, Garcés was working hard to finish his diary, for which both Querétaro and Mexico City were clamoring.[43] He first obtained the transcription and composition assistance of Díaz and several other friars at the mission of San Ignacio in late 1776.[44] Then he polished it with the help of Font at the mission of Tubutama. As a fortified town—perhaps the first such in the Pimería Alta—Tubutama was a relatively safe place to hole up for work. It was to find safety, in fact, that Font had come there with Garcés on December 30, 1776, as he continued to recover from his near-death experience in Magdalena.[45] Tubutama's houses were built into the ramparts and had doors that opened into the plaza. All its people—there were only eight families at the time—and animals were locked behind the town's two gates after sunset, and there were three guns for defense. The priest at Tubutama was the dedicated Father Antonio Barbastro, president of the Pimería Alta missions. During breaks in the padres' writing Barbastro prayed and said Mass with Font and Garcés at the little adobe church, built in 1764, dodging the bats that flew in through the glassless windows.[46] Garcés shared with Barbastro a devotion to their late friend Father Gil, whose rosary, medals, and broken crucifix Barbastro had kept as relics.[47]

The extraordinary map made of Garcés's 1775–76 travels by Fray
Pedro Font at Tubutama in 1777. *From the Newberry Library.*

For Garcés, having the capable assistance of Fathers Font and
Barbastro in composing his diary from the rough field notes he
had kept was a monumental blessing. Not only did the gloomy
Font help with the diary proper, he also drew a map of Garcés's
wanderings that has ever since been regarded as an astonishing
piece of cartography. Garcés also took advantage of Font's help,
as well as the help of Barbastro and others, to compose a narrative supplement to his diary, in which he provided his reflections
on what he had seen—for, as he put it, "it has happened that I
have come to understand in the nation next visited what I had
not understood when in the one I had just left. Moreover, subsequent happenings have made me now and then doubt the truth
of something earlier vouched for."[48]

Garcés divided his reflections into eight points.[49] First, he
named every "nation" with whom he had come into contact
or about which he had heard, along with their locations and

variations on their names (he realized better than most that groups were known by different names depending on who was talking). "In no nation have I found any signs of religion," he reported. "I have seen some medicine men, and they have their superstitions, but I surmise that they have no formal idolatry." Apparently the "idols" Garcés said he had been given by the Kohuanas on the lower Colorado did not count, religion being, to an eighteenth-century European like him, about doctrine and patterns of worship rather than its objects.

Second, Garcés explained the alliances and enmities that existed among the various groups he encountered. Third, he identified the peoples who were ready to receive missions and where these missions ought to be placed; it turned out that now he believed there should be no fewer than seventeen. No friendly tribes were left out of Garcés's accounting. From the Halyikwamais to the Papagos to the Mohaves, everyone deserved a mission. Font thought it insane to consider establishing new missions on the Gila, on the Colorado, or anywhere else when the ones already in existence were so threatened.[50] But unlike Font, and for better or worse, Francisco Garcés was a man of vision.

Naturally, Garcés next outlined where presidios ought to be placed, carefully prefacing his remarks by saying that the "number and stationing of presidios and of soldiers is a matter expressly for the Viceregal Government." In fact, he exercised great self-restraint, suggesting no new presidios besides the two for the Colorado and Gila already approved, and adding only that at each mission a guard of ten to twelve soldiers ought to be kept. When it came to how the military might subdue the Apaches, however (Garcés's fifth point), Garcés could not help but suggest that the presidio on the Gila be put instead on the Salt (the Río de la Asunción) and be given besides the usual fifty men fifty additional leatherjacket soldiers and eighty dragoons.[51] Such a presidio would provide "a formidable safeguard against the Apaches" and could even patrol as far as Oraibi; like most Spaniards at this time, Garcés believed the north-south distance between the Gila and Hopi lands to be shorter than it actually was, as Font's map makes clear. Indeed, he hoped that this presidio might over time bring the Hopis into line by attracting the Indian trade that usually went to them, forcing the Hopis to "humble themselves and want our friendship." Finally, this super-presidio on the Salt would lie along a new route that might be followed from Chihuahua diagonally northwest, crossing the Colorado River well north of Yuma and proceeding to Monterey by way of the Tehachapis or, at worst, San Gabriel.

For his sixth point, Garcés suggested potential routes between Monterey, Sonora, and New Mexico. He had not yet found a good one for "seven hundred or a thousand men," but for a small group virtually any of the routes he himself had taken between the three places would do. He was certain a shorter route from Oraibi to the Colorado River could be found. On this matter more exploration was needed. (Garcés remained overly optimistic about the possibilities of travel between the Colorado and the San Joaquín Valley by way of the Kern River.)

Garcés's seventh point had to do with a letter Fray Escalante had sent to Viceroy Bucareli in August 1775 but had not reached Garcés until his return to San Xavier in September 1776. Garcés wrote that unlike Escalante he had neither heard about nor seen anything like cannibalism on his travels. He encouraged Escalante to try to find a route from Santa Fe to Monterey north of the Colorado, perhaps by way of the big river of which the Yokuts had told him. He then spent several paragraphs speculating about this river, or another large one to the north, and its relation to earlier exploration reports. No less than others did Garcés hold the firm opinion that a large river flowing westward into the Pacific *must* exist.

Last, Garcés expounded on the question of how to equip the new missions on the Colorado and Gila, especially in light of what he had seen among the missions in California. Provisioning them via ships sailing up the Gulf of California and Colorado River to Yuma or somewhere to its south he thought the best and wisest choice. He added that the soldiers at San Diego should be under the same command as those on the Colorado, in case the former should be needed not only to help with provisions but also to prevent unauthorized travel by Spaniards between there and the northern California missions. Garcés made this suggestion in the hope of preventing further assaults on the Indians living in between.

Not that the friar had any misgivings about the Spaniards' project. "Thanks be to God, I see reviving in our time the old Spanish passion for discovering and taking possession of new lands in order to gather precious pearls, the souls of men!" he concluded. "I see the great steps that are being taken for having us press farther into the interior, and I firmly believe that God will favor our enterprise by bringing to us the most savage nations, if we please Him by adding at once to His church so many thousands of souls as today are disposed to join it, and are awaiting us with open arms."

✳ ✳ ✳

Garcés's recommendations were a stirring call to aggressive action that, unfortunately for he and his fellow friars, would ultimately be addressed to a man for whom aggressive action was not natural. That man was a forty-seven-year-old nobleman by the name of Teodoro de Croix, nephew of former viceroy Carlos Francisco de Croix. He arrived in Mexico City soon after Garcés and Font, on January 3, 1777, had put the finishing touches on the story of Garcés's pathbreaking journey of 1775–76. Gálvez had become Spain's minister of the Indies in January 1776, and soon thereafter he had appointed Croix to be the first commandant-general of the Provincias Internas, a concept Gálvez had been nurturing since he had visited New Spain's frontier in 1768. As with most major initiatives in the Spanish empire, it had taken years to come to fruition. The idea was that the six northern provinces of California, Sonora, Nueva Vizcaya, Coahuila, Texas, and New

Teodoro de Croix, known as "the Caballero," commandant-general of the Provincias Internas. *From Thomas,* Teodoro de Croix, *iv. Used by permission of the University of Oklahoma Press.*

Mexico were too distant, and their problems too complex, to be ruled effectively by an overworked viceroy in distant Mexico City. Much better for them to be governed by someone whose boots were on the ground, thought Gálvez, someone who retained a direct line to the crown. This arrangement would also allow the king to raise more revenue, reduce expenses, and implement some of the political, economic, and ecclesiastical reforms that had been intended when the Jesuits were expelled in 1767.[52] The governors of the six provinces included within the Provincias Internas would therefore report directly to Croix, with Viceroy Bucareli vaguely enjoined to aid and supply him. Naturally, Bucareli was irritated by this new arrangement. He had trouble viewing it as implying anything but a lack of confidence in his leadership.

Despite their admiration of Bucareli, the friars were at first less skeptical. News of the establishment of the Provincias Internas

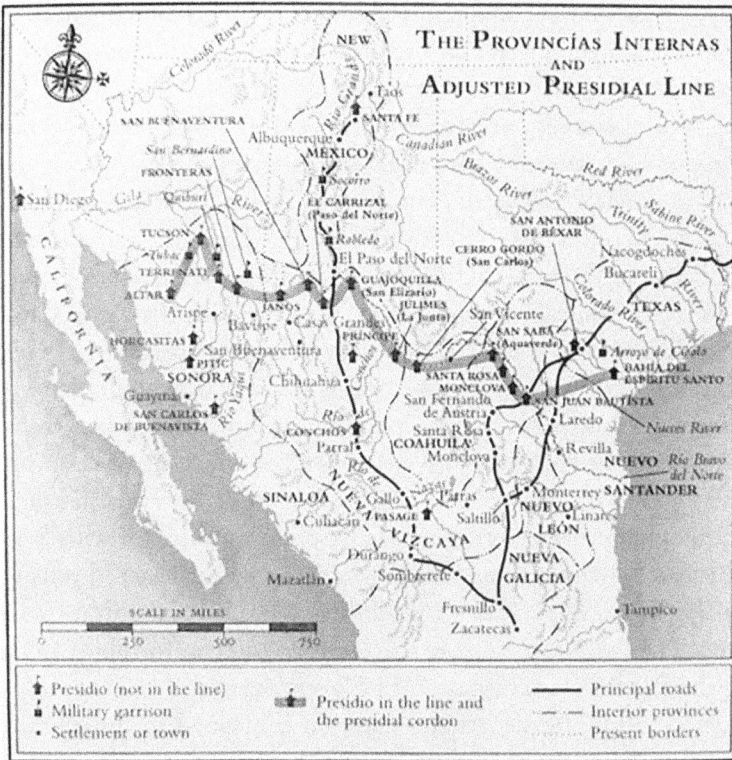

The Provincias Internas, a special administrative unit that as of 1776 consisted of the six northern New Spain provinces California, Sonora, Nueva Vizcaya, Coahuila, Texas, and New Mexico. The map also shows the new presidial line that came to fruition in the last half of the 1770s. *From Kessell*, Spain in the Southwest, *310. Used by permission of the University of Oklahoma Press.*

reached them, both in Mexico City and on the frontier, well before Croix did. The College of Santa Cruz looked upon the concept with "guarded optimism," in that the padres hoped it would mean more protection for their new missions.[53] Their optimism gradually waned, however, as the character of Croix revealed itself. Croix was not a bad or vicious man. He simply lacked the experience and spiritedness demanded by the moment, despite his having been given the Cross of the Teutonic Order in 1756, since which he had gone by the title Caballero de Croix.

Croix had served in New Spain from 1766 to 1772, but during that time he had gone nowhere near the northern frontier. After his arrival in Mexico City in January 1777, he set about learning that frontier's conditions. The more he learned, the more depressed he became. Bucareli and O'Conor painted a relatively rosy picture and encouraged him to move forward with their plans, but the testimony of everyone and everything else portrayed a bleak situation. Not knowing how to meet it, Croix hesitated. He took his sweet time gathering information. He dawdled in Mexico and elsewhere, toured part of the new presidial line, became seriously sick, and made a sure-to-be-declined request for two thousand more soldiers—this at a time when Spain, because war with Britain was brewing, needed all the military might it could muster in the Mississippi Valley and Gulf of Mexico. Incredibly, Croix would not arrive at Arizpe, the small and uncomfortable capital of the Provincias Internas, until November 1779.[54]

Meanwhile the situation in Sonora continued to deteriorate. Anza marched north with Palma and his fellow Quechans in the spring of 1777, stopping in Durango so that the newly baptized Indians could receive the sacrament of confirmation at its cathedral. At the presidio of Horcasitas, Anza formally assumed command as Sonora's interim military governor. He kept the post for nearly a year, even after being named governor of New Mexico in 1778, since Croix had not yet made his way to the northwest. It did not take long for Anza to conclude that the move of the Tubac, Fronteras, and Terrenate presidios had been a huge mistake. The plan had looked good on paper, but it had left Sonora even more unprotected. To push forward to the Gila, he now believed, would be the height of stupidity.[55]

From Garcés's perspective, however, at least the mission at San Xavier del Bac was now better defended. This was thanks both to the presidio that was now in Tucson and to its commander, the energetic Captain Allande. Allande was a Spanish-born officer who had worked in Sonora since 1768, and he had that borderline psychotic personality typical of so many effective military leaders. He was proud, prickly, and often violent with his troops, and he believed strongly in giving no quarter or rest to the enemy.[56]

After his arrival at Tucson, Allande finished the presidio walls—making each one roughly 750 feet in length and ten to twelve feet high—and built adobe houses for the troops and settlers on the walls' interiors. He surrounded the presidio with a rough-log palisade and built guardhouse bastions at its four corners. He also constructed within the presidio a magazine and a solid church, all at his own expense.[57] The result was essentially a walled city, with but a single gate, containing the largest community of Spaniards in the Pimería Alta.[58]

Soon Allande had his soldiers in good enough shape to begin an offensive against the Apaches, one characterized by a policy of merciless offensive warfare. Allande's exploits against the Apaches were epitomized by an episode of November 6, 1779, when a reported 350 Apaches attacked the Tucson presidio. With just fifteen men, he gave chase, and catching up with the warriors he was able to kill one of the Apache chiefs. He proceeded to cut off the man's head before his kinsmen's eyes, then charged their battle line with the chief's head thrust forward on the tip of his lance.[59] Such unusual bravery, if not insanity, generally made the few Spaniards now living at Tucson and San Xavier feel safer.

Those unfortunate enough to still be living at Tubac and points south felt otherwise. Many had not acted as O'Conor had supposed they would and migrated to Tucson. Instead, they formed a militia for self-protection. Eventually they formed a citizens' committee and pled, in November 1777, with Allande for the presidio's return to Tubac. Allande asked Garcés for his informed opinion on the matter. We do not have Garcés's response, but as under the committee's plan only ten to twelve soldiers were to be left at San Xavier it seems highly unlikely that he supported the Tubac citizens' argument. In any case, they were rebuffed;

Allande detached only a dozen or so soldiers to protect Tubac and the surrounding missions. That was too few to help Father Barbastro's companion Fray Felipe Guillén, who in April 1778 was speared through the chest by Apaches as he rode through country long considered reasonably safe.[60] When Croix received the news, he commented simply and laconically that it was "a lamentable occurrence but hardly surprising." The Caballero's indolence, combined with Anza's departure for New Mexico in March 1778, made New Spain's northwestern frontier feel like a more dangerous place than ever.

It must have been somewhat comforting to Garcés and his clerical brethren that there were now more priests around with whom to share that danger.[61] In early 1777, after a short stay at Tumacácori, there arrived at San Xavier the strong-willed Father Juan Bautista de Velderrain, a tall, dark-haired Basque. Garcés took him in and taught him the Piman tongue. Velderrain had presided over the construction of a new church at his last stop, Suaqui. It was his destiny to begin construction of a new one at San Xavier, too—the magnificently beautiful church that still stands there today.[62] Also at San Xavier for part of this time was another Basque, Father Joaquín Antonio Belarde, one of six priests who had gathered for mutual protection at the mission of Ímuris in November 1776 after the Indian attack that almost killed Father Font. The five-foot six-inch, blue-eyed, brown-haired Belarde had arrived in Sonora in 1773.[63] San Xavier was now almost crowded.

Garcés also found comfort in Bucareli's sympathetic understanding and the knowledge that the king had taken personal pleasure in his explorations. In response to Garcés's concern that Captain Rivera y Moncada might make good on his threat to arrest or detain Indians who came to the coastal missions from the Colorado River, Bucareli told Garcés in March 1777 that he would order that nothing of the kind be done.[64] The viceroy also assured Garcés that instructions for the establishment of missions on the Colorado and Gila would soon be issued. Then, on August 9, 1777, Bucareli passed along, by way of Gálvez, a message to the friar from Charles III himself. The king had "learned with much satisfaction of the information given by this religious of his peregrinations" and was awaiting receipt of the promised diary. In the meantime, he asked Bucareli to "give thanks in his royal name to Father Garcés for the zeal and fervor with which he acts in discovering, treating with, and attracting these ignorant nations." Bucareli added his own thanks for "the tenacity" Garcés had shown in his journeys, "regardless of fatigue."[65]

Garcés replied to Bucareli from Tucson on January 21, 1778:

[Receipt of this message from the king] filled my spirit with satisfaction, considering that it emanated from a King as wise and magnificent as he whom God has given us, and I hold it as certain that God will do some great work in payment of the ardent desires of his Catholic Majesty. As to what concerns me, I know well that such a great honor is not fitting for so insignificant a subject. I have been informed of how much the most illustrious Senor Gálvez is doing for the conversion and of what your Excellency has done in this particular; you will not suffer on the day of judgment for what you are doing to serve God in this matter.[66]

✳ ✳ ✳

The crown officially approved a mission and presidio for the Yumas on February 10 and 14, 1777.[67] Croix received these orders, acknowledged them—and did nothing. Garcés tried to spur things along by sending the Caballero a congratulatory letter and the map Font had drawn of Garcés's travels. Croix thanked him and said he personally wished to visit the site on the Colorado where the Spaniards were to plant their flag so that he could superintend the placement of new presidios there and on the Gila. But then he got sick.[68] Precious days, weeks, months passed as Croix's inactivity, his insistence on paying a visit to the Colorado before committing resources to the project, and problems elsewhere combined to stall movement on the frontier.

Meanwhile, Palma and the Quechans were waiting with increasing impatience for the Spaniards to fulfill their promises, not only of missions but more importantly of the food and gifts that would come with them. For Palma the situation was particularly dire. Since his return from Mexico City, he had conveyed many Spanish promises to his people. Those promises remained unfulfilled. With his prestige eroding, the Quechan chief traveled to the presidio of Altar in March 1778 to ask its captain, Pedro Tueros, why there had been a delay. Tueros explained that Croix was touring the presidios to the east (it was on this tour that Croix fell ill, like so many newcomers to the region) and that as soon as he returned he would visit the Quechans and establish missions there.

This explanation appeased Palma for a time. In eager anticipation of Croix and the priests' arrival, in the fall he laid in a large supply of wheat, corn, beans, and squash. But still his Spanish friends did not come. Every morning, at the break of dawn, the Quechans would scan the horizon for some sign of their expected visitors. Every morning they were disappointed. They and their neighbors began calling Palma a liar until he could take it no longer. In January 1779, a nearly distraught Palma led a multi-tribe party from the lower Colorado to Sonora to go see Tueros again. Thinking of every angle he could, Palma told Tueros that his people thought he was making fools of them, that he had ensured there would be plenty of food on hand to feed the comandante-general and the padres when they arrived, and that many of his people sought baptism. He also lamented that one of his children had died without being baptized. Tueros consoled him as best he could and assured his Cajuenche, Halchidhoma, Halyikwamai, Kohuana, and Cocopah companions that Palma was telling the truth about the Spaniards' words and intentions. Croix was coming. The friars were coming. Missions were coming.[69]

Everyone left these conferences satisfied, but the wise and sympathetic Tueros could plainly see that the Spanish window of opportunity on the Colorado was fast closing. He begged Croix— who had met Palma in Mexico City but clearly did not have Anza's or Garcés's emotional attachment to the Quechan and his people—finally to act. He must immediately send Garcés—and it had to be Garcés, for no other missionary knew so well how to deal with the Indians—and another priest chosen by Garcés to go live with the Quechans. They should be able to prevent any uprisings and protect Palma until Croix should decide how precisely to proceed.[70]

This time the Caballero got the message. On February 5, 1779, he dashed off three letters.[71] To Barbastro he relayed the substance of Palma's conversations with Tueros and asked that the father-president waste no time in sending Garcés and the clerical companion of his choice to the Colorado. He would see to it that they had whatever supplies they needed, transportation, and an escort. He wrote Tueros to say he had put the plan in motion and to order him to give Garcés however many soldiers he requested as an escort, and to allow Garcés to handpick them. Finally, he wrote Garcés directly, relaying Palma's situation and arguing that the grand enterprise of advancing to the Colorado River would fail if they did not act quickly. Garcés, of course, had been saying just that for several years. Not knowing his man very well, the Caballero expended a good deal of ink flattering Garcés: only he, with his experience, prudence, discretion, and talent, could do the job. He would give the padre whatever he needed, and he would go to the Colorado in person as soon as he could.

Upon receiving the Caballero's letter, Barbastro summoned Garcés to Tubutama for a discussion. He also sent for Father Díaz, whom the Quechans knew well from his 1774 sojourn there. Croix's ideas on how to proceed were unexpected. The friars had thought mission and presidio would be founded simultaneously, according to something like the usual model; indeed, Anza had argued that along with the usual garrison an especially strong military contingent would be needed at each of the missions themselves. Croix was now proposing that Queretaran missionaries advance to the Colorado only with a small guard taken from Tueros's command. With all the problems he was experiencing with rebellious Seris and Piatos in the Sonoran interior, Croix

claimed he could not afford to transfer the presidios of Horcasitas and Buenavista northward, as the padres had once thought
to be a fait accompli. And though he had ordered that the priests
be provisioned with whatever they needed, hard experience made
the friars skeptical this order would be followed, given the violence engulfing the entire country.[72] Finally, they knew well that
the establishment of a new mission with few soldiers to protect
it invited catastrophe; it was precisely such an arrangement that
had gotten their good friend Father Gil killed a few years earlier.

In short, this new plan was extraordinarily risky, even by the
friars' highly risk-tolerant standards. The nearest garrison would
be more than 250 miles away, and the Spaniards had disappointed Palma and his people for more than two years. Garcés
and Díaz understood, as Croix in all probability did not, that
Palma wasn't really in charge of all three thousand Quechans.
They knew that with respect to the Spaniards the tribes' moods
might soon darken, or rather that they had already darkened.[73]
But they decided to go ahead anyway. Practically speaking,
were they to refuse the Caballero's request they would surely
be blamed if the Quechans became hostile to the Spanish. But,
more basically, why else were they here? Why else had they gone
on the 1774 expedition? Why else had Garcés done all he had
to prepare for this moment? Plus, Garcés must have reflected,
hadn't he argued just a few years earlier that priests preparing to
establish new missions ought to enter into Indian communities
quietly and with little or no show of force? Providence was giving him a chance to put those words into action. "Where there is
a will, there is a way," he had written the colegio's guardian the
year previous, in a letter in which he had stressed how deeply he
cared about the missionary enterprise, "and a lot can be done if
the desire is great."[74]

By the close of their conference with Barbastro, Garcés and
Díaz had decided to move forward. On March 23, 1779, Garcés
wrote a long and serious letter to Tueros to make sure everyone
was on the same page.[75] First, he repeated what he understood his

charge to be: to travel to the Colorado River with the purpose of instructing, catechizing, and baptizing all those Quechans who wished to be baptized. Then he went into his conditions. He would need fifteen men, or at least twelve of his choosing from the presidios of Altar and Tucson. He would need a competent carpenter. He would need good mules. Thinking like Junípero Serra, he requested that the soldiers bring their wives with them; otherwise there were bound to be serious problems with the Quechan women, and hence the Quechan men. He would need plenty of food; apparently Garcés did not think Palma had stored enough for so many men, an intuition that would prove correct. He would need the soldiers to be held accountable for their behavior and to help with everything, including the erection of buildings and serving at Mass. Last, it would be helpful if settlers and retired soldiers were incentivized to join the enterprise by being promised land at the settlement, which he thought could be done without stealing any from the Quechans and other peoples who lived along the river, and if neophytes from settlements in Sonora were sent to serve as examples and interpreters. To all this the authorities readily assented, with the caveat that it might be difficult to persuade soldiers to take their wives. As Tueros wrote Garcés, few soldiers were eager to take such risks with their spouses.[76] One suspects that few wives were excited about the prospect of starting life anew so far away from Spanish civilization, either.

The friars spent the next several months collecting what provisions they could. Díaz met with Intendant-Governor Corbalán to get a draft for two thousand pesos, with which the Franciscans' factor at La Cieneguilla, Don Antonio Enriques de Castro, helped him obtain religious articles, mules, utensils, tobacco, and gifts for the Quechans. With Tueros's blessing, Garcés handpicked soldiers for the venture from the presidios of Tucson and Altar.[77] The plan was to leave in the spring, before the advent of the intense summer heat, but things were not ready until August 1, 1779. On that day, Garcés, Díaz, an Ópata scout, and eleven leatherjacket soldiers, led by twenty-five-year-old sergeant and Querétaro native José Darío Argüello, set off from Altar for Yuma.

In a few days the party reached Sonoita, where the men rested and refreshed themselves with their Papago hosts. The terrible Camino del Diablo lay ahead. On the 10th they resumed their journey. It had been a dry summer, and they feared that the few water holes along their route would be dry. It did not take long to discover that their fears were well-founded. Soon they were back in Sonoita, slaking their terrible thirst.

The prudent thing to do was to wait for the monsoon rains to arrive and fill up the *tinajas*. But every delay decreased the Spaniards' chances of meeting with friendliness among the Quechans. Argüello and the soldiers argued that the project should be given up, but Garcés and Díaz convinced them to adopt another plan. Garcés, two soldiers, and a native scout would forge ahead while Díaz and the others waited at Sonoita for the skies finally to open. It was not long until Garcés and his three companions were again on their way across the sun-baked Sonoran Desert, taking with them only what they needed to survive. On August 31, 1779, they arrived at Palma's ranchería. Francisco Garcés had reached his final earthly home.

CHAPTER II

Not Peace, but a Sword

1779–1781

O n the blazing hot day of August 31, 1779, Salvador Palma
and his village greeted Francisco Garcés and his three
companions hospitably. The rest of the Quechans,
unfortunately, were as surly as Garcés had feared. They had been
promised gifts—tobacco, cloth, beads, food. Where were they?
Garcés could only ask them to be patient, while turning on as much
charm as he could. Nothing he did could brighten the Quechans'
mood. They would not provide food except in exchange for Spanish goods, and Garcés had few goods to give them.[1]

It was all so heartbreakingly different than in 1771, 1774, 1775,
and 1776, when the Quechans had been so welcoming and generous. Now they were truculent, hostilities between the Quechans
and their neighbors had resumed, and Palma could do little if
anything about it. Garcés, as he would explain a bit later, decided
to approach the situation with resignation. "When I reached this
nation of the Yumas, I found it moved only by motives of selfish-
ness on account of the talks of Palma, to whom promises were

made at Mexico of I do not know what sort," he wrote his religious superiors. But he did not despair, believing not only that God himself could work changes of heart among the Quechans but also that presents for the Indians—presents that would surely arrive at some point—would work toward the same end. Therefore, Garcés "said nothing to the Caballero or to anyone else" but instead "swallowed the whole affair and resolved to establish the mission."[2]

Garcés himself was still well liked. Soon after his arrival, Palma roasted a lamb in the friar's honor and began building him a wattle-and-daub house on the high hill that overlooked El Puerto de la Concepción on the Colorado's western bank, the same location at which Fathers Eixarch and Garcés had had their home in 1775–76. Garcés repaid his hosts by again trying to make peace—this time between the Quechans and the Halchidhomas—and by baptizing a few infants and adults. Preaching, he lamented, was difficult, since the Quechans were scattered for miles up and down the riverbanks, planting and tending their fields.

On September 2, 1779, three days after his arrival in Yuma, Garcés wrote letters to the Caballero and to Intendant-Governor Corbalán informing them of his tenuous situation among the "turbulent" Quechans. He begged that gifts be sent as soon as possible. The few he had brought with him were already gone, given away or bartered for food upon his arrival. Without more supplies, the problem of survival would soon become acute. To further win over his hosts and the natives that surrounded them, Garcés also requested *bastones*—canes of office—for bestowal upon their chiefs, as well as more Ópata scouts to act as muleteers, carpenters, millers, and workmen. Garcés still believed in the peacemaking power of economic development more than he did the force of arms.

As always, Garcés's thinking stretched well beyond his immediate needs, no matter how urgent those needs might be. To Croix, he returned to his familiar theme that not just one or two but many missions ought to be established on the Colorado and the Gila. After the mission of La Purísima Concepción had been established on the hill where Garcés's house was being built, the Kohuanas, who maintained fertile fields downstream from the Quechans, ought to get the next mission. One could also be established among the Cocopahs. And the Halchidhomas. And the Mohaves. Nor should the Cocomaricopas and Pimas along the Gila be forgotten—indeed, they were currently much vexed at having been passed over in favor of their Quechan enemies. Garcés mused that perhaps no presidio at all would need to be established on these rivers if each of the missions had its own larger-than-usual military escort—an idea he later might have regretted floating. In any case, he clearly imagined a web of Spanish missions binding together the peoples of the northern frontier in a common faith and way of life, thereby putting a halt to their destructive wars.

On September 3, Garcés sent the two soldiers who had accompanied him to the Colorado back to Sonoita with his letters for Croix and Corbalán, along with a report for Father Díaz that included a request to come along soon—and regardless, to send food and goods immediately. For the next month Garcés lived among the Quechans alone, attempting to assuage their anger and minister to their spiritual needs, as he saw them.

If only he had had gifts to share. The friar had known how important presents would be for winning back the Quechans' allegiance, given both their inflated expectations and their sense of betrayal. Croix had provided no gifts or funds for purchasing any, so Garcés had written Bucareli on March 11, 1779, asking whether the viceroy, out of his personal piety and fortune, would be so kind as to provide alms for the purpose:

> Great has been our need to appeal to the piety of devotees in order to be able to encourage the zeal of those natives with the usual gifts, especially since there is only one mission, all the neighboring nations have recourse to it, and since these provinces are in such a deplorable state it is not possible to secure in them all that is necessary for these pious ends. The great charity of your Excellency has in this an opportunity

to vent itself. It will be very pleasing to God, and I shall always keep it in mind in order to pray that his Majesty will preserve for me your important life for many years in the highest exaltation and greatness.[3]

Bucareli had enough respect for Garcés, and enough genuine piety, that in all likelihood he would have responded generously to the friar, had his life in fact been preserved. But Bucareli died on April 9, 1779, having not yet received Garcés's letter. Hope for a happy ending on the Colorado died with him.[4]

✳ ✳ ✳

While Garcés renewed relationships with the testy Indians of the lower Colorado, Díaz was dealing with dangers and frustrations of his own. First there came a message to Sonoita that a Papago group was so angry at what they saw as the Spaniards' preference for the Quechans that they intended to descend on and kill Díaz and the five soldiers accompanying him (four of the nine troops had temporarily returned to Altar). Sergeant Argüello's response to this frightening news was to prepare hastily for flight, but Díaz persuaded him to stay. Garcés's letter from Yuma arrived shortly thereafter. It wasn't very comforting. Then the four soldiers who had gone to Altar returned bearing a missive from Captain Tueros. Following orders from Croix, Tueros commanded Díaz and Garcés to abandon their project entirely and return to Sonora to meet with the Caballero. This directive struck Díaz as so massively wrongheaded and ill-timed that he simply refused to comply. He was soon on his way to Yuma with Argüello and his men; they arrived on October 2, 1779. Once again, the Quechans cheered the arrival of the magnificent bonanza of supplies Palma had been promising since returning from Mexico City. Once again, they were bitterly disappointed.

At first there was great happiness. Clothes and tobacco and beads were distributed to all, and the Quechans responded by presenting more than two hundred children for baptism. But the

Spanish supplies—it was clothing, evidently, that the Quechans most coveted—soon ran out, and as far as the Quechans were concerned their quantity fell far short of what Palma had led them to expect. The lavish distribution of gifts that had accompanied the Spaniards' expeditions through Yuma, the many promises made by the missionaries and secular authorities, Palma's journey to Mexico City—all had now backfired on the Spanish, raising expectations among the Quechans to impossible heights. Argüello noted that within a few days there was "a sort of muttering" among the Indians. Palma had told them all would be outfitted like him, that the Spanish "would bring them many bales of clothing so that all could dress themselves to their satisfaction."[5] Desire had been awakened, and unhappiness predictably trailed in its wake.

As the mild Sonoran Desert autumn took hold, Palma's authority became even more attenuated. It was not obvious to Argüello that he possessed the ability to check whatever the Quechans might wish to do. Garcés acknowledged that Palma now wielded authority only among those living in his own small ranchería, although when it came to martial matters his authority was somewhat broader.[6] Palma's loss of prestige was the Spaniards' loss as well. With the help of the soldiers (and probably some friendly Quechans), Garcés and Díaz were able to finish building a house for themselves and a rude chapel for saying Mass at La Purísima Concepción. But only with extreme difficulty did they prevent a fresh war from breaking out between Quechans and the Halchidhomas and Kohuanas after some downstream Quechans itching for battle killed two Halchidhomas, and the Kohuanas, avenging the deaths of their allies, killed two Quechan warriors in response.[7] The priests found it impossible to persuade the Quechans to live near them in traditional mission style, lacking the gifts and food usually used as inducements, and were therefore unable to make much spiritual headway with them. They were horrified by the illicit sexual relations the Spanish soldiers—who had not, as yet, brought their families with them, as Garcés had requested—had with Quechan women. And they were only barely able to ward off starvation—for themselves and their soldier escorts—by trading tobacco and supplies for food.

Unless the Caballero provided more gifts, more supplies, more soldiers, more artisans, and more support, wrote Garcés to Croix on November 6, 1779, the sacred project being pursued at Yuma was highly unlikely to succeed. His requests, he added with that touch of sarcasm that entered Garcés's correspondence whenever he was truly irritated, did not seem unreasonable. Surely the mission at Monterey had received much more from the authorities when *it* was founded.

During that same month, Croix, recovered from his illness, finally arrived at Arizpe, capital of the Provincias Internas. Having addressed as well as he could the Apache problem on the northeastern frontier, his attention was now turned to the northwest. Alas, the Spanish crown had put him in a tight spot. Spain was now at war with Britain, and Charles III was therefore in no position to expend resources on offensive warfare in this comparatively unimportant corner of his empire. The king had ordered Croix henceforth to take only defensive military action in the Provincias Internas, husbanding resources and consolidating gains.[8] How Croix was to do that while subduing the rebellious Seris, Apaches, and other groups outside his front door, and simultaneously fulfilling the king's orders to move forward to the Colorado-Gila junction, was one of those insoluble dilemmas that made frontier officials wish they had never left Spain. The Caballero decided he ought at least to reverse the northward move of the presidios overseen by O'Conor, returning them to more southerly positions. This move did not augur well for the Queretarans' dreams of mission expansion. They were now losing ground.

Whatever the extent to which they understood Croix's difficulties, Garcés and Díaz were too concerned about their own problems to display sympathy. Besides a lack of food, supplies, and workers, these problems included the fact that the Quechans

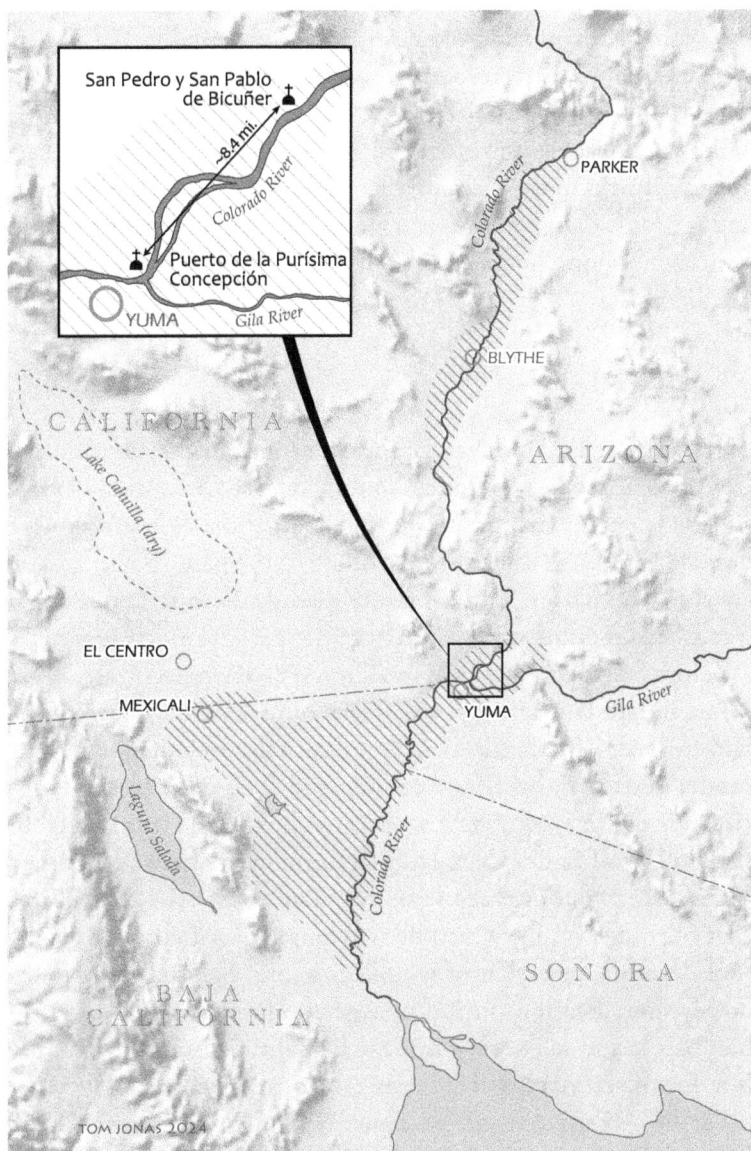

The sites of La Purísima Concepción and San Pedro y San Pablo Bicuñer. Today, a historical marker stands at the site of the latter. St. Thomas Indian Mission is perched on the hill where the former once stood. Hatched area represents a relatively settled region. *Map by Tom Jonas.*

living downstream had become especially unfriendly. The padres were hesitant to baptize even those who presented themselves, given that Croix had wanted to abandon the project some months earlier. And they were worried about the criticism that was apparently circulating about their methods.[9] Garcés was tired and anxious. Being on the road made him happy. Trying to build a mission among people who were ill disposed toward mission life did not.

✳ ✳ ✳

As they passed a lonely and hungry autumn in their hut on the Colorado, it seemed to Garcés and Díaz that Croix did not have an adequate understanding of their situation. They therefore decided that Díaz, the more articulate of the pair, should go and lay their troubles in front of Croix directly. Permission to do so was asked for and soon received from their superiors at Querétaro.

Before Díaz left, Father Juan Antonio de Barreneche arrived at Yuma in late January 1780 to replace him. As a boy, Barreneche had crossed the Atlantic as an apprentice to a rich merchant. His master settled in bustling Havana, and Juan entered the Franciscan order in 1768. A few years later, in 1773, he transferred to the College of Santa Cruz at Querétaro, where he was ordained a priest in 1776. For three years his main role at the colegio was that of confessor, for which he was amply qualified by his spiritual devotion, rejection of worldliness, and habitual practice of bodily mortification (including extreme fasting, the wearing of hair shirts, and self-scourging). Such qualities also helped qualify him for the hardships of frontier missionary life. In late 1779 the order he secretly longed for came; he was to go into the field, joining Garcés on the Colorado. From the moment he met the man who was now a living legend at Querétaro, the two friars got along swimmingly.[10]

Díaz set out for Arizpe soon after Barreneche appeared at the Colorado. He arrived on February 12, 1780, and immediately presented to Croix his and Garcés's latest requests and recommendations.[11] A general war between the Quechans and their allies (the Mohaves, principally) and the Halchidhomas, Kohuanas, and their allies (the Cocomaricopas, Pimas, and northern Papagos) was clearly in the offing, Díaz told the Caballero. To prevent this catastrophe, Díaz pleaded for two new missions among the Halchidhomas and Cajuenches, along with at least twenty additional soldiers, another carpenter, a stone mason, a mule driver, and other workmen. If that was impossible, he continued, it was at least necessary to launch a second mission among the Quechans, with each mission being staffed by two friars. Díaz also presented to the Caballero a letter from Garcés that sought to assure the commandant-general that the friars were adapting their methods to their particular circumstances and were asking for nothing other than what was genuinely needed. In response, a weary Croix took counsel with his legal advisor, the exceptionally frugal *asesor* Don Pedro Galindo y Navarro, a man not much loved or trusted by any frontier missionary.[12] Together, they came up with a new plan.

Croix and Galindo suggested starting another mission, just as Díaz had requested. But it would not be just a mission; rather, it and the aborning settlement at Puerto de la Concepción would be "military colonies," each including ten soldiers, ten farmers with their families, five workmen with their families, and two priests.[13] That much would clearly make Garcés and Díaz happy, as would Croix's charge that "the Reverend Fathers proceed with the reduction of the Indians in conformity with the sovereign laws and many cédulas of their Majesties." But Croix and his *asesor* also seized the opportunity to put into effect the money-saving, power-enhancing Enlightenment reforms that the Spanish crown still wanted to see implemented. These reforms included the restriction of the friars' authority to the spiritual realm alone, with military and civil authority wielded by a military commandant who would also serve as *juez político*, or civil judge; limitation of the extent to which Indian labor could be requisitioned for the missionaries' support; minute agricultural instructions intended to spur production and industry; and an insistence that the "reduction" of the Indians—presumably meaning Christian Indians—not include forcing them to live in the new settlements until they had "been attracted" to do so "by the good example and gentle treatment of the settlers."[14]

There was much in the plan that was innovative, in comparison to traditional mission practices, and one sees in Croix's plan a good-faith effort to meet Díaz and Garcés at least halfway. The friars would get another mission, more soldiers, more padres, and more settlers and laborers (the latter group to be approved by Díaz and Garcés themselves). Díaz, realizing that he and Garcés had gotten much of what they wanted, accepted most of Croix's conditions when he was presented with a draft on February 17. The most important components of his counterproposal were that Croix give the friars authority to control the missions' finances and extra money for the purchase of gifts and supplies. Croix acceded to both requests. These adjustments made, on March 7, 1780, Teodoro de Croix signed his official command to go forward with the establishment of the two Colorado River colonies.[15]

✳ ✳ ✳

Franciscan commentators, writing in hindsight after the bloody tragedy of July 1781, would complain bitterly about the unorthodox methods Croix used in establishing and governing the Colorado River missions.[16] Among their many other complaints, most of which revolve around the restriction of the clerics' authority, was that Croix acted with callous disregard for the safety of the missionaries in not putting a presidio on the river. They conveniently overlooked that the Croix plan had much in common with the Garcés plan of late 1779; it combined larger soldier escorts at the missions with the settlement of families in those places. Nevertheless, historian Mark Santiago is correct in pointing out that aspects of the Croix plan—and by extension, the Garcés plan—"were pure fantasy," especially those parts that presumed the availability of unclaimed, arable land for use by Spanish settlers; the assumption that the preaching of the friars and the good example of the settlers would in time lure the Quechans into leaving their rancherías and fields to live in a traditionally designed Spanish pueblo; and the overall premise that "fifty families of settlers and soldiers could merge blithely and happily among three thousand independent" natives.[17] The naïveté of the Spanish camp was not insubstantial.

The man tasked by Croix with the implementation of his instructions was Ensign Santiago Yslas, an Italian noncommissioned officer who had served on the frontier since 1776, when his regiment of dragoons was assigned to Nueva Vizcaya. In May 1777, Yslas had gained his current rank when he joined one of the "flying companies" of horsemen formed as a result of Hugo O'Conor's presidial reforms. Soon the Third Flying Company was assigned to the presidio of Horcasitas, where Yslas met and married Doña María Ana Montijo, daughter of one of the northwestern frontier's most wealthy and prominent families. Yslas was then transferred to Altar, where he distinguished himself in combat and was commended for the discipline of his troops. There is nothing to indicate he was not an exceptionally able military man.[18]

Able as he was, it was no easy task to gather the settlers, animals, and supplies Croix had called for in settling the Colorado. For six months Yslas scoured the impoverished settlements of Sonora for all that was needed. In Altar, Tubac, and Tucson he eventually found twenty families who would commit to living on the Colorado for at least ten years. It helped that each was promised not only free land but also two oxen, two cows, one bull, two horses, and one hoe. From the ranches and missions he scrounged more than 200 sheep and nearly 250 cattle and horses—but no oxen, a failure that would prove to make plowing all but impossible. Meanwhile, Croix detailed soldiers from the Altar, Buenavista, and Tucson presidios for the Colorado River assignment, including three whom Garcés knew from their service on Anza's expeditions.[19]

While Yslas gathered men and materiel, Díaz rode to Tubutama to obtain supplies, a muleteer, and two workmen. This done, he remained at Tubutama, waiting for Yslas to finish his tasks so that together they could journey to Yuma. Months dragged by until the conscientious Díaz decided he could wait no longer. On September 12, 1780, he informed Croix that, inasmuch as Garcés, Barreneche, and the other Spaniards at Yuma must by now be sorely in need of various provisions, he was going ahead without Yslas. He suggested that Yslas follow him no later than early January so the settlers could get their crops planted on time.

Garcés wrote Croix at about the same time. Provisions were indeed nearly gone, to the point that Argüello and all but three or four soldiers had returned to Altar. Those left behind were "without a cigar or anything else that they could trade for a little maize to preserve their lives." That was bad enough; the posture of the Quechans toward the Spaniards was worse. Palma's brother Ygnacio and a young man named Pablo, son of the now-deceased Chief Pablo, both of whom had been baptized in Mexico City, had apparently seen an opening for increasing the prestige conferred by that trip. They had adopted an anti-Palma, anti-Spanish stance, wrote Garcés, and as a consequence "the rumor had already spread among the youths that on coming to the Colorado River, the Fathers and Spaniards were to be killed."[20]

Garcés often waved off such rumors. This one he was inclined to believe. One wonders if he had heard about, and been shaken by, the gruesome torture and murder of fellow Queretaran Fray Francisco Perdigón, chaplain of the Tucson presidio, earlier that summer by a group of Apaches.[21] Díaz was equally convinced; he confirmed Garcés's report shortly after returning to the Colorado.[22] In his view, the situation at Yuma was now disastrous. First, crops had failed because the river had not flooded to its usual extent. Then Ygnacio had led an attack on the Kohuanas— "without any motive except [a] whim," wrote Díaz—and killed some of them, captured others, burned many of their houses and fields, and stole "all the corn that they could carry." The result was that the Kohuanas were completely without food and all the people of the Colorado were suffering from a lack of provisions. "These, sir, are the evils resulting from the delay of the soldiers and settlers who might have been here on time and prevented this disaster," wrote Díaz with some bitterness. In his view, it would be better for Yslas and the settlers not to come until spring 1781. Were they to arrive now, they would stress the already bad food-supply situation more than they would relieve it. The Spaniards there did not have the "things that are very necessary to make life passable," reported Díaz. "Their total resources are reduced to the little that the religious brought, and these are gradually being left without provision through ministering to their need."

That the Spanish had thus far failed to keep their promises was the reason the Quechans and other peoples were restless, explained Díaz. They also made war on one another to take captives. These they then sold at towns in the Pimería Alta or to the Papagos, who resold them farther south at a profit and therefore had a vested interest in the wars' continuance. Díaz warned that, until the slave trade was ended, "we shall not be freed here from these unjust outbreaks so pernicious and so contrary to all law." He asked Croix to outlaw the sale and purchase of captives among the Spaniards and to warn the Papagos that if they were found with any slaves in their possession they would be taken from them without compensation and returned to their people.

Finally, Díaz explained that Ygnacio had won a great following among the younger Yumas. Palma opposed him, and Ygnacio therefore desired to kill him. Ygnacio had also "circulated many statements against the Spaniards and (if it is true what many say) has incited his followers to take the life of the Fathers and soldiers, although I do not suppose these Indians will carry out their intention on account of their cowardice." This was either bravado or a classic Spanish underestimation of a potential foe. Regardless, Díaz thought Ygnacio ought to be deported from the

Colorado by Yslas when he arrived. A little later, Garcés reported to Croix that for a while even Palma had grown troublesome. Fortunately, he had "changed completely ever since we appointed him 'justicia' about a month ago," even helping with the catechizing of others and bringing them to Mass and to the church to pray. Palma, it seems, still desperately wanted to see realized his long-formed plans for a beneficial alliance.[23]

❋ ❋ ❋

Díaz's letter arrived in Sonora too late to stop Yslas and his settlers from proceeding to the Colorado. The group arrived at Yuma on December 27, 1780, and according to the ensign was received "with much applause, pleasure, and rejoicing."[24] Yslas swiftly got to work preparing the site for the establishment of the second town—to be called San Pedro y San Pablo Bicuñer—at a grassy site among some hills about eight miles upstream from La Purísima Concepción.[25] Garcés had made note of the site's advantages for a mission back in 1776.[26]

Work at both missions started with the construction of irrigation channels. Seed corn was scarce, Yslas reported, but there were plenty of beans and squash seeds to plant, and he was hopeful that with proper cultivation the yield would be plentiful enough to feed settlers and soldiers. Unfortunately, the few settlers who had come earlier with Díaz had neither sown crops nor cultivated fields because they lacked oxen. This tragedy would befall the settlers who came with him, too, Yslas fretted, if the new pueblos did not acquire oxen by March, when the planting season ended.

Croix attempted to relieve the situation.[27] He ordered Don Andrés de Arías Caballero to transport oxen, cattle, and various provisions and equipment to Yuma for the soldiers and their families. He also ordered a stop to the sale of captives in the Pimería. "This iniquitous trade has not until now reached my notice," he wrote Father Díaz, a statement that if honest indicates the Caballero's failure to comprehend actual frontier dynamics. Finally, he notified Yslas to confer with Díaz and Garcés with respect to Ygnacio and to then act as he thought best. If it was decided to deport the Quechan troublemaker, it should "be done in such a way that disorders shall not result nor these tribes be given any reason to doubt in the least the friendship and good faith that has been promised them."

Bad as the situation was, there was now little the Spaniards on the Colorado could do but continue with the project. On January 7, 1781, while a group of Quechans "looked on and saluted us with shouts," Yslas formally transferred San Pedro y San Pablo Bicuñer to Díaz and the settlers in the name of the king.[28] The total population of the new pueblo was seventy-seven, slightly less than that at La Purísima Concepción. It included a new priest, Father José Matías Moreno, who would with Father Díaz minister to the settlement's residents. Moreno had arrived in late December with the Yslas group. Born in Soria, Spain, in 1744, he was a lively, intellectually gifted man, talented enough to have held "a chair of philosophy or theology" had he remained in Spain rather than enter the mission field, in one historian's opinion.[29] Moreno had entered the College of Santa Cruz in 1769 and been assigned to the Pimería Alta in 1773. For the ensuing seven-plus years he had served at Tumacácori and, as Font's companion, at Caborca. During that time he had become amply familiar with Garcés's ideas and visions. Perhaps not coincidentally, he expected—and desired—to one day suffer martyrdom.[30]

As Díaz and Moreno began their work at Bicuñer, Garcés and Barreneche, working from their base at La Purísima Concepción, preached, baptized, anointed, and consoled the settlers and those Quechans who had not turned against them. The former quickly built a dozen mud huts on stone foundations around a small plaza on top of the mission's hill, doing their best to approximate a proper Spanish pueblo.[31] As for the latter, Garcés hoped that Croix would change his mind and go forward with a "complete reduction of the tribe," as he wrote the Caballero on December 30, 1780, since "more than half of the tribe cannot receive

Christian instruction without removing them from their lands, a thing difficult to bring about, because they are attached to their own soil and derive profit from it."[32] Clearly, Garcés had become less patient, and perhaps disillusioned, with the Quechans. He now complained about "their insubordination." He told Croix that they were "too stupid to be attracted to things spiritual."[33] This was far from his usual charitable tone. Was Garcés not well suited to the grinding, tedious, patient work of building a mission? Was he experiencing a dark night of the soul?

It was an uncharacteristically bitter and depressed Garcés who, along with Barreneche, now began to baptize and teach the catechism to any willing Quechan, not just those who had decided to settle at La Purísima Concepción—a substantial break from tradition that set tongues wagging among other Queretaran friars, but precisely the sort of innovation that Croix wished to see. A number of Quechan children and elderly formally became Christians in this manner. Because Díaz was not certain this method of missionizing was appropriate, the priests wrote their superiors for a judgment.[34] Garcés argued that ministering to the natives living outside settlement boundaries offered the only realistic way forward. "This conversion would be very sterile if we followed the rigorous method" that the church preferred, he wrote the authorities at Querétaro. He therefore baptized every boy and girl who was presented, figuring that if their families would not come to live in the settlements they might at least attend Mass there on Sundays, and he could preach to them in their fields. Barreneche agreed. He could not bear to see so "many innocent souls . . . die . . . without the grace of baptism."[35] He and Garcés even built a small hut in which they could say Mass and minister to the sick a few miles from Concepción. Díaz eventually came to agree with his brother friars' methods, at least with respect to the propriety of baptizing all children under the age of three.

Ensign Yslas, for his part, was intent on doing his duty. Taking advantage of the relatively cool winter days, he worked hard in the first months of 1781, overseeing the construction of wood-and-earth houses for the settlers, the completion of the irrigation system for their fields, and the planting of gardens, fruit trees, beans, and squash.[36] He gave each settler baize with which to barter for seeds with the Indians. And he disciplined the blacksmith and carpenter who had come to the Colorado with Díaz for not doing work "equivalent to the salary which they receive," docking the carpenter's pay and even requiring the blacksmith to make a written promise in front of witnesses to do the necessary ironwork for the building of the church, the padres' houses, his own house, and "other public buildings."

Lazy Spanish laborers were the least of Yslas's troubles. Conflict was growing with the Quechans over resources. Pasturage for the horses and sheep was "very scarce," which meant that the hundreds of animals that now roamed the riverbanks often wandered into the Quechans' fields and trampled and ate their crops, many of which were needed not only for food but also for seed.[37] There were arguments over water rights. There was harsh Spanish justice; when one Quechan "wounded a horse belonging to a corporal," Yslas unwisely had him beaten—by Palma, acting as justicia. And there were constant complaints. A Kohuana chief, for example, complained to Yslas about ill treatment at the hands of the Quechans, and Palma complained about not being given a new suit of clothes promised him by Viceroy Bucareli. Yslas thought he was well justified when, on January 17, 1781, he asked Croix for ten pairs of irons and two artillery pieces. The latter "would not fail to be of use some day in case there should be an uprising among these Indians."[38]

This request alarmed Croix. Yslas was supposed to be defusing conflict by killing the Quechans with kindness, not threatening them with confinement and artillery. He ordered Yslas to use "gentleness, kind treatment, and discretion to maintain and promote" good feeling among the Quechans. Likewise, Yslas was to try to reconcile the Quechans with the Kohuanas using argument rather than any "harsh treatment." Furthermore, when punishing any Indian, he reminded the ensign, he should

act with "moderation and justice" in order to "make attractive
to them the communication and valuable friendship which they
themselves have sought with the Spaniards."[39] Admirable sen-
timents, all. But Yslas could not help but feel that Croix failed
to understand how badly relations had deteriorated among all
peoples on the Colorado. Gentleness and kindness—assuming
that these qualities were much manifested at all—went only so
far, thought Yslas. He was a soldier, not a diplomat.

Still, Yslas did his best. He tried to win over Ygnacio by making him the governor of Bicuñer and his ally Pablo the fiscal. He
claimed, on May 28, 1781, to have brokered a new peace between the
Quechans and Kohuanas, as well as between the Quechans and
Halchidhomas. And he clarified that he had requested irons and
cannons not because he wished to be severe with the Quechans
but only because he wished to be prepared in case trouble should
arise. "I desire and wish very much that your Lordship might turn
into a celestial spirit so that you might observe closely my management of the Indians, which is such that when I give an order to one
of them and he commits some offense deserving of punishment, I
make use of his own 'justicias' for his punishment and reprimand,
in order that no feeling may be aroused against me."[40]

Within a few weeks, the Quechans would make clear that they
saw things rather differently.

✻ ✻ ✻

The profound differences between Quechans and Spaniards had
been evident to both sides for years, even generations. The two
peoples represented two cultures elaborated along drastically different lines. Some cultural differences were more or less superfi-
cial. Quechan men wore their long hair piled on top of their heads,
dusted it with a "powder the color of luminous silver," and protected it by sleeping sitting up.[41] Quechan women were incredibly
"dexterous swimmers," even better than their men, "for they are
the ones who cross the river loaded with children, provisions,

and other things," as Eixarch observed during the second Anza expedition.[42] Quechan girls—like many others in the region—were initiated into womanhood though an elaborate ceremony on the occasion of their first menstruation, during which for four days they fasted and were buried up to their necks in the sand, quite to Eixarch's amazement.[43] Quechan boys experienced their own four-day initiation rituals. When a Quechan lad was ten, or slightly younger, his nose was pierced. On each of the next four days, he ran ten to fifteen miles in one of the cardinal directions. During the entire period no sleep was allowed.[44]

Other differences bespoke divergent conceptions of the divine, morality, and justice. The Quechans had their own complex, partly historical creation story, and they had their own deities, including their creator Kwikumat, whose death they commemorated in their traditional mourning ceremony.[45] The Spaniards seemed to know little about Quechan religion, or at least to be little interested in it. They were much more troubled by Quechans' sexual ethics, which included multiple partners, easy divorce, and polygamy. Salvador Palma may have accepted, at least for a time, the practice of monogamy. But as Father Barreneche wrote, "The experience we have . . . is that if they remain single after baptism they do not refrain from living like the gentiles [unbaptized Indians], and if they are married by us, there is little hope they will be content with one woman." An incomprehension, or rejection, of Christian sexual ethics was the main reason few Quechans between the ages of twenty to sixty accepted the faith, thought the friars. Garcés was not sure this obstacle to conversion could ever be overcome, given "the concubines that [Quechan men] habitually take and leave."[46]

The Quechans were as little inclined to accept premodern Spanish notions concerning criminal justice, especially the legitimacy of painful corporal punishment. In contrast to the representations he made to Croix, Ensign Yslas ordered alleged Quechan malefactors to be flogged at the stake. Resentment festered. Then, sometime in the spring of 1781, he was told that Ygnacio

and Pablo, the native leaders at Bicuñer, had threatened to kill
a soldier named José Cayetano Mesa. He arrested them and put
them in the stocks. An irate Ygnacio began to dream of expelling
the Spaniards from Quechan lands. Another Indian, a Halyikwamai called Francisco Xavier who had been sold into slavery
at Altar and pressed into service as a Spanish interpreter, joined
him in spreading dissension. He was neither the first nor the last
Indian for whom familiarity with the Spanish bred contempt.

Then came the tipping point. In early June 1781 there arrived
at the Yuma crossing Captain Fernando Rivera y Moncada, the
man who five years earlier, at Mission San Gabriel, had refused
Garcés supplies and support. With Rivera were forty soldiers and
their families and approximately one thousand horses, mules,
and cows. Sixty more soldiers arrived soon thereafter. It is not
clear that anyone at the Colorado had received advance notice of
his arrival.

Rivera had been replaced as governor of the Californias by
Felipe de Neve in 1777. He had wished for nothing more than to
retire. Instead, he was commanded to recruit soldiers and families for the Alta California colonization effort. The soldiers were
to be stationed at the three new missions Junípero Serra had long
wished to establish along the Santa Barbara Channel, while the
settlers were to found a new town near Mission San Gabriel. It
was to be named El Pueblo de Nuestra Señora, la Reina de los
Angeles del Río de Porciúncula—Los Angeles, for short. Some
troops and colonists had been sent to Alta California by sea. The
others were now here at Yuma with Rivera, making use of the
new road Garcés had done so much to open.[47]

It was necessary for Rivera to linger here on the Colorado so
that his animals could regain their strength; having come by way
of El Camino del Diablo, they were in pitiful shape. Unfortunately, they regained their strength by trampling and eating the
Quechans' crops and plants, many of which bore precious seeds.
The needs of Rivera's people and animals were so enormous that
the captain even sent parties upstream and down to requisition

food from the Kohuanas and Halchidhomas.[48] First Yslas, and now Rivera. Once again, the best-laid plans of the friars were being undermined by a military they seemingly could neither live with nor live without.

Matters quickly became tense. A solder named Cayetano Limón noted that soon after Rivera's arrival Palma moved his residence out of the little village at Concepción, and that he and other Quechans displayed "insolence." Another soldier who was sent to requisition supplies found himself being "screamed" at by Quechans who tried to make him understand "that the cows and horses destroyed their mesquite, tornillo, and corn fields" and that the animals needed to be corralled, post haste.[49] Yslas seemed unconcerned by it all, but after ten days Rivera sent the colonists, those animals fit to travel, and most of his troops ahead to San Gabriel. Along with nineteen soldiers and a handful of servants, he would stay for a few weeks yet on the south side of the Colorado River, allowing the remaining 257 horses and mules to recuperate.[50]

Rivera must have thought he had deescalated the situation. But he had only opened himself to attack.

※ ※ ※

In July 1781, the Spanish advance beyond the Devil's Road into today's American interior came to an abrupt end. The events of those violent days shattered Franciscan dreams of a Catholic empire stretching northward to the Grand Canyon and beyond, military dreams of a fully pacified frontier, and royal dreams of a flourishing New Spain securely connected on its northern fringe from Louisiana to Alta California. Had the Yuma crossing remained open, would Spain have found the energy and resources to move forward as friars like Garcés dreamed? Would it have made much difference, historically? Would the Southwest have a different shape, character, or even boundaries than it does today? The Quechans ensured that answers to such questions would never be known. By the summer of 1781 a large contingent

of Quechans, perhaps a majority, had definitively concluded that
the benefits of an alliance with the Spaniards no longer out-
weighed the costs—especially when personal and regional power
might be won by casting them out once and for all.

The explosion came on the days of July 17–21. We know what
happened on those sunny, bloody days—from the Spanish point
of view—thanks to the reports of survivors. One of those reports,
certainly the one that tells us the most about those days with
respect to Garcés, was made by María Ana Montijo, Santiago
Yslas's wife.[51]

On the morning of Tuesday, July 17, Montijo attended Mass at
the chapel of La Purísima Concepción. Mass was said by Father
Barreneche. Immediately afterward, Garcés said his own Mass,
with Ensign Yslas serving. Tensions were by this time so high
that Yslas had taken the precaution of posting a guard—Corporal Pascual Baylón—at the chapel door. As Yslas "was moving
the missal from one side of the altar to the other for the gospel
of the Mass," Montijo recalled, "the war whoops of the Indians
began." A momentarily stunned Garcés stopped the liturgy. Barreneche, from somewhere outside the church, rushed to Baylón's
side, forcing his way through the Indians and absorbing many of
their blows. Baylón received more; he squeezed the priest's hand
as he died. Miraculously, the padre was somehow then taken into
the church.

Realizing that a full uprising was under way, Doña Montijo
quickly gathered together the female settlers and their children
and fled with them to the church. Other refugees had already
taken sanctuary there and, in all-too-human fashion, when Montijo and the women and children arrived they were involved in an
argument about who was to blame for the rebellion. "Let's forget
now whose fault it is, and simply consider it God's punishment for
our sins," said Garcés, to calm the crowd. "His voice was compassionate," Montijo remembered, but "his face was an ashen gray."

Time now passed very slowly, and the agony of those inside
the little church became unbearable. At some point Yslas bravely

left to see what he could do to fend off the attackers. He did not get far. Montijo endured the torture of seeing her "beloved husband . . . clubbed to death" before her very eyes. When night fell, the Quechans burned the settlers' houses and belongings and killed whomever they could find. After a while the warriors left, and Barreneche and Garcés stole out of the church and "moved stealthily about the village, administering the sacraments to the wounded and dying, consoling them in their hour of death."

Wednesday, July 18, dawned with a terrifying silence. Barreneche rose to the occasion, encouraging the Spaniards by saying, "The devil is on the side of the enemy, but God is on ours. Let us sing a hymn to Mary, most holy, that she favor us with her help, and let us praise God for sending us these trials." He led the settlers in the hymn, "Arise, arise!" which he sang "with great fervor of spirit," according to Montijo, and said Mass. After Mass, Barreneche pulled the arrows and spears out of the church walls and climbed onto the roof to observe and report on the Indians' movements. He could see hundreds of Quechans on the other side of the river, where they were attacking Captain Rivera and his party, none of whom would survive. Climbing down on the chapel's exterior, Barreneche took the opportunity of the Indians' absence to attend "to the last of the dying." When he returned, he had come to a conclusion: since the Quechans were now occupied with Rivera but would surely soon return, "each of us should try to escape as best we could." He, Garcés, and everyone else started off. Barreneche asked Garcés if they should check on the settlement at Bicuñer, but Garcés "assured him that it was completely destroyed and its inhabitants killed."

He was right. San Pedro y San Pablo had, like La Purísima Concepción, been attacked the previous morning. In the wee hours of the day, Fathers Díaz and Moreno had been called to the bedside of an old, sick woman. They anointed her with oil, administered the last rites, and gave her communion. A little later, just after dawn, they were walking across the plaza to the church to say Mass when Quechan and Mohave warriors sprung from concealment with war cries. Every Spaniard who could be caught was killed. There was nowhere for Moreno and Díaz to go. Father Moreno was clubbed until he crumpled to the ground. While still alive he was decapitated with an axe. Díaz was shot with a captured gun. As he lay on the earth, his skull was smashed by the warriors' heavy clubs.[52]

Back at La Purísima Concepción, as the surviving Spaniards left the church on the morning of the 18th, Fray Barreneche found and followed a trail of blood left by a man named Pedro Burgues, who had somehow sent word for the priest to come and hear his confession. The trail led the party to one of the many lagoons that lay alongside the Colorado's main channel. Barreneche waded in, but the water was much deeper than he expected. Soon the padre, who like Garcés did not know how to swim, was flailing for his life. Finally, he was able to "grasp a log and some roots. By pulling himself along the roots, he was able to reach the other bank," Doña Montijo remembered. "Though he miraculously escaped drowning, he lost his breviary and crucifix."

Whether Barreneche found Burgues on the other side Montijo does not say. In any case, Garcés, who had stayed back with the women and children (Montijo implies that only women and children were left), told them to stay together, and that if they did not resist capture the Quechans would not harm them, another intuition that would prove correct. He then "plunged into the lagoon" himself—an act for which the nonswimmer Garcés must have had to summon great courage—and joined Barreneche on the other side.

As Montijo learned later from Gertrudis Cantud, the wife of Pedro Burgues, after leaving the lagoon the fathers encountered a friendly Quechan man whose wife was a devoted Christian; the spiritual work of Garcés and his companions had not been entirely fruitless. The man took the padres to his house. Here the friars holed up and gathered their thoughts, no doubt wondering what they should do next. Were they overcome with fear?

An overwhelming sense of failure and loss? They must have been tormented by dark thoughts concerning the fates of Díaz and Moreno. Perhaps the Quechans with whom they were hiding told them what happened at Bicuñer. They must have hoped that Palma might yet try to save them; it was later said he had ordered that Garcés, at least, be spared, so they may have heard rumors to that effect. And they must have wondered whether they would be tortured before they were killed, if there was any way to escape this fate, and if it was because of their sins that the Quechans had erupted in rage.

We can safely assume that as they huddled on the floor of the stuffy hut Garcés and Barreneche heard each other's confessions and prayed. Somehow they had brought with them, or had brought to them, some chocolate (perhaps it was given them by other Spanish captives who had in the meantime been brought to the same ranchería). Garcés and Barreneche were drinking it on the morning of July 21 when their presence was discovered by a search party of warriors sent by Palma to find the friars and bring them back safely, for, as he put it, "what the Fathers said was good, and they did no harm to anyone."[53] Unfortunately for the priests, among the searchers was the angry anti-Spanish rebel Francisco Xavier, and it was his group that found the hut in which the priests were hiding.

At about ten o'clock, Francisco's group approached the house and began to shout. Garcés and Barreneche heard the Halyik-wamai man haranguing the others that Palma's wishes should be disregarded. "If these survive all is lost, for these are the worst!" Francisco told his companions. Soon one of the group's leaders stepped inside to find the friars sipping their hot drink, a last vessel of grace in their desolation. "Stop drinking that," he demanded. "We're going to kill you." "We'd like to finish our chocolate first," Garcés replied, finding within himself a vein of black humor. "Just leave it!" was the warrior's irritated response. The two priests rose, commended themselves to God, and followed him out the door. As soon as they stepped outside, they were viciously clubbed to

A late-eighteenth-century oil painting by an unknown artist depicting Francisco Garcés (left) and Juan Barreneche (right) as martyrs. Note the background scene. *From Museo Municipal, Querétaro, Mexico.*

within an inch of their lives. A captive named María Gertrudis Cantú watched the horrible scene unfold. She could hear the friars' "piteous moans as they lay dying."[54]

"The Indians tell the story that at the first attack of the executioners, Father Garcés disappeared from their sight, and they were left clubbing the air," Montijo told Father Barbastro, repeating what she heard when in captivity among the Quechans. "Word had spread among the Yuma nation that he was more powerful than their own witch-doctors. Time and again I heard that many of the Yumas did not want to see the Fathers killed. Nevertheless, their blood was spilled."

On September 25, 1781, a distraught Father Antonio Barbastro wrote Father Juan Agustín Morfi from Tubutama. Father Morfi had himself written Barbastro on July 17. That very day, Barbastro lamented, "saw the willows wither, the poplars turn pale, the birds become sad, the fishes take flight, the sun covered with clouds, and all nature horror-stricken, while the current of the Colorado River became swollen, and changed the muddy color of its waters to brilliant carmine, or the even redder coral, with the innocent blood of our four dear brothers," Fathers Garcés, Díaz, Moreno, and Barreneche.[55]

Morfi had probably heard the news by now, Barbastro figured, but it was necessary and proper to provide details the secular authorities may have overlooked. The sacred objects of the missions had been destroyed or used blasphemously, wrote Barbastro. Reports said that the altar cloths had been used by the Quechans as breechcloths, chasubles as handkerchiefs, albs as jackets. Those sacred vessels and images deemed of no use, or perhaps as especially symbolic of the religion the Quechans wished to decisively reject, had been thrown into the river. Garcés and Barreneche, meanwhile, had been buried or half-buried while still alive and thus "exposed to the ferocity of the animals and served as food for the beasts of the field." This report seems to have been false, for other witnesses said that the husband of the Christian Quechan who had sheltered Garcés and Barreneche buried them side by side in a shallow grave. His wife then directed him to make two small wooden crosses and place them on top of the grave to mark the missionaries' resting place.

Barbastro was the head of the Pimería Alta missions. He had just lost four friars, at least two of whom were beloved friends. Two or three of the other friars serving in his missions seemed on the verge of death, and it seemed that everyone else was sick. The new capital of Arizpe burdened him with many duties, a smallpox epidemic was spreading in one pueblo, hostile Apaches surrounded his territory, and a hostile bishop of the new diocese of Sonora—none other than the ambitious Antonio de los

Reyes—was pushing through reforms that only made his, Barbastro's, job more difficult.[56] That Barbastro sensed it was the end of an era, that he knew the extraordinary forward-looking energy of a Francisco Garcés would not be replaced, is evident in that he was already looking backward and thinking about posterity. He hoped to compose a history of the missions on the Colorado, Barbastro wrote Father Morfi, so that it might "teach centuries."

Croix was less interested in teaching the centuries than he was in teaching the Quechans a lesson. Soon after the revolt, an apparently conflicted and sorrowful Palma had written the authorities at Altar to ask for pardon. His tribesmen were not so remorseful. They managed to elude a large-scale battle with Captain Pedro Fages, whom Croix put in charge of a punitive expedition. Fages's main success lay in killing fifty-four Quechans in retribution— none of them instigators of the rebellion—and securing the return of all seventy-four Spaniards, mostly women and children, the Quechans had taken captive. From these Fages took depositions.[57] They had been treated well, they testified, perhaps in part because of what not only they, but also the Quechans (they claimed), had witnessed after the violence had ended.

> It is stated that after the burning of the missions had taken place, as soon as night fell, a procession of people dressed in white, all having burning candles in their hands, was seen. They were preceded by a cross and acolytes' candles. They marched around the area where the mission had been, and sang some unknown song. After marching around many times, they disappeared. This was seen to occur on many nights, not only by the Christians, but by the pagans; and this injected . . . fear into the latter and . . . frightened them.[58]

Fages recovered the remains of the Spanish dead, including the four friars, in December 1781. On the 10th of that month, the bodies of Garcés and Barreneche were found when one of the soldiers noted a conspicuously green and flower-strewn patch of earth. Fages gave orders to dig there, and soon the bodies of the two friars, "with their under-garments still on, and . . . not much decayed," had been exhumed. The bodies were transported to

San Pedro y San Pablo Bicuñer and were placed, along with the remains of Díaz and Moreno, on the altar of the ruined church. This structure, the captain reported, "although burned, still had its walls almost intact, especially those of the high altar."[59] There were no vessels with which the priest who was with him could say Mass, so Fages had candles lit on the altar and gathered everyone to recite a rosary for the missionaries' souls. Two days later, Fages had his men carefully wrap the friars' remains in a blanket and placed in two cigarette boxes. The remains were then taken to the presidio at Altar before being handed over to Father Barbastro at Tubutama.[60]

Thus did the body of Francisco Garcés depart the Colorado River. For his fellow friars, if not for his erstwhile ally Salvador Palma, Garcés's failure was his success. As a reflective Serra wrote when he heard the news of the massacre on the Colorado, "All we can do is to offer our sympathy for the sufferings of" Garcés, Díaz, Barreneche, Moreno, and the others "who met their death there and bow before the inscrutable will of God." "I do not know," Serra added, "that they lack anything to be considered martyrs."[61]

Epilogue
Blood of the Martyrs

The remains of Francisco Garcés, Juan Díaz, Juan Antonio de Barreneche, and José Matías Moreno remained at Tubutama until 1793, when Father Barbastro successfully gained permission for their transfer to the Church of Santa Cruz in Querétaro. Fray Diego Bringas preached a stirring sermon on the occasion of their reburial in the church's crypt on July 19, 1794.[1] The colegio had been blessed with worthy martyrs, he reminded his listeners. He did not dwell on the fact that the energy behind the Franciscans' mission project in Pimería Alta was already fading, that in reality the colegio had lost the frontier.

In the years that ensued, the dynamic Bringas, the colegio's last high-profile friar, would become embroiled in counterrevolutionary politics, and Mexico's successful separation from Spain would bring an end to his and his brother Queretarans' missionizing dreams. A succession of anticlerical regimes would to various degrees oppress, even terrorize, the Catholic Church in Mexico for many generations. Garcés and his fellow martyrs faded into obscurity. Until an amateur historian named Clarence Cullimore brought their reburial in Querétaro to the world's attention in 1954, it was not even generally known that their bodies and ashes had been removed from Tubutama.[2]

Things might have been different had Garcés and his companions been perceived as successful. That was not, and is not, the perception. On the contrary, it is typically believed, as Daniel Matson and Bernard Fontana concluded, that "Spain's conversion effort among the northern Piman Indians generally failed"— indeed, that this "is a matter of historical record." In 1795, Bringas reported that since the order had arrived in the Pimería Alta in 1768 the Franciscans had performed nearly one thousand baptisms.[3] He presented the figure as impressive. Considering that by that time the priests from Querétaro had spent twenty-seven years of grinding effort on New Spain's northwestern edge, during which six of their number had been martyred, it really wasn't.

Besides, baptisms were one thing; conversions were another. Even among those northwestern frontier natives (mostly O'odham, some Quechan) who did accept baptism from the Franciscans, many did not embrace Christian doctrine and practices, let alone understand them. Curiosity and opportunism led some of the Pimería Alta's Indians to ask for baptism, but the pull of their own peoples' traditions and ways kept many from genuinely converting to the new religion. James Sandos—a scholar who unlike many of his peers is open to the possibility that a significant number of mission Indians became serious Christian converts—estimates that as few as 10 percent truly did so.[4]

The Franciscans' success in the Pimería Alta was further limited by the gradual diminution of the region's Indian population. When Father Eusebio Kino arrived in 1680 there were an estimated 32,000 natives living in the area; by 1800 that number had fallen to about 9,000.[5] When they recognized this decline the friars lamented it. It was not their intention for native numbers to decrease. Even so, the high Indian death rate and low Indian birth rate were due largely to the diseases, despair, and cultural destruction introduced by the fathers. Both were manifestations of their project's failure.

Finally, the Franciscans' efforts on New Spain's northwestern frontier led to no lasting strategic victories for their country. At the onset of the Mexican War of Independence in 1810 there were native peoples still unsubdued. Neither the Franciscans' missions nor Spanish civilization had advanced beyond Tucson to the Gila River. The Yuma crossing remained closed. Within a generation or two, the Americans—not the Russians, not the English—swept in to colonize the world beyond El Camino del Diablo. Soon after his death, Francisco Garcés's former companion, Father Juan Bautista de Velderrain, managed to build a new, spectacular church at San Xavier del Bac. But that accomplishment stands out as New Spain's only significant achievement on the frontier after the Quechan uprising of 1781.

Failure, then, on all sides. And yet … when one zooms out to take a broader, long-term perspective, the picture looks quite different.

※ ※ ※

The last friar to maintain a connection to the Spanish missionary effort in the Pimería Alta left the region in 1843. For more than fifty years, no Catholic missionaries worked among those O'odham who lived north of the Devil's Road. With the exception, at times, of San Xavier del Bac, there were no established churches at which regular services were held.[6] If Christianity exerted no attraction for the O'odham, it should have died. But it didn't. The O'odham themselves kept the friars' faith alive. They built chapels in many of their villages in which they practiced a kind of folk Catholicism they called *santo himdag*—the saint way.[7] They kept in memory the prayers taught to them by the long-gone friars. They even kept in safekeeping many of their sacred vessels.[8]

Such surprises greeted the Franciscans upon their order's
return to Arizona in 1895. As they filtered out into the desert
from their base at St. Mary's in Phoenix, they found themselves
welcomed by many Papagos and Pimas. In some of their villages
Catholic chapels had been erected. In others the friars worked
with the O'odham to build them. The first church built by this
new wave of Franciscan missionaries was at Ali Chukson in 1912.
By 1976, thirty-five more had been erected, until nearly every village in the Papaguería had its own tiny, brilliantly whitewashed
chapel.[9] The vast majority remain standing and are in use today.[10]

Many of the Franciscans who led this twentieth-century missionizing effort were German. Unlike the German Jesuits of the
mid-eighteenth century, they worked in cooperation with and
maintained high respect for the O'odham. They were in turn
well liked. Garcés found a spiritual successor in the dedicated
and warmhearted Father Bonaventure Oblasser, who like him
tended toward impracticality and was universally beloved.[11] During his time in the desert Oblasser became familiar with Garcés's
work and consciously sought to extend his legacy. "Where Father
Garcés planned two missions, one at Santa Rosa and one at
Sonoita," announced Oblasser in 1936, he and his fellow Franciscans could "now point with pride to twenty churches, not counting smaller chapels, eight schools, 2,500 baptized neophytes, and
as many catechumens in the eleven Papago pueblos north of the
international boundary." By that date a catechism, dictionary,
and grammar in the Piman language had been composed, and
the Sunday gospel readings had been translated into the native
O'odham tongue.[12]

All this was accomplished without soldiers, without "reduc-
tions," without terror, threats, or violence—in other words, in a
highly Garcésian manner. The friars' way of thinking about missions had changed drastically over the previous 150 years, and better results followed. Garcés anticipated many of these changes,
intuiting that effective evangelization required submersion into,

imaginative identification with, and as much respect for other cultures as Christian doctrine could allow. The missiological concept of inculturation or, more accurately, what Joseph Ratzinger would later call "interculturality"—a concept according to which all cultures are to various degrees open to "the truth about God and reality as a whole"—was not and could not have been articulated by Garcés, but he exemplified that ideal in action more than any other missionary of his time.[13]

In 1938 the Franciscan scholar Maynard Geiger estimated that one-third of the five thousand Pimas in southern Arizona were Catholics.[14] Geiger counted just shy of four thousand baptized Catholics among the Papagos. The Franciscans had made headway among the Apaches; of the 2,900 living on the San Carlos Reservation, 250 were Catholics, and on the Fort Apache Reservation there had been 185 baptisms. The order had returned to the lower Colorado, too. In the late-nineteenth century, Father Zephyrin Engelhardt became the first friar assigned to Yuma since Garcés and his companions met their ends there. In 1922, Father Tiburtius Ward built a new church on the hill where the modest La Purísima Concepción church once stood. St. Thomas Mission Church still stands there today.[15] In front is a dignified concrete statue of Garcés and two Quechans, unveiled in 1928. Appropriately, inlaid in the base is petrified wood from the Castle Dome district of Arizona where Garcés once roamed. Even more appropriately, there is a Quechan Indian museum next door.[16]

On April 16, 2021, I had lunch with Father Anthony Tinker, pastor of St. John's Catholic Church in the Akimel O'odham town of Komatke, fifteen miles southwest of downtown Phoenix. Father Tinker is a cofounder of the Franciscan Friars of the Holy Spirit, whose headquarters on the banks of the Gila is located precisely where Garcés traveled on his journey downriver in 1770. The friars came to Komatke in 2017 at the invitation of Phoenix's Bishop Thomas Olmsted, himself acting on the request of

This statue of Garcés and two Quechans was erected on the former
site of La Purísima Concepción in 1928. *Photo by author.*

O'odham and Maricopas who had not had resident priests at
their missions for more than forty years. With the Consolata
Missionary Sisters and lay native leaders, these Franciscans serve
eleven mission parishes within the diocese's borders.

Father Tinker estimates that more than 90 percent of Akimel
O'odham identify as Christian, with somewhere between 50 and
80 percent of those identifying as Catholic (many others, thanks
largely to the efforts of a missionary named Charles H. Cook,
are Protestant).[17] A few Akimel O'odham are syncretists—that
is, adherents of a religious system that combines elements of

The limestone statue of Garcés, sculpted by John Palo-Kangas, that stands at the intersection of State Route 204 and Chester Avenue in Bakersfield, California, is twenty-two feet high. *Photo by author.*

traditional O'odham beliefs and spirituality with Catholic influences and has its own rites, ceremonies, and pastoral leaders— but not many. Syncretism among the Tohono O'odham is more popular, Father Tinker told me, but even among them he believed only 10 percent or so to be hard-core syncretists. Nearly all the O'odham, he said, tend to be attracted to Saint Kateri Tekakwitha (an Algonquin-Mohawk who lived from 1656 to 1680) and Nicholas Black Elk (Oglala Lakota Sioux, 1863–1950), whose lives and examples are perceived as meaningful and empowering.

Father Tinker's estimates appear to be accurate. The Tohono O'odham and the Akimel O'odham—the descendants of those to whom Father Garcés once ministered—are significantly more Christian than are their surrounding societies, and the Tohono O'odham Nation is one of the most Catholic areas in the United

St. Catherine Mission, located several miles south of Komatke,
Arizona. The Sierra Estrella range, on which Garcés stood
in October 1770, is in the background. *Photo by author.*

States.[18] It came about very differently than he had imagined, but
to Francisco Garcés that is the only kind of success that would
have mattered.

✳ ✳ ✳

It is not very hard to find in today's desert Southwest priests who
like Father Tinker carry on Garcés's legacy, some consciously
and some not. Father Ponchie Vásquez ministers to Catholics

living in the Tohono O'odham Nation. Father George Decasa does the same at St. Thomas Indian Mission; he calls himself Father George "of the Desert." In Phoenix, Father John Nahrgang, until recently the diocese's vicar for evangelization and education, finds in Garcés's life an inspiring story useful for his work. Father Charlie Urnick labors in Laughlin, Nevada. This is the homeland of the Mohaves, but on Saturdays and Sundays Father Charlie usually preaches to a motley crowd of retirees and casino visitors. He has dedicated a room in the back of his church to the memory of Garcés, the man whose patient, meet-them-where-they-are methods he seeks to emulate.

As the 250th anniversary of the Anza expeditions approaches, some of these priests seek to advance Francisco Garcés's cause for canonization. It is impossible to say whether that effort will or should succeed. But whatever the outcome, surely the most fitting monuments to Garcés's legacy will remain those sunbaked, stark-white churches that stand in hamlets scattered across the Sonoran Desert. Churches where for believers grace is dispensed and spiritual solace found. Churches where Catholic Christianity is preached but *himdag* is not forgotten. Churches where a once unfathomably large chasm has been—at least partly—bridged.

Appendix

Anza's Requested Supplies for the 1775–76 Expedition

With Don José de Echeveste, Anza provided to Bucareli the following list of items necessary to outfit the second expedition to Alta California, along with their probable expenses (omitted here).

(Adapted from Bolton's translation and annotations on the Echeveste memorandum of December 5, 1774, in Bolton, *Anza's California Expeditions*, vol. 5, 225–33.)

Clothing for One Man

3 good linen shirts
3 pairs of underdrawers of Puebla cotton
2 cloth jackets with linings and trimmings
2 pairs of breaches
2 pairs of hose
2 pairs of buckskin boots
3 pairs of buttoned shoes

1 cloth cape lined with baize
1 hat
2 blankets
Ribbon for hat and hair

Clothing for One Woman

3 chemises
3 white petticoats of Puebla cotton
2 skirts, 1 of serge and the other of baize, and 1 underskirt
2 varas [1 vara = ca. 33 inches] of linen for 2 jackets
2 pairs of Brussels stockings
2 pairs of hose
2 pairs of shoes
2 rebozos [headscarfs or shawls]
1 hat
6 varas of ribbon

Clothing for Ninety Boys

5 pieces of cloth containing 180 varas
12 pieces of Puebla cotton for linings and white breeches
270 varas of linen for shirts
50 hats
8 dozen pairs of shoes for boys of all sizes

Clothing for Ninety Girls

270 varas of linen for chemises
4 pieces of cotton cloth for petticoats and linings
90 pieces for rebozos of all sizes
2 pieces of baize for little skirts
4 pieces of cloth of 34 varas each for underskirts
12 pieces of ribbon for trimming
16 pieces of ribbon with a satin border
8 dozen pairs of shoes for girls of all sizes
120 single blankets
120 coarse blankets

Arms

20 carbines
20 gun cases of good quality of the kind called ords
20 swords
20 lances
22 leather jackets
30 shoulder belts with the name San Carlos de Monterrey
20 cartridge boxes with 14 charges each

Mounts and Their Equipment for the Men

60 horses
20 saddles
20 pairs of spurs
20 fine mule bridles
20 pairs of saddle bags

Mounts for the Wives and Families

60 mares
30 saddles
30 fine mule bridles

Rations

60 rations, 3 for each family, for 40 days [enough to get to Tubac for resupply]

Baggage

20 mules
20 pack saddles with attachments
30 leather portmanteaus for the clothing of the soldiers and their families

OUTFIT

1 banner with the royal arms
11 camp tents of unbleached canvas with wooden frames
4 Biscayan hand axes with a good steel edge
4 hoes of the same kind
4 spades of the same kind
1 crowbar
10 cartridge boxes with ball
40 leather powder flasks with primer
8 iron frying pans
10 copper camp kettles
12 large chocolate pots of the same kind
1 box of iron well dressed and prepared, two-thirds for horseshoes and one-third for mules, with a double supply of nails
1 bag with tools for shoeing horses
2 blank books for keeping records

CATTLE AND PROVISIONS TO RATION THE PEOPLE

100 beef cattle, one for each day
30 loads of flour tortillas
60 bushels of pinole
60 bushels of beans
6 boxes of common chocolate
2 tierces of white sugar, weighing 16 arrobas [one arroba = ca. 25 lbs or 4 gallons]
12 pesos' worth of white soap
3 barrels of brandy for needs that arise

FOR THE TABLE OF THE COMMANDER AND THE CHAPLAIN, WHICH ECHEVESTE SUGGESTS TO THE MOST EXCELLENT SEÑOR VICEROY, CONTRARY TO THE WISHES OF THE PERSON INTERESTED

1 box of hams weighing 7 arrobas
25 pounds of sausage
6 boxes of biscuits
1 box of fine chocolate

1 barrel of wine
6 arrobas of cheese
4 pounds of pepper
1/2 pound of saffron
4 ounces of cloves
4 ounces of cinnamon
1 jar of olive oil
1 jar of vinegar
Guangoche mats, sacks, and ropes
140 skin bags for provisions

Pack Train for Transportation

4 droves, comprising 132 mules
100 complete pack saddles for the four droves
20 muleteers

Provisions and Aid for the New Establishments

200 head of cattle, bulls, and cows
6 Indian vaqueros
Gifts for the Indians
6 boxes of beads, not including any black beads but an abundance of
    red ones
1 cloak of blue cloth trimmed with gold
1 jacket and pair of breeches of buckskin
2 shirts
1 cap with its cockade, like that of the dragoons
2 bales of first-class tobacco weighing 350 pounds

Notes

1. Novelist Luis Albreto Urrea provides an arresting account of the peoples and cultures associated with the contemporary Camino del Diablo in *The Devil's Highway: A True Story* (New York, Back Bay Books, 2004). The Spanish-era history he provides is a bit fanciful.

INTRODUCTION

1. This physical description of Garcés is taken from Kessell, "Making of a Martyr," 188.

2. The following summary account of Garcés's journey to Oraibi comes from his published diary (Garcés, *Record of Travels*, 68–75). At the time Garcés met them, the Mohave Indians lived along the Colorado River in an area centered around today's Laughlin, Nevada. Garcés called them Jamajabs.

3. For the history of Franciscans among the Hopis, see Brooks, *Mesa of Sorrows*, from which I draw for the uncited information given in this and the next paragraph. See Sheridan et al., *Moquis and Kastiilam*, for more extensive discussions.

4. Rushforth and Upham, *Hopi Social History*, 106.

5. As Beebe and Senkewicz write in their biography of Junípero Serra, "For most Spaniards, whose emerging national identity was tied up with the Reconquista, there was little meaningful difference between responding

349

to [the] biblical summons to make Indigenous people Christian and making those same people Hispanic" (*Junípero Serra*, 60).

6. Prior to 1775, the Spanish knew of no overland route whatsoever between Monterey and Santa Fe. By the time Garcés visited the Hopis in 1776, such a route could be said to exist, in theory, but it was incredibly circuitous, not to mention dangerous, and it is likely that no one had ever taken it. From Santa Fe it would have led southward along the Río Grande to El Paso and fairly deep into modern Mexico before swinging northwest through Sonora, crossing the Colorado River at what is now Yuma, bearing west until reaching the recently founded mission of San Gabriel (just east of today's Los Angeles), and finally heading north along the coast to Monterey. Finding a better east-west route between New Mexico and Alta California was a high Spanish priority. See Simmons, "Spanish Attempts."

7. Garcés, *Record of Travels*, 75.

8. Garcés, *Record of Travels*, 75.

9. The 22-foot-high limestone statue, created by the Finnish sculptor John Palo-Kangas (whose name is spelled in multifarious ways) in 1939, is located at the intersection of State Route 204 and the Chester Avenue overpass (see Epilogue for photo). Palo-Kangas also created the original clay sculpture of Father Junípero Serra that until 2020 stood in Ventura, California.

10. This is not my judgment alone. Statements such as this can be found throughout the literature that touches on Garcés. One example: Garcés was "one of the greatest explorers in the history of the American West" (Hague, "Search for a Southern Overland Route," 153).

11. Garcés's writings are, for example, key sources for archaeologist Peter Whiteley's work on the historical ethnography of the Southwest; see Whiteley, "Who Were the Napac?" and Whiteley, "Francisco Garcés' 1775–76 Diary." Alfred Kroeber, the great cultural anthropologist, cited Garcés frequently in his pioneering early twentieth-century works on California's native peoples; see, e.g., Kroeber, *Handbook of the Indians of California*. Studies of the Quechans, Chemehuevis, Mohaves, Havasupais, and other groups as they existed at the time of contact, some of them no longer extant, do the same.

12. Bannon, *Herbert Eugene Bolton*, 234 (Bolton was perennially overcommitted, to the exasperation of his publishers). Bolton unearthed the archive of Garcés's College of Santa Cruz, four unknown Garcés diaries, and numerous other reports and letters related to Garcés's missionary work and expeditions, none of which had previously been used by English-speaking historians. He insisted that the materials proved that Garcés was "the real

pathfinder" for the first Spanish overland expedition to California in 1774, and that the friar was therefore a pivotal figure in American history. For more on Bolton, see Hurtado, *Herbert Eugene Bolton.*

13. Bolton, *Bolton and the Spanish Borderlands,* 47; Bolton, *Outpost of Empire,* 31.

14. Bolton, *Outpost of Empire,* 43.

15. Bolton, *Outpost of Empire,* 32, 104, 88.

16. Garcés, *Record of Travels,* viii; Kessell, *Friars, Soldiers, and Reformers,* 31; Bannon, *Spanish Borderlands Frontier,* 185; Herrera, *Juan Bautista de Anza,* 64. A Franciscan historian, Maynard Geiger, wrote that Garcés "easily ranks first in accomplishments and personality" among the Franciscan missionaries of Arizona (*Kingdom of St. Francis,* 16).

17. John Kessell, a leading historian of the Spanish borderlands, nurtured a desire to write Garcés's biography and gathered much material toward that end, but he was never able to get to it (personal interview, February 22, 2020). Jack Holterman corresponded with Bernard Fontana for many years about a biography of Garcés that Holterman was writing, a copy of which in 2021 came into the possession of the Southwest Mission Research Center, which is considering preparing it for publication. In 1932, Honoré Morrow published a highly fictionalized portrait of Garces, *Beyond the Blue Sierra.* In 1980, Peter R. Odens, an amateur historian based in Southern California, self-published a pamphlet titled *Father Garcés: The Maverick Priest.* This slim volume is mainly useful for the quotations and information Odens collected from contemporary Quechans (Yumas).

18. Kittle, *Franciscan Frontiersmen.*

19. It is surprising, for example, that Steven Hackel takes no notice of Garcés in his lengthy treatment of California Indian communities as they existed at the time of contact in *Children of Coyote.*

20. Mathes, in Arricivita, *Apostolic Chronicle,* vol. 1, xiv.

21. Cervantes, "Devils of Querétaro," 51.

22. Thomas, *Rivers of Gold,* 15.

23. Meier, "Franciscans in the New World," 77–78. On the character and antecedents of the Franciscans' typical worldview(s), see Phelan, *Millennial Kingdom;* Cervantes, *Conquistadors,* esp. 203; Elliott, *Imperial Spain,* 60; and Scine, "Anti-apocalyptic Thought."

24. Indian missions were supposed to last only ten years, after which they were to be secularized—that is, integrated into ordinary state and church structures. This virtually never happened, at least within the prescribed timeframe.

25. See Cohen, Harrison, and Rex Galindo, *Franciscans in Colonial Mexico*, 7–8, for an overview of how historians, for their part, have tended to depict the Franciscan experience in North America.

26. Robert Goodwin, for example, misunderstands Garcés when he calls him a "maverick missionary," although he is not necessarily wrong to portray him as "one of those classic romantic colonial figures who (like Lawrence of Arabia) was more at home traveling among the 'natives' than living and working alongside Europeans" (*América*, 273).

27. Happily, the story of Spanish America has recently begun to find a larger audience. See the major synthetic histories published by Goodwin (*América*), Gibson (*El Norte*), Starr (*Continental Ambitions*), and Saunt (*West of the Revolution*).

28. James Sandos labels this approach "Christophobic Nihilism" (*Converting California*, xiii–xiv). In a similar vein, another scholar of Spanish history, Darío Fernández-Morera, has argued that Occidentalism, "a pervasive negative interpretation of the West that often culminates in a denial of its very existence," as well as "Christianophobia" are endemic in modern academic history. See Fernández-Morera, *Myth of the Andalusian Paradise*, 242–43.

29. For an early, sustained argument to this effect, see Costo and Costo, *Missions of California*.

30. As Sandos writes, "Hitler and the Nazis intended to destroy the Jews of Europe and created secret places to achieve that end, ultimately destroying millions of people in a systematic program of labor exploitation and death camps. Spanish authorities and Franciscan missionaries, however, sought to bring Indians into a new Spanish society they intended to build on the California frontier and were distressed to see the very objects of their religious and political desire die in droves. From the standpoint of intention alone, there can be no valid comparison between Franciscans and Nazis" (*Converting California*, 179). Besides Sandos, many contemporary scholars have contributed to the creation of a nuanced, critical, and historically sensitive understanding of the Spanish colonial enterprise in the American Southwest—not that all or perhaps any of them would necessarily agree with Sandos's, or my, particular judgments. See, for example, Cervantes, *Conquistadores*; Brooks, *Mesa of Sorrows*; Torre Curiel, *Twilight of the Mission Frontier*; Herrera, *Juan Bautista de Anza*; Hackel, *Junípero Serra*; Wasserman-Soler, *Truth in Many Tongues*; Rex Galindo, *To Sin No More*; and Wilson, *Peoples of the Middle Gila*, to name just a few worthy titles published in the past decade alone.

31. Ironically, concern for the violence done by Christian actors to non-Christian peoples is itself one of the fruits of the triumph of Christian ideas, in the sense that Christianity wrought "a truly massive and epochal revision of humanity's prevailing vision of reality," a revision "so pervasive in its influence and consequences as actually to have created a new conception of the world, of history, of human nature, of time, and of the moral good" (Hart, *Atheist Delusions*, xi).

32. Cervantes, *Devil in the New World*, 4.

CHAPTER 1

1. Morata's history and geography are described in the *Gran Enciclopedia Aragonesa* and by Kittle in *Franciscan Frontiersmen*, 9–10.

2. The palace of the counts of Morata, known as Palacio de los Luna, is one of the principal attractions in today's Zaragoza.

3. Kessell, "Making of a Martyr," 182.

4. Kittle, *Franciscan Frontiersman*, 9–10. Garcés was likely a healthy child, for Geiger (*Life and Times of Fray Junípero Serra*, vol. 1, 5) says that at the time robust Spanish children were usually baptized a day or two after they were born, whereas the sickly were baptized on their day of birth.

5. Elliott, *Imperial Spain*, 18.

6. Petrie, *King Charles III of Spain*, 151.

7. Arricivita, *Apostolic Chronicle*, vol. 2, 259. Arricivita's history is one of our foundational documents in providing information on the lives and activities of Francisco Garcés and other Franciscan missionaries from the College of Santa Cruz in Querétaro. Along with the primary documents unearthed by historian John Kessell and Robert Kittle, it provides nearly all we know about Garcés's early life; since Arricivita's intention was to edify as much as it was to inform, his narrative surely must be taken with a grain of salt.

8. Kessell, "Making of a Martyr," 183.

9. Information in this paragraph taken from Noel, "Missionary Preachers in Spain," quote at 883.

10. Kessell, "Making of a Martyr," 184. Those men whose veins ran with the blood of *conversos*—Jewish converts to Catholicism—were considered at the time to be unworthy, or at least unwelcome, candidates for Franciscan service; see Rex Galindo, *To Sin No More*, 87. Elliott (*Imperial Spain*, 212–13) points out that purity of faith became tightly linked in the Spanish mind with purity of blood—*limpieza de sangre*—as early as the sixteenth

century, thanks to popular anxiety about the possibility that converted Jews and Muslims might in fact be secret heretics.

11. A letter from the College of Santa Cruz's guardian says that Garcés, at thirty years old, had taken the Franciscan habit fourteen years earlier (Araujo to de la Vega, AHPFM, Letter M, Legajo 3, Number 1).

12. María's story is told well in Fedewa, *María of Ágreda*, from which I draw for this account of her life, unless otherwise noted.

13. For their part, during the colonial era Indians throughout the frontier of New Spain often reported having been visited, in the distant past, by friars or a "Lady in Blue." At least that is what the padres *thought* the Indians were saying. The Jesuit Eusebio Kino and his companion Captain Juan Matheo Mange, for example, reported that elderly Indians living along the Colorado River told them in 1699 that a beautiful white woman clothed in garments of white, brown, and blue had appeared to them when they were children, carrying a cross and speaking an unknown language (Geiger, *Life and Times of Fray Junípero Serra*, vol. 1, 291).

14. Junípero Serra cites this promise, reported by María to Father Alonso de Benavides, in one of his letters to his friend and colleague Father Francisco Palóu. See Palóu, *Palóu's Life of Fray Junípero Serra*, 125.

15. Orfalea, *Journey to the Sun*, 74.

16. For Cabeza de Vaca's amazing story, see Adorno and Pautz, *Narrative of Cabeza de Vaca*; and Reséndez, *Land So Strange*.

17. Colombo, "Franciscans, Jesuits, and the Desire for Martyrdom in New Spain," 339, in Cohen, Harrison, and Rex Galindo, *Franciscans in Colonial Mexico*, 339.

18. Matthew 28:19, New Revised Standard Version.

19. Traditionally, the Feast of the Epiphany was more highly celebrated than the Feast of the Nativity in the Latin American world (Geiger, *Life and Times of Fray Junípero Serra*, vol. 1, 15).

20. Kittle, *Franciscan Frontiersmen*, 10, provides a contemporary description of both the ruins and the peacefulness that reigns at the Convento de San Cristóbal today.

21. For the words of the Franciscan vows, see Geiger, *Life and Times of Fray Junípero Serra*, vol. 1, 21–22.

22. Geiger points out that books chronicling the exploits of the order's missionaries were often the most thrilling part of a Franciscan's education. Geiger was a Franciscan priest himself, and his description of a novice's life is worth quoting: "The year's novitiate in a religious Order, required by the canon law of the Church before a novice takes his vows and becomes a full member of the Order, is a year of strict seclusion and rigorous discipline

during which he imbibes the spirit of the Order. During that year dedicated to the acquisition of virtue, the novice must prove to himself and to his superiors that he has a true vocation to lead the life of his choice. He is expected to attend exclusively to the serious business of becoming Christlike and of absorbing the spirit and traditions of the Order. Prayer, meditation, choir attendance, spiritual reading, daily instructions, acts of mortification, silence, regularity and promptness in attending the daily routine, and physical chores about the convent constitute each day's unvarying horarium, lightened somewhat on the occasion of great feasts" (Geiger, *Life and Times of Fray Junípero Serra*, vol. 1, 19–20). On the background of Franciscans like the Recollects, and their association with missionary activity, see Cohen, Harrison, and Rex Galindo, *Franciscans in Colonial Mexico*, 7–8.

23. Borges Morán, "Expediciones misioneras," 840. Whether or not Garcés would by today's standards be considered dyslexic, his writing often befuddles its would-be English translators, as Rose Marie Beebe and Constanza López Lamerain discovered to their consternation in providing me with translations for this biography. For her part, Beebe thinks Garcés was not dyslexic but rather an oral learner. He could have been both.

24. The word used to describe Garcés on his embarkation papers from Cádiz in 1763 ("Despacho de embarcacion, Cadiz, July 18, 1763," AGI, Contratación, 5545A).

25. This story, which is surely embroidered and perhaps totally fabricated, is told by Arricivita in *Apostolic Chronicle*, vol. 2, 260.

26. I am assuming that six years of study were required—three in philosophy and three in theology—because that was the usual requirement of Franciscans on their way to the priesthood. Subjects within those disciplines included logic, dialectics, metaphysics, cosmology, moral theology, and dogmatic theology (Geiger, *Life and Times of Fray Junípero Serra*, vol. 1, 24–25). Kessell, "Making of a Martyr," 185, characterizes La Almunia as "bawdy."

27. For an extensive discussion of what colegio recruiters were looking for, see Rex Galindo, *To Sin No More*, 71–116. Recruiters were supposed to select candidates first from Spain's mainland colegios, but when these could not fill all the vacancies men from the regular Franciscan provinces could be selected (Geiger, *Life and Times of Fray Junípero Serra*, vol. 1, 40).

28. On María de Ágreda's veneration in the colegios, see Beebe and Senkewicz, *Junípero Serra*, 77, 83–84.

29. Rex Galindo, *To Sin No More*, 101, gives twenty-nine as the average age of colegio recruits.

30. Rex Galindo, *To Sin No More*, 99. This was the way recruiters were supposed to operate, anyway. We do not know exactly what was said to Garcés.

31. Rex Galindo, *To Sin No More*, 107.

32. Kessell, *Friars, Soldiers, and Reformers*, 31. Gil, Garcés, and their companions would have been as clean-shaven as circumstances allowed since, as Brown notes, "It was a clean-shaven century" (Font, *With Anza to California*, 16).

33. On Gil, see Arricivita, *Apostolic Chronicle*, vol. 2, 231–32; Kessell, *Friars, Soldiers, and Reformers*, 29–34; and Kessell, "Making of a Martyr."

34. Geiger, *Life and Times of Fray Junípero Serra*, vol. 1, 56; Kittle, *Franciscan Frontiersmen*, 8; Font, *With Anza to California*, 16–17. Another of the friars on board was Antonio de los Reyes, a tall, blond, ambitious Murcian with whom Garcés would a few years later serve on New Spain's northern frontier. Reyes would ultimately become the first bishop of Sonora. For more on his life and personality, see Stagg, *First Bishop of Sonora*.

35. Quoted in Orfalea, *Journey to the Sun*, 62.

36. Arricivita, *Apostolic Chronicle*, vol. 2, 232, is the source of information on the friars' activities at Cádiz. At the very least it tells us how pious friars were supposed to conduct themselves there. Rex Galindo, *To Sin No More*, 101, says that friars often used this time to familiarize themselves with the lands to which they were sailing.

37. It was not uncommon for recruits to get cold feet, especially if they were seeing the inexpressibly vast ocean for the first time in their lives. For example, five friars who were supposed to sail with the party that ultimately brought Fathers Junípero Serra and Francisco Palóu to New Spain changed their minds when they looked on the Atlantic, allowing Serra and Palóu to come as substitutes (Palóu, *Palóu's Life of Fray Junípero Serra*, 11; Geiger, *Life and Times of Fray Junípero Serra*, vol. 1, 42).

38. Kessell, "Making of a Martyr," 187.

39. See Kessell, *Friars, Soldiers, and Reformers*, 29–33, for this story.

CHAPTER 2

1. Geiger describes the route from Veracruz to Mexico City at length in *Life and Times of Fray Junípero Serra*, vol. 1, 76–81.

2. Kinnaird, *Frontiers of New Spain*, 48.

3. Santa Cruz was named such because local Catholics had cultivated a devotion to a "miraculous stone cross" found in the area in the sixteenth century (Beebe and Senkewicz, *Junípero Serra*, 75).

4. Rex Galindo, *To Sin No More*, 171. This work is my primary resource for most of the information in this chapter about the colegios and the College of Santa Cruz at Querétaro in particular.

5. Cervantes notes that the formation of the first colegios apostólicos de propaganda fide in the late seventeenth century revived, for a time, the missionary fervor and hopefulness that accompanied the first Franciscans' arrival in Mexico in 1524 ("Devils of Querétaro," 52).

6. One scholar, Pedro Borges Morán, calculated that 8,441 Franciscan missionaries came from Spain to America between 1493 and 1822. That was 60 percent of the total number of missionaries who made that journey during the same period (cited in Cohen, Harrison, and Rex Galindo, *Franciscans in Colonial Mexico*, 12).

7. For more on this debate see Radding, *Wandering Peoples*.

8. These were the words Father Romualdo Cartagena used to describe Garcés in a letter written to Viceroy Bucareli, January 29, 1773. The letter is included in Bolton, *Anza's California Expeditions*, vol. 5, 55–56.

9. Jay Harrison, an expert on the College of Santa Cruz, is the source for the contention that as a relatively young priest Garcés would have been expected to act as a confessor for teens and preteens. Later, he would have graduated to young men, married persons, and finally single women (Harrison, personal interview, November 24, 2020).

10. See Arricivita, *Apostolic Chronicle*, vol. 2, 260–261, which, again, is virtually our only source for information on Garcés's years at Querétaro.

11. Rose Marie Beebe pointed this out to me (personal correspondence, October 24, 2022).

12. Rex Galindo, *To Sin No More*, 118.

13. Rex Galindo, *To Sin No More*, 119.

14. That is, not observed at midnight but rather at a more convenient time. See Rex Galindo, *To Sin No More*, 128. If any man unfit for this life made his way through the recruitment screening, the difficulty and rigidity of the colegio's routines soon revealed that fact. Five out of thirty-eight new recruits who arrived in 1770 begged to be released from their commitments after only six months; two more were released because of mental illness (Kessell, *Friars, Soldiers, and Reformers*, 67).

15. Rex Galindo, *To Sin No More*, 122–23. See also Matson and Fontana, *Friar Bringas Reports to the King*, 27.

16. Rex Galindo, *To Sin No More*, 130.

17. Rex Galindo, *To Sin No More*, 131–32.

18. Rex Galindo, *To Sin No More*, 148. Rex Galindo writes that "Franciscan libraries were among the most important concentrations of knowledge

in New Spain, comparable in their number of books to the famous libraries in America and even in Europe" ("Conferences on Theology," 260).

19. Roberts, for example, makes this claim in *Escalante's Dream*, 238. Hackel emphasizes that the Franciscans knew that learning native languages was of surpassing importance in their efforts to reach and convert the Indians effectively (*Children of Coyote*, 136).

20. On the number of languages spoken in California, see Hackel, *Children of Coyote*, 22. On the languages spoken on New Spain's northern frontier, see Spicer, *Cycles of Conquest*, 10–12. The churchmen of New Spain encountered more than three hundred languages, and at least twelve linguistic families, in Mexico and Central America. Many of them learned more than one of these languages. And though at certain times and in certain places it was considered inexpedient to encourage or teach in a particular language, the use of local languages was more encouraged than not. It should also be kept in mind that the church did not necessarily regard communication in the vernacular as necessary for conveying the essence of doctrine or for advancing conversion. More important were participation in the sacraments and growth in virtue. See Wasserman-Soler, *Truth in Many Tongues*, for an extended discussion of this topic.

21. Matson and Fontana deny that this was the case for the Piman language, which they claim was and is "as complex as any in the world," fully "capable of expressing ideas as intricate and as abstract as any concepts peculiar to Indo-European cultural traditions" (*Friar Bringas Reports to the King*, 25).

22. Rex Galindo, *To Sin No More*, 156–58; Beebe and Senkewicz, *Junípero Serra*, 94.

23. Fray Francisco Antonio Barbastro, when he became president of the Quereteran missions in the Pimería Alta, said that Garcés and Father Juan Díaz were so proficient in the Piman language that he sent them to preach in outlying villages where Spanish was all but unknown (McCarty, *Spanish Frontier*, 75).

24. A wonderful example of such surprising misinterpretation can be seen in a January 17, 1996, letter from Bernard L. Fontana, who was both an important scholar of the borderlands as well as a practicing Catholic, to aspiring Garcés biographer Jack Holterman. Fontana writes, "It's hard for us to imagine in the 1990s the strange encounter between people, the missionaries, who believed that the human body and everything about it was repugnant and sinful, and Native Americans for whom there was nothing so wonderful as a good fart or a piece of ass" (BFLP, Box 28, Folder 18).

25. Arricivita, *Apostolic Chronicle*, vol. 1, 32–33. As the text implies, the historical accuracy of Arricivita's account of Margil's life is open to question. The point is that this is the kind of high ideal Garcés and his peers were presented with.

26. So wrote one of the chroniclers of the colegio at Querétaro, Father Isidro Félix de Espinosa. Quoted in Matson and Fontana, *Friar Bringas Reports to the King*, 28.

27. Francisco Palóu reports this incident in his early biography of Serra (*Palóu's Life of Fray Junípero Serra*, 41–42). The story is likely apocryphal, or at least exaggerated.

28. In 1700 there were five thousand Franciscans in the Spanish Americas, and there were another fifteen thousand in Spain. No other order had so many members in either location.

29. It is not difficult to find in the scholarship on, and literature of, colonial New Spain examples of native interest in the Christian faith. See Pérez de Ribas, *My Life among the Savage Nations*, 117; Bannon, *Mission Frontier in Sonora*, 41, 67–68; John, *Storms Brewed*, 75–76; Spicer, *Cycles of Conquest*, 25, 36, 48–49; and Hu-DeHart, *Missionaries, Miners, and Indians*, 38.

30. Besides the factors mentioned here, it has been speculated that another reason the Indians of northern New Spain so readily accepted the Jesuits in the 1600s was that epidemics, among other causes, had for a century brought significant population decline, and hence a good deal of "social disintegration." The Jesuit missionaries may have "served as a point of reference for social reorganization." See Jackson, "Northwestern New Spain," 78.

31. John, *Storms Brewed*, 79.

32. Cervantes, *Devil in the New World*, 62.

33. Cervantes, *Devil in the New World*, 60.

34. John, *Storms Brewed*, 79.

35. The hechiceros remained Christian missionaries' chief opponents centuries later. Shaw writes that, when a Protestant missionary named Charles H. Cook was working to convert the O'odham in the early twentieth century, it was the hechiceros who "were especially opposed to the Gospel message, for they felt it would destroy the old beliefs. Probably they also feared losing their customers" (*Pima Past*, 91). In the colonial period, it was not unknown for hechiceros to pay for their opposition to Christianization with their lives, sometimes at the hands of their own kin; see Bannon, *Mission Frontier in Sonora*, 105, for one example.

36. Bannon points out that the Jesuits' work in Sinaloa in the late sixteenth century was made difficult because the natives there well remembered the

"tradition of Spanish ruthlessness dating back to the days of Nuño de Guzmán," a tradition too often marked by "indiscriminate reprisals by the soldiery" (*Mission Frontier in Sonora*, 3).

37. The Seris, Hopis, and Apaches stand out as notable exceptions, but even the last of these groups "initially embraced Catholicism" (Babcock, *Apache Adaption*, 9, 19–23). John L. Kessell, one of the most accomplished scholars of the Spanish Southwest, has written that "the novelty of new religion" often "had strong appeal" (Smith, Kessell, and Fox, *Father Kino in Arizona*, 58). For a theologically sophisticated discussion of Indians' resistance to monotheism and the notion that the one god was all-good, see Cervantes, *Devil in the New World*, 40–47. In my opinion Cervantes is generally the most reliable authority on the relationship between Native American religions and Christianity. See also his *Conquistadores* and his contributions to Griffiths and Cervantes, *Spiritual Encounters*.

38. For many native men, paring down to just one all-powerful and all-good god could be as cognitively bewildering and distressing as paring down to just one wife.

39. Spicer, *Cycles of Conquest*, 33.

40. See, e.g., Spicer, *Cycles of Conquest*, 49.

41. See Hastings, "People of Reason and Others," 324–25.

42. It was "an old adage among the missionaries on the Western Slope that faith had come to the Indians through their stomachs and that through their stomachs they must be kept Christians" (Bannon, *Mission Frontier in Sonora*, 113). Father Francisco Pangua, guardian of the College of San Fernando in Mexico City from 1774 to 1777, candidly referred to missionaries' gifts of beads, food, and clothing as "the bait and means for spiritual fishing" (Webb, *Indian Life at the Old Missions*, 25).

43. Spicer, *Cycles of Conquest*, 29, 36.

44. See, e.g., Reséndez, *Other Slavery*, 89, 95, 136, 141, for just a few examples.

45. Spicer, *Cycles of Conquest*, 31, 32.

46. Spicer, *Cycles of Conquest*, 32.

47. Donohue, *After Kino*, 89.

48. Spicer, *Cycles of Conquest*, 52.

49. Cervantes concludes that even into the eighteenth century there were "very few movements of Indian resistance, however nativistic or even anti-Spanish in purpose, which at the same time adopted an anti-Christian attitude" (*Devil in the New World*, 69). This is not to say that some rebellions weren't opposed to the established church, or even anticlerical (*Devil in the New World*, 71).

50. See Matson and Fontana, *Friar Bringas Reports to the King*, 23–24. Another distinct group of O'odham, the Hia Ced O'odham ("In-the-Sand People"), colloquially called Sand Papagos, lived in the extreme northwest of this region, west of today's Organ Pipe Cactus National Monument to the Sierra Pinacate in an area that includes the Cabeza Prieta Wildlife Refuge, the Goldwater Air Force Range, and the lower Sonoyta River valley. See Nabhan, Hodgson, and Fellows, "Meager Living?"

51. Fontana's *Of Earth and Little Rain* captures the beauty of this land and the virtues of its peoples well.

52. On the population of the Pimería Alta around 1700, see Torre Curiel, *Twilight of the Mission Frontier*, 51–52.

53. Wilson, *Peoples of the Middle Gila*, 12.

54. His legacy was carried forward by Father Agustín de Campos, who so consistently took the side of the O'odham in disputes with both settlers and the church that he was removed from his post by his Jesuit brethren in 1736. See Brenneman, "Learning the Landscape."

55. This was a boomtime for the Jesuits of German Europe, thanks to the effect the published letters of missionaries working overseas had on the populace. That was a good thing for Spain, whose holdings in the New World were too large to be served solely by Spanish Jesuits. Still, the crown took care to post the German-speaking Jesuits in outlying lands where they could not engage in any geopolitical treachery. See Treutlein, "Non-Spanish Jesuits," 224–25, 230.

56. Och, *Missionary in Sonora*, 119.

57. Dunne writes that "as a rule" the German missionaries were "less charitable than the Latins" (*Juan Antonio Balthasar*, 30). Even in Europe, the German clergy of the eighteenth century tended to be far more moralistic and negative than their Spanish and Portuguese counterparts—as seen, for instance, in their practice of stigmatizing illegitimate children (Lehner, *Catholic Enlightenment*, 84).

58. Dunne, *Juan Antonio Balthasar*, 78.

59. Thompson, *Jesuit Missionary*, 166, 149.

60. Och, *Missionary in Sonora*, 123, 119.

61. Quoted in Bannon, *Mission Frontier in Sonora*, 14.

62. Nentvig, *Rudo Ensayo*, 55.

63. On Luis and the Pima Revolt of 1751, see Ewing, "Pima Outbreak"; Salmón, "Marginal Man"; Martínez, "Paradox of Friendship"; along with the other sources cited in this discussion.

64. See Dunne, *Juan Antonio Balthasar*, 47–48.

65. Nentvig, *Rudo Ensayo*, 27.

66. Nentvig, *Rudo Ensayo*, 120. Hastings presents evidence that Nentvig exaggerated somewhat, at least with respect to the situation in southern Sonora (see "People of Reason and Others," 338). Torre Curiel provides data showing that as of 1753, in the Pimería Alta portion of the province, there were twenty-one towns, two mines, fourteen ranches and haciendas, and three abandoned settlements (*Twilight of the Mission Frontier*, 23).

67. Unless otherwise noted, for the story of the Jesuits' expulsion I rely on Dunne, "Expulsion of the Jesuits."

68. Dunne, "Expulsion of the Jesuits," 6. Only Croix and two others— José de Gálvez and the viceroy's nephew, Teodoro de Croix—knew the content of this letter beforehand.

69. The evidence indicates that Jesuits really were involved in instigating those riots to some extent (Lehner, *Catholic Enlightenment*, 36).

70. See McCarty, *Spanish Frontier*, 1–7.

71. In their diaries and letters, the Franciscans generally offered no evaluation of the expulsion, positive or negative. Arricivita does not mention the Jesuit expulsion as the reason the Franciscans were sent to Sonora, and he makes no mention of the Jesuits being in Guaymas when the Queretarans passed through there in April and May 1768. Palóu, in his biography of Serra, also passes over the Jesuit expulsion in silence. Priestley notes that in San Luis de la Paz a Franciscan friar circulated pamphlets urging defiance of the order of expulsion, for which act he was imprisoned. In another location, however, the Franciscan provincial helped persuade an Indian mob to assist with rather than resist the expulsion (Priestley, *José de Gálvez*, 215–19).

72. The commissary-general reported directly to the commissary-general of the Indies in Madrid, at the royal court.

73. McCarty, *Spanish Frontier*. The following discussion draws on this work.

74. For Querétaro, this meant withdrawing from the mission field in Texas, an area that would henceforth be staffed by Franciscans from the colegio at Zacatecas.

CHAPTER 3

1. This account of the missionaries' departure and journey from Querétaro to Sonora comes from Arricivita, *Apostolic Chronicle*, vol. 2, 88–94; and McCarty, *Spanish Frontier*, unless otherwise noted.

2. Palóu described the climate on the way to Guadalajara as "hot and intemperate," and Geiger notes that thanks in part to the daily rains the road was often in bad shape (*Life and Times of Fray Junípero Serra*, vol. 1, 184).

3. He was probably so because he had been asked by the viceroy to assess the practicality of sending supplies to the northern frontier by sailing up the Gulf of California and into the Gila via the Colorado River (Kinnaird, *Frontiers of New Spain*, 5–6). McCarty does not mention this potential reason, speculating instead that Gálvez was worried about soldiers deserting if they traveled north overland (*Spanish Frontier*, 28). Priestley notes, too, that the construction of two brigantines for plying the Gulf of California had long been urged by the Council of the Indies (*José de Gálvez*, 235). Here, then, was a chance to comply with royal wishes while also meeting a pressing need.

4. With characteristic energy, Serra proposed in September that the friars redeem the time by preaching a mission to the area's residents. Geiger, in *Life and Times of Fray Junípero Serra*, implies that Serra was persuaded by Buena not to launch a mission (vol. 1, 185), but Palóu, in *Palóu's Life of Fray Junípero Serra*, states clearly that the mission took place (52). It is not clear who is correct.

5. For more on Reyes's personality and life, see Stagg, *First Bishop of Sonora*.

6. Thurman, *Naval Department of San Blas*, 32.

7. Dunne, "Expulsion of the Jesuits," 22.

8. Hu-DeHart, *Missionaries, Miners, and Indians*, 96. McCarty also concluded that the Franciscans had no opportunity to communicate with their Jesuit peers (*Spanish Frontier*, 61).

9. At least, they do not mention it in any of the letters or diaries I was able to consult, both published and unpublished. Additional research may turn something up.

10. The Jesuits finally left Guaymas on May 20, 1768, but their travails were far from over. On June 12, having been battered by high winds at sea, the ship carrying them anchored at Loreto to make repairs and replenish supplies. The Jesuits were in bad shape, but they were not allowed to disembark for fifteen days. Serra came down to the port to offer them consolation, and settlers and soldiers gave them generously of what they had. The Jesuits did not get back to San Blas until August 9, 1768. A shocking twenty of the fifty Jesuit priests who left Guaymas in May died before leaving New Spain. See Dunne, "Expulsion of the Jesuits," 21–25; and Kessell, *Friars, Soldiers, and Reformers*, 25.

11. Stagg observes that Governor Pineda and Father Reyes liked to indulge in word play and classical references in their correspondence with one another. Such features are utterly absent from Garcés's letters. See Stagg, *First Bishop of Sonora*, 22–23.

12. The Queretaran missions and their posts in the Pimería Alta as of summer 1768 were as follows: San Francisco del Ati, Father José Soler; Purísima Concepción de Caborca, Father Juan Díaz; San Ignacio de Cabúrica, Father Diego Martín García; Los Santos Ángeles de Guevavi, Father Juan Chrisostome Gil de Bernabe; Nuestra Señora de los Dolores de Sáric, Father Juan José Agorreta; San Xavier del Bac, Father Francisco Garcés; Santa María Suamca, Father Francisco Roch; San Pedro y San Pablo de Tubutama, Father Mariano Antonio Buena y Alcada (mission president) and Father José del Río.

13. Garcés to Anza, July 29, 1768, in McCarty, *Desert Documentary*, 8–10.

14. Herrera, *Juan Bautista de Anza*, 43.

15. This information about Anza's curriculum vita is taken from a report Anza filed from Tubac on September 1, 1767. The report is included in McCarty, *Desert Documentary*, 5–7. I also draw from Herrera, *Juan Bautista de Anza*, 31–54, for a few of the details in this paragraph.

16. Information in this paragraph is derived from Garcés's letter to Anza of July 29, 1768, and from Herrera, *Juan Bautista de Anza*, 47–48.

17. Writing two weeks later to Father Sebastián Flores, after sharing some rather convoluted thoughts on this and that, including his anxieties about having enough money to keep the mission going, he confessed that he was "incredibly happy," not least because at San Xavier he did not have to deal with any Spaniards (August 13, 1768, JKLP, Box 6, Folder 5).

18. It is possible that Garcés exaggerated this point to justify the need for the Franciscans and to emphasize the poor job done by the Jesuits. But given what we know about the spotty, weak presence of the Jesuits at San Xavier and Garcés's own record of transparency, I doubt it.

19. Treutlein, "Father Gottfried Bernhardt Middendorff," 311. Herbert Bolton translated this phrase as *Rim of Christendom*, the title of his biography of Eusebio Kino.

20. Bolton, *Rim of Christendom*, 268–69.

21. See Bolton, *Rim of Christendom*, 428–44.

22. Fontana, *Gift of Angels*, 5.

23. Donohue, "Unlucky Jesuit Mission," 128.

24. Thompson, *Jesuit Missionary*, 126.

25. Thompson, "Letters from Eighteenth-Century Sonora," xiii, xxxv.

26. See Thompson, *Jesuit Missionary*, 143–47. Several years later, some, but by no means all, of the items Segesser had asked for finally arrived.

27. Thompson, *Jesuit Missionary*, 134, 157.

28. Thompson, *Jesuit Missionary*, 151.

29. Thompson, *Jesuit Missionary*, 207. In another letter Segesser writes: "It seems that this country has hitherto been the very dwelling place of the accursed Satan. Although no particular idolatry is found here, there are in fact very many people who have conversations with the devil at night. He appears to them in different shapes, sometimes in the form of a wolf, sometimes a monkey, frequently a black Moor, and then teaches them how to harm people and kill them" (152). Segesser's naïveté is revealed not so much by these beliefs, which were typical during the colonial period among both Jesuits and Franciscans—indeed, among most Europeans generally—as by his penchant for believing tall tales such as the one recounted by Father Agustín de Campos, who told Segesser that "people who have only one foot can be seen in this . . . region who are yet able to walk as rapidly as people with two" (204). On the presence, real or ascribed, of diabolism among New Spain's natives, and how it ought to be interpreted, see Cervantes, *Devil in the New World*.

30. Segesser went on to note that the uninstructed San Xavier Christians called themselves *"Cósua* instead of Joseph, *Mánalas* instead of María" (Thompson, *Jesuit Missionary*, 149.)

31. Quoted in Officer, Schuetz-Miller, and Fontana, *Pimería Alta*, 90.

32. On the typical features of borderlands churches during this era, see Morgan, *Guide to Historic Missions and Churches*. It is probable that the interior walls of the Espinosa church at San Xavier were covered with whitewash, but this is uncertain.

33. The details given here about Fathers Paver and Espinosa are drawn primarily from Donohue, "Unlucky Jesuit Mission," 132–36. On the Espinosa church and other details in this paragraph, see Fontana, *Gift of Angels*, 5; Fontana, "Revealing the First Church," 7–8; Gann, "'Reconstructing' the Espinosa Church," 8; Reyes, "Report on the Missions of Arizona and Sonora" (UASC, Kieran R. AZ 261); and Officer, Schuetz-Miller, and Fontana, *Pimería Alta*, 92.

34. See Kessell, *Friars, Soldiers, and Reformers*, 19–20. During this interim, the civil commissioners often took the opportunity to cheat and lie to the natives, steal mission property, and let the rest deteriorate. This is not what the Enlighteners had had in mind. Gálvez would find that a third to half the goods originally entrusted to the civil commissioners had disappeared (Matson and Fontana, *Friar Bringas Reports to the King*, 58).

35. Torre Curiel, *Twilight of the Mission Frontier*, 53. The Indian population at San Xavier in 1766 was 187, so there had been only a small reduction

in numbers after the expulsion of the Jesuits. There were no Spanish settlers living either at San Xavier or in Tucson when Garcés arrived. As to what the mission came with, note not only that the Jesuits had both spiritual and temporal authority over their missions but also that they even received six months of Piman-language training before being assigned to their posts. See Thompson, *Jesuit Missionary*, xviii.

36. McCarty, *Spanish Frontier*, 54, 62.

37. Fontana, *Gift of Angels*, 5. Reyes says in his 1772 report that many of the "ornaments for the altar and divine services" were in "very poor" shape (48).

38. Fontana, *Gift of Angels*, 62.

39. In 1766 the reported Indian population of Tucson was 139 (Torre Curiel, *Twilight of the Mission Frontier*, 53). No number was officially reported for 1768, but Garcés provided his estimate in his letter to Flores of August 13, 1768. Garcés noted that many others lived in the surrounding area. The name "Tucson" was a Hispanization of the O'odham place name Chuk Shon, meaning "black base," in reference to the black rock on top of a nearby hill (Griffith, *Beliefs and Holy Places*, 29).

40. Information in this paragraph comes from Treutlein, "Father Gottfried Bernhardt Middendorff."

41. Only 178 Spaniards, not including soldiers and their families, lived in the entire Pimería Alta as of 1769 (Jones, *Los Paisanos*, 193).

42. The O'odham dialect group that likely lived at San Xavier in Garces's time is the *totokowany*. This group has a guttural speech pattern and was traditionally thought by other Papagos to be particularly skilled as medicine men and as runners (Joseph, Spicer, and Chesky, *Desert People*, 68).

43. Garcés to Pineda, July 29, 1768, in Dobyns, *Spanish Colonial Tucson*, 27–28 (the translation is Dobyns's). Garcés did not trust Pineda, but he may have connected with him a bit better than some others because they were both Aragonese.

44. Garcés to Pineda, July 29, 1768 (JKLP, Box 6, Folder 4).

45. Garcés to Pineda, July 29, 1768. The translation is Kessell's.

46. Dobyns, *Spanish Colonial Tucson*, 26. One wonders what other kind of conscience Garcés could possibly have had.

47. Garcés to Pineda, July 29, 1768 in Dobyns, *Spanish Colonial Tucson*, 28 (Dobyns translation).

48. See Garcés to Pineda, July 23, 1769, in Dobyns, *Spanish Colonial Tucson*, 30–31.

49. Dobyns, in *Spanish Colonial Tucson* (29), suggests that this was in part so that the young man could spy on Garcés, which may be true but for which there is no evidence.

50. See Garcés to Flores, August 13, 1768; and Maughan, "Francisco Garcés," 45–47.

51. Maughan, "Francisco Garcés," 41; Garcés to Flores, August 13, 1768.

52. Arricivita says they came at Garcés's invitation, but this does not seem to be the case. In his August 13, 1768, letter to Flores, he says that "two governors came down from the mountains to see me."

53. Garcés, *Copia de las noticias sacadas*. Even Arricivita, writing in 1792, apparently did not have access to Garcés's original 1768 diary, so it must have been lost quite soon after it was written. Perhaps that was why Garcés later made this summary of its contents.

54. Bolton, *Bolton and the Spanish Borderlands*, 256. There were probably a handful of other clerical visitors to the area, including Father Agustín de Campos, but Father Campos left no written account of his travels.

55. Maughan identifies this officer as Anza.

56. Wilson, *Peoples of the Middle Gila*, 37.

57. Garcés, *Copia de las noticias sacadas*. A Spanish league was the distance a person could walk in an hour. Thus, it was usually roughly two and a half miles in length, or perhaps a little more, depending on the terrain. Kessell estimates that on this entrada Garcés traveled about two hundred miles (*Friars, Soldiers, and Reformers*, 46).

58. McCarty, *Spanish Frontier*, 87.

59. I think Kessell is right in saying that physically "Garcés was a very average Joe" ("Making of a Martyr," 195).

60. McCarty, *Spanish Frontier*, 87.

61. The translation of this sentence is from Arricivita, *Apostolic Chronicle*, vol. 2, 99.

62. Probably Sacaton because (1) this was a heavily populated area, and Garcés mentions that many people were gathered there; and (2) he mentions in the diary of his 1770 entrada that he had been at this village in 1768, and we are fairly certain that the village in 1770 was Pitaique, located at or near today's Sacaton (see chapter 4). On this 1768 entrada, Garcés also apparently visited Pitac, at or near today's Blackwater (Garcés to Araujo, FMCC, 201:77).

63. Winter, "Cultural Modifications," 72, 74.

64. Font, *With Anza to California*, 103–4.

65. Jay Harrison pointed out to me that this was how Franciscan missionaries at least since the time of Margil approached preaching to local peoples (personal correspondence, June 14, 2023).

66. Officer, Schuetz-Miller, and Fontana, *Pimería Alta*, 16.

67. Officer, Schuetz-Miller, and Fontana, *Pimería Alta*, 27.

68. Officer, Schuetz-Miller, and Fontana, *Pimería Alta*, 59. Matson and Fontana, who otherwise tend to present an idealized view of O'odham society and culture, write that prior to contact with the Spanish O'odham "existence must have been harsh. Life expectancy was very short. In dry years there were probably starvations; in good years people weren't likely to get fat. . . . Spanish cattle, sheep, and horses—to say nothing of crops such as wheat—must have looked very good to the Pimans. It is small wonder that Piman villages sometimes sent out emissaries to urge a visit by the missionary. It was he who distributed the largesse of European foodstuffs" (*Friar Bringas Reports to the King*, 25).

69. There is disagreement over just when the Apaches arrived from the north into the American Southwest, but it seems to have been no earlier than 1100 and possibly as late as the late 1400s or even early 1500s.

70. This was the story told by virtually all actors on this part of the frontier at this time. See, e.g., Kinnaird, *Frontiers of New Spain*, 106. Seymour thinks that some Sobaípuris may have remained on the San Pedro after 1762 or returned there shortly thereafter, but even if true this argument does not change the fact that after 1762 some Apache bands had easier access to the frontier's interior than they had had before. See Seymour, "1762 on the San Pedro."

71. See Buena to Flores, November 10, 1768 (FMCC 201:50); and Kessell, *Friars, Soldiers, and Reformers*, 46–47.

72. This account comes from a letter written by Juan de Pineda to Viceroy Croix on October 17, 1768 (McCarty, *Desert Documentary*, 11–12). Pineda had gotten the information from the ensign at Tubac presidio. It was customary for the Spanish to appoint, or to ask the residents of a mission to elect from a vetted list, a gobernador, among a handful of other officials.

73. Nentvig discusses some of the characteristic diseases found in the Pimería Alta, as well as their remedies, in *Rudo Ensayo*, 25–26, 47–48.

74. McCarty speculates that, because the area was hit by torrential rains that July and August, there was a considerable amount of stagnant water and attendant mosquitoes around the missions, and that the illness therefore may have been malaria. Other sick missionaries included Fathers Agorreta, Salazar, and Roch. Father Gil was hit too, but only with a mild case. He nursed not only Garcés back to health but also Father Roch, who was stationed at nearby Suamca (*Spanish Frontier*, 97–98).

75. Arricivita, *Apostolic Chronicle*, vol. 2, 99.

76. Maughan, "Francisco Garcés," 51.

CHAPTER 4

1. Garcés tells the story of the raid in a letter he wrote to Governor Pineda the next day (McCarty, *Desert Documentary*, 13–15).

2. The Apaches also stated that this forthcoming attack would be at night, for reasons that are unclear. Some additional detail on this attack is found in Kessell, *Friars, Soldiers, and Reformers*, 49–50.

3. Petrie, *King Charles III of Spain*, 42, xx.

4. On the Stamp Act, see Petrie, *King Charles III of Spain*, 136.

5. See Bobb, *Viceregency of Antonio María Bucareli*, 13–14, for everything in this paragraph unless otherwise noted. Petrie, *King Charles III of Spain*, 90–91, also says that Gálvez's reforms made many things better in New Spain.

6. Gálvez's was a rags-to-riches story. He began life as a poor shepherd boy. Managing to obtain a legal education, he made a fortunate marriage to a French woman of higher social status. He then parlayed his new connections into a secretaryship under minister of state Jerónimo Grimaldi. See Priestley, "Reforms of José de Gálvez," 349.

7. Among those Gálvez served well were, in one scholar's judgment, the Indians of New Spain, who were "freed from much illegal oppression" by some of his reforms (Petrie, *King Charles III of Spain*, 145).

8. Petrie, *King Charles III of Spain*, 147–48; Priestley, *José de Gálvez*, 243.

9. Kessell, *Friars, Soldiers, and Reformers*, 50.

10. The information in this paragraph is from Maughan, "Francisco Garcés," 53–55.

11. Babock, *Apache Adaption to Hispanic Rule*, 5–6.

12. Moorhead, *Apache Frontier*, 3.

13. Moorhead, *Apache Frontier*, 8. Hugo O'Conor, who had wide experience fighting Apaches, would write in 1777 that at the hands of Apaches "babies were torn to bits at the breasts of their mothers and even in their wombs, carrying out on the dead bodies the most detestable excesses of ferocity and cruelty" (Cutter, *Defenses of Northern New Spain*, 37).

14. Reyes to Pineda, July 6, 1768, in McCarty, *Spanish Frontier*, 85.

15. Hutton, *Apache Wars*, 12.

16. See Moorhead, *Apache Frontier*, 6–8. The Apaches, or Ndé, also often raised a few crops and, of course, engaged in economic exchange. See Babcock, *Apache Adaption to Hispanic Rule*, 4–5.

17. Moorhead, *Apache Frontier*, 15.

18. Maughan, "Francisco Garcés," 56, drawing in part from Garcés's July 23, 1769, letter to Pineda (AC, ms. 1094).

19. Garcés to Pineda, July 23, 1769; Kessell, *Friars, Soldiers, and Reformers*, 50.

20. Garcés to Pineda, July 23, 1769 (translation from Kessell, JLKP, Box 6, Folder 8). Indeed, the Apaches liked to joke that the Spanish were their shepherds (Hutton, *Apache Wars*, 12).

21. Garcés to Pineda, July 23, 1769.

22. See Priestley, *José de Gálvez*, 239, for more on the circumstances and context surrounding Gálvez's work in this respect.

23. McCarty, *Spanish Frontier*, 104.

24. In his biography of Gálvez, Priestley notes not only the episode of insanity Gálvez suffered in Sonora but also a two-month vacation Gálvez took while in Spain in 1775 because of "fevers in his head," as well as another episode that preceded and perhaps led to his death on June 17, 1787 (*José de Gálvez*, 6, 11).

25. For this discussion of Gálvez in Sonora, see Maughan, "Francisco Garcés," 54–56; McCarty, *Spanish Frontier*, 100–105; and Priestley, *José de Gálvez*, 267–95.

26. Garcés made clear his preference for "priestly governance" of the missions in his July 23, 1769, letter to Governor Pineda.

27. Matson and Fontana, *Friar Bringas Reports to the King*, 19; Kessell, "Friars versus Bureaucrats," 153. Gálvez further clarified the missionaries' authority in a September 1769 decree. A few more concessions were made by Viceroy Bucareli in 1773, thereby fully abrogating the Enlighteners' post-Jesuit reforms (Kessell, "Friars versus Bureaucrats," 154).

28. Reyes, *Reyes Report of 1772*, July 6, 1772 (UASC, AZ 261).

29. Bells were "so central to the project of congregation and evangelization," so important for the friars' ability "to establish an orderly pattern of life, communicate information, increase productivity in labor, and instill religious discipline and devotion," that they were named and even, after a fashion, baptized (Mann, "Defining Time and Space," 276, 271).

30. Another native official not mentioned by Reyes, the *temastián*, was sometimes appointed to take care of the church and its objects, much like a sexton (Torre Curiel, *Twilight of the Mission Frontier*, 97).

31. For a detailed description of religious instruction at the missions in their contemporaneous California instantiation, see Hackel, *Children of Coyote*, 127–81.

32. Father Cartagena reported this style of greeting to Viceroy Bucareli in a letter of September 30, 1772 (AGN, PI, 152).

33. Reyes, *Reyes Report of 1772*, July 6, 1772.

34. For more on this distinction, see Lehner, *Catholic Enlightenment*, 37; and Cervantes, *Conquistadores*, 214–23. On the uses of "smells and bells," see Hackel, *Children of Coyote*, 171.

35. Hackel, *Children of Coyote*, 80.

36. Hackel's analysis makes clear that even in the more rigorously administered California missions the Franciscans displayed flexibility in the matter of dances, hunting and fishing, and so on—in large part because the Indians were determined to have freedom in such matters (*Children of Coyote*, 85–86).

37. Torre Curiel, *Twilight of the Mission Frontier*, 198.

38. Sandos, *Converting California*, 178.

39. Jackson, "Northwestern New Spain," 82.

40. Jackson, "Northwestern New Spain," 78. To say that there was less resistance is not to say there was *no* resistance, of course.

41. Sandos, *Converting California*, 10.

42. Hackel, *Children of Coyote*, 322.

43. Examples of abuse are easier to come by in the annals of the California missions than in those of the Pimería Alta. At San Gabriel, for instance, Father José Zalvidea chained suspected shamans together at San Gabirel and made then work as sawyers in large underground pits (Sandos, *Converting California*, 26). Indians who fled Mission San Francisco in 1797 charged that they had been abused by the alcaldes and flogged for such misdeeds as crying at family members' deaths, not working when they were sick, not taking back an adulterous wife, and hunting clams when hungry (Sandos, *Converting California*, 161). Such examples notwithstanding, Sandos concludes that in the California missions excessive punishment was not universal (*Converting California*, 179). Surely the same was true of the Pimería Alta missions.

It is worth noting that, even among "leading Catholics" in New Spain, this era saw the growth of a movement to limit the use of corporal punishment by priests and missionaries (Hackel, *Children of Coyote*, 324). Ironically, the association of this movement with secular reformers may only have intensified the missionaries' commitment to using whip and irons.

44. See Hackel, *Children of Coyote*, 283.

45. See, e.g., Joseph, Spicer, and Chesky, *Desert People*, 9–10; and Underhill, *Papago and Pima Indians*, 43.

46. The Piman-speaking group or groups living at Bac when Garcés arrived in 1768 is not entirely clear. There may well have been a shifting mix present at and around the mission, including Sobaípuris, Tohono O'odham,

a group called Koahadk, and a group called *totokwany*. For various and somewhat conflicting ideas on this score, see Torre Curiel, *Twilight of the Mission Frontier*, 57; Seymour, "1762 on the San Pedro," 177; Dejong, "None Excel Them," 24; and Joseph, Spicer, and Chesky, *Desert People*, 68.

47. Underhill, *Papago and Pima Indians*, 2, 5.

48. Underhill, *Papago and Pima Indians*, 6.

49. See, e.g., Pérez de Ribas, *My Life among the Savage Nations*, 64; and Font, *With Anza to California*, 387.

50. Webb claimed that these houses' openings always faced east, to catch the morning sun (*Pima Remembers*, 57).

51. Underhill, *Papago and Pima Indians*, 6.

52. Webb, *Pima Remembers*, 15.

53. See Joseph, Spicer, and Chesky, *Desert People*, 40.

54. Matson and Fontana, *Friar Bringas Reports to the King*, 24.

55. Joseph, Spicer, and Chesky, *Desert People*, 28–29; Underhill, *Papago and Pima Indians*, 9. Officer, "Kino and Agriculture in the Pimería Alta," 298–99, states that additional crops introduced by Kino into the region included pomegranates, figs, pears, quinces, apricots, peaches, grapes, sugar cane, chickpeas, lentils, cabbages, lettuce, onions, leeks, garlic, cilantro, and anise.

56. Underhill, *Papago and Pima Indians*, 11–21. Father Segesser said the baskets, "woven as tightly as Capuchin bottles," could hold water for "at least an hour" (Thompson, *Jesuit Missionary*, 194).

57. Underhill, *Papago and Pima Indians*, 35–36; Webb, *Pima Remembers*, 7.

58. Underhill, *Papago and Pima Indians*, 38; Webb, *Pima Remembers*, 36. The O'odham were especially accomplished long-distance runners. A favorite game (*We-ch* or *wuichutha*) was to race one another through the desert, kicking or throwing a wooden ball with one's feet until the goal line was reached. Such races could take place over ten or more miles. Webb recalled that Pimas would usually lose to American soldiers in short-distance races but nearly always win over long distances (*Pima Remembers*, 40). See also McCarthy, *Papago Traveler*, 9, 19–20; and Shaw, *Pima Past*, 86–89.

59. Joseph, Spicer, and Chesky, *Desert People*, 9–10.

60. Underhill, *Papago and Pima Indians*, 39–40.

61. Thompson, *Jesuit Missionary*, 192.

62. Underhill, *Papago and Pima Indians*, 41–43; Joseph, Spicer, and Chesky, *Desert People*, 73.

63. See Cavanaugh, *Myth of Religious Violence*, for an extended discussion of this point.

64. Matson and Fontana, *Friar Bringas Reports to the King*, 24. The O'odham believed that other peoples, even animals and plants, had their own distinct "ways" as well.

65. "The Report of Fr. Diego Miguel Bringas de Manzaneda y Encinas, O.F.M., to the King of Spain, 1796–97," in Matson and Fontana, *Friar Bringas Reports to the King*, 54.

66. Sandos, *Converting California*, 6, 168.

67. Reyes, *Reyes Report of 1772*, July 6, 1772. Father Antonio Barbastro, when he was president of the missions in 1780, confirmed this policy with respect to widows, orphans, and the sick or disabled (Torre Curiel, *Twilight of the Mission Frontier*, 201). Such had been the case in the Jesuit missions as well (Treutlein, "Economic Regime of the Jesuit Missions").

68. McCarty, *Spanish Frontier*, 63. Father Och complained that when he sent food to a sick person it was often eaten instead by members of that person's family (*Missionary in Sonora*, 135). Serra noted that among the Indians of Carmel the unweaned infants of mothers who died were often buried with them, if no family members could or would take care of the unfortunate babies (Geiger, *Life of Times of Fray Junípero Serra*, vol. 1, 261). Hackel proposes that in Alta California, "widows with children especially might have found some aspects of life in the missions preferable to life outside of them" (*Children of Coyote*, 66).

69. On this point, see Holland, *Dominion*; many of the works of the renowned ancient historian Peter Brown, including *Through the Eye of a Needle*; and many of the works of the eminent sociologist Rodney Stark, including *Rise of Christianity*.

70. Och, *Missionary in Sonora*, 135. Like so many of the practices discussed here, this was not a uniquely Sonoran practice. Members of Junípero Serra's party, on approaching San Diego in 1769, were offered women in exchange for cloth (Geiger, *Life and Times of Fray Junípero Serra*, vol. 1, 226). A Chumash chief offered Sebastián Vizcaíno's men ten women when he discovered they had none with them (Engelhardt, *Missions and Missionaries of California*, vol. 1, 63–64).

71. Sandos, *Converting California*, 23.

72. For articles arguing that native women found several reasons to be attracted to Christianity, see Shoemaker, "Kateri Tekakwitha's Tortuous Path"; and Purdue, "Women, Men, and American Indian Policy."

73. Shaw, *Pima Past*. See also Webb, *Pima Remembers*.

74. Underhill, *Papago and Pima Indians*, 40.

75. Webb, *Pima Remembers*, 38. Dobyns suggests that this practice was not ancient but was started in response to the epidemics that began to

plague the O'odham after their contact with the Spanish (*Pima-Maricopa*, 27). But since burning the belongings and houses of the dead was practiced by many other native groups across the Southwest (and beyond), this seems highly doubtful.

76. See Griffith, *Beliefs and Holy Places*, for an extended discussion of the modern O'odham embrace and, to some extent, adaptation of Christianity.

77. Kessell, *Friars, Soldiers, and Reformers*, 56. I am assuming Anza was dressed in the typical fashion of a presidio captain.

78. The following account of Anza's visits and orders is taken largely from McCarty, *Desert Documentary*, 16–25; and Kessell, *Friars, Soldiers, and Reformers*, 56.

79. Garcés to Buena, February 20, 1771 (HEBP, Box 20, Folder 25).

80. Wilson says it was measles, malignant fevers, and diarrhea (*Peoples of the Middle Gila*, 39). Kessell mentions only measles (*Friars, Soldiers, and Reformers*, 57). Much depends on the translator's choice from original Spanish accounts, themselves not always very specific.

81. As Kessell notes in *Friars, Soldiers, and Reformers*, 56.

82. I get this detail about the Christian woman from Arricivita, *Apostolic Chronicle*, vol. 2, 112. In his letter to Father Joseph de Araujo of November 23, 1770 (FMCC, 201:77), Garcés mentions that one reason he embarked on this trip was that a married woman had run away from the mission. Another reason was that an Indian who lived "inland" had taken ill. Arricivita may have conflated these women. The reason for this woman's flight may well have been to escape the epidemic or to receive care from a native healer. Hackel points out that the most common reasons baptized Indians fled the missions were to escape hunger and disease, to obtain greater food variety, and simply to regain their freedom (*Children of Coyote*, 91–93).

83. The following account of Garcés's 1770 entrada comes primarily from the extensive narrative he provides in his *Diario que se ha formado por el viaje hecho al Río Gila* (HEBP, Carton 20, Folder 23). I also draw from the shorter version he recounted in the *Copia de las noticias sacadas* (HEBP, Carton 21, Folder 11). Because this second version is not only briefer but was written several years later, whenever there are contradictions I privilege the *Diario . . . Gila*. For example, the *Diario . . . Gila* says Garcés left San Xavier on October 19, whereas the *Copia* says it was October 18 (as does Garcés's letter to Araujo of November 23, 1770, FMCC, 201:77). The former date is apparently the right one since, as John P. Wilson points out, in that diary's entry for October 23 Garcés tells us he names two rancherías after Saint John Capistrano, and October 23 is that saint's feast day. Wilson, perhaps the foremost scholar of the Gileño Pimas, has done a tremendous job in

reconstructing Garcés's route and interpreting the diaries; my account owes much to his work. Finally, in narrating the story of this entrada I also draw, in some places, on the interpretations of Arricivita (*Apostolic Chronicle*), Maughan ("Francisco Garcés"), and Kessell (*Friars, Soldiers, and Reformers*).

84. Garcés seems to imply in his summary diary (*Copia de las noticias sacadas*) that on this first day he retraced at least part of his former route. Since other diaries mention Quitoa and El Aquitum (or Aquituni) as being situated along the Santa Cruz, with the latter place located near today's Picacho Peak, we can be reasonably sure of his path. Garcés writes in his November 23, 1770, letter to Araujo that he started off to the northeast; this is likely a typo, however, since he clearly states that he went northwest in both his 1770 diary and in the *Copia de las noticias sacadas*. Furthermore, in the letter he says that his first objective was to visit some Papagos, who did not not typically live east of the Santa Cruz.

85. The chief's name may have been Cojo, if he is identical with the Gileño "governor" mentioned by Captain Anza in a letter to Sonoran governor Pineda on August 20, 1769 (Bolton, *Anza's California Expeditions*, vol. 5, 1–2).

86. In Tubac, Anza heard this news as early as August 20, 1769, the date on which he wrote Governor Pineda to tell him that the son of a Gileño Pima chief had come to Tubac and reported hearing from the Cocomaricopas to the west that among another tribe even farther to the west had come "four Spaniards [who] carried very long muskets and wore long garments." Anza surmised that these men were part of the Serra expedition. One would think that he relayed this report to Garcés at San Xavier del Bac, but in his diary the friar implies that the Gileños were giving him fresh information.

87. Garcés to Araujo, November 23, 1770.

88. See Smith, Kessell, and Fox, *Father Kino in Arizona*, for a concise account of Kino's explorations in the region Garcés was now visiting.

89. Father Kino ascended to the top of Gila Butte, located a little to the north of Sweetwater, in the hope of seeing where the Colorado River emptied into the Gulf of California. Needless to say, he was disappointed (Wilson, *Peoples of the Middle Gila*, 17).

90. See, e.g., Webb, *Pima Remembers*, 29. It is possible that the Jesuit remembered by these old men was actually Father Keller, or perhaps even Father Sedelmayr, both of whom came through these parts. Keller was trying to find a way north to the Hopis, in compliance with a royal cédula of 1742. His party was attacked a little north of the Gila by Apaches, lost all its animals and one of the accompanying soldiers, and gave up the journey (Dunne, *Juan Antonio Balthasar*, 50–51).

91. See Wilson, *Peoples of the Middle Gila*, 3, for more discussion of this area. Sedelmayr noted in 1744 that the Gila, having gone underground for about ten miles, once again emerged aboveground here. Indeed, *sutaquisón* means "where the water comes up" (Wilson, *Peoples of the Middle Gila*, 1, 21).

92. Webb said that the thicket in his boyhood, around 1900, ran for eight miles west to east and three miles north to south (*Pima Remembers*, 76).

93. From the heights of the Estrellas, Garces said he could also see the Sierra Azul, "which is very high." It is not clear to which mountains he was referring. Because the Spaniards of the time often called today's Verde River the Azul, he may have been referring either to the Mazatzal, or Superstition Mountains, which rise from the northeastern horizon in the direction of the Verde's entrance into the Salt and would have been familiar to Garcés from his previous trips to the Gila. Alternatively, Garcés might have meant the Bradshaw Mountains, which do indeed rise "very high" (up to 8,000 feet) to the north of Phoenix, if by this time he no longer referred to the Verde River as the Azul. The Sierra Azul was apparently a mystery to Garcés and his contemporaries; it was mentioned in early Spanish accounts of the region, but its location was not definitely known. Anza says that throughout his 1774 expedition he asked natives for its whereabouts, without success (Bolton, *Anza's California Expeditions*, vol. 2, 118).

94. This detail comes from Garcés's letter to Araujo, November 23, 1770.

95. In his November 23, 1770, letter to Araujo, Garcés says that, because of a lack of pasturage, at night two Opa boys would bring the horses food to eat.

96. Spier, *Yuman Tribes of the Gila River*, xiii. Spier attributes this talent to all the Yuman-speaking peoples, not just the Opas.

97. Wilson, *Peoples of the Middle Gila*, 42.

98. This last observation Garcés made in his November 23, 1770, letter to Araujo. See also Wilson, *Peoples of the Middle Gila*, 41.

99. Garcés later wrote to Araujo (November 23, 1770) that the Opas, "until they feel they are not being deceived and are confident of the Father, ... tell all manner of lies. They deny the roads and say that there are no waterholes and that every place is full of enemies. . . . One must not ask for other peoples, as the Jesuits did for the Hopi" (Wilson, *Peoples of the Middle Gila*, 42). He may not have understood precisely why the natives acted as they did, but Garcés was gaining an understanding of their ways.

100. Father Jacobo Sedelmayr was one such Spaniard. Upon reaching the confluence of the Bill Williams and Colorado Rivers in 1743, he believed he was on the "borders of the celebrated province of Moqui." He wasn't (Dunne, *Jacobo Sedelmayr*, 20). A map drawn by Nicolás de Lafora in the

late 1760s shows Moqui as just above the Gila (although if anything, on this map the Hopi homeland is presented as too far east rather than west). See map included in Kinnaird, *Frontiers of New Spain*.

101. Thompson, *Jesuit Missionary*, 204. The Cocomaricopas—Spanish spelling of the Pima word *Kokmalik O'p*—had been driven onto the Gila by their Quechan enemies (Dobyns, *Pima-Maricopa*, 29). Apparently the Cocomaricopas inspired fear in many people. In 1699, Father Kino found it necessary to visit them in order to refute reports that they were cannibals (Wilson, *Peoples of the Middle Gila*, 17). The Cocomaricopas and Opas were closely related Yuman-speaking groups considered by archaeologists to belong to the Patayan culture. They are now known as the Maricopas, or the Piipaash—which, per usual, translates into English as "the people"— although Spier argued that those who lived downstream from Gila Bend were Kaveltcadom, a distinguishable group (*Yuman Tribes of the Gila River*).

102. Garcés notes in his November 23, 1770, letter to Araujo that he had intended to be gone from his mission for only five days, and that no friar was overseeing San Xavier in his absence.

103. One clue to their return route is given by Garcés in one of the diaries of his 1771 entrada (*Diario desde ocho de agosto*), in which he notes that in 1770 near his route back from the Gila was a village he calls Anica, which he says was west of the village of Santa Rosa. Today, we find in that area a small village called Emika.

104. As he says in his letter to Araujo of November 23, 1770.

CHAPTER 5

1. Wilson, *Peoples of the Middle Gila*, 42. Torre Curiel is incorrect in saying that Garcés showed "little concern for the features proper to each one of the tribes that he encountered on his travels" (*Twilight of the Mission Frontier*, 39). Rather, I would agree with Stewart that Garcés was "the best ethnographer among the Spanish explorers of the lower Colorado River," if not several other regions ("Mohave Indians in Hispanic Times," 32).

2. Garcés to Araujo, November 23, 1770 (FMCC, 201:77).

3. Kessell, *Friars, Soldiers, and Reformers*, 34–45.

4. Jackson, "Northwestern New Spain," 75.

5. Jackson, "Demographic Change," 465. For context, Jackson notes that roughly half of European children in the seventeenth through nineteenth centuries also died before age ten. It was not just epidemics that decimated Indian populations at missions like Tumacácori but increased susceptibility to disease caused by the stress of incorporation into the mission system;

lower birth rates; a shift in the sexual division of manual labor from women to men; abandonment of the practice of periodically burning residences, which killed vermin; poor sanitation; the introduction of new woolen clothing to which parasites could cling; and higher population densities, which allowed disease to spread more readily (466–67). Increased rates of venereal disease also led to higher death rates (Sandos, *Converting California*, 111), as did Indians' participation (sometimes unwillingly) in military campaigns versus other tribes (Torre Curiel, *Twilight of the Mission Frontier*, 53). For a detailed discussion and statistical analysis of population decline in the California missions, see Hackel, *Children of Coyote*, 96–123.

6. "As if the Indians did not have any reason," noted Father Serra somewhat caustically, with regard to the term gente de razón, in a letter of December 8, 1782 (Geiger, *Life of Times of Fray Junípero Serra*, vol. 2, 194). Serra was certainly not the only cleric, or only Spaniard, who knew full well that, taken literally, the term was inaccurate. Father Antonio Barbastro, for example, said that the O'odham had "at least as much talent, I would say more," than the so-called gente de razón he encountered on the frontier (Kessell, *Friars, Soldiers, and Reformers*, 69). The locution was nevertheless widely used.

7. See Kessell, *Friars, Soldiers, and Reformers*, 45–57.

8. Kinnaird, *Frontiers of New Spain*, ix.

9. Maughan, "Francisco Garcés," 10–11.

10. Kinnaird, *Frontiers of New Spain*, 2.

11. See Kinnaird, *Frontiers of New Spain*, 20–21, 23, 108.

12. Kinnaird, *Frontiers of New Spain*, 23.

13. Kinnaird, *Frontiers of New Spain*, 24.

14. See also Maughan, "Francisco Garcés," 62–63, and Garcés to Río, March 8, 1771 (JLKP, Box 6, Folder 11).

15. Obtaining for his native charges at Tucson their own permanent missionary was for many years one of Garcés's major objectives. See his letter "Reasons for Urging a Minister for San Agustín del Tucson," which was written sometime after May 1771 (HEBP, Box 20, Folder 25).

16. Maughan, "Francisco Garcés," 62–63.

17. Maughan, "Francisco Garcés," 61.

18. Garcés to Buena, February 20, 1771 (HEBP, Box 20, Folder 25).

19. Garcés was far from alone in making this assessment, at least among his fellow missionaries. Father Reyes claimed in a September 4, 1771, letter that the "Apaches have never been so bloodthirsty" as they had become in 1771 (Stagg, *First Bishop of Sonora*, 28).

20. Garcés called it the Río Azul. As far as I can tell, he had never seen this river, which flows from the Mogollon Rim of central Arizona into the Salt River at the eastern edge of today's metropolitan Phoenix area.

21. The Yumas already were the chief members of an alliance that included the Mohaves, Yavapais, Kumeyaay (called Diegueños, then, and sometimes still today), and Chemehuevis. This alliance had as its primary enemy another alliance, which included the Cocomaricopas, Opas, Halchidhomas, Cocopahs, Hualapais, Gileño Pimas, and Papagos. Adding the Apaches to the Yuma alliance would have greatly tilted the balance of power between these two groups.

22. Garcés to Río, March 8, 1771.

23. Garcés, *Copia de las noticias sacadas.*

24. McCarty, *Spanish Frontier*, 68.

25. Bolton, *Bolton and the Spanish Borderlands*, 268.

26. Garcés to Buena, February 20, 1771.

27. As he reports in the *Copia de las noticias sacadas.*

28. From the notes he made on this trip, Garcés compiled a diary called the *Diario que se ha formado con la ocasión de la entrada que hiço a los vecinos gentiles* (HEBP, Carton 20, Folders 22–23). This version was quick and dirty, even by Garcés's standards, and he apparently did not consider it a full and true diary. Thus, some months later he also compiled another diary of this entrada known as the *Diario desde ocho de agosto, con la ocasión de la visita de los próximos gentiles* (HEBP, Carton 20, Folder 23), a fuller version that not only amplifies but sometimes contradicts the first diary. Father Esteban de Salazar also created a compressed narrative of Garcés's 1771 entrada based on his extensive conversations with the friar upon his return from the wilderness at Tubutama on October 31 of that year. Finally, the 1771 entrada is covered by Garcés in the summary of his entradas written in 1775—the *Copia de las noticias sacadas* (HEBP, Carton 21, Folder 11)—and this account differs somewhat from the others. None of these diaries has been published in English.

Because Garcés was traveling in wholly unfamiliar territory and was not a very clear writer to begin with, there are obscurities and confusions in each of these primary source documents—obscurities and confusions that have led later historians to different conclusions as to what happened to Garcés, where, and among whom on this historic 1771 journey. In short, there is much room for interpretation when it comes to reconstructing the story of Garcés's 1771 entrada. Generally speaking, I follow Bolton's "Early Explorations of Father Garcés," Maughan's "Francisco Garcés," or

mapmaker Tom Jonas's intuitions when I have had questions about interpreting the source materials, although it should be noted that Bolton's
account appears to rely on only one of the two 1771 extant diaries (*Diario
que se ha formado con la ocasión de la entrada que hiço a los vecinos gentiles*).
Arricivita, the earliest historian of this journey, did not know the territory
well and generally perpetuates confusion in his *Apostolic Chronicle*, and
Coues's *On the Trail of a Spanish Pioneer* was (correctly) shown by Bolton
to be often unreliable in relating the stories of Garcés's journeys. (Coues
was an unreliable historian generally, and I refrain from using any of his
translations, summaries, or interpretations in this book.) In sum, I have
had to make many choices in how to understand Garcés's entrada and have
surely gotten a number of things wrong—it is simply hard if not impossible
to know *which* things.

29. Garcés, *Diario desde ocho de agosto*. The original plan had been to go
north to the Gila, then down the Gila to the Colorado. Why Garcés ultimately abandoned this plan is unclear. The excitement of seeing new lands
probably had something to do with it.

30. Horgan, *Lamy of Santa Fe*, 342.

31. In this section I draw from the *Diario que se ha formado . . . gentiles*
unless otherwise noted. In the quotation above, although Garcés was often
not literally alone on this journey, even when he was in the company of
native guides it is not difficult to believe that he felt a profound sense of
loneliness.

32. He alludes to this in the *Diario que se ha formado . . . gentiles* but elabo-
rates a bit more in the *Copia de las noticias sacadas*.

33. The *Diario desde ocho de agosto* puts this on August 12 and has Garcés
staying at the next place for two days rather than at Santa Rosa for two days.

34. This village, called in one of the diaries El Comaquibuto, may have
been today's Quijotoa. Another possibility is Vainom Kug.

35. In the *Diario desde ocho de agosto*, Garcés says he went only three
leagues on this day to arrive at Santa Ana de Cuboc (called Cubba in the
Diario que se ha formado . . . gentiles). Kupk is about that distance from
Vainom Kug and a little farther from Quijotoa.

36. Nothing remains of this church today. For an account of Sonotya's
mission history, including Ruhen's death and the 1751 uprising, see Ives,
"Mission San Marcelo del Sonoydag."

37. The provenance of the spring's name has been much discussed, including by Garcés. Hoy ("A Quest for the Meaning of Quitobaquito") concludes that its most likely origin is from *ki-to*, meaning a completed Papago
house, and *bac*, meaning springs. To the south of Quitobaquito there was a

ranchería called Quitobac ("houses near springs"). When the Spanish kept going north and found another, small village near springs, they naturally called it Quitobaquito.

38. Garcés was actually probably riding somewhat south of today's Camino del Diablo, but not far enough south to make a material difference. Based on the evidence given in his diary, most of his journey here likely took place just south of today's international border.

39. On the lifeways of the In-the-Sand People, see Nabhan, Hodgson, and Fellows, "Meager Living?" It is also possible that these people were *xapu´k*, considered to be semi-Papago by their O'odham neighbors in the Papaguería. They too were friends with the Yumas. See Spier, *Yuman Tribes of the Gila River*, 7.

40. He had to promise them a hunting knife, since he had promised knives to each of the two guides who accompanied him from Sonoita. At this point, when he learned that he would not get a knife, the annoying man from near El Carrizal turned back, for which decision Garcés thanked God.

41. He says in the *Copia de las noticias sacadas* that he struck the Gila about ten leagues upstream from its junction with the Colorado. Of course, he didn't know that at the time.

42. At the end of the *Diario que se ha formado . . . gentiles* Garcés says it is "possible" that the Indians who took him across the river were Yumas. In the *Diario desde ocho del agosto* he speaks directly about Palma being the "governor of the Yumas," though he does not use Palma's name. This diary was almost certainly written in mid-1772, after the *Diario que se ha formado . . . gentiles*, when Garcés had come to understand more about where he had been, and with whom. Bolton, in "Early Explorations of Father Garcés," states with confidence that the "governor" met by Garcés was none other than Palma.

43. I mostly refer to him as Salvador Palma rather than his Quechan name in the rest of this narrative, not only out of sympathy with my non-Quechan readers but also because Palma himself seems not to have objected to the name, or indeed to Christianization, until shortly before the Yuma uprising of 1781 (if then).

44. Forbes, *Warriors of the Colorado*, 68–69.

45. Guerrero, "Lost in the Translation," 330. The name Salvador is said to have been given to Palma several years after Garcés's 1771 entrada by a mission escapee the Spanish called Sebastián Taraval, whom we meet later and to whom Palma acted as a savior when Taraval emerged half-dead from the desert into one of the Quechan villages. If that is true, then at the time Garcés met him Olleyquotequiebe was presumably known to the Spaniards simply as Palma.

46. A good summary of these visits is provided by Forbes, *Warriors of the Colorado*, 118–24.

47. Dunne, *Jacobo Sedelmayr*, 61.

48. Dunne, *Jacobo Sedelmayr*, ii, 7.

49. As translated in Arricivita, *Apostolic Chronicle*, vol. 2, 116.

50. Garcés, *Copia de las noticias sacadas*.

51. Garcés, *Copia de las noticias sacadas*. Had it not been a rainy monsoon season, Garcés would have had even more trouble crossing the desert both to and beyond the Colorado.

52. Garcés, *Diario desde ocho de agosto*, 5.

53. Very little is known about the Kohuanas, who spoke a Yuman dialect and have disappeared as a distinct people. Much if not most of what we do know is provided by Garcés, who encountered them on this and subsequent trips to the river.

54. Bolton believed this to be near Heintzelman's Point, approximately fifty miles north of the Colorado River's mouth and the place where tide-water stops. He also believed Garcés did not go any farther south along the Colorado. See Bolton, "Early Explorations of Father Garcés," 325.

55. See Bolton, "Early Explorations of Father Garcés," 326.

56. See Bolton, *Outpost of Empire*, 32.

57. Bolton, *Outpost of Empire*, 32, concludes that the Cocopah Range was the western limit of Garcés's travels on this entrada.

58. In this section I continue to draw from the *Diario que se ha formado . . . gentiles* unless otherwise noted. The Quechan mourning ceremony is called *Karʔúk* and commemorates a battle with the Cocopahs. The ceremony takes four days. See Zappia, *Traders and Raiders*, 30.

59. Garcés noted the slave-taking and -trading that routinely took place among all the peoples of the region, a practice he argued the Spanish would also have to eradicate. He did not understand that the slave trade, although it predated Spanish entry into the Americas, had only intensified among the natives of the lower Colorado with the introduction of the Spanish slave market and more desirable goods—horses, cattle, tools—for which to trade people. See Zappia, *Traders and Raiders*, 8.

60. Bolton, "Early Explorations of Father Garcés," 328.

61. Yuma is the sunniest place in the world. It is sunny 90 percent of the time from sunrise to sunset. It is also one of the hottest (mean annual temperature of 76 degrees, and 133 days a year over 100 degrees, based on 1991–2020 data) and one of the driest (3.2 inches of precipitation a year, based on the same data set).

62. In March or April 1774, when he was at either the mission of San Gabriel or the mission of San Diego, Garcés was shown for the first time the diary of Jesuit Father Ferdinand Konščak, who from his base in Baja California had explored the lower Colorado River in 1746 (see Konščak, *Life and Works of the Reverend Ferdinand Konščak*). The diary confirmed for Garcés that in 1771 he had been very close to the mouth of the Colorado, and that the size of the river varied greatly depending on the season. He noted in 1771, "[I had] expected to see in the Colorado an immeasurable river, but this was my mistake. Being ignorant of the location of the junction, and thinking that the Indians were deceiving me, I did not wish to affirm what I did not know from a certainty" (Bolton, *Anza's California Expeditions*, vol. 2, 358).

63. Arricivita, *Apostolic Chronicle*, vol. 2, 125.

64. Kessell, *Friars, Soldiers, and Reformers*, 61–62.

65. Salazar to Buena, November 13, 1771 (HEBP, Box 20, Folder 25). Salazar wrote Father Buena very soon after Garcés's arrival at Tubutama, for Buena was one of the people most concerned about Garcés's well-being. In this letter Salazar provides a thumbnail summary of Garcés's journey. He also notes that Garcés said it was "less trouble" for him to go nurse Fathers Gil and Agorreta than to be put temporarily in charge of Agorreta's mission at Sáric, another clue that mission administration was not exactly his passion.

CHAPTER 6

1. Kessell, *Friars, Soldiers, and Reformers*, 68–69.

2. Quotes in this paragraph from diary as cited in Arricivita, *Apostolic Chronicle*, vol. 2, 116–17.

3. Corbalán to Bucareli, January 21, 1772 (HEBP, Box 20, Folder 22). The intendant system was introduced by José de Gálvez as a way of increasing funds to the royal treasury by replacing the corrupt alcaldes mayores with more professional regional executives. See Priestley, *José de Gálvez*, 290.

4. Bucareli to Arriaga, March 25, 1772 (HEBP, Box 20, Folder 22).

5. McCarty, *Desert Documentary*, 25.

6. Garcés, "Report on the Founding of Missions, 1772" (HEBP, Box 20, Folder 25). Garcés had been pushing for Tucson to receive its own resident priest almost since the moment he arrived at San Xavier. See his undated letter, "Reasons for Urging a Minister for San Agustín del Tucson" (HEBP, Box 20, Folder 25). Tucson was fated never to receive its own resident Franciscan, however.

7. See Harrison, "Franciscan Concepts of the Congregated Mission and the Apostolic Ministry in Eighteenth-Century Texas," in Johnson and Melville, *From La Florida to La California*; and Harrison, "Franciscan Missionaries and Their Networks."

8. Garcés to Araujo, November 23, 1770 (FMCC, 201:77).

9. See Kessell, "Anza Damns the Missions," which includes the text of the letter Anza wrote Bucareli from Tubac on December 15, 1772. The impetus of Anza's letter was a recent widely circulated report from Father Reyes that the missions were in a disastrous state. Anza laid it on thick, perhaps, in order to curry favor with the viceroy's fiscal, José Antonio de Areche, who was known to agree with Reyes. Among the criticisms of the missions leveled by Anza were that they failed to teach their native residents Christian doctrine effectively, that they precluded Indians on the frontier from assimilating into Spanish society, and that where they were introduced the Indian populations declined. Anza was correct on all three points.

10. Garces to Buena y Alcalde, "Comment on the New Cordon of Presidios," n.d. (HEBP, Box 20, Folder 25).

11. I am presuming Garcés is referring to O'Conor in speaking of "the commander" in this letter. O'Conor had fled Ireland as a young man to enter Spain's foreign service, as had many other Irish in the hope of throwing off the yoke of English Protestants—or at least in the hope of exacting some revenge for the British crown's repression of Irish Catholics. On O'Conor's life and work, see McCarty and Santiago, "Founder of Spanish Tucson Petitions the King"; and Cutter, *Defenses of Northern New Spain*.

12. On all this, see also Maughan, "Francisco Garcés," 63–64.

13. Bobb, *Viceregency of Antonio María Bucareli*, 19.

14. Portrait on frontispiece in Bobb, *Viceregency of Antonio María Bucareli*. Bobb obtained the portrait from Manuel Rivera Cambas, *Los gobernadores de México*, vol. 1, 422.

15. Bobb, *Viceregency of Antonio María Bucareli*, 16–17.

16. Bobb, *Viceregency of Antonio María Bucareli*, 30.

17. John, *Storms Brewed*, 443.

18. In describing the first two problems mentioned here and the way the Spanish viewed them, I am drawing heavily from Bolton, *Outpost of Empire*, 27–29.

19. The fledgling mission at San Diego was about to be abandoned for lack of food when on the last day of a novena (nine-day prayer) to Saint Joseph, patron saint of the 1769 expedition, a ship was sighted on his feast day (March 19, 1770; see Palóu, *Palóu's Life of Fray Junípero Serra*, 86–88, for

the classic account). Pedro Fages led a highly successful three-month bear hunt near San Luis Obispo in the spring and summer of 1772 that provided much-needed meat for the missions of San Carlos and San Antonio.

20. As was pointed out by Costansó to Bucareli in his letter of September 5, 1772, in Bolton, *Anza's California Expeditions*, vol. 5, 8–11. These missions were administered by the Dominicans as of 1772.

21. See Bolton, *Outpost of Empire*, 47–48.

22. Anza to Bucareli, May 2, 1772, in Bolton, *Anza's California Expeditions*, vol. 5, 3–7, the source of additional Anza quotes in this section.

23. Although Anza does not mention it here, he had in 1769 mentioned the idea of opening up a road to Alta California to Gálvez, who had recommended it to Viceroy Croix. But other priorities intervened, and the matter was temporarily dropped. It was the "zeal and knowledge furnished by . . . the intrepid Francisco Garcés" that led to Anza becoming more firmly committed to pursuing the notion (Bolton, *Outpost of Empire*, 31). See Gálvez to Arriaga, March 8, 1774, in Bolton, *Anza's California Expeditions*, vol. 5, 102–6.

24. Costansó to Bucareli, September 5, 1772.

25. The nature of this network is one of the primary subjects of Zappia's *Traders and Raiders*.

26. Areche to Bucareli, October 12, 1772, in Bolton, *Anza's California Expeditions*, vol. 5, 12–24. The fiscal in colonial Spain was akin to an attorney general.

27. In a letter to Minister Arriaga of January 27, 1773, an optimistic Bucareli said that "the spiritual and apostolic labors of Father Garcés not only are worthy of praise but promise the rich fruit of an abundant harvest of souls willing to submit themselves to the pale of our sacred religion" (Maughan, "Francisco Garcés," 78).

28. Anza to Bucareli, January 22, 1773, in Bolton, *Anza's California Expeditions*, vol. 5, 50–52.

29. Sastre to Bucareli, October 19, 1772, in Bolton, *Anza's California Expeditions*, vol. 5, 33–40.

30. Sastre to Bucareli, January 21, 1773, in Bolton, *Anza's California Expeditions*, vol. 5, 47–49. In this letter Sastre suggests that Anza and Garcés go alone, without soldiers, so that they can advance "quietly, without arousing any fears which might be caused among the Indians by seeing the troops, which certainly would happen and might prevent the accomplishment of any good results." This advice was ultimately rejected.

31. "I have repeatedly asked for it and . . . it appears to be one of the documents most necessary for making the decision," Bucareli had complained

the previous October (Bucareli to Arriaga, October 27, 1772, in Bolton, *Anza's California Expeditions*, vol. 5, 41–45).

32. Cartagena to Bucareli, January 29, 1773, in Bolton, *Anza's California Expeditions*, vol. 5, 55–56.

33. Bucareli to Arriaga, April 26, 1773, in Bolton, *Anza's California Expeditions*, vol. 5, 77–78.

34. Bucareli to Arriaga, January 27, 1773, in Bolton, *Anza's California Expeditions*, vol. 5, 53–54.

35. Anza to Bucareli, March 7, 1773, in Bolton, *Anza's California Expeditions*, vol. 5, 57–67.

36. Garcés to Bucareli, March 8, 1773, in Bolton, *Anza's California Expeditions*, vol. 5, 68–76.

37. In this letter to Bucareli, Garcés mentions that he had made diaries of each of his three journeys (in 1768, 1770, and 1771), as well as of his journey to the Apachería in 1769, and that he had sent them all to Querétaro. To my knowledge, the diaries of Garcés's 1768 and 1769 entradas have never been found. We know about them only through various letters and the summary Garcés wrote of all his entradas in 1775.

38. The information in this section is drawn from Geiger, *Life and Times of Fray Junípero Serra*, vol. 1, 354–57, 371–77, except where otherwise noted.

39. Bucareli scarcely had a higher view of the common Spanish soldier than did Serra or the rest of the friars. He claimed that a third of the militia in Mexico City spent most of their time in jail. He also complained that they were impossible to train, thanks to their lack of fear of punishment and their lack of any sense of honor (Bobb, *Viceregency of Antonio María Bucareli*, 92).

40. This is precisely what the Escalante expedition would attempt to achieve in 1776–77 (see chapter 10).

41. Bucareli to Arriaga, September 26, 1773, in Bolton, *Anza's California Expeditions*, vol. 5, 95–98. Geiger, *Life and Times of Fray Junípero Serra*, vol. 1, 380.

42. Council of War and Royal Exchequer, Mexico, September 9, 1773, in Bolton, *Anza's California Expeditions*, vol. 5, 82–93. I have modernized some spellings in this quote.

43. Bucareli to Rivera y Moncada, September 19, 1773, in Bolton, *Anza's California Expeditions*, vol. 5, 94.

44. Arriaga to Bucareli, March 9, 1774, in Bolton, *Anza's California Expeditions*, vol. 5, 107.

45. Council of War and Royal Exchequer, September 9, 1773, in Bolton, *Anza's California Expeditions*, vol. 5, 91–92.

46. Bolton, *Anza's California Expeditions*, vol. 2, 1.

47. See Kessell's notes from a letter written by Garcés from Tumacácori on September 1, 1773 (JLKP, Box 6, Folder 16). The Tiburones were a subgroup of the Seris. Gil's reputation for sanctity was such that the possibility of his being a saint was bandied about directly after his death. His cause was formally opened in 1782, but after a while it became dormant.

48. Garcés to Ximénez, December 25, 1776 (FMCC 201:18). Some of those conflicts were stirred up by Father Reyes, who at this time, to the horror of his Queretaran brethren, was advocating a "new method" of mission administration that would reduce the role of the colegio. This effort fizzled by the end of 1774. See Kessell, *Friars, Soldiers, and Reformers*, 76–77.

49. Garcés wrote later that it was his desire not to follow the Gila downstream from the villages of the Gileños but to travel from there cross-country northwest to the Colorado. Whether Anza had assented to or even seriously considered this plan is not clear. See Bolton, *Anza's California Expeditions*, vol. 2, 391.

50. We know the names of seventeen of these soldiers from a list that was later assembled. Because they typically remain nameless both in the expedition's official reports and in the historical narratives that have followed, it seems appropriate to record them here: Marcial Sánchez (corporal), Juan de Espinosa, Joseph Marcos Ramírez, Juan Antonio Valencia, Joseph Torivio Corona, Juan Joseph Rodríguez, Joseph María Martínez, Joseph Pablo Corona, Francisco Figueroa, Juan Martínez, Joseph Antonio Acedo, Ysidro Martínez, Joseph Antonio Romero, Pasqual Rivera, Juan Miguel Palomino, Joseph de Ayala, and Juan Angel Castillo (Bolton, *Anza's California Expeditions*, vol. 5, 203).

51. Geiger, *Franciscan Missionaries in Hispanic California*, 63.

52. Here I am following Beebe and Senkewicz, *Junípero Serra*, 209, both in telling Taraval's California story as well as in spelling his last name Taraval rather than Tarabal. Both spellings are extant in the literature.

53. Guerrero, "Lost in the Translation," reviews Palma's possible motives.

54. Bolton, *Anza's California Expeditions*, vol. 2, 33.

55. Bolton, *Anza's California Expeditions*, vol. 2, 3–4. Díaz clarifies in his diary that the horses were stolen on January 2 (Bolton, *Anza's California Expeditions*, vol. 2, 248).

56. In a later diary entry, Garcés wrote, "I confess the extreme repugnance which I had for going to experience the trials suffered during my previous journey in those horrible sand dunes" (Bolton, *Anza's California Expeditions*, vol. 2, 391).

57. Bolton, *Anza's California Expeditions*, vol. 2, 249. Díaz was very familiar with the road from Sáric to Caborca and beyond, thanks to his six years
in the mission field in that territory.

CHAPTER 7

1. I try to tell the story of the expedition from original sources, but in
places I also draw from the wonderful narrative of Bolton (*Anza's California
Expeditions*, vol. 1).
2. Kessell, *Friars, Soldiers, and Reformers*, 95.
3. Bolton, *Anza's California Expeditions*, vol. 2, 1–2.
4. For a description of what the route to Altar was like just a few years before
the expedition came through, see Kinnaird, *Frontiers of New Spain*, 109–12.
5. Bolton, *Anza's California Expeditions*, vol. 2, 3–4. Route 43 today connects Sáric to Tubutama, Atil, Oquitoa, and Altar, where it strikes Highway
2. That highway goes west to Caborca before turning nothwest to Sonoyta.
Thus, most of the expedition's route in Sonora can easily be followed today
if one doesn't mind assuming the usual risks of Sonoran travel.
6. Perhaps Garcés met with Díaz when he came through Caborca and
decided that Díaz's temperament and knowledge of the country made him
the most suitable companion friar for the current expedition. Alternatively,
it may have been College of Santa Cruz Father President Antonio Ramos
who suggested Díaz, if he did not simply confirm Garcés's choice (Kessell,
Friars, Soldiers, and Reformers, 95). Arricivita says that Garcés "took" Díaz
(*Apostolic Chronicle*, vol. 2, 156).
7. Bolton, *Anza's California Expeditions*, vol. 2, 17–19.
8. Garcés does not say so, but it seems probable that this was the "governor" both he and Father Salazar praised so highly in 1771.
9. Bolton, *Anza's California Expeditions*, vol. 2, 315.
10. Bolton, *Anza's California Expeditions*, vol. 2, 254–55.
11. Bolton, *Anza's California Expeditions*, vol. 2, 30.
12. Bolton, *Anza's California Expeditions*, vol. 2, 31.
13. Both Anza and Garcés report that Luis said that Indians *upstream*
from the Yumas—apparently meaning upstream on the Gila rather than
the Colorado, since Palma's village was then on the former river—posed
a threat. Bolton says (*Anza's California Expeditions*, vol. 1, 95), erroneously,
that the threat came from downstream, and specifically from an Indian the
Spaniards named Captain Pablo or Captain Feo (Captain Ugly Face). We
meet this man later.

14. Bolton, *Anza's California Expeditions*, vol. 2, 318. According to Garcés, Palma later told him that it was Opa Indians from along the Gila who had stirred up the unrest. They were angry at the change of route that had left them unvisited by the Spaniards.

15. Bolton, *Anza's California Expeditions*, vol. 2, 37.

16. Bolton, *Anza's California Expeditions*, vol. 2, 37.

17. But see note 14. It may have been both the Cocomaricopas and the Opas who were causing trouble. They were closely related groups.

18. Bolton, *Anza's California Expeditions*, vol. 2, 259.

19. Bolton, *Anza's California Expeditions*, vol. 2, 39–40.

20. Bolton, *Anza's California Expeditions*, vol. 2, 45.

21. This place, the future site of one of the Colorado River missions, became in the nineteenth century the site of Fort Yuma. St. Thomas Indian Mission is located there now, along with a fine statue of Garcés; see photo in this volume's Epilogue.

22. Bolton, *Anza's California Expeditions*, vol. 2, 46. The Quechans called this hill Avie Quah-la-Altwa (Zappia, *Traders and Raiders*, 21).

23. Bolton, *Anza's California Expeditions*, vol. 2, 47.

24. Bolton, *Anza's California Expeditions*, vol. 2, 265. Anza wrote that the Quechans displayed an "affability such as is never seen in an Indian toward a Spaniard" (Bolton, *Anza's California Expeditions*, vol. 5, 115).

25. Kittle, *Franciscan Frontiersmen*, 83.

26. On Quechan homosexuality and transgenderism, see Forbes, *Warriors of the Colorado*, 57. Neither practice was peculiar to the Quechans, of course, but it may have been more visible than with most of the other peoples the friars had contacted.

27. See Bolton, *Anza's California Expeditions*, vol. 2, 365; Arricivita, *Apostolic Chronicle*, vol. 2, 160; and Barbastro, "Sonora Report, 1768–1783" (FMCC, 202:35).

28. As Kittle notes (*Franciscan Frontiersmen*, 84), and as travelers on Interstate 8 can observe for themselves, directly west of Yuma is a huge field, or erg, of sand dunes running for forty-five miles from northwest to southeast. The dunes are six miles wide.

29. Pourade, *Anza Conquers the Desert*, 42.

30. Bolton believed this location was near the foot of Cerro Prieto, about thirty miles southeast of Mexicali. Bolton, *Anza's California Expeditions*, vol. 2, 272.

31. Bolton, *Anza's California Expeditions*, vol. 2, 64.

32. Garcés, *Copia de las noticias sacadas*.

33. Bolton, *Anza's California Expeditions*, vol. 2, 68. Anza told this story to Font in 1776 (Font, *With Anza to California*, 386–87); this account clarifies that it was Pablo who was being spoken of, as does a diary entry from Garcés. Garcés, however, did not believe Pablo's story, "especially since he was wearing the mule's shoes suspended from his neck and did not give them up" (Bolton, *Anza's California Expeditions*, vol. 2, 360). This sort of enigmatic explanation is characteristic of Garcés's writing. Apparently he meant to suggest that Pablo had killed one of the mules for its meat, not the wife of its alleged thief.

34. Bolton, *Anza's California Expeditions*, vol. 2, 368.

35. Garcés, *Copia de las noticias sacadas*. While Garcés was exploring downstream, wrote Father Díaz in his diary, some Indians living on the river "brought the idols which they have and delivered them voluntarily, in order that we might smash them to pieces." Destroying "idols" was a favorite and well-established topic of missionary reports, although few items perceived to be idols tended to be found among the tribes of the far-northern New Spain frontier (Bolton, *Anza's California Expeditions*, vol. 2, 274).

36. Bolton identified the spring's location as Pinto Canyon, just south of modern Mexicali along Highway 2.

37. Bolton, *Anza's California Expeditions*, vol. 2, 78.

38. A year and a half later the Kumeyaay at San Diego rebelled and killed a priest and two others (see chapter 9). Incidents such as these may have contributed, however slightly, to their suspicion and resentment of the Spaniards.

39. The location is a few miles south of Interstate 8 and a few miles east of California 98. The flat rocks, Herbert Bolton found, were "black, flat flakes of shale" (*Anza's California Expeditions*, vol. 1, 143). If they were there at the time, Anza and his men did not notice the huge geoglyphs made in this former inland sea by the Kumeyaay, abstract rock designs hundreds of yards in extent that could be seen as a whole only from an aerial view.

40. Bolton speculates that Garcés either learned about Fages's journey from Taraval, who would have heard about it when he was resident at San Gabriel, or inserted this information later, after arriving at San Gabriel himself ("In the South San Joaquín," 9).

41. The geological history and landscape of this route are described very well by Pourade in *Anza Conquers the Desert*, 49–61.

42. As did other southern California Indians (Kroeber, *Handbook of the Indians of California*, 704).

43. Bolton, *Anza's California Expeditions*, vol. 2, 343.

44. In the *Copia de las noticias sacadas,* written in May 1775, Garcés said that the Danzarines resembled the "mountain Cajuenches [Kohuanas]" and spoke a language similar to that of the Gabrielinos. In his 1775–76 diary, Garcés, using a name he heard used by the Indians of the Colorado River, called this group the Jequiches. George Hammond and Agapito Rey identify them as Cocopahs (Arricivita, *Apostolic Chronicle,* vol. 2, 341), but this seems highly unlikely given that Garcés elsewhere identified and named the Cocopahs, who were concentrated much farther south, and did not link the two groups himself. Most likely the Danzarines were a Cahuilla subgroup. See Font, *With Anza to California,* 160, for another memorable description of this group.

45. The description of the Santa Ana Valley is Díaz's, in Bolton, *Anza's California Expeditions,* vol. 2, 287.

46. Bolton, *Anza's California Expeditions,* vol. 2, 199, 202.

47. Bolton, *Anza's California Expeditions,* vol. 2, 96.

48. These particular bells were called *esquilas.* They were rung on happy occasions. Webb provides a description: "These bells have flat headstocks pierced usually by three or four eyelets, or slots. They are hung suspended from a yoke in which they are secured by bolts passed through the eyelets of the headstock. The yokes, which serve as counter balance for the bells, turn in bearings set in the side-walls of the bell-arches. These bells are fashioned to turn completely over and over, producing a joyous ringing" (*Indian Life at the Old Missions,* 33). For a more contemporary account of the use and importance of bells in the missions, see Mann, "Defining Time and Space."

49. Bolton, *Anza's California Expeditions,* vol. 2, 347.

50. I draw mainly from Kenneally, *Writings of Fermín Francisco de Lasuén,* 38–43, for these biographical details.

51. In a letter of May 2, 1774, Lasuén made sure that the College of San Fernando was told about these kindnesses from the colegio's Quereteran brethren. Neither Garcés nor Díaz mentions these acts of generosity in his diary.

52. Palóu, *Palóu's Life of Fray Junípero Serra,* 119.

53. See Miller, *Gabrielino,* for a brief introduction to this people, their culture, and their beliefs. Next to the Chumash, the Gabrielinos were the most prosperous people living on the California coast. Regarding their baskets, Hackel notes that "California Indians were among the world's most sophisticated basket makers" (*Children of Coyote,* 25).

54. For more details, see Geiger, *Life and Times of Fray Junípero Serra,* vol. 1, 302–4, 307.

55. That it had been "forced" to dock because its masts were too long and had to be cut down was the story told by the Franciscans. Others said that it was the pleas of Serra, who knew how badly San Diego needed some of the provisions on board, which led Captain Pérez to land there. Bucareli was somewhat peeved when he learned this, since he had expressly charged Pérez to sail directly to Monterey, but it was a darn good thing his orders were countermanded. Besides, Bucareli seemed never to be able to stay angry at Serra. See Bolton, *Anza's California Expeditions*, vol. 5, 156–57, 179–80.

56. Serra to the Guardian, March 31, 1774, in Bolton, *Anza's California Expeditions*, vol. 5, 126–27; Palóu, *Palóu's Life of Fray Junípero Serra*, 181.

57. Kenneally, *Writings of Fermín Francisco de Lasuén*, 42.

58. Geiger, *Life and Times of Fray Junípero Serra*, vol. 1, 412–13.

59. Bolton, *Anza's California Expeditions*, vol. 2, 100. Two soldiers ended up escorting Valdés from Yuma to Altar. One continued with him as far as Horcasitas. Valdés then rode alone to Mexico City (Bolton, *Anza's California Expeditions*, vol. 5, 159).

60. Actually, Anza was apparently still of the mind that on his return from Monterey he would cut eastward from San Luis Obispo, strike the Colorado, and journey south from there to Yuma. He states this as his plan in a letter to Bucareli written on April 10, the day of his departure from San Gabriel, and he repeated it to Fray Francisco Palóu when he met him at Mission San Carlos on April 18. Why he abandoned this plan is unclear; it may be because he had heard that Father Díaz was waiting for him at San Gabriel, or perhaps because he had to obtain more food at that mission. Regardless, Palóu was delighted by Anza's accomplishment. It was "a great service to God and the king, and a universal benefit for these missions, as I expect that time will show" (Bolton, *Anza's California Expeditions*, vol. 5, 135).

61. Mostly in stride, anyway. The possibility of Anza leaving before Garcés returned had come up, and Anza had said he would leave behind two or three soldiers as an escort that would allow Garcés to catch up with him. But this he decided he could not do, which left Father Garcés mildly disappointed, as he mentioned to Bucareli in a letter of April 27, 1774 (Bolton, *Anza's California Expeditions*, vol. 5, 143–47).

62. Geiger, *Life and Times of Fray Junípero Serra*, vol. 1, 413.

63. Garcés "fully understood that the order for a person of good character and conduct to accompany [him] was not given for [his] consolation, but that he might make the observations." So Garcés writes to Bucareli on April 27, 1774. This party consisted, besides Garcés, of twelve soldiers and two muleteers, according to Valdés (Bolton, *Anza's California Expeditions*,

vol. 5, 158). Garcés himself said that he had with him sixteen other individuals, but he was not always the most reliable source for such quotidian details (Garcés to Bucareli, April 27, 1774).

64. Garcés specifies the Danzarines as the horse-killers in the *Copia de las noticias sacadas*. "Perhaps the contortions of their limbs make them more accurate," chuckled Arricivita in one of the lighter moments of his chronicle (*Apostolic Chronicle*, vol. 2, 160).

65. Bolton, *Anza's California Expeditions*, vol. 2, 351–52. Garcés is not clear as to whether these were the same Danzarines that caused the expedition so much mirth on the way to San Gabriel. It seems likely that they were.

66. Garcés actually intended to send Bucareli, via Valdés, only a short letter in which he brought the viceroy up to date. He apologized for his brevity ("I do not know how to write well") and explained that he was sending his diary first to one of his brother priests in the Pimería Alta so that it could be copied out in better handwriting. As Bolton notes, this was not done, and Bucareli ultimately received the diary in Garcés's own hand (Garcés to Bucareli, April 27, 1774).

67. Bolton, *Anza's California Expeditions*, vol. 2, 360.

68. Along the way, the Danzarines shot and wounded three horses in the same place where the Garcés party had lost a horse to native arrows. Anza—doubtless grumpy from so much hunger and time on the road—was not in the same forgiving mood as Garcés. He found the man whom he believed to be the "chief culprit" and gave him "a beating" (Bolton, *Anza's California Expeditions*, vol. 2, 113).

69. Bolton, *Anza's California Expeditions*, vol. 2, 115–16.

70. Bolton, *Anza's California Expeditions*, vol. 2, 121.

71. The village was near a lava-topped granite hill called in more recent times Pilot Knob. It is on the northwest side of the river in California, a couple miles north of today's international border.

72. Bolton, *Anza's California Expeditions*, vol. 2, 298–99.

CHAPTER 8

1. The quote is from Garcés to Cartagena, January 12, 1775 (FMCC 201:16).

2. As Peter Whiteley has shown, Garcés consistently used the name Yavapai, with or without modifiers, to refer to upland Yumas living east of the Colorado River; indeed, Yavapai probably meant "eastern people" in Yuman, argues Whiteley. Over time Garcés came to distinguish Yavapais from the Hualapais and Havasupais living to their north and the Apaches living to their east (Whiteley, "Who Were the Napac?").

3. Bolton, *Anza's California Expeditions*, vol. 2, 376. For the details of this journey I draw both from Garcés's main diary, included in Bolton, *Anza's California Expeditions*, vol. 2, 375–92, and his summary in the *Copia de las noticias sacadas*.

4. At this point he called them *niforas*, a name the Spaniards often heard applied to the natives living in this area. It was not the name of any distinctive people, however, but a term used by Quechans to refer to western Yavapai, western Apache, and Halchidhoma captives (see Dobyns et al., "What Were Nixoras?"). At other times Garcés called the Yavapais Tejuas or Tejua Apaches. *Tejua* was likely a Pai term meaning "enemy" (Whiteley, "Who Were the Napac?").

5. Bolton, *Anza's California Expeditions*, vol. 2, 377.

6. See Forbes, "Development of the Yuma Route before 1846."

7. Bolton writes that Garcés's route took him "generally west-northwest, between Eagle Tail Mountains and Castle Dome Mountains" (*Anza's California Expeditions*, vol. 2, 377). He is surely right about Castle Dome, which would have been to Garcés's left, since the friar mentions a "cliff which looks like a castle," a description that matches Castle Dome Peak in the Castle Dome Mountains. Garcés also mentions some wells at the northern end of that range, which could easily mean today's Horse Tanks. However, the Eagle Tails are a good thirty miles northeast of where Garcés rode and would not have been visible from King Valley.

8. Bolton, *Anza's California Expeditions*, vol. 2, 379.

9. Later, the Halchidhomas would be driven off the Colorado by the Quechans. They moved to the middle Gila, where they eventually adopted their modern identity as Maricopas, even as they continue to maintain a distinctive identity within that larger one.

10. The quote is from Garcés, *Copia de las noticias sacadas*.

11. Garcés's location can be pinpointed by the approximate distance he had traveled north since coming to the Colorado (about sixteen and a half leagues, or perhaps forty miles), the fact that the Riverside Mountains fit his description, and the fact that he notes that from where he stood "to the northeast and east there is seen a very large opening which indicates level land." This describes well the Cactus Plain, which lies in that direction from Mesquite Mountain. Garcés's 1775–76 diary further allows us to home in on his location during this May–June 1774 trip up the Colorado. Bolton thought that the Riverside Mountains were Chemehuevi Mountain (*Anza's California Expeditions*, vol. 2, 385), but this would put Garcés way too far north.

12. Bolton, *Anza's California Expeditions*, vol. 2, 385.

13. Garcés, *Copia de las noticias sacadas*.

14. Bolton, *Anza's California Expeditions*, vol. 2, 387.

15. Wilson identifies Uturituc with Sweetwater (*Peoples of the Middle Gila*, 40).

16. Bolton, *Anza's California Expeditions*, vol. 2, 389. It is probable but not definite that Garcés visited Uturituc/Sweetwater in 1768. He certainly came there on his 1770 entrada.

17. Baldonado, "Missions San José de Tumacácori," 23–24. Indeed, after 1773 the Pimas abandoned the Santa Cruz River and left it to the Papagos, possibly because of the Santa Cruz's increasing salinity (Winter, "Cultural Modifications," 72–73).

18. Kessell, *Friars, Soldiers, and Reformers*, 98.

19. Bucareli had previously received the letter Anza wrote him on February 9 after crossing the Colorado at Yuma (Bolton, *Anza's California Expeditions*, vol. 5, 113–16), as well as a letter Anza wrote on February 28, in which he explained that he was leaving some men and provisions with Palma (Bolton, *Anza's California Expeditions*, vol. 5, 117–20).

20. Bolton, *Anza's California Expeditions*, vol. 1, 192.

21. Bolton, *Anza's California Expeditions*, vol. 1, 194.

22. The bonus was paid to the seventeen soldiers who went at least as far as San Gabriel. Bolton says that an escudo could also be a silver coin worth a single peso. It is not clear which coin Bucareli meant, although in context it seems likelier to have been the gold coin. Soldiers were paid a peso per day, at the time, so a bonus of a single extra peso per month would have been rather minor (Bolton, *Anza's California Expeditions*, vol. 5, 175).

23. Or, as they were then known, the missions of Monterey.

24. A 1770 flood had left some of this region's residents homeless. The decline of mining in the region had increased the poverty of others (Hackel, *Children of Coyote*, 57).

25. Anza to Bucareli, November 17, 1774, in Bolton, *Anza's California Expeditions*, vol. 5, 209.

26. Anza to Bucareli, November 17, 1774, in Bolton, *Anza's California Expeditions*, vol. 5, 212.

27. Decree by Bucareli, November 28, 1774, in Bolton, *Anza's California Expeditions*, vol. 5, 215.

28. Font, *With Anza to California*, 31–32.

29. Memorandum by Don José de Echeveste, in Bolton, *Anza's California Expeditions*, vol. 5, 231.

30. Bucareli to Garcés, January 2, 1775, in Bolton, *Anza's California Expeditions*, vol. 5, 271. It was at Anza's request that Garcés was ordered to remain at the Colorado once the expedition reached that point.

31. In anticipation of the new missions to be founded in the Pimería Alta, the College of Santa Cruz formally petitioned Bucareli to give up its missions in the Pimería Baja on December 6, 1774. Bucareli accepted this petition on May 24, 1775. The Pimería Baja missions were transferred to the Franciscans' Jaliscan province.

32. Garcés to Cartagena, January 12, 1775 (FMCC 201:16). It seems that Anza did not wish for Garcés to go to Mexico City, either, at least in his company, for he did not deliver a letter to Garcés in which the colegio summoned Garcés to the capital until two or three days before he was to leave himself, thus depriving Garcés of time to find a replacement at San Xavier. Garcés reports this in the same letter to Cartagena. Anza claimed he had misplaced the letter and only recently found it.

33. Garcés and Díaz to Bucareli, March 21, 1775, in Bolton, *Anza's California Expeditions*, vol. 5, 276; Maughan, "Francisco Garcés," 126.

34. Garcés and Díaz to Bucareli, March 21, 1775, in Bolton, *Anza's California Expeditions*, vol. 5, 278.

35. See Garcés, *Record of Travels*, 8, where he says that Captain Bernardo de Urrea also did an inspection of potential mission sites on the Gila.

36. Garcés repeats many of the same recommendations at the end of the *Copia de las noticias sacadas*, which he wrote two months later at San Xavier del Bac.

37. When it came to the Apaches, Garcés and Díaz were no more inclined toward mercy than were other Spaniards (and Indians) living on the frontier. By placing presidios at the Apaches' doorstep, they hoped, "it may be possible to punish them for their great boldness and inspire them with fear, if, indeed, their entire reduction or extermination is not effected. Experience teaches us that this is the best method to expatriate them and the correct way to punish them" (Garcés and Díaz to Bucareli, March 21, 1775, in Bolton, *Anza's California Expeditions*, vol. 5, 281–82).

38. Bucareli to Arriaga, May 27, 1775, in Bolton, *Anza's California Expeditions*, vol. 5, 295.

39. Bucareli wrote to Gálvez on October 27, 1775, that he believed maintaining six presidios in Sonora would be necessary, but that before proceeding with any more moves he had counseled O'Conor to wait and see what information and ideas emerged from Anza's second expedition (see Galvéz to Bucareli, February 14, 1776, in Bolton, *Anza's California Expeditions*, vol. 5, 326–27).

40. Garcés to Bucareli, August 20, 1775, in Garate, *Captain Juan Bautista de Anza*, 121.

41. Garcés to Anza, July 7, 1775, in Garate, *Captain Juan Bautista de Anza*, 109.

42. See Garcés to Cartagena, January 12, 1775, FMCC 201:16. Garcés emphasized that his companion must be prepared to face extraordinary difficulties; he didn't want to have to babysit anyone. Father Juan Gorgoll offered to join him, and Garcés informed Anza in a July 7, 1775, letter that Gorgoll would be his companion (letter included in Garate, *Captain Juan Bautista de Anza*, 109), but for reasons unexplained Father Eixarch ended up replacing Gorgoll on the journey. For biographical information on Eixarch, see Kessell, "Father Eixarch." Eixarch arrived at the College of Santa Cruz in 1770. He was about five feet, two inches tall.

43. For this part of the story, besides the primary sources cited here, see Kessell, *Friars, Soldiers, and Reformers*, 112–13.

44. Anza to Bucareli, January 7, 1775, in Garate, *Captain Juan Bautista de Anza*, 35–36. Bucareli confirms Anza's full authority over the expedition, including its friars, in a letter of January 9, 1775. Anza "should ask their opinion only in such case that the subject coincides with their ministry" (Garate, *Captain Juan Bautista de Anza*, 39).

45. Bucareli explained in a later letter to Minister Arriaga that he had wanted Garcés to remain on the Colorado so that he could build stronger relationships with the Quechans and others living there, increasing the chances that missions could be established. "The presence of this father among these tribes, while Anza performs his mission to the port of San Francisco, I have considered most desirable, on account of the talents which adorn him, his zeal, and his acquaintance with the tribes, or most of them, and their progress," wrote Bucareli (Bucareli to Arriaga, March 27, 1776, in Bolton, *Anza's California Expeditions*, vol. 5, 334).

46. English translations of the diaries written by Anza, Font, and Eixarch, as well as accounts provided by Lieutenant José Joaquín Moraga and Father Francisco Palóu of the founding of San Francisco, are collected in Bolton, *Anza's California Expeditions*, vol. 3. Garcés's diary has been translated and published in English by Elliott Coues (*On the Trail of a Spanish Pioneer*) and John Galvin (*A Record of Travels in Arizona and California, 1775–1776*), working from somewhat different manuscript copies; Galvin's is the better of the two. A new translation of Font's diary was translated by Alan K. Brown and published in 2015 as *With Anza to California, 1775–1776*.

47. The 1775–76 expedition is a major subject of Bolton's *Outpost of Empire* (which is also vol. 1 of *Anza's California Expeditions*). The expedition's story is also told by Pourade in *Anza Conquers the Desert* and Guerrero in *Anza*

Trail. Even so, the second Anza expedition still awaits a first-class, in-depth, book-length treatment.

48. See "Mapping Historic Campsites of the Anza Colonizing Expedition," a project conducted in the summer and fall of 2015 by the National Park Service, www.nps.gov/juba/learn/historyculture/mapping-historic -campsites-of-the-anza-colonizing-expedition.htm, accessed January 1, 2022.

49. See Los Californianos website, www.loscalifornianos.org.

50. Anza to Bucareli, May 1, 1775, in Garate, *Captain Juan Bautista de Anza*, 67. The original plan was for all settlers to be soldiers, but by the time he reached El Fuerte Anza had modified that plan to include nonmilitary settlers.

51. Font, *With Anza to California*, 19.

52. Anza to Bucareli, October 20, 1775, in Garate, *Captain Juan Bautista de Anza*, 156.

53. Anza reported to Bucareli on October 20, 1775, that he left Horcasitas four days later than intended because Font was very sick (Garate, *Captain Juan Bautista de Anza*, 179).

54. Font, *With Anza to California*, 73; Garate, *Captain Juan Bautista de Anza*, 188–89.

55. Kessell, *Friars, Soldiers, and Reformers*, 98; Garcés to Cartagena, January 12, 1775 (FMCC 201:16). This letter also makes clear that there was significant tension between Father Díaz and Anza, as well. In another letter, Garcés allowed himself to complain to Bucareli that "on occasion" Anza made serving both "God and King a difficult thing" (Garcés to Bucareli, August 20, 1775, in Garate, *Captain Juan Bautista de Anza*, 124).

56. Anza to Bucareli, January 4, 1775 (AGN, PI, 23).

57. Maughan, "Francisco Garcés," 134–35. It was Galvéz, actually, who had first suggested that Garcés be put in charge of the new missions contemplated for the Colorado and Gila Rivers (Galvéz to Bucareli, December 18, 1773, AGI, Guad 418).

58. Garcés provided the following population estimates in the *Copia de las noticias sacadas*: Papagos, 4,000; Gileño Pimas, 2,500; Opas and Cocomaricopas, 3,000; Yumas, 3,000; Kohuanas, 6,000; Danzarines, 500; Halchidhomas, 3,000.

59. Just when Gamarra arrived at San Xavier is not known, but on September 3, 1775, he signed the Tumacácori Register of Administration as "Minister of San Xavier del Bac" (Stoner and Dobyns, "Fray Pedro Antonio de Arriquibar," 73).

60. McCarty, *Desert Documentary*, 26–27; Kessell, *Friars, Soldiers, and Reformers*, 109–10.

61. Garcés was ever after anxious to keep O'Conor apprised of the information he had gathered and suggestions he had for strengthening Spanish presence on the frontier. He came to see O'Conor, whom he quite liked, as a key supporter of the missionaries, as he wrote Father Diego Ximénez, then the guardian of the College of Santa Cruz, on January 3, 1777 (FMCC 201:19).

62. The infant, christened José Antonio Capistrano Feliz, reached California but died before his first birthday at Mission San Gabriel (Garate, *Captain Juan Bautista de Anza*, 188–89). Garcés omits any mention of this episode in his diary, which is especially sparse for that part of the expedition he traveled with Font. He was always happy to let someone else handle the writing, if possible.

63. One of these new brides was María Micaela Bojórquez, age twelve. She was the youngest wife among the settlers, nine of whom were eighteen years or younger (Garate, *Captain Juan Bautista de Anza*, 190).

64. Font, *With Anza to California*, 86.

65. Moore and Beene, "Interior Provinces of New Spain," 278.

66. I supplement Anza's list of supplies with Oakah Jones's descriptions of what the country people of northern New Spain typically wore at the time. See Jones, *Los Paisanos*, 186–87.

67. Jones, *Los Paisanos*, 189.

68. Font, *With Anza to California*, 90. Neither Garcés nor Anza mentions this episode.

69. Garcés, *Record of Travels*, 6.

70. Garcés, *Record of Travels*, 73–74.

71. Font, *With Anza to California*, 91, 100–101; Wilson, *Peoples of the Middle Gila*, 40.

72. Font, *With Anza to California*, 99.

73. This site would later become known as Maricopa Wells.

74. Bolton, *Anza's California Expeditions*, vol. 3, 21.

75. Font, *With Anza to California*, 102.

76. Bolton, *Anza's California Expeditions*, vol. 3, 22.

77. Garcés, *Record of Travels*, 9.

78. Font, *With Anza to California*, 106.

79. Font, *With Anza to California*, 135. This delicacy on the part of the Spaniards was difficult for the Quechans to understand. Font continues: "Chief Palma, who previously behaved like the rest, had already begun to improve in this respect. At first, when he was told this was not a good thing to do in front of people, he answered he could not do otherwise, since if he did not, he would burst." Of course, Palma (and the others) could simply have been pulling their visitors' legs.

80. Geiger, *Life and Times of Fray Junípero Serra*, vol. 1, 222.

81. Font, *With Anza to California*, 109.

82. Garcés, *Record of Travels*, 10. Arricivita, the colegio's chronicler, would later write of this episode, "The clarity and native intelligence that the Lord bestowed upon these savages for the knowledge of His precepts is surprising, for it is almost extinct in the abominable lives of many Catholics" (*Apostolic Chronicle*, vol. 2, 171).

83. Bolton, *Anza's California Expeditions*, vol. 3, 29–30.

84. Garate, *Captain Juan Bautista de Anza*, 189–90. The mother was Ana María de Osuna. She and her husband had two other children with them, girls age eight and seven (Kittle, *Franciscan Frontiersmen*, 104). Font concluded at this point in the journey that four missions along the Gila would be adequate for all the people who lived in the region: one at Agua Caliente, one at Gila Bend, one at Sacate, and one at Sweetwater.

85. It is worth remembering that we have only Anza's account of this conversation. Neither Garcés nor Font say anything about it. See Bolton, *Anza's California Expeditions*, vol. 3, 38–41.

86. Bolton, *Anza's California Expeditions*, vol. 3, 39.

87. Kittle, *Franciscan Frontiersmen*, 133–38, provides a good, brief account of the uprising and its motivations.

88. It is Font who properly introduces Pablo to us, and Font who tells the story of his speech on the evening of the 27th. See Font, *With Anza to California*, 115–16.

89. Font, *With Anza to California*, 117.

90. Font, *With Anza to California*, 118.

91. Font, *With Anza to California*, 121.

92. In his diary entry for this day, Garcés adds that a man from the Halchidhoma embassy told the Spaniards an "odd story" about a man among them "who had come from the new missions in California; he had been killed and reduced to ashes by the nations through which he had passed: but that he had the power to turn himself into a whirlwind; that he carried with him a viper, and was a great wizard; that he could make the Jalcheduns [Halchidhomas] do what he wanted and therefore they were much in awe of him. Our Commander showed some vexation, even in spite of the very great patience he has with the Indians—a trait worthy of being imitated by all who are sent on such enterprises. I asked him for some beads, which I gave to these Indians" (Garcés, *Record of Travels*, 13–14).

93. These interpreters and servants had likely been assigned to the priests since they joined the expedition, as discussed in various letters among Bucareli, Anza, and Garcés. Eixarch tells us, in his diary entry for

January 11, 1776, that one of these servants was named Joseph María Araiza. He was from Tubac and had volunteered to come along on the expedition as Garcés's unpaid assistant. Eixarch says he proved to be of "no account" and a "useless man" (Bolton, *Anza's California Expeditions*, vol. 2, 338). Garcés never names or complains about Araiza.

94. Font, *With Anza to California*, 144.

95. Font, *With Anza to California*, 125, 127.

CHAPTER 9

1. For the narrative of and quotes related to this downstream journey, I draw from Garcés, *Record of Travels*, 15–24, except where otherwise noted.

2. Font, *With Anza to California*, 144.

3. It was especially difficult to extirpate on the lower Colorado, where such violence was more intense and destructive than in most other regions. As Johnson points out, whereas among most Native Californian groups there was no "formal, institutionalized warrior class," the Yuman-speaking peoples of the lower Colorado represented a possible exception. Among them "and their enemies, battles tended to be bloodier and often arranged, and there was typically no reconciliation. In fact, there was territorial conquest" ("Ethnohistoric Descriptions of Chumash Warfare," 75, 76).

4. In this diary, Garcés refers to the Halyikwamais as Jalliquamais. At times they have also been called Quiquimas. As with the Kohuanas, very little is known about this people and their way of life in the colonial period except for what Garcés and two or three other explorers tell us.

5. See Dutton, *American Indians of the Southwest*, 175–77, as well as various citations in Kroeber's classic *Handbook of the Indians of California* for a brief introduction to the Cocopahs. See Zappia, *Traders and Raiders*, 28–29, for the creation story they shared with other Yuman speakers. As with so many other peoples, much of what we know about them before the American period comes from Garcés's writings.

6. See Kroeber, *Handbook of the Indians of California*, 723–25.

7. Eixarch's diary is included in Bolton, *Anza's California Expeditions*, vol. 3, 309–81. Unless otherwise noted, I draw from this diary in telling the story of Eixarch's time on the Colorado.

8. See Font, *With Anza to California*, 124–76.

9. Bolton, *Anza's California Expeditions*, vol. 3, 322–23.

10. Bolton, *Anza's California Expeditions*, vol. 2, 343. In a later passage, Eixarch clarified that he "greatly" loved the Quechans, and that his annoyance

came at having always to give them tobacco and other gifts, of which he was running very low (Bolton, *Anza's California Expeditions*, vol. 2, 351).

11. Eixarch said that the house "contains one room fourteen and a half varas long with a partition in the middle, where there is an altar better than in some churches. . . . From the door of the house one can see the water on both sides of the pass, and being situated on the skirts of a hill it has a site as good as anyone might wish or could find in the best valley. In a word, it is as good a site as could be desired for the establishment of a mission" (Bolton, *Anza's California Expeditions*, vol. 2, 349). A vara was just under thirty-three inches, so this new house was quite large.

12. At Eixarch's request, Taraval left for Tubutama to retrieve wine for Mass on January 11, taking with him (and not bringing back) his servant, Joseph María Araiza (see chap. 8, n. 93). Taraval returned on February 6.

13. Forbes, *Warriors of the Colorado*, 65.

14. Garcés, *Record of Travels*, 26. Another old man, apparently a visiting Cocomaricopa, spoke with Garcés on January 20 and told him that he "loved God much and he would very gladly be a Christian," according to Eixarch (Bolton, *Anza's California Expeditions*, vol. 2, 341).

15. Garcés, *Record of Travels*, 26–27.

16. Bolton, *Anza's California Expeditions*, vol. 2, 341.

17. Garcés, *Record of Travels*, 28. Garces called them Yavapais Tejua and said they were "known to us as Apaches." I use the modern term here, though, to avoid confusion. Whiteley ("Who Were the Napac?" 74) has shown that this term, when used by Garcés at this point, almost certainly referred to "Yavapais proper."

18. Eixarch wrote in his diary of January 14, 1776: "I think that all of these tribes will remain friendly if the appropriate measures are taken by the superior authorities, but if they delay long in establishing soldiers and a presidio of Spaniards, such an abundant harvest as is offered by this great vineyard may go to waste" (Bolton, *Anza's California Expeditions*, vol. 2, 339).

19. Garcés wrote Bucareli on January 12, 1776 (Bolton, *Anza's California Expeditions*, vol. 5, 314–15).

20. The route described here as taken by Garcés from Yuma to Needles represents my best guess, based on the information regarding topography, distances, and water sources Garcés provides in his diary.

21. The Chemehuevis' name for themselves is Nümü—meaning "people," as usual. Theirs was not a highly elaborated culture, socially or religiously. Some now live on the Colorado River Reservation. Garcés is the sole Spanish source for information on this people. See Stewart, "Brief History of the Chemehuevi Indians."

22. This was likely true. Garcés was the first European to visit the Mohave Valley (Scrivner, *Mohave People*, 24; Stewart, "Mohave Indians in Hispanic Times," 25).

23. Garcés, *Record of Travels*, 33.

24. Stewart, "Witchcraft among the Mohave Indians," 320.

25. Scrivner, *Mohave People*, 10–11.

26. The interpreter who took the Halchidhoma girls back to their homeland had not yet caught up with Garcés and the others. What happened to the other interpreter Garcés does not say.

27. To Kroeber, "the religious dominance of the Mohave," from their myths to their song cycles, over their neighbors as far as away as the Zuñis was clear (*Handbook of the Indians of California*, 599).

28. From the textual evidence he gives, it seems that as Garcés traveled westward he angled somewhat south of today's Mojave Road, leaving it by as much as seven or eight miles until he came to a pass in the Providence Mountains, when he turned northwest. For instance, he notes that he angled southwest soon after leaving the Colorado River; the Mojave Road leads somewhat northwest. He says that he passed through a mountain range that had some "small pines" through "a good pass." This sounds like the Foshay Pass in the Providence Mountains. He then says that after passing through this pass he "entered a small valley with sandy knolls at its sides," which sounds like the Kelso Sand Dunes or the dunes of the Devil's Playground. See Garcés, *Record of Travels*, 35. Wood ("Francisco Garcés," 191) agrees that this was likely Garcés's route to the Mojave River. And Scrivner points out that this more southerly route was often the one taken when there had been considerable rain (*Mohave People*, 44).

29. On the petroglyphs and backpacks I am speculating; Garcés does not mention them. Other writers do. See Zappia, *Traders and Raiders*, 23.

30. On trips such as this, Mohaves would survive on chuckwallas and other lizards, ground squirrels, and pack rats, all of which they would kill with a stick, lance, or arrows. "To secure a small meal, they would take a stick and tap the chuckwalla on the nose, as he had inflated himself in some clefts of a rock. The lizard soon deflates himself and backs into the waiting hand" (Scrivner, *Mohave People*, 29).

31. Zappia says not only that trails through the Mojave Desert often consisted of "paved tightly packed gravel surfaces" but also that many of them "were manicured with a ridge of stones on each side to prevent the traveler from getting lost" (*Traders and Raiders*, 49).

32. The path went through or near modern Barstow, Harvard, and Victorville (Wood, "Francisco Garcés," 191–92).

33. Johnson, "Ethnohistoric Descriptions of Chumash Warfare," 78. Garcés was the first to apply the name Beñemés to this people. They are sometimes referred to as the Vanyume. The Serranos (Yuhaviatam, or "people of the pines," in their own language) traditionally lived in the San Bernardino Mountains, with related groups residing in both the Mohave Valley and the Antelope Valley. Some Serranos were gathered at the San Gabriel mission. Jedediah Smith encountered them in 1826 and, like Garcés, found them to be both poor and generous.

34. The Mohaves thought it disgusting to eat such fare (Scrivner, *Mohave People*, 29).

35. Garcés, *Record of Travels*, 37.

36. Garcés, *Record of Travels*, 37.

37. On the importance of acorns, which provided dietary carbohydrates and fats, see Hackel, *Children of Coyote*, 25. For decades, most scholars believed Garcés crossed the San Bernardino Mountains via Cajón Pass or perhaps either Devil Canyon or Cable Canyon (Wood, "Francisco Garcés," 192). Weaver, however, has used a close reading of the various diarists' texts to argue that from the vicinity of Victorville Garcés traveled southwest, then south, until he struck Oro Grande Wash, which he followed up the mountains to its head, whence he crossed to the Lytle Creek streambed and followed it upward until he summitted the range in the area of San Sevaine Flat ("1776 Route of Father Francisco Garcés").

38. Font, *With Anza to California*, 179. See also Engelhardt, *San Gabriel Mission*, 21–30.

39. Font, *With Anza to California*, 179.

40. See Beebe and Senkewicz, *Junípero Serra*, 17–19. Johnson notes that in 1775 two Chumash towns known as Dos Pueblos, both located along the Santa Barbara Channel, had engaged in aggressive warfare toward other Chumash villages ("Ethnohistoric Descriptions of Chumash Warfare, 96).

41. Garcés, *Record of Travels*, 40.

42. Font, *With Anza to California*, 368–70. It should be noted that Rivera was not just proud and somewhat sensitive but also generous and charming, including with clerics who were more patient and understanding than the pushy Serra or single-minded Garcés. At San Gabriel, Father Paterna, like Father Lasuén before him, came to like Rivera immensely. In Baja California, Rivera served with the Jesuit Fathers Konščak and Linck, who both spoke highly of him. The Spanish government used Rivera poorly, failing to pay him a single peso of his three thousand pesos-per-year salary from 1774 until his death in 1781. For more on Rivera, see Burrus, "Rivera y Moncada."

43. Kittle notes that the woman, María Feliciana Arballo, was a "mulata libre, that is, a woman of mixed African and Latin forebears" (*Franciscan Frontiersmen*, 118). She had come with her two children on the journey, doubtless not unaware that the many unmarried soldiers who would be met along the way would present her with good marriage prospects. Font tells us that at one point during the expedition she entertained the travelers with some singing that they greatly enjoyed but that he found inappropriate. Brown adds that the descendants of Arballo and her soldier-husband, Juan Francisco López, would include some of early California's most prominent families (Font, *With Anza to California*, 154).

44. The account of Garcés's exploration in this section, including quotations, is drawn from Garcés, *Record of Travels*, 43–51.

45. So Herbert Bolton thought, and so I think, based on what little evidence Garcés provides in his diary. It is certainly possible that we are wrong.

46. See Kroeber, *Handbook of the Indians of California*, 611–13, for this and other details about Kitanemuk culture.

47. The baskets were probably made by these people or their neighbors in the San Joaquín Valley. They would trade them to the Chumash for shell beads manufactured by the Chumash. These beads, called *olivella* by the Mojaves and *chok* by the Yokuts, were the common currency of native trade networks stretching from California to Sonora and New Mexico. See Zappia, *Traders and Raiders*, 16–22, 39.

48. This narcotic was called *pespibata* (Johnson, "Ethnohistoric Descriptions of Chumash Warfare," 101).

49. On the Kitanemuks' "vastness of conception and profoundness of feeling" with respect to religion, see Kroeber, *Handbook of the Indians of California*, 511.

50. Although their conflicts were not as bloody as among the peoples of the lower Colorado, there was much intergroup hostility among Yokuts groups, and between those groups and the Chumash. "In the popular imagination and in scholarly treatments, California Indians are frequently depicted as peaceable peoples, living in harmony with each other and the environment at the advent of European contact," writes Johnson. "This common perception is at variance with both the written record of contemporary Spanish observers and direct testimony of elderly California Indians interviewed by ethnographers during the late nineteenth and early twentieth centuries. Intervillage raids, ritualized battles, larger-scale hostilities among opposing allied groups, and even territorial conquest were all part of the spectrum of enmity relations in Native California" ("Ethnohistoric Descriptions of Chumash Warfare," 74–76). Pablo Tac, an Indian who grew up at the San

Luis Rey mission, recalled in his memoir that, prior to the missions' establishment, there "was always war, always strife day and night, with those who speak another language" ("Memories of Life at a Mission").

51. The reader will by now not be surprised that the word Yokuts, in its various dialectical forms, meant "person" or "people." See Kroeber, *Handbook of the Indians of California*, 488, 492–543, for an extended discussion of their social institutions, material culture, and religion.

52. Garcés struck the Kern east of Bakersfield. A monument has been placed along State Highway 178, eleven miles east of Bakersfield, where it is thought he crossed the river. Garcés writes that, once he was on the northern side of the Kern, he traveled northwest for three leagues—about eight miles—before heading north for roughly twenty miles until he met another river. Once he turned north, Garcés's route from the Kern likely paralleled today's Porterville Highway.

53. Font, *With Anza to California*, 233.

54. Zappia, *Traders and Raiders*, 22, 36.

55. See Kroeber, *Handbook of the Indians of California*, 522–23. A Yokuts sweat lodge was for males only and was "small, not over fifteen feet in length. . . . Often on retiring, the inmates sang and sweated, perhaps in competition along the two sides, the fire being added to make the opposite row cry out first that they had had enough. Then came a plunge into the stream, and a return to dry and sleep."

56. The elderly Yokut guide abandoned Garcés on May 1 because he was too tired to continue.

57. Another reason Garcés did not feel he had to physically trace a route from the San Joaquín Valley to San Luis Obispo was that by this time he knew Fages had already done so.

58. Quotations from Garcés in this section are from Garcés, *Record of Travels*, 53–60, unless otherwise noted.

59. The foothills of the mountains on the eastern side of the San Joaquín Valley are indeed gashed with numerous gulches, canyons, and draws.

60. Font would later moan that, having lent "an ordinary quadrant" to Garcés, the father "broke it for me" somewhere along his way. The self-pitying wording is classic Font (Font to Ximénez, in Matson, "Letters of Friar Pedro Font," 265).

61. Along with Garcés, *Record of Travels*, see his undated letter to Ximénez titled "Report to Fray Diego Ximénez on the Indians of the Gila, Colorado, and Moqui" (HEBP, Box 21, Folder 10).

62. To my knowledge, neither of these two letters has been found. We know their contents only through the somewhat conflicting reports

of Anza, Garcés, and Font in their respective diaries. Anza says that on May 12 he "sent a messenger with a letter from me for Father Garcés, telling him of my return and that I am waiting to see if he wishes to go out with me, summoning him, in case he should be at the place where they have said," which was among the Halchidhomas, rather than the Mohaves, "and assuring him that in case he does not come I shall leave him various provisions for his subsistence, as he by a letter requests me (Bolton, *Anza's California Expeditions*, 177). Garcés, on the other hand, simply says that Anza's letter urged him "to return to the Yumas" and that by its terms he felt "obliged" to do so, which implies rather different content. Why Garcés should have felt obliged, given that by the time he received the letter he must have known that Anza was long gone from Yuma, is another mystery. Font, for his part, says that Anza's letter gave Garcés three days to return to Yuma before the expedition would be moving on and that it stated that "we wished him to come at once," which aligns more with Garcés's account than Anza's (Font, *With Anza to California*, 381–82).

63. At this point in his own diary, Anza refers to Garcés as "that tireless soul." Though the missionary may have driven him crazy, Garcés had the commander's respect (Bolton, *Anza's California Expeditions*, vol. 4, 177).

64. Ewing, "Pai Tribes," provides a memorable description of the Hualapais, as does Iliff in *People of the Blue Water*.

65. Bolton, *Anza's California Expeditions*, vol. 2, 357.

66. Garcés, undated letter to Ximénez titled "Report to Fray Diego Ximénez on the Indians of the Gila, Colorado, and Moqui."

67. Garcés does say that on his return to the Mohaves' territory on July 25, 1776, he was told by them that "Sebastián was bad, that he had given away the shells and other things I had left." The friar makes no further comment on this report.

68. Quotations from Garcés in this section are from Garcés, *Record of Travels*, 61–67, except where otherwise noted. On Pai hunting and food-gathering practices, see Martin, "On the Estimation of the Sizes of Local Groups."

69. From the details he gives in his diary, it seems likely that Garcés traveled eastward roughly along the path taken by Highway 68 today.

70. Had he known about them, Garcés would have recognized such corruption in the Hualapais' practices of strangling disabled and mixed-race children at birth and their occasional abandonment of infants and the elderly in the wilderness in the name of self-preservation (Ewing, "Pai Tribes," 70). Iliff attests to what she viewed as the Hualapais' poor treatment of the elderly infirm and disabled (*People of the Blue Water*, 35–37).

71. The Yavapais and Hualapais were usually bitter enemies, but the Hualapais and Havasupais intermarried freely (Ewing, "Pai Tribes," 62). The Pais were descended from the prehistoric Cerbat, a lower-Colorado Yuman-speaking people (Martin, "Prehistory and Ethnohistory of Havasupai-Hualapai Relations," 136).

72. We learn later in the diary that they were Havasupais. Garcés called them Jabesua. The Havasupai people were heavily influenced in certain cultural practices by their Hopi neighbors (Martin, "Prehistory and Ethnohistory of Havasupai-Hualapai Relations," 136).

73. Traveling today from Kingman to Peach Springs via Route 66 would put one on Garcés's route. From Peach Springs to Supai he followed a path traced by today's Indian Road 18.

74. The Havasupais typically split their time between farming in the Grand Canyon and hunting and gathering on top of the Coconino Plateau.

75. Hirst writes that the Hopis may have been particularly well disposed toward the Havasupais because the latter lived on a southern tributary to the Grand Canyon, from which kind of stream the Hopis believed they originally came. One of the Hopis' kachinas is a stylized Havasupai in traditional dress (*Life in a Narrow Place*, 38)

76. Iliff, *People of the Blue Water*, 94.

77. Ives's experience is recounted by editor John Galvin in Garcés, *Record of Travels*, 65.

78. The Canfranc Pass is on a branch of the Camino de Santiago that leads from Arles.

79. Hirst identifies this trail as the Moqui (*Life in a Narrow Place*, 46).

80. It is Bolton who speculates that Garcés was standing on Point Quetzal (*Pageant in the Wilderness*, 5).

Chapter 10

1. Garcés refers to them all as Yavapais at this point in his diary. Five of them were Havasupais, whom Garcés then considered to be a subtype of Yavapai. This we know from what an Acoma Indian named Lázaro told Fathers Domínguez and Escalante (see narrative below), as well as from the text of Garcés's undated letter to Father Ximénez ("Report to Fray Diego Ximénez on the Indians of the Gila, Colorado, and Moqui," HEBP, Box 21, Folder 10). Apparently the Mohave guides did not come this far.

2. See Garcés, "Report to Fray Diego Ximénez." Unless otherwise noted, I draw from this long letter (evidently written in late 1776) as well as Garcés,

Record of Travels, in giving this account of Garcés's entrada. Quotations from Garcés's visit to the Hopi village are from *Record of Travels*, 69–75.

3. Recall that a vara was a few inches shorter than an English yard.

4. Father Mariano Rosete to Father Francisco Atanasio Domínguez, July 6, 1776, in Adams and Chávez, *Missions of New Mexico*, 284.

5. We know this man's name, and the fact that he was from Acoma Pueblo, from the testimony he later gave to Father Mariano Rosete at Zuñi, as reported by Rosete in a letter he wrote to Father Francisco Atanasio Domínguez on July 6, 1776. See Adams and Chávez, *Missions of New Mexico*, 283–85. Lázaro's testimony confirms the essentials in Garcés's account of his time among the Hopis and fills in certain gaps.

Zuñi was the dusty city of Cíbola that a thoroughly frightened Fray Marcos de Niza had espied from afar in 1539 and reported to have been larger than Mexico City, a report that led to Francisco Vázquez de Coronado's expedition of 1540.

6. Rosete to Domínguez, July 6, 1776.

7. It is possible that Garcés was advised to try Walpi but was not accompanied there, because his presence at Oraibi was inhibiting his Pai companions' trading efforts (see Arricivita, *Apostolic Chronicle*, vol. 2, 192).

8. Lázaro reported that the village chief had threatened to punish any Hopi who helped the friar (Rosete to Domínguez, July 6, 1776).

9. Anza, when he was governor of New Mexico, reported in 1779 a belief extant among the Hopis that they attributed their subsequent misfortunes—famine, disease, war with the Navajos—to their rejection of Fray Garcés (Maughan, "Francisco Garcés," 181).

10. My discussion of Escalante and Domínguez and their connection to Garcés relies on Adams and Chávez, *Missions of New Mexico*; Briggs, *Without Noise of Arms*; Roberts, *Escalante's Dream*; and Bolton, *Pageant in the Wilderness*.

11. See Bolton, *Pageant in the Wilderness*, for this story. In part thanks to information he obtained from Garcés's travels, José de Gálvez had been thinking about finding a direct route from Santa Fe to Monterey for some time. In 1773 he recommended that expeditions simultaneously leave both places and try to meet in the middle. Mendinueta's request of Escalante represented his attempt to address the minister's concern.

12. Thomas speculates that, because they had thrown off the yoke of Chacoan elites in the 1300s or 1400s and adopted a more democratic and decentralized social arrangement, the Hopis and other Puebloan Indians of northern New Mexico and Arizona were "pre-adapted" to resist the

hierarchical, top-down rule of the Spanish ("War and Peace on the Franciscan Frontier," 128).

13. Garces's letter is included in Adams and Chávez, *Missions of New Mexico*, 283.

14. Rosete to Domínguez, July 6, 1776, in Adams and Chávez, *Missions of New Mexico*, 285. Rosete included a copy of Father Garcés's letter, in which he had made several corrections because Garcés's "hand is rather poor" (285). Few people could resist commenting on Garcés's poor handwriting and imprecise style upon first encountering them.

15. Quotations from Garcés's return to San Xavier del Bac taken from Garcés, *Record of Travels*, 77–87, unless otherwise noted.

16. Garcés's only food while among the Hopis seems to have been a little *atole* he made from cornmeal he had brought with him.

17. Garcés, "Report to Fray Diego Ximénez."

18. Font, *With Anza to California*, 381. Font took this opportunity in his diary to again criticize Anza, who in sending his letter northward to Garcés had also asked the courier to bring back any animals he found that belonged to Garcés. What if Garcés needed those animals? Font's question was a fair one. It is not clear why Anza gave such an order.

19. Anza to Bucareli, November 20, 1776, in Bolton, *Anza's California Expeditions*, vol. 5, 385.

20. Indeed, it was to try to create peace among the peoples of the whole region that Garcés had continued downriver from the Halchidhomas to the Quechans rather than cutting cross-country, or southeast, to the Gila along the path he had taken in 1774 (Arricivita, *Apostolic Chronicle*, vol. 2, 194).

21. Garcés survived many rumors of his death. Even the residents of San Gabriel heard that he had been killed after leaving there in April 1776. Rivera went looking for him and found tracks that had been left after the supposed time of his death, thus quashing the rumor (Palóu, *Historical Memoirs of New California*, vol. 4, 87).

22. See Moore and Beene, "Interior Provinces of New Spain," 277–78. Hugo O'Conor wrote Garcés on December 13, 1775, saying, "Everything proposed by me concerning the moving of the presidios of Horcasitas and Buena Vista to the Gila and Colorado Rivers has been approved, and although the order to implement this is in my hands, the transfer cannot be accomplished until you return from your pilgrimage. It is important that no one learns of this decision until the very moment of carrying it into effect" (Barbastro, "Sonora Report, 1768–1783," FMCC, 202:35). Bucareli wrote Minister Arriaga on March 27, 1776, that he was "entirely dedicated to considering" the move of the presidios, but that he was waiting for Anza's return to

make a final decision (Bolton, *Anza's California Expeditions*, vol. 5, 335). On August 27, 1776, Bucareli told Gálvez he had the "preliminaries" for making these presidial moves "before me" (Bolton, *Anza's California Expeditions*, vol. 5, 353). On December 25, 1776, Bucareli wrote Felipe de Neve, the new governor of the Californias, to the same effect (Geiger, "Antonio María Bucareli's Christmas").

23. See Kessell, *Friars, Soldiers, and Reformers*, 127–28. O'Conor had not been impressed with the Tubac garrison when he visited in August 1775. He was especially harsh in his assessment of Anza's godson, an ensign by the name of Juan Felipe Belderrain (see Dobyns, *Lance Ho!*, 6; and Kessell, *Friars, Soldiers, and Reformers*, 104). Belderrain's character is partly revealed by the idiotic practical joke he played on Father Eixarch as the friar was making his way back from Yuma to Tumacácori in 1776, the "joke" being that the Apaches had completely destroyed the mission. It wasn't true, but Eixarch was forced to worry about it all the way from Caborca (Font, *With Anza to California*, 394–95; Kessell, *Friars, Soldiers, and Reformers*, 120–21).

24. Kessell, *Friars, Soldiers, and Reformers*, 135.

25. Kessell, *Friars, Soldiers, and Reformers*, 117–18.

26. Font to Ximénez, November 30, 1776, in Matson, "Letters of Friar Pedro Font," 274.

27. Font to Ximénez, November 30, 1776, in Matson, "Letters of Friar Pedro Font," 276, 282. Arricivita writes that the Indians of the Pimería Alta "continued their raids and attacks all through the year 1777, the missionaries of necessity also being exposed to their brutality." He complains that the authorities did little to provide for the friars' protection (*Apostolic Chronicle*, vol. 2, 200).

28. Kessell, *Friars, Soldiers, and Reformers*, 129–30.

29. Font to Ximénez, November 30, 1776, in Matson, "Letters of Friar Pedro Font," 277. Garcés himself would no longer travel alone in certain parts of the Pimería Alta, as he implies in Garcés to Ximénez, January 3, 1777 (FMCC, 201:19).

30. Garcés to Ximénez, September 24, 1776 (FMCC, 201:17).

31. Garcés to Bucareli, September 24, 1776, in Bolton, *Anza's California Expeditions*, vol. 5, 319–20.

32. Garcés, "Report to Fray Diego Ximénez."

33. Font heard the same thing while traveling along the Santa Barbara Channel with the expedition. This reprobate's "reputation became so widespread among the Indians that they call every soldier Camacho. We had nothing but questions from them asking about Camacho. Where was Camacho? Was Camacho coming?" (Font, *With Anza to California*, 220).

34. See Anza to Bucareli, December 15, 1772 (AGN, PI, 152); and Kessell, "Anza Damns the Missions."

35. Palma to Bucareli, November 11, 1776, in Bolton, *Anza's California Expeditions*, vol. 5, 365–77.

36. Guerrero ("Lost in the Translation") argues convincingly that Anza neither composed the petition, as Bolton thought, nor dictated its contents. Palma knew what he was doing, writes Guerrero, and the letter likely reflects well the views he intended to convey. There are extant Anza paraphrases of each of Palma's answers, so a real conversation definitely took place. Even so, I do not think Guerrero is warranted in concluding that everything in Palma's petition was "conceived on [Palma's] initiative and pursued without encouragement from Anza" (348). How could we know that?

37. Arricivita, *Apostolic Chronicle*, vol. 2, 203.

38. Font, *With Anza to California*, 381–83. This version of events does seem to comport a bit better with Anza's own diary, although that diary could also be read as not in contradiction with the petition. See Bolton, *Anza's California Expeditions*, vol. 4, 177–78.

39. Bolton, *Anza's California Expeditions*, vol. 1, 500.

40. Bucareli to Gálvez, November 26, 1776, in Bolton, *Anza's California Expeditions*, vol. 5, 395–97.

41. Velázquez, "Baptism of Captain Palma, Chief of the Yuma Indians, and Three Others of His Tribe," in Bolton, *Anza's California Expeditions*, vol. 5, 402–5. Font is our source for the detail about the Kohuana boy, whom he says "ever since Father Garcés visited his tribe had . . . made up his mind to go to Mexico City (Font, *With Anza to California*, 382).

42. As Kittle notes, the cathedral, "still the largest church in the Americas, was dominated by four ornate facades with portals flanked by columns and statues of the saints. The interior was a masterpiece of sixteen gilded chapels, with stunning altarpieces, Baroque paintings, and sculptures. It also featured two of the largest organs in the world" (*Franciscan Frontiersmen*, 218).

43. Font complained that the colegio had asked that he and Garcés not come to Querétaro to report in person on their journeys, but to report in writing instead (Font to Ximénez, January 20, 1777, in Matson, "Letters of Friar Pedro Font," 282).

44. Garcés told Ximénez on December 25, 1776 (FMCC, 201:18) that he had left for the "missions in the west" at the end of November, having waited for some time for a priest to arrive at San Xavier to replace him.

45. Font to Ximénez, January 20, 1777. Font had come to Tubutama after first gathering with others for some time at Ímuris. See Font, *With Anza to California*, 406.

46. Officer, Schuetz-Miller, and Fontana, *Pimería Alta*, 67–68.

47. Barbastro would formally open Gil's cause for sainthood in 1782. Kessell, *Friars, Soldiers, and Reformers*, 80–81.

48. Garcés, *Record of Travels*, 89. Garcés told Ximénez in a January 3, 1777, letter (FMCC 201:19) that he obtained input from several friars in drafting this supplement, including, besides Fathers Font and Barbastro, Fathers Eixarch, Gomarra, and Espinosa.

49. This discussion of the Garcés's eight points is drawn from *Record of Travels*, 89–102.

50. Font to Ximénez, January 20, 1777, in Matson, "Letters of Friar Pedro Font, 286.

51. Regular presidial troops wore arrow-proof leather jackets with up to seven layers of hide. They carried carbines, saddlebags with water and food, a lance, pistols that hung on hooks attached to the saddle blanket, a shield, and a cartridge belt. See Moore and Beene, "Interior Provinces of New Spain," 274.

52. In July 1776, Gálvez also appointed as intendant-governor of Sonora Pedro Corbalán, another relative of the Marqués de Croix (now deceased). He had been intendant of Sonora prior to this. The intendant-governorship gave him control over both political and economic affairs. Military affairs would at first be under control of Anza, until Croix arrived at Arizpe (Kessell, *Friars, Soldiers, and Reformers*, 125).

53. Kessell, *Friars, Soldiers, and Reformers*, 126.

54. On Croix, see Cutter, *Defenses of Northern New Spain*, Introduction; and Thomas, *Teodoro de Croix*. Thomas provides a more positive assessment of Croix than almost any other scholar. Jones notes that in 1778 Arizpe had 118 adobe houses and 1,534 residents, including 1,020 Christian Indians, mostly Ópatas. Very few persons of European ancestry lived north of this Spanish outpost (*Los Paisanos*, 181).

55. Kessell, *Friars, Soldiers, and Reformers*, 131.

56. McCarty, *Desert Documentary*, 27–30.

57. McCarty, *Desert Documentary*, 43.

58. Some of the details in this paragraph are taken from Jones, *Los Paisanos*, 192–94.

59. McCarty, Desert Documentary, 41, 43–44.

60. Kessell, *Friars, Soldiers, and Reformers*, 132–33. Guillén's murderers may have been Seris, according to Arricivita (*Apostolic Chronicle*, vol. 2, 200). The two groups were allied at this time.

61. Garcés to Ximénez, December 25, 1776 (FMCC, 201:18). Garcés worried that too many of the friars being sent to the frontier were lacking in the

virtues of charity and obedience, and that some were downright licentious; he does not name names. One notes that in stressing the need to be obedient Garcés manifests anything but the mindset of a maverick or antiestablishment rebel.

62. Kessell, *Friars, Soldiers, and Reformers*, 127.

63. Kessell, *Friars, Soldiers, and Reformers*, 133.

64. Arricivita, *Apostolic Chronicle*, vol. 2, 203–4.

65. Bucareli to Garcés, August 9, 1777 (HEBP, Carton 21, Folder 10).

66. Garcés to Bucareli, January 21, 1778 (HEBP, Carton 21, Folder 10).

67. See Gálvez to Croix, February 10, 1777; Gálvez to Bucareli, February 14, 1777; and Gálvez to Croix, February 14, 1777, in Bolton, *Anza's California Expeditions*, vol. 5, 400–401, 406–7, 408–9.

68. Arricivita, *Apostolic Chronicle*, vol. 2, 204.

69. Tueros to Croix, January 22, 1779; and Tueros to Croix, February 3, 1779 (both in AGI, Guad 277).

70. Tueros to Croix, January 22, 1779.

71. Croix to Barbastro, Croix to Tueros, and Croix to Garcés, February 5, 1779 (AGI, Guad 277).

72. Arricivita, *Apostolic Chronicle*, vol. 2, 206–7.

73. Kessell, *Friars, Soldiers, and Reformers*, 138–39.

74. Garcés to Ximénez, February 19, 1778 (FMCC, 201:20).

75. Garcés to Tueros, March 23, 1779 (AGI, Guad 277).

76. Tueros to Garcés, April 14, 1779 (AGI, Guad 277). Garcés had already made clear how important it was that the missionaries assigned to new frontier outposts have both prior missionary experience and a deep generosity of spirit. See Garcés to Ximénez, February 19, 1778.

77. Kessell, *Friars, Soldiers, and Reformers*, 139–40.

CHAPTER 11

1. Garcés to Croix, November 6, 1779 (AGI, Guad, 277). The narrative in this chapter relies on primary sources as much as possible, including the letters cited throughout. In recent years, the story is told very well by Santiago, *Massacre at the Yuma Crossing*, on whom I sometimes also rely for translations and interpretation.

2. Arricivita, *Apostolic Chronicle*, vol. 2, 208.

3. Garcés to Bucareli, March 11, 1779 (HEBP, Box 21, Folder 18).

4. News of Bucareli's death hit the Franciscan missionaries hard, as Palóu reports (*Palóu's Life of Fray Junípero Serra*, 209).

5. Santiago, *Massacre at the Yuma Crossing*, 70–71, for quotes.

6. Garcés to Croix, November 6, 1779; and Garcés to Croix, December 27, 1779 (both in AGI, Guad, 277).

7. Garcés to Croix, November 6, 1779.

8. Park, "Spanish Indian Policy in Northern Mexico."

9. Garcés to Croix, December 27, 1779 (AGI, Guad 277). On this criticism, See also Garcés to Guardián and Discretorio, March 23, 1781 (FMCC, 201:23).

10. On Barreneche's background and personality, see Geiger, *Franciscan Missionaries in Hispanic California*, 28–29; and Santiago, *Massacre at the Yuma Crossing*, 86–87.

11. Díaz to Croix, February 12, 1780 (AGI, Guad 277).

12. Pedro Galindo y Navarro assumed his post in 1777 and kept it, with a couple of interruptions, until 1797. The man was exceptionally frugal. He "repeatedly and consistently took a stand in favor of thrift and economy of the royal treasury against requests of bishops, missionaries, and of anyone else connected with the religious establishment," and one churchman characterized him as "fidgety, debauched, confused, and a paper-shuffler" (Matson and Fontana, *Friar Bringas Reports to the King*, 8).

13. Croix to Díaz, February 17, 1780 (AGI, Guad 277).

14. Matson and Bringas, *Friar Bringas Reports to the King*, 105, 102. Croix's formal instructions are included in their entirety at 97–105. For an extensive discussion of the new method of mission administration, see Weber, *Bárbaros*, 102–7.

15. Díaz to Croix, February 19, 1780 (AGI, Guad 277). For some of the information in this paragraph, see Santiago, *Massacre at the Yuma Crossing*, 81–82.

16. See, for example, Palóu, *Palóu's Life of Fray Junípero Serra*, 216–17; Arricivita, *Apostolic Chronicle*, vol. 2, 211–16; and Matson and Fontana, *Friar Bringas Reports to the King*, 105–11.

17. Santiago, *Massacre at the Yuma Crossing*, 82–83.

18. Santiago, *Massacre at the Yuma Crossing*, 84–85.

19. Santiago, *Massacre at the Yuma Crossing*, 85.

20. The quotations here are Arricivita's (*Apostolic Chronicle*, vol. 2, 216), purportedly paraphrasing Garcés.

21. Kessell, *Friars, Soldiers, and Reformers*, 135. Garcés likely knew Perdigón personally.

22. Díaz to Croix, November 8, 1780 (HEBP, Box 21, Folder 20).

23. Garcés to Croix, December 30, 1780 (HEBP, Box 21, Folder 20).

24. Yslas to Croix, December 30, 1780 (HEBP, Box 21, Folder 20).

25. A marker was dedicated at the site on May 4, 1980. It is located on the north side of County Road S24 (or 11th Street) in Winterhaven, California,

just east of that road's intersection with Heyser Road. For some time, thanks to Arricivita, it was thought that San Pedro y San Pablo Bicuñer was downstream from Yuma, but the location of the site upstream at or near the current marker is certainly correct. See Yates, "Locating the Colorado River Mission San Pedro y San Pablo de Bicuñer."

26. Santiago, *Massacre at the Yuma Crossing*, 94.

27. Croix wrote both Yslas and Díaz on January 12, 1781 (HEBP, Box 21, Folder 20).

28. Yslas to Croix, January 17, 1781 (HEBP, Box 21, Folder 20).

29. Geiger, *Franciscan Missionaries in Hispanic California*, 157.

30. See Santiago, *Massacre at the Yuma Crossing*, 95–96. Although the expectation of and desire for martyrdom were often real enough, we should note that in retrospective hagiographies of actual martyrs their joyful anticipation of such an end is always emphasized.

31. Santiago, *Massacre at the Yuma Crossing*, 103.

32. Garcés to Croix, December 30, 1780, in Roberts, *Spanish Missions at Yuma*.

33. Garcés to Guardián and Discretorio, March 23, 1781 (FMCC 201:23), quoted in Arricivita, *Apostolic Chronicle*, vol. 2, 220.

34. Garcés to Guardián and Discretorio, March 23, 1781.

35. Garcés to Guardián and Discretorio, March 23, 1781; quote from Santiago, *Massacre at the Yuma Crossing*, 104.

36. Yslas to Croix, January 17, 1781 (HEBP, Box 21, Folder 20).

37. Bolton, *Anza's California Expeditions*, vol. 3, 375–76. A similar scene had played out in spring 1776, when Father Eixarch lamented that the animals left behind by the second Anza expedition had eaten nearly all the Quechans' wheat.

38. Yslas to Croix, January 17, 1781.

39. Croix to Yslas, February 22, 1781 (HEBP, Box 21, Folder 20).

40. Yslas to Croix, May 28, 1781 (HEBP, Box 21, Folder 20).

41. Kittle, *Franciscan Frontiersmen*, 84.

42. Bolton, *Anza's California Expeditions*, vol. 3, 353.

43. Bolton, *Anza's California Expeditions*, vol. 3, 335–37. See Bee, *Yuma*, 28–29, for another description of this ceremony.

44. Bee, *Yuma*, 27–28.

45. Forbes, *Warriors of the Colorado*, 22.

46. Santiago, *Massacre at the Yuma Crossing*, 104.

47. Palóu, *Palóu's Life of Fray Junípero Serra*, 216–17; Geiger, *Life and Times of Fray Junípero Serra*, 269.

48. Santiago, *Massacre at the Yuma Crossing*, 112–13.

49. The soldier was José Darío Argüello; quoted in Santiago, *Massacre at the Yuma Crossing*, 113–14.

50. Santiago, *Massacre at the Yuma Crossing*, 114.

51. Montijo wrote her account in December 1785 at the request of Father Francisco Antonio Barbastro, the superior of the Franciscan missions in Sonora. Doña Montijo's account in this section is drawn from McCarty, *Desert Documentary*, 36–39, except where otherwise noted.

52. Santiago, *Massacre at the Yuma Crossing*, 114–15.

53. Santiago, *Massacre at the Yuma Crossing*, 124.

54. Santiago, *Massacre at the Yuma Crossing*, 124–25.

55. Santiago, *Massacre at the Yuma Crossing*, 125.

56. See Stagg, *First Bishop of Sonora*, 57–87.

57. Santiago, *Massacre at the Yuma Crossing*, 146.

58. Palóu, *Palóu's Life of Fray Junípero Serra*, 227.

59. Priestley, "Colorado River Campaign" 51. The remains of Díaz and Moreno were in such a state that Fages first had them cremated.

60. Palóu, *Palóu's Life of Fray Junípero Serra*, 227.

61. Geiger, *Life and Times of Fray Junípero Serra*, vol. 2, 310.

Epilogue

1. See Cullimore, "California Martyr's Bones," for this story.

2. Bancroft, Coues, Bolton, and the contemporary priest at Tubutama were all among those who did not realize the priests' final burial place was Querétaro. See Cullimore, "California Martyr's Bones."

3. Matson and Fontana, *Friar Bringas Reports to the King*, 54, quote at 30.

4. Sandos applied his estimate to the California missions. "I estimate conservatively that 10 percent of the mission Indian population was directly affected by the choir members and that they formed the nucleus of converts" (*Converting California*, 152). Since the Pimería Alta's mission regimes tended to be less intense, whatever the true percentage was in California, it was probably lower in the Pimería Alta.

5. Jackson, "Demographic Change in Northwestern New Spain," 467. Note that this number does not count those Indians living on the Colorado and Gila and beyond.

6. Griffith, *Beliefs and Holy Places*, 37, 69.

7. Griffith, *Beliefs and Holy Places*, 76.

8. Geiger, *Kingdom of St. Francis*, 35–36.

9. Griffith, *Beliefs and Holy Places*, 70, 68.

10. It is estimated that today forty Tohono O'odham villages have a church or chapel. See "Serving Desert People on a Vast Reservation." This is to say nothing of the Akimel O'odham, discussed below.

11. Fontana, "Builders" (BLFP).

12. Geiger, *Kingdom of St. Francis*, 35, 41.

13. Ratzinger (who would become Pope Benedict XVI) argued that living cultures are not static but open, and that the greater they are the more open they are, interiorly, to the truth about human beings and nature. All cultures, Ratzinger maintained, are intrinsically potentially universal ("Christ, Faith, and the Challenge of Cultures").

14. Geiger, *Kingdom of St. Francis*, 33.

15. Today, Immaculate Conception Catholic Church has migrated across the river to Yuma.

16. Geiger, *Kingdom of St. Francis*, 43–45.

17. See Cook and Whittemore, *Among the Pimas*.

18. Catholic Extension estimates that 11,000 residents of the Tohono O'odham Nation are Catholic, or about 85 percent of the total population; see "Serving Desert People on a Vast Reservation."

Bibliography

ARCHIVES

Archivo General de Indias, Seville, Spain. Cited as AGI.

Archivo General de la Nación, Mexico City. Cited as AGN.

Archivo Histórico de la Provincia Franciscana de Michoacán, Convento de San Francisco, Celaya, Guanajuato, México. Cited as AHPFM.

Arizona Historical Society Library and Archives, Tucson, AZ. Cited as AHSLA.

Ayer Collection, Newberry Library, Chicago, IL. Cited as AC.

Bernard L. Fontana papers, Special Collections, University of Arizona, Tucson, AZ. Cited as BLFP.

Father Marcellino Civezza Collection, Pontifical University of St. Anthony (Antonianum) Library, Rome. Cited as FMCC.

Fondo del Colegio de la Santa Cruz de Querétaro, Archivo Histórico de la Provincia Franciscana de Michoacán, Convento de San Francisco, Celaya, Guanajuato, México. Cited as FCSQC.

Herbert E. Bolton papers, The Bancroft Library, University of California, Berkeley, CA. Cited as HEBP.

Huntington Library, San Marino, CA. Cited as HL.

John L. Kessell Papers. University of New Mexico Center for Southwest Research and Special Collections, Albuquerque, NM. Cited as JLKP.

Latin American Library, Tulane University, New Orleans, LA. Cited as LAL.

Special Collections, University of Arizona Libraries, Tucson, AZ. Cited as UASC.

GARCÉS DIARIES

Garcés undertook significant journeys in 1768, 1769, 1770, 1771, 1774, and 1775–76. He made at least one diary of each of these entradas. The 1768 and 1769 diaries appear to have been lost, although it is certainly not impossible that an enterprising researcher may one day discover them in some dusty and neglected archival corner. Fortunately, Garcés discussed those journeys in a summary diary he wrote in 1774. That diary covers in brief not only his 1768 and 1769 trips but also those of 1770, 1771, and 1774.

In this work, I draw from the following English-language versions of the Garcés diaries. For the unpublished versions, I relied on translations made by Herbert Bolton or his students, with additional translation support from Constanza López Lamerain and Rose Marie Beebe. For purposes of clarity, spelling and capitalization for the titles of each diary have been corrected, regularized, or modernized where necessary.

Copia de las noticias sacadas, y remitidas por el Padre Predicador Fr. Francisco Garcés de los diarios que ha formado en las cuatro entradas practicadas desde el año de '68 hasta el presente de '75 a la frontera septentrional de los gentiles de Nueva España. Dated May 21, 1775, this diary summarizes Garcés's 1768, 1769, 1770, 1771, and 1774 entradas. HEBP, Carton 21, Folder 11.

Diario que se ha formado por el viaje hecho al Río Gila, quando los indios Pimas Gileños me llamaron a fin de que baptisase sus hijos que estavan enfermos del sarampión. Diary of Garcés's 1770 entrada. HEBP, Carton 20, Folder 23.

Diario que se ha formado con la ocasión de la entrada que hiço a los vecinos gentiles. First diary of Garcés's 1771 entrada. HEBP, Carton 20, Folders 22 and 23.

Diario desde ocho de agosto, con la ocasión de la visita de los próximos gentiles, que practiqué para poder dar noticia del actual estado y proporción para adelantar y propagar nuestra santa fe y dominios del rey nuestro señor, que Dios guarde. Second, longer diary of Garcés's 1771 entrada. HEBP, Carton 20, Folder 23.

Expediente formado á consecuencia de Representación del Padre Fr. Francisco Garcés con que acompaña el diario de su expedición á los Ríos Gila y Colorado: en que expone su dictamen sobre fundación de misiones en estos parages. Includes Garcés's first, brief diary of the 1774 Anza expedition. Included in Herbert Eugene Bolton, ed., *Anza's California Expeditions*, vol. 2: *Opening a Land Route to California: Diaries of Anza, Díaz, Garcés, and Palóu.* Berkeley: University of California Press, 1930, 363–72.

Diario de la entrada que se practica de orden del Excelentísimo Sr. Virrey Don Antonio María Bucareli y Ursúa producida en Junta de Guerra i real acienda a fin de abrir camino por los Ríos Gila y Colorado para los nuevos establecimientos de San Diego y Monterey el Capitán Comandante Don Juan Baptista de Anza. Garcés's second, fuller diary of the 1774 Anza expedition. Included in Herbert Eugene Bolton, ed., *Anza's California Expeditions,* vol. 2: *Opening a Land Route to California: Diaries of Anza, Díaz, Garcés, and Palóu.* Berkeley: University of California Press, 1930, 307–60.

Expediente formado á consecuencia de Representación del Padre Fr. Francisco Garcés con que acompaña el diario de su expedición á los Ríos Gila y Colorado: en que expone su dictamen sobre fundación de misiones en estos parages. Includes Garcés's diary of his sidetrip to the Halchidhomas and return to San Xavier del Bac in 1774, after splitting off from the main body of the Anza expedition. Included in Herbert Eugene Bolton, ed., *Anza's California Expeditions, vol. 2: Opening a Land Route to California: Diaries of Anza, Díaz, Garcés, and Palóu.* Berkeley: University of California Press, 1930, 375–92.

Diario y derecho que siguió el M.R.P. Fr. Francisco Garcés en su viaje hecho desde Octubre de 1775 hasta 17 de Septiembre de 1776, al Río Colorado para reconocer las naciones que habitan sus márgenes, y á los pueblos del Moqui del Nuevo México. Garcés's diary of his travel with the Anza expedition in 1775, as well as his subsequent travels in 1775–76. Published in English as *A Record of Travels in Arizona and California, 1775–1776: A New Translation.* Edited by John Galvin. San Francisco: John Howell Books, 1995.

BOOKS

Adams, Eleanor B., and Fray Angélico Chávez, eds. *The Missions of New Mexico, 1776.* Santa Fe, NM: Sunstone Press, 2012.

Arricivita, Juan Domingo. *Apostolic Chronicle of Juan Domingo Arricivita: The Franciscan Mission Frontier in the Eighteenth Century in Arizona, Texas, and the Californias.* 2 vols. Translated by George P. Hammond and Agapito Rey. Berkeley, CA: Academy of American Franciscan History, 1996.

Babcock, Matthew. *Apache Adaption to Hispanic Rule.* New York: Cambridge University Press, 2016.

Bannon, John Francis. *Herbert Eugene Bolton: The Historian and the Man.* Tucson: University of Arizona Press, 1978.

———. *The Mission Frontier in Sonora, 1620–1687.* New York: United States Catholic Historical Society, 1955.

———. *The Spanish Borderlands Frontier, 1513–1821.* New York: Holt, Rinehart and Winston, 1970.

Bee, Robert L. *The Yuma*. New York: Chelsea House, 1989.

Beebe, Rose Marie, and Robert M. Senkewicz. *Junípero Serra: California, Indians, and the Transformation of a Missionary*. Norman: University of Oklahoma Press, 2015.

Benavides, Fray Alonso de. *The Memorial of Fray Alonso de Benavides, 1630.* Albuquerque: Horn and Wallace, 1965.

Bobb, Bernard E. *The Viceregency of Antonio María Bucareli in New Spain, 1771–1779.* Austin: University of Texas Press, 1962.

Bolton, Herbert Eugene, ed. *Anza's California Expeditions.* 5 vols. Berkeley: University of California Press, 1930.

———, ed. *Bolton and the Spanish Borderlands.* Norman: University of Oklahoma Press, 1964.

———. *Guide to Materials for the History of the United States in the Principal Archives of Mexico.* Washington, DC: Carnegie Institution of Washington, 1913.

———. *Outpost of Empire.* New York: Alfred A. Knopf, 1939.

———. *Pageant in the Wilderness: The Story of the Escalante Expedition to the Interior Basin, 1776, Including the Diary and Itinerary of Father Escalante Translated and Annotated.* Salt Lake City: Utah State Historical Society, 1951.

———. *Rim of Christendom: A Biography of Eusebio Francisco Kino, Pacific Coast Pioneer.* New York: Russell and Russell, 1960.

Brague, Rémi. *The Kingdom of Man: Genesis and Failure of the Modern Project.* Notre Dame, IN: University of Notre Dame Press, 2018.

Briggs, Walter. *Without Noise of Arms: The 1776 Dominguez-Escalante Search for a Route from Santa Fe to Monterey.* Flagstaff, AZ: Northland Press, 1976.

Brooks, James F. *Captives and Cousins: Slavery, Kinship, and Community in the Southwest Borderlands.* Chapel Hill: University of North Carolina Press, 2002.

———. *Mesa of Sorrows: A History of the Awat'ovi Massacre.* New York: W. W. Norton, 2016.

Brown, Peter. *Through the Eye of a Needle: Wealth, the Fall of Rome, and the Making of Christianity in the West, 350–550 AD.* Princeton, NJ: Princeton University Press, 2014.

Burrus, Ernest J., trans. and ed. *Wenceslaus Linck's Reports and Letters, 1762–1778.* Los Angeles: Dawson's Book Shop, 1967.

Cabeza de Vaca, Álvar Núñez. *The Narrative of Cabeza de Vaca.* Edited and translated by Rolena Adorno and Patrick Charles Pautz. Lincoln: University of Nebraska Press, 2003.

Calloway, Colin G. *One Vast Winter Count: The Native American West before Lewis and Clark*. Lincoln: University of Nebraska Press, 2003.

Cavanaugh, William T. *The Myth of Religious Violence: Secular Ideology and the Roots of Modern Conflict*. New York: Oxford University Press, 2009.

Cervantes, Fernando. *Conquistadores: A New History*. London: Allen Lane, 2020.

———. *The Devil in the New World: The Impact of Diabolism in New Spain*. New Haven, CT: Yale University Press, 1994.

Chacón Richard J., and Rubén G. Mendoza, eds. *North American Indigenous Warfare and Ritual Violence*. Tucson: University of Arizona Press, 2007.

Clayton, Lawrence A. *Bartolomé de Las Casas: A Biography*. Cambridge: Cambridge University Press, 2012.

Cohen, Thomas M., Jay T. Harrison, and David Rex Galindo, eds. *The Franciscans in Colonial Mexico*. Norman: University of Oklahoma Press, 2021.

Cook, Charles H., and Isaac T. Whittemore. *Among the Pimas, or the Mission to the Pima and Maricopa Indians*. Albany, NY: n.p., 1893.

Cook, Sherburne F. *Population Trends among the California Mission Indians*. Berkeley: University of California Press, 1940.

Corle, Edwin. *Desert Country*. New York: Duell, Sloan and Pearce, 1941.

———. *Fig Tree John*. Los Angeles: Ward Ritchie Press, 1955 [1935].

———. *Listen, Bright Angel*. New York: Duell, Sloan and Pearce, 1946.

Costo, Rupert, and Jeannette Henry Costo, eds. *The Missions of California: A Legacy of Genocide*. San Francisco: Indian Historian Press, 1987.

Coues, Elliott. *On the Trail of a Spanish Pioneer: The Diary and Itinerary of Francisco Garcés*. 2 vols. New York: Francis P. Harper, 1900.

Cullimore, Clarence. *The Martyrdom and Interment of Padre Francisco Garcés*. Bakersfield, CA: Kern County Historical Society, 1954.

Cutter, Donald C., trans. and ed. *The Defenses of Northern New Spain: Hugo O'Conor's Report to Teodoro de Croix, July 22, 1777*. Dallas: Southern Methodist University Press, 1994.

Dobyns, Henry F. *Lance Ho! Containment of the Western Apaches by the Royal Spanish Garrison at Tucson*. Lima, Peru: Editorial Estudios Andinos, 1964.

———. *The Pima-Maricopa*. New York: Chelsea House, 1989.

———. *Spanish Colonial Tucson: A Demographic History*. Tucson: University of Arizona Press, 1976.

Donohue, John Augustine, S.J. *After Kino: Jesuit Missions in Northwestern New Spain, 1711–1767*. Rome: Jesuit Historical Institute, 1969.

Douglass, John G., and William M. Graves, eds. *New Mexico and the Pimería Alta: The Colonial Period in the American Southwest*. Boulder: University Press of Colorado, 2017.

Dunne, Peter Masten. *Jacobo Sedelmayr: Missionary, Frontiersman, Explorer in Arizona and Sonora; Four Original Manuscript Narratives, 1744–1751*. Tucson: Arizona Pioneers' Historical Society, 1955.

———. *Juan Antonio Balthasar, Padre Visitador to the Sonora Frontier, 1744–1745*. Tucson: Arizona Pioneers' Historical Society, 1957.

Dutton, Bertha P. *American Indians of the Southwest*. Albuquerque: University of New Mexico Press, 1983.

Elliott, J. H. *Imperial Spain, 1469–1716*. New York: St. Martin's, 1964.

Engelhardt, Zephyrin. *The Franciscans in Arizona*. Harbor Springs, MI: Holy Childhood Indian School, 1899.

———. *The Missions and Missionaries of California*, vol. 1, 2nd ed. Chicago: Franciscan Herald Press, 1929.

———. *San Gabriel Mission and the Beginnings of Los Angeles*. San Gabriel, CA: Mission San Gabriel, 1927.

Faulk, Odie B. *Destiny Road: The Gila Trail and the Opening of the Southwest*. New York: Oxford University Press, 1973.

———. *The Leather Jacket Soldier: Spanish Military Equipment and Institutions of the Late Eighteenth Century*. Pasadena, CA: Socio-Technical Publications, 1971.

Fedewa, Marilyn H. *María of Ágreda: Mystical Lady in Blue*. Albuquerque: University of New Mexico Press, 2009.

Fergusson, Erna. *Dancing Gods: Indian Ceremonials of New Mexico and Arizona*. Albuquerque: University of New Mexico Press, 1931.

Fernández-Morera, Darío. *The Myth of the Andalusian Paradise: Muslims, Christians, and Jews under Islamic Rule in Medieval Spain*. Wilmington, DE: ISI Books, 2016.

Font, Pedro. *With Anza to California, 1775–1776: The Journal of Pedro Font, O.F.M.* Translated by Alan K. Brown. Norman: Arthur H. Clark Company and University of Oklahoma Press, 2011.

Fontana, Bernard L. *A Gift of Angels: The Art of San Xavier del Bac*. Tucson: University of Arizona Press, 2010.

———. *Of Earth and Little Rain: The Papago Indians*. Flagstaff, AZ: Northland Press, 1981.

Forbes, Jack D. *Warriors of the Colorado: The Yumas of the Quechan Nation and Their Neighbors*. Norman: University of Oklahoma Press, 1965.

Friede, Juan, and Benjamin Keen, eds. *Bartolomé de Las Casas in History: Toward an Understanding of the Man and His Work*. DeKalb: Northern Illinois University Press, 1971.

Fustel de Coulanges, Numa Denis. *The Ancient City: A Study of the Religion, Laws, and Institutions of Greece and Rome.* Mineola, NY: Dover, 2006.

Garate, Donald T., ed. *Captain Juan Bautista de Anza: Correspondence on Various Subjects, 1775.* San Leandro, CA: Los Californianos. 1995.

————, ed. *The Juan Bautista de Anza–Fernando de Rivera y Moncada Letters of 1775–1776: Personalities in Conflict.* San Diego: Los Californianos, 2006.

Garcés, Francisco. *A Record of Travels in Arizona and California, 1775–1776: A New Translation.* Edited by John Galvin. San Francisco: John Howell Books, 1995.

Geiger, Maynard J. *Franciscan Missionaries in Hispanic California, 1769–1848: A Biographical Dictionary.* San Marino, CA: Huntington Library, 1969.

————. *The Kingdom of St. Francis in Arizona.* Santa Barbara, CA: n.p., 1939.

————. *The Life and Times of Fray Junípero Serra, O.F.M., or The Man Who Never Turned Back.* 2 vols. Washington, DC: Academy of American Franciscan History, 1959.

Gibson, Carrie. *El Norte: The Epic and Forgotten Story of Hispanic North America.* New York: Atlantic Monthly Press, 2019.

Girard, René. *The Girard Reader.* New York: Crossroad, 1997.

————. *The Scapegoat.* Baltimore: Johns Hopkins University Press, 1989.

————. *Violence and the Sacred.* Baltimore: Johns Hopkins University Press, 1979.

Goodwin, Robert. *América: The Epic Story of Spanish North America, 1493–1898.* New York: Bloomsbury, 2019.

Greater America: Essays in Honor of Herbert Eugene Bolton. Berkeley: University of California Press, 1945.

Griffith, James S. *Beliefs and Holy Places: A Spiritual Geography of the Pimería Alta.* Tucson: University of Arizona Press, 1992.

Griffiths, Nicholas, and Fernando Cervantes. *Spiritual Encounters: Interactions between Christianity and Native Religions in Colonial America.* Birmingham, UK: University of Birmingham Press, 1999.

Guerrero, Vladimir. *The Anza Trail and the Settling of California.* Berkeley, CA: Heyday, 2006.

Hackel, Steven W. *Children of Coyote, Missionaries of Saint Francis: Indian-Spanish Relations in Colonial California, 1769–1850.* Chapel Hill: University of North Carolina Press, 2005.

————. *Junípero Serra: California's Founding Father.* New York: Hill and Wang, 2013.

Harney, Martin P., S.J. *The Jesuits in History: The Society of Jesus through Four Centuries.* Chicago: Loyola University Press, 1962.

Hart, David Bentley. *Atheist Delusions: The Christian Revolution and Its Fashionable Enemies.* New Haven, CT: Yale University Press, 2010.

Herrera, Carlos R. *Juan Bautista de Anza: The King's Governor in New Mexico.* Norman: University of Oklahoma Press, 2015.

Hirst, Stephen. *Life in a Narrow Place: The Havasupai of Grand Canyon.* New York: David McKay, 1976.

Holland, Tom. *Dominion: How the Christian Revolution Remade the World.* New York: Basic Books, 2019.

Horgan, Paul. *Lamy of Santa Fe: A Biography.* New York: Farrar, Strauss, Giroux, 1975.

———. *Under the Sangre de Cristo.* Flagstaff, AZ: Northland Press, 1985.

Hu-DeHart, Evelyn. *Missionaries, Miners, and Indians.* Tucson: University of Arizona Press, 1981.

Hurtado, Albert L. *Herbert Eugene Bolton: Historian of the American Borderlands.* Berkeley: University of California Press, 2012.

Hutton, Paul Andrew. *The Apache Wars: The Hunt for Geronimo, the Apache Kid, and the Captive Boy Who Started the Longest War in American History.* New York: Crown, 2016.

Iglesia, Ramón. *Columbus, Cortés, and Other Essays.* Berkeley: University of California Press, 1969.

Iliff, Flora Gregg. *People of the Blue Water: A Record of Life among the Walapai and Havasupai Indians.* Tucson: University of Arizona Press, 1985 [1954].

Jackson, Robert H., ed. *New Views of Borderland History.* Albuquerque: University of New Mexico Press, 1998.

Jackson, Robert H., and Edward Castillo. *Indians, Franciscans, and Spanish Colonization: The Impact of the Mission System on California Indians.* Albuquerque: University of New Mexico Press, 1995.

James, Harry C. *Pages from Hopi History.* Tucson: University of Arizona Press, 1974.

John, Elizabeth A. H. *Storms Brewed in Other Men's World: The Confrontation of Indians, Spanish, and French in the Southwest, 1540–1795.* 2nd ed. Norman: University of Oklahoma Press, 1996.

Johnson, Timothy J., and Gert Melville, eds. *From La Florida to La California: Franciscan Evangelization in the Spanish Borderlands.* Berkeley, CA: Academy of American Franciscan History, 2013.

Jones, Oakah L., Jr. *Los Paisanos: Spanish Settlers on the Northern Frontier of New Spain.* Norman: University of Oklahoma Press, 1979.

Joseph, Alice, Rosamond P. Spicer, and Jane Chesky. *The Desert People: A Study of the Papago Indians of Southern Arizona.* Chicago: University of Chicago Press, 1949.

Kenneally, Finbar. *Writings of Fermín Francisco de Lasuén.* 2 vols. Washington, DC: American Academy of Franciscan History, 1965.

Kessell, John L. *Friars, Soldiers, and Reformers: Hispanic Arizona and the Sonora Mission Frontier, 1767–1856.* Tucson: University of Arizona Press, 1976.

———. *Mission of Sorrows: Jesuit Guevavi and the Pimas, 1691–1767.* Tucson: University of Arizona Press, 1970.

———. *Spain in the Southwest: A Narrative History of Colonial New Mexico, Arizona, Texas, and California.* Norman: University of Oklahoma Press, 2002.

Kinnaird, Lawrence, trans. and ed. *The Frontiers of New Spain: Nicolas de Lafora's Description, 1766–1768.* Berkeley, CA: Quivira Society, 1958.

Kittle, Robert A. *Franciscan Frontiersmen: How Three Adventurers Charted the West.* Norman: University of Oklahoma Press, 2017.

Konščak, Ferdinand. *Life and Works of the Reverend Ferdinand Konščak, S.J., 1703–1759.* Boston: Stratford, 1923.

Kroeber, A. L. *Handbook of the Indians of California.* New York: Dover, 1976 [1925].

Las Casas, Bartolomé de. *Account, Much Abbreviated, of the Destruction of the Indies.* Indianapolis: Hackett, 2003.

Lehner, Ulrich L. *The Catholic Enlightenment: The Forgotten History of a Global Movement.* New York: Oxford University Press, 2016.

Lynch, John. *New Worlds: A Religious History of Latin America.* New Haven, CT: Yale University Press, 2012.

Madariaga, Salvador de. *Hernán Cortés: Conqueror of Mexico.* Coral Gables, FL: University of Miami Press, 1942.

Matson, Daniel S., and Bernard L. Fontana, eds. *Friar Bringas Reports to the King: Methods of Indoctrination on the Frontier of New Spain, 1726–1797.* Tucson: University of Arizona Press, 1977.

McCarthy, James. *A Papago Traveler: The Memories of James McCarthy.* Tucson: University of Arizona Press, 1985.

McCarty, Kieran. *Desert Documentary: The Spanish Years, 1767–1821.* Tucson: Arizona Historical Society, 1976.

———. *A Spanish Frontier in the Enlightened Age: Franciscan Beginnings in Sonora and Arizona, 1767–1770.* Washington, DC: Academy of American Franciscan History, 1981.

McClure, Julia, ed. *The Franciscan Invention of the New World.* New York: Palgrave Macmillan, 2016.

McNamee, Gregory. *Gila: The Life and Death of an American River,* updated and expanded ed. Albuquerque: University of New Mexico Press, 2012.

McWilliams, Carey. *Southern California Country: An Island on the Land.* New York: Duell, Sloan and Pearce, 1946.

Miller, Bruce W. *The Gabrielino.* Los Osos, CA: Sand River Press, 1991.

Moorhead, Max L. *The Apache Frontier: Jacobo Ugarte y Loyola and Spanish-Indian Relations in Northern New Spain, 1769–1791.* Norman: University of Oklahoma Press, 1968.

Morgan, Richard J., Jr. *A Guide to Historic Missions and Churches of the Arizona-Sonora Borderlands.* Tucson, AZ: Adventures in Education, 1995.

Morrow, Honoré. *Beyond the Blue Sierra.* New York: A. L. Burt, 1932.

Neihardt, John G. *Black Elk Speaks: The Complete Edition.* Lincoln: University of Nebraska Press, 2014.

Nentvig, Juan. *Rudo Ensayo: A Description of Sonora and Arizona in 1764.* Edited and translated by Alberto Francisco Pradeau and Robert R. Rasmussen. Tucson: University of Arizona Press, 1980.

Och, Joseph. *Missionary in Sonora: The Travel Reports of Joseph Och, S.J., 1755–1767.* Translated by Theodore E. Treutlein. San Francisco: California Historical Society, 1965.

Odens, Peter R. *Father Garcés: The Maverick Priest.* Yuma, AZ: Sun Graphics, 1980.

Officer, James E. *Hispanic Arizona, 1536–1856.* Tucson: University of Arizona Press, 1987.

Officer, James E., Mardith Schuetz-Miller, and Bernard L. Fontana, eds. *The Pimería Alta: Missions and More.* Tucson, AZ: Southwestern Mission Research Center, 1996.

O'Kane, Walter Collins. *The Hopis: Portrait of a Desert People.* Norman: University of Oklahoma Press, 1953.

———. *Sun in the Sky: The Hopi Indians of the Arizona Mesa Lands.* Norman: University of Oklahoma Press, 1950.

Orfalea, Gregory. *Journey to the Sun: Junípero Serra's Dream and the Founding of California.* New York: Scribner, 2014.

Palóu, Francisco. *Historical Memoirs of New California.* 4 vols. Edited by Herbert Eugene Bolton. Berkeley: University of California Press, 1926.

———. *Palóu's Life of Fray Junípero Serra.* Translated by Maynard J. Geiger. Washington, DC: Academy of American Franciscan History, 1955.

Pérez de Ribas, Andrés. *My Life among the Savage Nations of New Spain.* Los Angeles: Ward Ritchie Press, 1968.

Petrie, Sir Charles. *King Charles III of Spain: An Enlightened Despot.* London: Constable, 1971.

Pfefferkorn, Ignaz. *Sonora: A Description of the Province*. Translated and annotated by Theodore E. Treutlein. Tucson: University of Arizona Press, 2016 [1989].

Phelan, John Leddy. *The Millennial Kingdom of the Franciscans in the New World*, 2nd ed. Berkeley: University of California Press, 1970.

Polzer, Charles W. *Kino: A Legacy: His Life, His Works, His Missions, His Monuments*. Tucson: Jesuit Fathers of Southern Arizona, 1998.

———. *Rules and Precepts of the Jesuit Missions of Northwestern New Spain*. Tucson: University of Arizona Press, 1976.

Pourade, Richard F. *Anza Conquers the Desert: The Anza Expeditions from Mexico to California and the Founding of San Francisco, 1774 to 1776*. San Diego: Copley, 1971.

Priestley, Herbert Ingram. *José de Gálvez, Visitor-General of New Spain (1765–1771)*. Berkeley: University of California Press, 1916.

Radding, Cynthia. *Wandering Peoples: Colonialism, Ethnic Spaces, and Ecological Frontiers in Northwestern Mexico, 1700–1850*. Durham, NC: Duke University Press, 1997.

Repplier, Agnes. *Junípero Serra*. Garden City, NY: Doubleday, 1933.

Reséndez, Andrés. *A Land So Strange: The Epic Journey of Cabeza de Vaca: The Extraordinary Tale of a Shipwrecked Spaniard Who Walked across America in the Sixteenth Century*. New York: Basic Books, 2009 [2007].

———. *The Other Slavery: The Uncovered Story of Indian Enslavement in America*. Boston: Houghton Mifflin, 2016.

Rex Galindo, David. *To Sin No More: Franciscans and Conversion in the Hispanic World, 1683–1830*. Palo Alto, CA: Stanford University Press, 2018.

Richman, Irving Berdine. *California under Spain and Mexico, 1535–1847*. New York: Cooper Square, 1965.

Rivera Cambas, Manuel. *Los gobernantes de México: Galería de biografías y retratos de los virreyes, emperadores, presidentes y otros gobernantes que ha tenido México, desde don Hernando Cortés hasta el c. Benito Juárez*. Mexico City: J. M. Aguilar Ortiz, 1872.

Roberts, David. *Escalante's Dream: On the Trail of the Spanish Discovery of the Southwest*. New York: W. W. Norton, 2019.

Roca, Paul M. *Paths of the Padres through Sonora: An Illustrated History and Guide to Its Spanish Churches*. Tucson: Arizona Pioneers' Historical Society, 1967.

Royal, Robert. *Columbus and the Crisis of the West*. 2nd ed. Manchester, NH: Sophia Institute Press, 2020.

Rushforth, Scott, and Steadman Upham. *A Hopi Social History*. Austin: University of Texas Press, 1992.

Russell, Frank. *The Pima Indians.* Tucson: University of Arizona Press, 1975.

Sánchez, Joseph P. *Spanish Bluecoats: The Catalonian Volunteers in Northwestern New Spain, 1767–1810.* Albuquerque: University of New Mexico Press, 1990.

Sandos, James A. *Converting California: Indians and Franciscans in the Missions.* New Haven, CT: Yale University Press, 2004.

Santiago, Mark. *Massacre at the Yuma Crossing: Spanish Relations with the Quechans, 1779–1782.* Tucson: University of Arizona Press, 2010.

Saunt, Claudio. *West of the Revolution: An Uncommon History of 1776.* New York: W. W. Norton, 2014.

Schwaller, John F., ed. *Francis in the Americas: Essays on the Franciscan Family in North and South America.* Berkeley, CA: Academy of American Franciscan History, 2005.

———. *The History of the Catholic Church in Latin America.* New York: New York University Press, 2015.

Scrivner, Charles. *Mohave People.* San Antonio, TX: Naylor, 1970.

Serra, Junípero. *Writings of Junípero Serra.* 4 vols. Translated by Antonine Tibesar. Washington, DC: Academy of American Franciscan History, 1955–66.

Shaw, Anna Moore. *A Pima Past.* Tucson: University of Arizona Press, 1974.

Sheridan, Thomas E., Stewart B. Koyiyumptewa, Anton Daughters, Dale S. Brenneman, T. J. Ferguson, Leigh Kuwanwisiswma, and Lee Wayne Lomayestewa, eds. *Moquis and Kastiilam: Hopis, Spaniards, and the Trauma of History.* 2 vols. Tucson: University of Arizona Press, 2015, 2020.

Siedentop, Larry. *Inventing the Individual: The Origins of Western Liberalism.* Cambridge, MA: Harvard University Press, 2014.

Silverberg, Robert. *The Pueblo Revolt.* Lincoln: University of Nebraska Press, 1994 [1970].

Smith, Fay Jackson, John L. Kessell, and Francis J. Fox, eds. *Father Kino in Arizona.* Phoenix: Arizona Historical Foundation, 1966.

Sonnischen, C. L. *Tucson: The Life and Times of an American City.* Norman: University of Oklahoma Press, 1987.

Spicer, Edward H. *Cycles of Conquest: The Impact of Spain, Mexico, and the United States on the Indians of the Southwest, 1533–1960.* Tucson: University of Arizona Press, 1962.

Spier, Leslie. *Yuman Tribes of the Gila River.* New York: Cooper Square, 1970 [1933].

Stagg, Albert. *The First Bishop of Sonora: Antonio de los Reyes, OFM.* Tucson: University of Arizona Press, 1976.

Stark, Rodney. *The Rise of Christianity: How the Obscure, Marginal Jesus Movement Became the Dominant Religious Force in the Western World in a Few Centuries.* San Francisco: Harper, 1997.

Starr, Kevin. *Continental Ambitions: Roman Catholics in North America: The Colonial Experience.* San Francisco: Ignatius Press, 2016.

Stephens, H. Morse, and Herbert E. Bolton, eds. *The Pacific Ocean in History.* New York: Macmillan, 1917.

Thomas, Alfred Barnaby. *Forgotten Frontiers: A Study of the Spanish Indian Policy of Don Juan Bautista de Anza, Governor of New Mexico, 1777–1787.* Norman: University of Oklahoma Press, 1932.

———. *Teodoro de Croix and the Northern Frontier of New Spain, 1776–1783.* Norman: University of Oklahoma Press, 1941.

Thomas, Hugh. *Conquest: Montezuma, Cortés, and the Fall of Old Mexico.* New York: Simon and Schuster, 1993.

———. *Rivers of Gold: The Rise of the Spanish Empire, from Columbus to Magellan.* New York: Random House, 2003.

Thompson, Augustine, O.P. *Francis of Assisi: A New Biography.* Ithaca, NY: Cornell University Press, 2012.

Thompson, Raymond H., ed. *A Jesuit Missionary in Eighteenth-Century Sonora: The Family Correspondence of Philipp Segesser.* Albuquerque: University of New Mexico Press, 2014.

Thurman, Michael E. *The Naval Department of San Blas: New Spain's Bastion for Alta California and Nootka, 1767 to 1798.* Glendale, CA: Arthur H. Clark, 1967.

Torre Curiel, José Refugio de la. *Twilight of the Mission Frontier: Shifting Interethnic Alliances and Social Organization in Sonora, 1768–1855.* Palo Alto, CA: Stanford University Press, 2013.

Turner, Christy G., II, and Jacqueline A. Turner. *Man Corn: Cannibalism and Violence in the Prehistoric American Southwest.* Salt Lake City: University of Utah Press, 1999.

Underhill, Ruth. *The Papago and Pima Indians of Arizona.* Palmer Lake, CO: Filter Press, 1979 [1941].

Vickery, Paul S. *Bartolomé de Las Casas: Great Prophet of the Americas.* New York: Paulist Press, 2006.

Wade, Maria F. *Missions, Missionaries, and Native Americans: Long-Term Processes and Daily Practices.* Gainesville: University Press of Florida, 2008.

Walker, Henry P., and Don Bufkin. *Historical Atlas of Arizona*. 2nd ed. Norman: University of Oklahoma Press, 1986.

Wasserman-Soler, Daniel I. *Truth in Many Tongues: Religious Conversion and the Languages of the Early Spanish Empire*. University Park: Pennsylvania University State Press, 2020.

Webb, Edith Buckland. *Indian Life at the Old Missions*. Lincoln: University of Nebraska Press, 1982 [1952].

Webb, George. *A Pima Remembers*. Tucson: University of Arizona Press, 1959.

Weber, David J. *Bárbaros: Spaniards and Their Savages in the Age of Enlightenment*. New Haven, CT: Yale University Press, 2005.

Weber, Msgr. Francis J. *Prominent Visitors to the California Missions*. Los Angeles: Dawson's Book Shop, 1991.

White, Helen Constance. *Dust on the King's Highway*. New York: Macmillan, 1947.

Wilson, John P. *Peoples of the Middle Gila: A Documentary History of the Pimas and Maricopas, 1500s–1945*. Sacaton, AZ: Gila River Indian Community, 2014.

Zappia, Natale A. *Traders and Raiders: The Indigenous World of the Colorado Basin, 1540–1859*. Chapel Hill: University of North Carolina Press, 2014.

ARTICLES, BOOK CHAPTERS, AND UNPUBLISHED THESES

Baldonado, Luis. "Missions San José de Tumacácori and San Xavier del Bac in 1774." *Kiva* 24 (April 1959): 21–24.

Bolton, Herbert Eugene. "The Early Explorations of Father Garcés on the Pacific Slope." In H. Morse Stephens, and Herbert E. Bolton, eds., *The Pacific Ocean in History*, 317–30. New York: Macmillan, 1917.

———. "In the South San Joaquín ahead of Garcés." *California Historical Society Quarterly* 10, no. 3 (September 1931): 211–19.

———. "The Mission as a Frontier Institution in the Spanish-American Colonies." *American Historical Review* 23 (October 1917): 42–61.

Borges Morán, Pedro. "Expediciones misioneras al colegio de Querétaro (Mejico), 1683–1822," *Archivo Ibero-Americano*, 2nd series, 42 (1982): 809–58.

Brenneman, Dale S. "Learning the Landscape: The O'odham Acclimation of Father Agustín de Campos." *Journal of the Southwest* 56 (Summer 2014): 269–91.

Burrus, Ernest J. "Rivera y Moncada, Explorer and Military Commander of Both Californias, in the Light of His Diary and Other Contemporary

Documents." *Hispanic American Historical Review* 50 (November 1970): 682–92.

Cavanaugh, Ray. "The Resilience of Native American Catholicism," *Catholic World Report*, November 23, 2017, accessed on June 6, 2020, at www .catholicworldreport.com/2017/11/23/the-resilience-of-native-american -catholicism.

Cervantes, Fernando. "The Devils of Querétaro: Scepticism and Credulity in Late Seventeenth-Century Mexico." *Past and Present* (February 1991): 51–69.

Chambers, George W. "The Old Presidio of Tucson." *Kiva* 20 (December–February 1955): 15–16.

Cullimore, Clarence. "A California Martyr's Bones." *California Historical Quarterly* 33 (1954): 13–21.

Dejong, David H. "None Excel Them in Virtue and Honesty: Ecclesiastical and Military Descriptions of the Gila River Pima, 1694–1848." *American Indian Quarterly* 29 (Winter and Spring 2005): 24–55.

Dobyns, Henry F. "Some Spanish Pioneers in Upper Pimería." *Kiva* 25 (October 1959): 18–21.

Dobyns, Henry F., Paul H. Ezell, Alden W. Jones, and Greta S. Ezell. "What Were Nixoras?" *Southwestern Journal of Anthropology* 16, no. 2 (Summer 1960): 230–58.

Donohue, J. Augustine. "The Unlucky Jesuit Mission of Bac, 1732–1767." *Arizona and the West* 2 (Summer 1960): 127–39.

Dunne, Peter Masten. "The Expulsion of the Jesuits from New Spain." *Mid-America* 19 (January 1937): 3–30.

Eckhart, George B. "A Guide to the History of the Missions of Sonora." *Arizona and the West* 2 (Summer 1960): 165–83.

Escalante, Fray Silvestre Vélez de. "Letter to the Missionaries of New Mexico." Translated by Eleanor B. Adams. *New Mexico Historical Review* 40 (October 1965): 319–36.

Ewing, Henry P. "The Pai Tribes." *Ethnohistory* 7 (Winter 1960): 61–80.

Ewing, Russell. "The Pima Outbreak in November, 1751." *New Mexico Historical Review* 13 (October 1, 1938): 337.

Fernández-Morera, Darío. "Ruthless Conquistadores and No Less Ruthless Indigenous Peoples." *Postil* (online), December 1, 2021.

Fontana, Bernard. "Revealing the First Church at Mission San Xavier del Bac." *Archaeology Southwest* 18 (Fall): 7–8.

Forbes, Jack D. "The Development of the Yuma Route before 1846." *California Historical Society Quarterly* 43 (June 1964): 99–118.

Fritts, Harold C., et al. "Tree-Ring Evidence for Climatic Changes in Western North America from 1500 A.D. to 1940 A.D." *Annual Report of the United States Weather Bureau* (Tucson, AZ: 1964).

Gann, Douglas W. "'Reconstructing' the Espinosa Church." *Archaeology Southwest* 18 (Fall): 8.

Geiger, Maynard. "Antonio María Bucareli's Christmas of 1776." *Southern California Quarterly* 50 (December 1968): 427–43.

Guerrero, Vladimir. "Lost in the Translation: Chief Palma of the Quechan." *Southern California Quarterly* 92, no. 4 (Winter 2010–11): 317–50.

Habig, Marion A. "The Builders of San Xavier del Bac." *Southwestern Historical Quarterly* 41, no. 2 (October 1937): 145–66.

———. "The Franciscan Provinces of Spanish North America." *Americas* 1, no. 3 (January 1945): 330–44.

Hague, Harlan H. "The Search for a Southern Overland Route to California." *California Historical Quarterly* 55 (Summer 1976): 150–61.

Hammond, George P. "Pimería Alta after Kino's Time." *New Mexico Historical Review* 4, no. 3 (July 1929): 220–38.

Harrison, Jay T. "Franciscan Missionary Theory and Practice in Eighteenth-Century New Spain: The Propaganda Fide Friars in the Texas Missions, 1690–1821." Ph.D. diss. Catholic University of America, 2012.

———. "Franciscan Missionaries and Their Networks: The Diffusion of Missionary Concepts in Eighteenth-Century New Spain." *Catholic Historical Review* 105 (Summer 2019): 457–79.

Hastings, James R. "People of Reason and Others: The Colonization of Sonora to 1767." *Arizona and the West* 2 (Winter 1961): 321–40.

Hattie Belle, Paul. "The Garcés Reports on the Southwestern Indians." M.A. thesis. University of California, 1917.

Heim, Mark. "Visible Victim: Christ's Death to End Sacrifice." *Christian Century*, March 14, 2001, 19–23.

Hoy, Wilton E. "A Quest for the Meaning of Quitobaquito." *Kiva* 34 (April 1969): 213–18.

Ives, Ronald L., ed. "From Pitic to San Gabriel in 1782: The Journey of Don Pedro Fages." *Journal of Arizona History* 9 (Winter 1968): 222–44.

———. "Mission San Marcelo del Sonoydag." *Records of the American Catholic Historical Society of Philadelphia* 66 (December 1955): 201–21.

———, ed. "Retracing Fages' Route from San Gabriel to Yuma, April 1782." *Arizona and the West* 17 (Summer 1975): 141–60.

———, ed. "Retracing the Route of the Fages Expedition of 1781." *Arizona and the West* 8 (Spring and Summer 1966): 49–70, 157–70.

Jackson, Robert H. "Demographic Change in Northwestern New Spain." *Americas* 41 (April 1985): 462–79.

———. "Northwestern New Spain: The Pimería Alta and the Californias." In Robert H. Jackson, ed., *New Views of Borderlands History*, 73–97. Albuquerque: University of New Mexico Press, 1998.

Johnson, John R. "Ethnohistoric Descriptions of Chumash Warfare." In Richard J. Chacón and Rubén G. Mendoza, eds., *North American Indigenous Warfare and Ritual Violence*, 74–113. Tucson: University of Arizona Press, 2007.

Kessell, John L., ed. "Anza Damns the Missions: A Spanish Soldier's Criticism of Indian Policy, 1771." *Journal of Arizona History* 13 (Spring 1972): 53–63.

———. "Father Eixarch and the Visitation at Tumacácori, May 12, 1775." *Kiva* 30, no. 3 (February 1965): 77–81.

———. "Friars versus Bureaucrats: The Mission as a Threatened Institution on the Arizona-Sonora Frontier, 1767–1842." *Western Historical Quarterly* 5 (April 1974): 151–62.

———. "The Making of a Martyr: The Young Francisco Garcés." *New Mexico Historical Review* 45 (Autumn 1970): 181–96.

———. "The Puzzling Presidio." *New Mexico Historical Review* 41, no. 1 (January 1966): 21–46.

Lambert, Patricia M. "The Osteological Evidence for Indigenous Warfare in North America." In Richard J. Chacón and Rubén G. Mendoza, eds., *North American Indigenous Warfare and Ritual Violence*, 202–21. Tucson: University of Arizona Press, 2007.

Lockwood, Frank C. "With Padre Kino on the Trail." *University of Arizona Bulletin* 5, no. 2 (February 15, 1934): 7–142.

Mann, Kristin Dutcher. "Christmas in the Missions of Northern New Spain." *Americas* 66, no. 3 (2010): 331–51.

Mann, Kristin Dutcher. "Defining Time and Space: Franciscans and Bells in Northern New Spain." In Thomas M. Cohen, Jay T. Harrison, and David Rex Galindo, eds., *The Franciscans in Colonial Mexico*, 259–86. Norman: University of Oklahoma Press, 2021.

Martin, John F. "On the Estimation of the Sizes of Local Groups in a Hunting-Gathering Environment." *American Anthropologist* 75 (1973): 1448–68.

———. "The Prehistory and Ethnohistory of Havasupai-Hualapai Relations." *Ethnohistory* 32 (Spring 1985): 135–53.

Martínez, Ignacio. "The Paradox of Friendship: Loyalty and Betrayal on the Sonoran Frontier." *Journal of the Southwest* 56 (Summer 2014): 319–44.

Matson, Daniel S., trans. and ed. "Letters of Friar Pedro Font, 1776–1777." *Ethnohistory* 22 (Summer 1975): 262–93.

Mattison, Ray H. "Early Spanish and Mexican Settlements in Arizona." *New Mexico Historical Review* 21 (October 1946): 273–327.

Maughan, Scott Jarvis. "Francisco Garcés and New Spain's Northwestern Frontier, 1768–1781." Ph.D. diss. University of Utah, 1968.

McCarty, Kieran. "The Colorado Massacre of 1781: María Montielo's Report." *Journal of Arizona History* 16 (Autumn 1975): 221–25.

McCarty, Kieran, and Mark Santiago. "The Founder of Spanish Tucson Petitions the King: Don Hugo O'Conor's 'Relación.'" *Journal of Arizona History* 39, no. 1 (April 1998): 85–98.

Meier, Johannes. "The Franciscans in the New World: Their Contribution to the Evangelization of North, Central, and South America." In Timothy J. Johnson and Gert Melville, eds., *From La Florida to La California: Franciscan Evangelization in the Spanish Borderlands*, 71–82. Berkeley, CA: Academy of American Franciscan History, 2013.

Moore, Mary Lu, and Delmar L. Beene. "The Interior Provinces of New Spain: The Report of Hugo O'Conor, January 30, 1776." *Arizona and the West* 13, no. 3 (Autumn 1971): 265–82.

"Morata," *Gran Enciclopedia Aragonesa*, accessed on January 11, 2021, at www .enciclopedia-aragonesa.com/voz.asp?voz_id=9092&tipo_busqueda=1 &nombre=morata%20de%20jalon&categoria_id=&subcategoria_id=& conImagenes=.

Nabhan, Gary Paul, Wendy Hodgson, and Frances Fellows. "A Meager Living on Lava and Sand? Hia Ced O'odham Food Resources and Habitat Diversity in Oral and Documentary Histories." *Journal of the Southwest* 31 (Winter 1989): 508–33.

Noel, Charles C. "Missionary Preachers in Spain: Teaching Social Virtue in the Eighteenth Century." *American Historical Review* 90 (October 1985): 866–92.

Officer, James E. "Kino and Agriculture in the Pimería Alta." *Journal of Arizona History* 34 (Autumn 1993): 287–306.

Park, Joseph F. "Spanish Indian Policy in Northern Mexico, 1765–1810." *Arizona and the West* 4 (Winter 1962): 325–44.

Porter, Charles R. "Querétaro in Focus: The Franciscan Missionary Colleges and the Texas Missions." *Catholic Southwest* 19 (2008): 9–51.

Priestley, Herbert Ingram, ed. "The Colorado River Campaign, 1781–1782: Diary of Pedro Fages." *Academy of Pacific Coast History Publications* 3 (May 1913): 135–233.

———. "Franciscan Exploration of California." *Catholic Historical Review* 6, no. 2 (July 1920): 139–55.

———. "The Reforms of José de Galvez in New Spain." In H. Morse Stephens and Herbert E. Bolton, eds., *The Pacific Ocean in History*, 349–59 (New York: Macmillan, 1917).

Purdue, Theda. "Women, Men, and American Indian Policy: The Cherokee Response to 'Civilization.'" In Nancy Shoemaker, ed., *Negotiators of Change: Historical Perspectives on Native American Women*, 90–114. New York: Routledge, 1995.

Radding, Cynthia. "Crosses, Caves, and Matachinis: Divergent Appropriations of Catholic Discourse in Northwestern New Spain." *Americas* 55, no. 2 (1998): 177–203.

Ratzinger, Joseph. "Christ, Faith, and the Challenge of Cultures." Address given on March 3, 1993, accessed on July 20, 2022, at www.vatican.va /roman_curia/congregations/cfaith/incontri/rc_con_cfaith_19930303 _hong-kong-ratzinger_en.html.

Rentería-Valencia, Rodrigo F. "Colonial Tensions in the Governance of Indigenous Authorities and the Pima Uprising of 1751." *Journal of the Southwest* 56 (Summer 2014): 345–64.

Rex Galindo, David. "Conferences on Theology and Indian Languages: A Program to Train Missionaries in New Spain." In Timothy J. Johnson and Gert Melville, eds., *From La Florida to La California: Franciscan Evangelization in the Spanish Borderlands*, 251–70. Berkeley, CA: Academy of American Franciscan History, 2013.

Roberts, Elizabeth E. "The Spanish Missions at Yuma, 1779–1781: A Translation of Original Documents." M.A. thesis. University of California, Berkeley, 1920.

Rowland, Donald. "A Project for Exploration Presented by Juan Bautista de Anza." *Arizona Historical Review* 7 (April 1936): 10–18.

Salmón, Roberto Mario. "A 1791 Report on the Villa de Arizpe." *Journal of Arizona History* 24 (Spring 1983): 13–28.

———. "A Marginal Man: Luis of Saric and the Pima Revolt of 1751." *Americas* 45 (July 1988): 61–77.

Sauer, Carl. "A Spanish Expedition into the Arizona Apachería." *Arizona Historical Review* 6, no. 1 (January 1935): 3–13.

Schaafsma, Polly. "Documenting Conflict in the Prehistoric Pueblo Southwest." In Richard J. Chacon and Rubén G. Mendoza, eds., *North American Indigenous Warfare and Ritual Violence*, 114–28. Tucson: University of Arizona Press, 2007.

Scine, Catherine. "Anti-apocalyptic Thought in Medieval and Modern Evangelism and Eschatology." In Timothy J. Johnson and Gert Melville, eds., *From La Florida to La California: Franciscan Evangelization in the Spanish Borderlands*, 61–69. Berkeley, CA: Academy of American Franciscan History, 2013.

Scrivner, Charles Fulsom. *Mohave People*. San Antonio, TX: Naylor, 1970.

"Serving Desert People on a Vast Reservation," accessed on July 20, 2022, at www.catholicextension.org/stories/missionary-pastor-serves-catholic -native-americans-arizona.

Seymour, Deni J. "1762 on the San Pedro: Reevaluating Sobaipuri-O'odham Abandonment and New Apache Raiding Corridors." *Journal of Arizona History* 52 (Summer 2011): 169–88.

Shoemaker, Nancy. "Kateri Tekakwitha's Tortuous Path to Sainthood." In Nancy Shoemaker, ed., *Negotiators of Change: Historical Perspectives on Native American Women*, 49–71. New York: Routledge, 1995.

Simmons, Marc. "Spanish Attempts to Open a New Mexico-Sonora Road." *Arizona and the West* 17 (Spring 1975): 5–20.

Stewart, Kenneth M. "A Brief History of the Chemehuevi Indians." *Kiva* 34 (October 1968): 9–27.

———. "The Mohave Indians in Hispanic Times." *Kiva* 32 (October 1966): 25–38.

———. "Witchcraft among the Mohave Indians." *Ethnology* 12 (July 1973): 315–24.

Stoner, Victor R. "The Spanish Missions of the Santa Cruz Valley." M.A. thesis. University of Arizona, 1937.

Stoner, Victor R., and Henry F. Dobyns. "Fray Pedro de Arriquibar, Chaplain of the Royal Fort of Tucson." *Arizona and the West* 1 (Spring 1959): 71–79.

Tac, Pablo. "Memories of Life at a Mission," accessed on July 20, 2022, at www.californiafrontier.net/pablo-tac.

Thomas, David Hurst. "War and Peace on the Franciscan Frontier." In Timothy J. Johnson and Gert Melville, eds., *From La Florida to La California: Franciscan Evangelization in the Spanish Borderlands*, 105–30. Berkeley, CA: Academy of American Franciscan History, 2013.

Thompson, Raymond Harris. "Letters from Eighteenth-Century Sonora: Father Segesser Writes to His Family in Switzerland." *Journal of the Southwest* 53 (Summer 2011): 225–37.

Treutlein, Theodore E. "The Economic Regime of the Jesuit Missions in Eighteenth Century Sonora." *Pacific Historical Review* 8 (September 1939): 289–300.

———. "Father Gottfried Bernhardt Middendorff, S.J., Pioneer of Tucson." *New Mexico Historical Review* 32 (October 1957): 310–18.

———. "Non-Spanish Jesuits in Spain's American Colonies." In *Greater America: Essays in Honor of Herbert Eugene Bolton,* 259–80. Berkeley, University of California Press, 1945.

Van Dyke, Dix. "A Modern Interpretation of the Garcés Route." *Annual Publication of the Historical Society of Southern California* 13 (1927): 353–59.

Weaver, Richard A. "The 1776 Route of Father Francisco Garcés into the San Bernardino Valley, California: A Reevaluation of the Evidence and Its Implications." *Journal of California and Great Basin Anthropology* 4, no. 1 (Summer 1982): 142–47.

Whiteley, Peter M. "Francisco Garcés' 1775–76 Diary and the Napac: A Further Inquiry." *Kiva* 80 (May 2016): 366–92.

———. "Who Were the Napac? Decoding an Ethnohistorical Enigma." *Kiva* 77 (Fall 2011): 59–86.

Winter, Joseph C. "Cultural Modifications of the Gila Pima: A.D. 1697–A.D. 1846." *Ethnohistory* 20 (Winter 1973): 67–77.

Wood, Raymund F. "Francisco Garcés, Explorer of Southern California." *Southern California Quarterly* 51, no. 3 (September 1969): 185–209.

Wyllys, Rufus K. "The Historical Geography of Arizona." *Pacific Historical Review* 21 (May 1952): 121–28.

Yates, Richard. "Locating the Colorado River Mission San Pedro y San Pablo de Bicuner." *Journal of Arizona History* 13 (Summer 1972): 123–30.

Index

www.ingramcontent.com/pod-product-compliance
Lightning Source LLC
Chambersburg PA
CBHW020447100426
42812CB00036B/3475/J